PRAISE FOR *THE BISHOP AND THE BUTTERFLY*

"A first-class murder mystery, unfolding addictively through its twists and crooked turns. But it's also a remarkable portrait of New York during the Prohibition Era, alive with speakeasies and forbidden cocktails, crime and corruption, the perfect setting for evil to thrive and heroes to emerge undaunted."

—**Deborah Blum**, Pulitzer Prize–winning journalist and author of
The Poisoner's Handbook: Murder and the Birth of Forensic Medicine in Jazz Age New York

"A real-life murder mystery that proves that fact is stranger than fiction. [It] starts with a tip-of-the-iceberg murder and ends with the sinking of an era. Michael Wolraich is a remarkably good writer who delivers history, alive and well, to the modern reader."

—**Nelson DeMille**, *New York Times* bestselling author

"The true crime tale of a woman obsessed with revenge against the crooked cop who put her behind bars, whose unsolved murder brought down New York City's mayor and propelled Franklin D. Roosevelt into the White House. With impeccable research, evocative details, and an extraordinary cast of characters, Michael Wolraich exposes the ugly underbelly of the Jazz Age."

—**Debby Applegate**, Pulitzer Prize–winning author of
Madam: The Biography of Polly Adler, Icon of the Jazz Age

"Vivian Gordon was a 'small forgotten thread in the glorious tapestry of New York City,' until Michael Wolraich trained his investigator's eye and writer's pen on her story. In meticulous, delicious detail, Wolraich paints a rich portrait of a teetering city, and the invisible—until now—woman who pushed it over the brink. Wolraich has a gift for language, a talent for reporting, and a detective's eye for mystery. Vivian Gordon and the jazz age live again in his prose."

—**Sarah Maslin Nir**, author, journalist, two-time finalist for the Pulitzer Prize

"Wolraich hasn't merely written a lurid urban tale of jazz molls, dirty cops, and crooked politicians. His story—which contains all that—matters more. It depicts that unrepeatable moment when New York's underworld reached up from the shadows and changed the course of the city's history."

—**Alan Feuer**, journalist and author of *El Jefe: The Stalking of Chapo Guzman*

"Rare is the book that is both a rip-roaring yarn and also [a] deeply researched social history, but Wolraich more than pulls it off here. This is a book that can be read in a great big gulp. . . . Surely one of the great New York City books in many years."

—**David Freedlander**, journalist and author of *The AOC Generation:
How Millennials Are Seizing Power and Rewriting the Rules of American Politics*

"It would be easy to write Vivian Gordon as a villain. . . . But in his insightful and deeply researched account of her death and its aftermath, Michael Wolraich resists that urge and does the hard work of distilling meaning from her chaotic life. In his account, her faults are a reflection of New York City's failings, and her traumas are a small portion of the human cost of political corruption. [It's] both a true crime tale and a political thriller, but in its sum it's a grander and more ambitious thing than either of those constituent parts."

—**Colin Asher**, author of *Never a Lovely So Real: The Life and Work of Nelson Algren*

PRAISE FOR *UNREASONABLE MEN*

"As Michael Wolraich argues in his sharp, streamlined new book, it was 'the greatest period of political change in American history.'"

—*Washington Post*, 50 Notable Works of Nonfiction

"Wolraich probes this historic moment in light of an American political reawakening to the idea of the interests of the citizens as separate from, and potentially victim to, the interests of corporations and capital holders; it is a mighty and relevant insight into the cyclical nature of history."

—*Publisher's Weekly*

"Exceptionally modern . . . lively, passionate, and cinematic. . . . The book almost reads like a political thriller."

—*LSE Review of Books*

"This is a fascinating, thoroughly readable account of the rise of Progressivism in America. . . . It sheds some crucial light on our current moment."

—**Mathew Rothschild**, senior editor at *The Progressive*

"Michael Wolraich has that special ability to be immersed in the present and bring its insights to the past. . . . A must read."

—**Josh Marshall**, editor and publisher of *Talking Points Memo*, Polk Award winner

"Wolraich presents an engaging survey of a movement's progress from radical extremism to conventional wisdom."

—*Kirkus Reviews*

"In a timely history of the birth of progressivism, political journalist Michael Wolraich explores the spectacular power struggle that shattered the Republican Party and split the country between the ideological factions that now define modern politics: progressive and conservative."

—*Daily Beast*

THE
BISHOP
AND THE
BUTTERFLY

THE
BISHOP
AND THE
BUTTERFLY

MURDER, POLITICS, AND THE
END OF THE JAZZ AGE

MICHAEL WOLRAICH

**UNION
SQUARE
& CO.**

NEW YORK

UNION
SQUARE
& CO.

NEW YORK

ISBN 978-1-4549-4802-5 (hardcover)
ISBN 978-1-4549-4803-2 (e-book)
ISBN 978-1-4549-5692-1 (paperback)

For information about custom editions, special sales, and premium purchases,
please contact specialsales@unionsquareandco.com.

Printed in the USA

2   4   6   8   10   9   7   5   3   1

unionsquareandco.com

Cover design by Studio Gearbox
Cover images: Bridgeman Images: © Museum of the City of New York (city);
Getty Images: Bettmann (Gordon); Shutterstock.com: Ela Kwasniewski (frame)
Interior design by Kevin Ullrich
Captions by Union Square & Co., LLC (except pages 189 and 221)
Picture credits: See page 325

For my parents,
Mark and Debra,
with love and gratitude

CONTENTS

PREFACE

"It was an age of miracles, it was an age of art,
it was an age of excess, and it was an age of satire."
—F. Scott Fitzgerald, "Echoes of the Jazz Age" (1931)

WHEN FITZGERALD PUBLISHED HIS WISTFUL EULOGY TO THE JAZZ AGE IN November 1931, he conceded that it was "too soon to write about the Jazz Age with perspective." Yet even then, only two years after the stock market came crashing down, he knew that it was over. The glorious era depicted in *The Great Gatsby* had "leaped to a spectacular death in October, 1929," he wrote, "as if reluctant to die outmoded in its bed."

Fitzgerald's nostalgia for the Jazz Age is understandable. The postwar boom had ushered in a decade of prosperity and permissiveness that fostered artistic innovation, cultural enlightenment, and sexual freedom. The Harlem Renaissance elevated Black writers and artists, and the popularization of jazz introduced white audiences to the revolutionary musical form, inspiring dance crazes, hit Broadway musicals, and dazzling nightclubs.

Yet, the spirit of tolerance that nurtured social and cultural progress was also exploited by darker elements. Gangsters trafficked in liquor, narcotics, gambling, and prostitution, virtually unchecked by police and prosecutors, many of whom were tainted themselves. New Yorkers tolerated the crime and corruption while the economy was booming, but their patience dried up with the arrival of the Great Depression in 1929, setting the stage for an explosive political crisis that permanently reshaped the city.

This conflict, while local in scope, reflects a more universal theme in American history—the clash between two national ideals, freedom and virtue. Our veneration of freedom is often associated with Revolutionary War heroes and intrepid pioneers, though the same impulse has also guided more notorious historical figures, like outlaws and robber barons who have interpreted liberty as license. By contrast, our fixation with virtue is usually linked to Puritan settlers seeking to build "a city upon a hill." While the moralizing impulse has occasionally provoked witch hunts and other forms of intolerance, it has also inspired abolitionists and civil rights leaders to fight the evils of slavery and racism.

These two competing aspirations, freedom and virtue, crashed together during the Jazz Age. At the dawn of the Roaring Twenties, moralists enacted Prohibition and other vice laws to preserve the nation from sin. Libertines fought back, defying the interdictions and casting off the old taboos. In big cities like New York, the latter gained the upper hand. Artists, entertainers, and ordinary citizens crowded into jazz clubs, speakeasies, theaters, and brothels, indulging in vice as a creative act of defiance. This was the joyful debauchery that F. Scott Fitzgerald eulogized.

Yet for every Fitzgerald, for every Duke Ellington, Josephine Baker, and Langston Hughes, there was an Arnold Rothstein, the inspiration for Meyer Wolfsheim in *Gatsby*, who grew rich from gambling and bootlegging. More ominous still were the crooked bosses of Tammany Hall, the political machine that controlled the city. Even Governor Franklin Delano Roosevelt, who needed Tammany's support to fulfill his presidential aspirations, dared not cross the bosses. At the head of the libertine parade marched New York's beloved mayor, Jimmy Walker. Known as the Night Mayor for his patronage of theaters and clubs—often accompanied by his mistress Betty Compton, a Broadway star—the charming playboy embodied both the hedonism and the corruption of the era.

Ten years later, as the decade came to a close, a new champion of American virtue rose to prominence, a former judge named Samuel Seabury whose sanctimonious manner led people to call him "the Bishop." Though he descended from generations of Protestant clergymen, Judge Seabury's crusade wasn't religious. He demanded honest government and denounced the corruption of Tammany Hall. Empowered by the governor to investigate corrupt cops and judges, he exposed the rot that permeated New York City's justice system.

In the midst of the furious confrontation between Seabury and Tammany, there emerged a woman of no obvious importance, all but forgotten today. Vivian Gordon was an actress turned prostitute and gold digger who seduced rich men and then blackmailed them. Her victims included some of the city's most prominent businessmen, but she was also a victim herself, twice over. In 1923, a dirty cop and a ruthless judge sent her to prison on a dubious prostitution charge, depriving her of her young daughter and destroying her reputation, which consigned her to a life of crime. Then in 1931, unknown killers strangled her with a dirty rope and dumped her body in a public park.

The story of Vivian Gordon's murder was irresistible to new tabloid-size newspapers like the *Daily News*, which eagerly published lurid details about the illicit activities of the "Broadway Butterfly." But what made the case explode across the headlines of every paper in the city and ricochet into newspapers around the world was the discovery that five days before her murder, she had met with one of Judge Seabury's investigators. Amid feverish speculation that police officers had executed her to keep her quiet, Governor Roosevelt reluctantly agreed to expand Seabury's authority. As the police hunted for Vivian Gordon's killers, Seabury's investigators worked their way up the Tammany hierarchy, culminating in a dramatic showdown between Judge Seabury and Mayor Walker in Governor Roosevelt's executive office. The outcome of their extraordinary confrontation ultimately liberated New York City from Tammany's grasp and transformed it into the modern metropolis that we know today.

Judge Seabury and Vivian Gordon, the Bishop and the Butterfly, are long gone. Yet the friction between those two paradoxical ideals, virtue and freedom, still shapes our destiny in ways both hopeful and ominous. The fascinating forgotten story of Vivian Gordon's murder and its dramatic consequences illuminates an exciting moment in American history, but it also offers clues to help us better understand and appreciate our world today.

DRAMATIS PERSONAE

The first list below includes people mentioned in this book in connection with Benita Franklin Bischoff, alias Vivian Gordon, a 39-year-old prostitute and extortionist murdered in the Bronx in 1931. A second list includes people associated with Samuel Seabury, a 58-year-old former judge selected by Governor Franklin D. Roosevelt to investigate corruption in New York City government.

VIVIAN GORDON (THE BUTTERFLY)

Adlerman, Israel J. P.: Assistant district attorney, Bronx county; lead prosecutor at the murder trial

Adler, Polly: Madam, associate of Vivian Gordon

Bischoff, Benita Fredericka: Daughter of Vivian Gordon and John Bischoff

Bischoff, Eunice M.: John Bischoff's second wife

Bischoff, John E. C.: Gordon's ex-husband; common-law marriage from 1915–24.

Bruckman, Henry Englebert: Bronx borough inspector, lead NYPD detective in the Gordon murder case

Butterman, David: Professional fence, associate of Harry Stein

Clayton, Cassie: Gordon's friend and former roommate

Cohen, Samuel "Chowderhead": Convicted burglar, associate of John Radeloff, arrested as a material witness in the Gordon murder case

Crater, Joseph Force: New York Supreme Court justice who mysteriously disappeared on August 6, 1930, alleged associate of Gordon

Diamond, Jack "Legs": Mobster, bootlegger

Doman, Harold: Pimp, friend of Gordon

Dorf, Helen: Gordon protégé

Flegenheimer, Arthur "Dutch Schultz": Bronx mobster, bootlegger

Franklin, Arnolda: Gordon's sister

Franklin, Pierre: Gordon's brother

Ganley, Richard: NYPD vice officer, partner of Andrew McLaughlin; accused of framing women for prostitution

Gibson, Ann Tomkins: Doctor and family friend of the Bischoffs

Greenberg, Samuel "Greenie": Convicted burglar, safe-cracking specialist, member of the Oslo expedition

Halsey, Leonora: Cuban maid who claimed to work for Gordon

Higgins, Charles "Vannie": Brooklyn bootlegger

Joralmon, Henry M.: Banker and chemical company president, Gordon's lover/benefactor

Kamna, Emmanuel G.: Bronx resident, discovered Gordon's body

Larson, Karl W.: Norwegian burglar, organizer of the Oslo expedition

Leibowitz, Samuel S.: Prominent NYC criminal defense lawyer who defended Stein

Lefkowitz, Louis L.: Assistant medical examiner at Fordham Hospital in the Bronx

Levine, Morris "Doc": Ex-convict, member of the Oslo expedition

Lewis, Izzy "English": Ex-convict, friend of Harry Schlitten

Marks, Al: Gordon's former lover, arrested with her in 1923

McLaughlin, Andrew: NYPD vice officer, arrested Gordon in 1923; partner of Ganley, accused of framing women for prostitution

McLaughlin, Charles B.: District attorney, Bronx County, who conducted grand jury inquiries into Gordon's murder

Mulrooney, Edward P.: New York City police commissioner

Radeloff, John A.: Brooklyn attorney; Gordon's lover, lawyer, and accomplice; arrested as a material witness in her murder case

Radlow, Joseph: Financial racketeer, Gordon's lover

Renaud, Henry Stanley: Manhattan magistrate, sentenced Gordon in 1923

Repez, Vernon: Lived with Doman, nursed Gordon after assault

Robinson, Grace B.: Crime reporter for the *Daily News*

Rothstein, Arnold: Mobster, gambler, criminal financier

Ryan, Frank: Taxi driver, witnessed possible abduction of Gordon

Scaffa, Noel C.: Private detective, associate of David Butterman, alleged source to Commissioner Mulrooney

Schlitten, Harry: Chauffeur, professional strikebreaker, murder trial witness

Schweinler, Frederic "Teddy": Magazine printer, sued by Gordon for alleged assault

Seibert, Erich: Superintendent at 156 East 37th Street, Gordon's apartment building

Stein, Harry: Convicted burglar, associate of Gordon and Radeloff, ringleader of the Oslo expedition

Stoneham, Jean: Gordon protégé, girlfriend of Vannie Higgins

Thurston, Lillian: Gordon's elder sister

Tully, Madeline: Harry Stein's landlady

Vigdor, William: Thrift shop owner in Revere, Massachusetts, Butterman's relative, corresponded with Gordon

SAMUEL SEABURY (THE BISHOP)

Acuna, Chile M.: Stool pigeon, Seabury hearings witness

Block, Paul: Advertising tycoon, New York City mayor Jimmy Walker's friend

Compton, Betty: Broadway actress, Walker's mistress

Cooper, Irving Ben: Lawyer, assistant to Seabury and Isidore Kresel

Crain, Thomas C. T.: District attorney, New York County

Curry, John F.: Boss of Tammany Hall, 1929–33

Cuvillier, Louis A.: New York state assemblyman (Democrat), member of the Hofstadter commission

Doyle, William F.: Horse veterinarian, real estate lobbyist, Tammany loyalist accused of bribing city officials

Ellis, James T.: Accountant, Seabury assistant

Ewald, George F.: Bronx magistrate, succeeded Albert Vitale

Farley, James "Jim" A.: Franklin Delano Roosevelt's campaign manager for his gubernatorial and presidential campaigns

Farley, Thomas "Tom" F.: Sheriff, New York County

Haberman, Phillip "Phil" W., Jr.: Lawyer, Seabury assistant

Hastings, John A.: New York state senator (Democrat)

Hearst, William Randolph: Newspaper magnate

Hofstadter, Samuel H.: New York state senator (R), chairman of the joint legislative committee to investigate New York City government

Kresel, Isidore J.: Lawyer, chief counsel for Seabury's investigation of the Magisrates' Courts

La Guardia, Fiorello H.: Mayor of New York City (R) (1934–45)

McNaboe, John J.: New York state senator (D), member of the Hofstadter commission

Moley, Raymond C.: Political science professor at Columbia University

Molloy, J. G. "Louis": Lawyer, Seabury assistant

Murphy, Charles Francis: Boss of Tammany Hall, 1902–24

Perkins, Frances: New York State industrial commissioner under Gov. Franklin D. Roosevelt, later US Secretary of Labor.

Plunkitt, George W.: Former district boss from Tammany Hall

Roosevelt, Franklin Delano: Governor of New York (D) (1929–33), President of the United States (D) (1933–45)

Roosevelt, Theodore: Governor of New York (R) (1899–1900), President of the United States (R) (1901–9)

Scanlan, William J.: Street-cleaner salesman; accused of bribing Walker

Seabury, Josephine "Maud": Samuel Seabury's wife

Sherwood, Russell T.: Walker's money manager

Sisto, J. A.: Investment banker, associate of Walker

Smith, Alfred "Al" Emanuel: Governor of New York (D) (1919–20, 1923–28), 1928 Democratic presidential nominee

Smith, J. Allen: Equitable Coach Company representative; accused of bribing Walker

Terranova, Ciro "Artichoke King": Harlem mafia gangster; allied with Dutch Schultz

Ungerleider, Samuel: Investment banker, associate of Walker

Untermyer, Samuel: Wealthy attorney, Thomas Crain's lawyer, Walker's friend

Valentine, Lewis J.: NYPD detective, demoted after investigating corrupt Tammany officials, later NYC police commissioner under Mayor Fiorello La Guardia

Vitale, Albert H.: Bronx magistrate; accused of ties to Arnold Rothstein, Ciro Terranova

Walker, James "Jimmy" John: Mayor of New York City (D) (1926–32)

Weston, John C.: Assistant district attorney, New York County, confessed to taking bribes

Wise, Stephen S.: Reform rabbi, founder of the City Affairs Committee

PART I
MURDER ON MOSHOLU

CHAPTER 1
A MOTH THAT LOVES THE FLAME

A PALE SUN EASED OVER THE HILLS OF VAN CORTLANDT PARK, POLISHING bare branches to a yellow glint, sketching faint shadows on frost-glazed grass. The warm weather had thawed the ancient brook that bisects the park. Free of winter's grip, it gurgled through the valley and washed into a narrow, slush-choked lake beside an overgrown golf course. Skaters and curlers were usually out on the ice this time of year, but the red ball that signaled safe skating had been lowered and DANGER signs posted for good measure. Most people in the park at this hour were passing through along the macadam-paved Mosholu Parkway that meandered east to west, curling around the lake. Traffic was light, mostly commuters and delivery trucks. Just below the embankment, in a gully 500 feet from the edge of the park, a single white glove hung from a bush, fluttering in the breeze.[1]

The forest had never left this corner of the Bronx. Unlike Central Park's sculpted gardens, Van Cortlandt's designers let the raw wilderness remain. Oak, maple, and hickory shaded the rocky highlands, giving way to marshes and meadows below. White-tailed deer, coyotes, and wild turkeys roamed the woods. "If you want to see what much of New York looked like before it was developed, this is it," a park administrator proclaimed. In the old days, the Wiechquaskeck tribe of the Lenape lived here, hunting and foraging in the forest, planting maize and beans in the fields, and fishing in the stream. There's a myth published in official park literature that Mosholu was the Wiechquaskecks' name for the creek, derived from an Algonquin phrase meaning "smooth or round stones." In fact, Mosholu was the name of a nearby settlement, likely christened in the early nineteenth century to honor Mushulatubbee, a Choctaw chief who fought with the Americans in the War of 1812. His name was an amalgamation of the words *amosholi*, "to try hard," and *ubi*, "to kill."[2]

OPPOSITE: Investigators stand on the Mosholu Parkway across from the ditch where Vivian Gordon's body was found in the Bronx's Van Cortlandt Park on February 26, 1931.

Three East 236th Street is a trim little house on the eastern border of the park, just north of where the old Mosholu Parkway once emerged from the woods. In the winter of 1931, a middle-aged man named Emanuel Kamna lived there with his wife, in-laws, and two daughters. He had enlisted with the National Guard in his twenties and never left the military. He'd patrolled the Mexican border during the Pancho Villa Expedition and survived the shell-shredded trenches of Flanders during the Great War. After returning from Europe with an honorable discharge, he found work at the Kingsbridge Armory, just south of the park, where he earned $7 a day maintaining guns and rifles for the National Guard's 27th Division. The wages were modest, but he was lucky to have a job. These were the early days of the Great Depression, before shantytowns mushroomed in the parks, when bankers and merchants still spoke wistfully about an imminent improvement in business conditions. But the unemployment rate was closing on 20 percent, and the breadlines grew longer with each passing day. The shock of the stock market crash had been replaced by a deepening sense of malaise.[3]

The armory was three miles from Kamna's house, an hour's walk with a pleasant stretch through the park. On February 26, 1931, he was crossing the Mosholu Parkway just before 7:00 a.m. when he saw it—the white glove caught on a bramble beside the roadway, just hanging there as if someone had left it to dry. Then he looked down into the gully and saw its owner. He had encountered enough corpses to recognize death. He saw it in the contortion of her neck, the hands folded neatly together as if smoothing out her dress, the eyes wide open. He lingered for a moment but did not approach. Instead, he turned back to the road and held up his arm to hail an automobile. A delivery truck from the Tidewater Oil Company rumbled to a stop. Kamna told the driver what he'd seen, and they drove out of the park in search of a phone. By the time the news hit the press later that day, the story had gotten mangled. The truck driver was credited with finding the body while walking to work. Kamna returned to the armory and faded into obscurity.[4]

But the news of his gruesome discovery blazed on without him as the mysterious murder ignited New York's collective imagination. Like a wildfire in a windstorm, it flared in unexpected directions, leaping from tree to tree until it scorched vast territories far from the original spark. By the time the conflagration burned out in 1932, the mayor had resigned in disgrace, and Tammany Hall, the fearsome political machine that had ruled New York City for a century, lay a smoldering ruin. Then, amid the ashes and rubble, a modern metropolis took root and reached for the sky.

Inspector Henry Engelbert Bruckman didn't look much like the chiseled heroes of detective films. His face was full and fleshy, with a soft chin that faded into his neck and an incongruously sharp nose. Congenital bags under his eyes made him look gloomy and fatigued. He was tough, though, six-foot-two and solid. As a rookie, he'd distinguished himself by knocking out five members of the Hudson Dusters gang in "one of the liveliest street fights ever seen in Greenwich Village." Yet his superiors were more impressed by his "quick, incisive mind," "amazingly retentive memory," and "uncanny eye for detail." His detective work was meticulous, characterized by dogged fact-finding rather than swift leaps of intuition. Faced with a challenging case, he would spend long hours searching for clues and fitting them into position like puzzle pieces until a picture emerged from the mosaic.[5]

He was one of the rare police officers of the era who won promotions for competence rather than political fealty. High-level hiring decisions were usually determined by the Tammany Hall bosses, who prized loyalty over independence. Bruckman's colleague, Inspector Lewis Valentine, had been demoted after he annoyed Tammany leaders by arresting well-connected gamblers. Bruckman wasn't a crusader like Valentine; he kept his head down and avoided politics. But he was honest, diligent, and tenacious. Raised in a tenement house in Yorkville on the Upper East Side of Manhattan by parents who were German immigrants, he spent twenty-five years on the force, methodically passing the required civil-service exams and climbing the ranks to become Bronx Borough Inspector* at the age of forty-five, despite having only an eighth-grade education.[6]

Bruckman's ascent coincided with a revolution in organized crime. The Hudson Dusters gang was old-school, an unruly crew of Irish

---

* The highest-ranking officer in the New York Police Department was the chief inspector, who reported directly to the police commissioner's office. The five borough inspectors ranked just below the chief inspector.

hoodlums reminiscent of the nineteenth-century ruffians portrayed in *Gangs of New York*. When Bruckman scrapped with the Dusters in 1905, they were already headed toward oblivion, soon to be supplanted by a new breed of gangster. A few of the Dusters played poker in the prop room of Oscar Hammerstein's Victoria Theatre. They were often joined by an awkward, pale-faced teenager who spoke little but carried a roll of bills that grew thicker over the course of the night. Sometimes he lent money to his fellow gamblers at steep rates. Within a few years, the teenager, Arnold Rothstein, had become one of New York's richest men. In addition to playing high-stakes poker, he waged hundreds of thousands of dollars on horse races and usually won. He bet on baseball, too, and was blamed for fixing the 1919 World Series, though his role in the scandal is a matter of dispute. Gambling was only one of his many revenue streams, however. He was also a bookmaker and a loan shark. He underwrote bail bonds, financed nightclubs and casinos, arranged police protection for criminal operations, and supplied thugs-for-hire to participate in violent labor strikes—as either strikers or strikebreakers, depending on who was paying. Known as "The Brain," "The Bankroll," and "The Man Uptown," he had dealings with almost every major criminal and corrupt politician in New York City. "Rothstein's main function was organization," wrote biographer Leo Katcher. "He provided money and manpower and protection. He arranged corruption—for a price. And, if things went wrong, Rothstein was ready to provide bail and attorneys. He put crime on a corporate basis when the proceeds of crime became large enough to warrant it."[7]

After the Volstead Act outlawed the sale of liquor in the United States in 1920, Rothstein swooped into the bootlegging business. He established a whiskey-smuggling operation from Canada—across Lake Ontario and down the Hudson River—and soon added overseas routes from Britain and Cuba. He also financed local bootleggers and provided them with trucks and drivers in return for a cut of the proceeds. Smuggling and bootlegging were highly profitable—a case of Scotch could be purchased for $75 in London and sold for $300 in New York—but the business was risky. Rothstein mitigated interference from authorities through bribes and political favors, but hijacking became a constant threat. A truck full of expensive liquor was an attractive target for bandits, and victimized bootleggers had no legal recourse to recover their stolen contraband.[8]

To protect his merchandise, Rothstein hired one of his labor-strike thugs, a former Hudson Duster named Jack Diamond. Skinny and pale, with brooding eyebrows and hard, gray eyes, Diamond was a dashing publicity hound who favored a chinchilla coat, white silk scarf, and wide-brimmed, white felt hat. People called him "Legs," possibly because of his youthful prowess as a truck bouncer—a petty thief who pilfered packages from delivery trucks and sprinted away. By the time he reached his twenties, Diamond was stealing entire trucks. He was vicious, cunning, and unencumbered by sentiment or conscience, a man well-suited for the violence of the Prohibition Era. Arnold Rothstein hired Legs and his brother Eddie to ride shotgun on his delivery trucks for $7.50 a day and didn't object when they moonlighted by hijacking his competitors.[9]

In 1921, Legs Diamond asked Rothstein to help him start his own bootlegging operation. Rothstein, who preferred to let others do the dirty work, agreed to provide financing, legal services, and protection from the cops. With his support, Legs established a well-organized crime gang with rackets all over town, including burglary, hijacking, bootlegging, and narcotics. Some of the most notorious gangsters of the era got their start under Diamond, including Charles "Lucky" Luciano and Arthur Flegenheimer, better known as Dutch Schultz. Unlike the clannish Hudson Dusters, they had diverse ethnic backgrounds. The Diamond brothers were second-generation Irish immigrants raised in Philadelphia and Brooklyn. Schultz was an Austrian Jew from Yorkville. Luciano was born in Sicily and grew up on the Lower East Side. "Diamond was the organizer of the first really modern mob in New York," recalled Schultz's lawyer, "Dixie" Davis. "As distinguished from the old loosely knit gangs, the mob was a compact business organization with a payroll of gunmen who worked for a boss."[10]

The Diamond mob was short-lived, however. Legs was a difficult boss: cruel and capricious, prone to explosive rages, and devoid of loyalty. When his minions split to start their own operations, brutal turf wars ensued. Diamond allied with a bellicose Brooklyn rum runner named Vannie Higgins to shut out his erstwhile protégé, Dutch Schultz. Meanwhile, Lucky Luciano went to work for Mafia boss Joe Masseria during the brutal Castellammarese War, which pitted the Italian crime families against each other. Flush with money, equipped with shotguns and modern submachine guns, the mobsters battled for power, profit,

A composite news photo from c. 1929, left to right: Ed Diamond, brother of Jack; Jack "Legs" Diamond, Thomas "Fatty" Walsh, and Charles "Lucky" Luciano.

and vengeance. "Prohibition has brought into existence an organization of crime and criminal such as no other country on the face of the globe has ever known," observed actuarial scientist Frederick Hoffman in 1930. "Gangsters and gunmen are being killed almost day after day, forming a not inconsiderable item in the large number of homicidal deaths."[11]

Arnold Rothstein was one of the statistics, gunned down during a business meeting at the glamorous Park Central Hotel in 1928, allegedly over a gambling debt. When a detective asked him who'd done it as he lay dying in the hospital, he put a trembling finger to his lips and whispered, "You know me better than that, Paddy."* Two years later, hit men busted

---

* "Paddy" was a derogatory label for Irish Americans.

into Jack Diamond's suite at the Monticello Hotel near Central Park and drilled him with five bullets—reportedly payback by Vannie Higgins after Legs double-crossed him. After they left him for dead, he swigged two shots of whiskey, stumbled out of his room in his red silk pajamas, and collapsed in the hallway. Fifty-one gangsters had already been killed that year, and the surgeon expected him to join their ranks, but Diamond, who had survived two previous shootings, pulled through again. "His ability to recover from what ambulance surgeons always declare at first to be fatal wounds have made him the clay pigeon of the underworld," marveled the *New York Herald Tribune*. Vannie Higgins, who was in Montreal to negotiate a bootlegging deal, sent Legs a sardonic telegram, "Better luck next time, old pal." But like Rothstein, Diamond confounded the police by refusing to name the shooters, dismissing all questions with a shake of the head and a twisted smile.[12]

The upsurge in violent crime was especially pronounced on Inspector Bruckman's home turf. When he moved to the Bronx in 1908, many of his colleagues scorned the city's northern borough as a rural backwater where inept and insubordinate cops were sent to patrol the unpaved roads on horseback. For Bruckman, an up-and-coming detective, it was a place to raise a family and train homing pigeons that he kept on the roof, not to advance his career, so he continued to commute to rougher Manhattan neighborhoods like Greenwich Village and the Tenderloin* for several years. But while he was pursuing gangsters and murderers downtown, new subway lines and elevated tracks snaked through the Bronx, followed by houses and apartment buildings that sprouted along the transit routes like saplings on a riverbank. The population of the Bronx sextupled between 1900 and 1930, transforming the sleepy borough of 200,000 into a teeming metropolis of 1.3 million, larger than Los Angeles, the country's fifth-biggest city at that time. As the population boomed, policing the Bronx

---

* The Tenderloin was a red-light district on the West Side of Manhattan between Fifth and Eighth avenues, originally concentrated in the mid-twenties in what is now Chelsea but eventually stretching north to include Times Square and Hell's Kitchen. It owed its name to a nineteenth-century police captain who was so excited about the bribes he anticipated from his new precinct that he crowed, "I've been having chuck steak ever since I was on the force, and now I'm going to have a bit of tenderloin."

became a serious business, and Bruckman eventually transferred to a precinct closer to home.[13]

But it was the Volstead Act that ignited the crime wave that blazed through the borough in the 1920s. After Dutch Schultz deserted Diamond's gang, he set up a sprawling beer distribution network in Harlem and the Bronx, which included trucks, warehouses, speakeasies, nightclubs, and a brewery in Yonkers. His only serious competition in the northern reaches of the city was an Italian syndicate controlled by Ciro Terranova, known as "the Artichoke King" because of his monopoly on artichoke imports into the city. To avoid conflict, Schultz formed an alliance with Terranova and offered the Italians a cut of the profits.[14]

Schultz was almost the anthesis of his former boss. Where Diamond was reckless, impulsive, and vain, Schultz was measured, methodical, and camera-shy. His appearance was plain—average height and weight, dark-haired, with a round face and a crooked nose—and he was a sloppy dresser. He also lacked Diamond's sadistic streak, though he didn't shy from using violence to muscle out the competition, and he allegedly dropped one of his own henchmen into the East River with cement shoes. Another of his lieutenants, Vincent "Mad Dog" Coll, pioneered the fine art of drive-by shooting. In the summer of 1930, Coll split from Schultz's gang and started up a rival bootlegging operation in the Bronx. Schultz went to war against his erstwhile lieutenant, and machine-gun fire rattled the streets of the formerly bucolic borough.[15]

Amid the bloody turf battles and vendettas, the Bronx Borough Inspector had plenty of work. A woman's body dumped in Van Cortlandt Park was not as shocking as it would have been a decade earlier, but it was still serious enough to merit Bruckman's personal attention. He worked out of the old Bathgate Station in the 48th Precinct, a boxy, yellow-brick, Renaissance-style edifice about four miles from the crime site. By the time his patrol car pulled onto the shoulder of the Mosholu Parkway, several officers had already arrived at the scene. Now that the sun was up, the body was plainly visible from the road, lying on its side in the leafless underbrush below the embankment. Bruckman could see that, even in death, the victim was a beautiful woman with wavy, reddish-brown hair, cut fashionably short. She looked to be in her late twenties or early thirties, of average height and weight. She was dressed as if for a party, in a black velvet cocktail dress trimmed with cream lace and gunmetal-gray stockings. One black velvet pump with a studded buckle lay on the ground nearby, along with a black straw hat and a white kid glove. There were bruises on her face, and her dress was torn and scrunched up to her hips, exposing pink silk panties. A noose, fashioned from what looked like a dirty, six-foot clothesline, squeezed her throat so tightly that it broke the skin. The killer had tied a single knot behind the slipknot to hold it in place, then wrapped the rope around her neck two more times for good measure.[16]

A *Daily News* photo of the clothesline, entangled with strands of Vivian Gordon's hair, used to strangle her, February 26, 1931.

A young doctor had already examined the body before Bruckman arrived. He introduced himself as Ralph Drews, a surgical resident from nearby Fordham Hospital, and confirmed that the victim had died of strangulation. He estimated that she'd been dead for four or five hours before her body was discovered, which would put her death at two or three in the morning. The evening wear suggested that she'd been to a nightclub or speakeasy. Noting that the dress was slightly worn on one side, Bruckman speculated that she might have been a waitress or cigarette girl and had perhaps abraded the material by brushing against the tables. Despite the stylish clothing, she wore no coat, purse, or jewelry, though her finger bore an impression from a ring, which suggested robbery. Yet simple thieves would not likely take the trouble to garrot their victim. There was no sign of struggle in the grass or bushes, so she'd probably been killed elsewhere and dumped at this spot. Lacking any obvious conventional explanation, Bruckman initially conjectured that she may have been the victim of a "maniac."[17]

The next step was to identify the body, which could be difficult since she wasn't carrying any papers or identification. Bruckman ordered

Police prepare to move Gordon's body from Van Cortland Park, February 26, 1931.

fingerprints taken as a matter of course, though these would only be useful if she had a criminal record. More likely, some relative would come forward once the story hit the press. Sensational homicides sold plenty of papers in New York, and the mysterious strangulation of a beautiful white woman was as sensational as it gets. The newfangled tabloid papers, the *Daily News* and the *Mirror*, which fixated on crime and sex, would go wild. Sure enough, a gang of reporters arrived at the scene almost immediately and began snapping pictures and poking around in the bushes. Bruckman gamely shared his theories with them as they scribbled notes.

As it turned out, he was wrong about the fingerprints. He soon received word that the wizards downtown, with their pigeonholes of index cards, had matched the loops and whorls from the dead woman's fingers. Her name, apparently, was Mrs. Benita F. Bischoff. In 1923, she'd been convicted of "vagrancy," a legal catchall for various misdemeanors, including alcoholism, homelessness, and prostitution—the most common charge against young women. The magistrate had sentenced her to a minimum of six months at the New York State Reformatory for Women at Bedford Hills, New York, an unusually harsh penalty for a first offense. Initially released after six months, she was returned twice for parole violations and finally completed her sentence in November 1926.[18]

Four months later, she was arrested again at a luxury hotel on Times Square. The assistant manager reported that she'd run through the halls shouting for the police and the fire department. When the cops arrived, she claimed that two men had invited her to their hotel suite and then robbed her of $50. But the men had disappeared, and she admitted that she'd been drinking, so she was booked for disorderly conduct, though the charges were later dismissed. Her fingerprints matched those of the vagrancy arrest from 1923, but this time she told the police that her name was Vivian Gordon.[19]

In May 1929, Vivian Gordon's name again appeared in the court record, this time as the victim of a robbery. She accused a young woman named Jean Stoneham, who had been staying with her, of stealing a dress and a hat. Stoneham was arrested, but Gordon ultimately chose not to press charges, and the case was dropped. Stoneham's name was known to the police. Later, in 1930, she had an affair with Vannie Higgins, the Brooklyn bootlegger, and detectives had interrogated her about the attempted assassination of Legs Diamond at the Monticello.[20]

On March 1 1930, Benita Bischoff, alias Vivian Gordon, was picked up at another Times Square hotel following a late-night party in one of the suites. The police found her on a fire escape at 7:00 a.m. with severe bruises on her face and head, screaming hysterically that she'd been assaulted and accusing her escort of orchestrating the attack. According to the hotel clerk, the couple had registered as Mr. and Mrs. Lerner of New Orleans, but the woman told the police that her name was Vivian Martin and that her escort was Frederick "Teddy" Schweinler, president of Schweinler Press. His ten-story printing house spanned an entire block in Greenwich Village, producing seven million magazines a month for *Harper's Weekly*, *McClure's Magazine*, and other prominent periodicals.* The woman said

---

* The building has since been converted into a luxury condo residence called the Printing House, featuring loft-style apartments.

that Schweinler had fled the scene, but as the cops began to question her, she referred them to her lawyer, John A. Radeloff, with offices at 66 Court Street in Brooklyn. Detectives later followed up with him to determine whether Vivian Martin wished to press charges. He informed them that his client's name was Vivian Gordon and that she did not wish to press criminal charges but had filed a civil suit against Schweinler for $50,000.[21]

A few months later, on August 7, 1930, the woman was once again arrested in the lobby of a Midtown hotel after a man named Joseph Radlow accused her of blackmailing him. In court, he testified that she told him, "If I don't get $1,000, I'll go down to the district attorney's office and to the United States attorney and prefer charges against you and also to the newspapers and tell them all about you." He said that she threatened to report him for sex trafficking and forgery. But Joseph Radlow lacked Teddy Schweinler's money and reputation. He was a convicted con man and sometime columnist for the *New York Evening Post* who wrote about securities fraud under the byline E. X. Swindler. The charges against Vivian Gordon were swiftly dismissed. Curiously, her attorney, John Radeloff, once again figured into the story. In addition to representing her, he was also Radlow's first cousin—Radeloff and Radlow were Americanized variants of the same Russian last name. According to Joseph Radlow, his cousin Radeloff advised him that "it was cheaper to send her some money than to have her squawking all over town."[22]

The woman had one other minor arrest, in 1930, for public intoxication and disorderly conduct after a dispute with a taxi driver over the fare. In that instance, as well as in the Radlow case, she'd given the name Vivian Gordon. And there was an address: 156 East 37th Street, Apartment 3C, in Manhattan. That was the information Inspector Bruckman needed. He gathered his team and headed downtown.[23]

Within a few years, East 37th Street would become a traffic-choked conduit for the new Queens–Midtown Tunnel, but in 1931, it was still a quiet side street in a fashionable neighborhood lined by elegant brownstones, a few blocks from J. Pierpont Morgan's mansion and Tiffany's jewelry store. Bruckman was impressed by the victim's residence—a brand-new ten-story apartment building with a modern elevator. According to the superintendent, the woman who called herself Vivian Gordon had lived there for a couple of years, paying $150 a month for a one-bedroom apartment. She'd told the staff that she was an artist and that her husband was a mining engineer. The super described her as quiet and polite but said that she kept odd hours, often departing late and returning after dawn. The elevator attendant reported that she'd left the building around 11:30 the night before, wearing a mink coat, diamond ring, and diamond-studded watch, none of which had been found at the crime scene. "It was her usual hour of departure," he added.[24]

Gordon's apartment was on the third floor in the rear of the building, shielded from street noise. The walls were painted orchid-purple and adorned with tapestries and paintings. Persian rugs and oak furniture with leather and velvet upholstery graced the living room. A small work studio contained an easel with oil paints, a sewing table with a half-finished dress, a violin and a clarinet. Two half-filled whiskey glasses and an empty pint flask stood on a porcelain table in the kitchen. In the bedroom, costumed boudoir dolls with papier mâché faces—a fad among sophisticated women—lounged on the double bed. A large oval mirror stood on a wooden dresser stuffed with French finery and lingerie. Beside it, a folding picture frame held two photographs. One pane presented a glamorous headshot of the murder victim. Bare-shouldered, she glanced sidelong and pursed her lips with a faint, sad smile. Her auburn hair billowed over her ears. Dark eyeliner emphasized the almond shape of her eyes, and lipstick molded her mouth into a Cupid's bow. She rested one hand gently against her chest and turned her head as if gazing at someone across her shoulder. The second pane held a full-length portrait of a young girl, about six years old, photographed from the side. Wearing ballet slippers, bedecked with clownish frills and ruffles, she balanced on tiptoes and leaned forward with her hands on her hips. Her round face turned toward the camera with a saucy pout that hinted at Gordon's expression in the opposite pane. Yet, there were no signs of a child in the apartment, no toys or children's clothes.[25]

There were documents, though, boxes of them. In one, Bruckman discovered a poem, apparently composed by Gordon, that hinted at her crimes and seemed to foretell her fate.

I'm a lady of the evening
And while youth and beauty last,
I never worry who will pay my rent.
For a while I'll be in clover,
And when easy days are over
I know I'll go the way that all
My predecessors went.

I'm a lady of the evening
With a morning glory's beauty.
The payment for my raiment
I get in devious ways.
When some big and wealthy brute
Wants to love me cause I'm cute,
I admit that I submit
Because it pays.

I'm a lady of the evening
Just like Cleopatra was.
The Queen of Sheba also played my game.
Though by inches I am dying,
There's not any use in crying.
I stay and play cause I'm that way,
A moth that loves the flame.[26]

Gordon's handwriting was quite legible, even graceful, with idiosyncratic flourishes. She dotted her *i*'s with circles and crossed her *t*'s with long, slanting slashes. Her capital *M* resembled a hut composed of three vertical bars with a horizontal line hovering above. The poetry spoke to her sophistication and artistry, apiece with the paintings on the walls, the musical instruments, and the half-finished dress. Whatever Vivian Gordon had been, she was no ordinary streetwalker.

Yet more pertinent to Bruckman's investigation were other writings that he discovered with the poems: three black, leather-bound datebooks for the years 1929, 1930, and 1931. Each day had its own page, with a time-line running down the left column, but the times had been ignored, and

freeform sentences tumbled down the pages like diary entries
were terse, sometimes just a few disjointed phrases. The first entry, on january 1, 1929, read simply:

J. A. R. 16.40 paid.

The same initials appeared again on January 31:

*Went to hospital—girl. (Kennedy). Riverdale, East New York.
J. A. R. paid Dr.—and hospital bill $600.*

The third entry, on February 12, took a sudden dark twist:

*Had to call Dr. Another operation necessary. Did not start this
diary for reason other than to remind me of dates but think—
advisedly so—that it's best to put down things as they happen concerning John A. Radeloff—he is not to be trusted. He would stoop
to anything.*

The tone of Gordon's ominous disclosure wasn't confessional. She
seemed to have recorded her suspicion for the sake of documentation
rather than private self-reflection, a trail of evidence in case something
happened to her. As Bruckman read on, it became apparent that Radeloff
wasn't just her lawyer; he was also her lover. According to the diary, the
two had a bitter fight in February—Gordon called it a "finale"—followed
by more death threats. "If anything happens to me, he is to blame," she
warned again. "He has henchmen."

The lovers soon made up, but Radeloff's threats continued. After
their reconciliation, he casually mentioned that one of his legal clients,
a convicted burglar named Sam Cohen, had offered to kill her for him.
Radeloff assured her that he'd rejected the idea, yet his purpose in telling
her this story was evident:

*The threat has been made Sam Cohen (who is a client of J. A.
R . . .)—has brought the thugs two of them—to J. A. R.'s office, so
J. A. R. told me and he refused to let them do the trick. But how did*

they know J. and I had a scrap? Unless he told S. C. And why make a confidante of a common loft thief. The above info was conveyed to me by J. A. R. in my apt. after a reconciliation on Feb. 23. There is no denying that I am in love with J. A. R. and have reason to believe he is with me but still I list this info—in case—his man is, according to his statement, supposed to have said: "We'll take her out somewhere no one will know what happened to her—every mark of identification will be missing, especially that ring"—meaning a $2,500 ring I wear.

At times, Gordon tried to extract herself from the relationship. "The end is here," she declared in May. "From now on it's just what I can get out of him until the ripe time to spring." A few months later, she wrote, "J. A. R., he thinks maybe he'll be friendly with me again. No! No! No! I've had enough of him." Yet she couldn't seem to quit him. Month after month, she obsessed over his criminal schemes, his marriage, his lovers, and the money he owed her. Her words smoldered with jealousy, contempt, and fear. Even after their love affair cooled, she continued to lend him money, employ his legal services, and collude with him in various schemes, both lawful and illicit.

At Radeloff's suggestion, she set up a real estate holding company called the Vivigo Corporation and purchased vacant lots in Brooklyn and rental houses in Jamaica, Queens. Radeloff handled the corporate operations from his Brooklyn office, which allowed him to manage the rental income and mortgage payments.

He also persuaded Gordon to finance a plot by some of his associates to rob a Norwegian bank in the summer of 1929. On August 17, she wrote,

Supposed to get money from Norway today—another one of J. A. R.'s rotten deals. I gave him $1,500 (on his say so)—to H. Saunders for passage to Oslo, Norway, for himself and two others to clean up a bank there. The money was supposed to be cabled to my bank on this date (for safe keeping) until their return.

But the operation apparently hit a snag. Radeloff told Gordon that H. Saunders required more money to finish the job. When she refused to pay, the death threats resumed. "J. A. R. here again hinted about my getting killed," she wrote, "saying 'I'd better get my collar and shirt out of here. If you should get killed they'd look for me.'"

On August 19, she confronted him in front of his wife over $500 that he owed her and revealed their affair to her. "Met him just as he and his wife were coming out for a walk," she wrote, "Read the riot act to him. She didn't say a word. Dumb! Dumb! Dumb!"

The incident marked an inflection point in Gordon's relationship with Radeloff. After the confrontation, she made another attempt to liberate herself from his influence, recorded for posterity in her diary:

> *J. A. Radeloff is the only one who is really an enemy of mine—because of certain things I have told his wife in retaliation for all the rotten things he has done to me—he was just using me for a "good thing," treating me half civil—a necessary evil—as it were, because he knew he could borrow money from me—besides I have a mortgage of $11,300 (Eleven thousand dollars) due to close October 30. It wouldn't surprise me a bit if he tried to have me killed so as to grab that money as there is no one close to me to put up a squawk if anything occurred—anything I have done to him he deserves 100 percent. more.*

Gordon's obsession with Radeloff did seem to abate after that, but she didn't sever the relationship. She continued to employ him as her lawyer and loan him money, and he continued taking advantage of her. In June 1930, he collected rent from some of her tenants and spent the money on a drunken bender. "Has been drunk since Wednesday making himself big shot with my $'s," she complained. "When I insisted on putting the screws to him, he gave one of his usual threats."

Radeloff's threats weren't the only ones Gordon recorded in her diary. On March 27, 1929, she discussed the arraignment of "Gene Stoneman," misspelling the name of Jean Stoneham, the gangster moll she'd accused of stealing her clothes:

> *10:30 court. Gene Stoneman out on bail. William Dinerstein of 257 W. 30th St. with her in court. Also a shady looking character who bears watching—Dinerstein paid bondsman. About one*

week before she left here she asked verbatim "Vivian, if you were found dead would I be questioned?" I answered "Yes." She also bears watching—she'll stoop to anything. Adjourned till Monday.

Gordon's diary also related the incident with Teddy Schweinler on February 28, 1930:

Jimmie Fritz an acquaintance of 5 yrs ago—phoned—wanted me meet a friend—Theodore Schweinler, 405 Hudson St. T. S. seemed charming(?). T. S. and I went to Villa D'Este—he had 2 old fashion cocktail—I had 1 but gave it to him—then went to Broadway "Itch" place at 135 W. 45—Ye Gods, nothing but gangsters there—T. S. was singing my praises about being an artist, etc.

About 4 or 5 A. M. we left 135 W. 45—went across street to girl's apt. Palace Hotel—presumably to have a drink with friends—two women & four men—also T. S. and S. W.—then the works—harrowing experience—I was nearly killed—everything taken from purse—while unconscious—went down fire escape to avoid more—police met on fire escape took me in lobby—Dr. wanted to get me morphine—I said NO nothing doing . . . about 10:15 Saturday A. M. Dr. came—ye Gods— concussion brain—2 broken ribs—bruises from head to foot.

And on August 7, Gordon described how Joseph Radlow, the con man, had entrapped her by offering to pay off a debt only to have her arrested on blackmail charges:

Joe Radlow—arrest—extortion—that—after I've given him three years to pay me—what he owes—first he cried his kid had mastoid— then his wife expected another child—then he went to jail (workhouse) then he got out—he pleaded for time—to get some money—then he phoned and agreed to meet me at McAlpin—saying he had 200—toward payment and would pay balance as soon as possible.[27]

But the $200 payment included marked notes used to incriminate her in the extortion charge. After the grand jury dismissed the charges, Gordon retaliated by filing a $50,000 lawsuit against Radlow.

After describing Radlow's accusations in August, the diary entries trailed off for the remainder of the year, resuming only in the third date-book, 1931, a few weeks before her murder. The final entries were terse and cryptic, mostly concerned with money she was owed:

January 2: Corey, 10,358

January 3:

> *Saunders, note 1500, due Oct. 5, 1929, not paid. Corey $10,000 note.*

> *J. Radlow handled by B. Fanger . . . lawsuit, 50,000 . . . money taken by police, 200.*

> *F. Schweinler law suit, assault and battery—50,000, handled by J. A. Radeloff.*

January 9: 450.—50—Dr. Eagle 20—Hartmann, 285 Madison Ave. 270 West 75th St.—3 a.

January 30: Saunders here.

January 31: Greenberg returned from A. C. Sunday

February 2: Stoney

February 4: I believe that John A. Radeloff and Sam Cohen pulled that jewelry deal alone.

February 5: Ring.

February 14: J. A. R. borrowed 25—to be returned Monday, 2/16/31.[28]

The final entry was a fitting coda to the contents of the three black date-books, yet another loan to John A. Radeloff. Gordon had mentioned other potential suspects in the diary, including Jean Stoneham, Teddy Schweinler, and Joseph Radlow, as well as two pimps named Zeno and Doman, with whom she'd quarreled, and someone named Corey, to whom she'd lent $10,000. The detectives also found a $1,500 promissory note signed by Harry A. Saunders, presumably the "H. Saunders" mentioned in the diary. But the obvious suspect was the man who had repeatedly threatened her life. Radeloff had many possible motives—to exact retribution for exposing their

John Radeloff, left, and Samuel "Chowderhead" Cohen, right, appear in court in March 1931, after being arrested as material witnesses in the Gordon murder case.

affair, to steal Gordon's mortgage payments, to escape his debts to her, and to prevent her from testifying about their criminal activities. He may have stopped her from talking, but her diary screamed accusations from beyond the grave. Inspector Bruckman immediately ordered the arrests of John A. Radeloff and his alleged henchman, Sam Cohen.[29]

There were still other mysteries to unravel, though. For one, the diaries didn't explain how Vivian Gordon made a living. Prostitution wouldn't cover a $150-per-month luxury apartment, let alone $10,000 loans and speculative real estate investments. Records found in her apartment indicated she'd invested over $75,000 in real estate—$1.5 million in today's dollars. The detectives also found $11,000 worth of securities and a key to a safe-deposit box at the Bank of America, which might hold even more riches.[30]

The source of Gordon's wealth was suggested by another black book the detectives found in the apartment, containing the names of hundreds of men. Some were gangsters, including Arnold Rothstein, Legs Diamond, and Vannie Higgins, but most were prominent businessmen and politicians: Jefferson Livingston, "the catsup king"; John A. Hoagland, "the baking powder playboy"; Broadway producer Murray Phillips; State Supreme Court Justice Selah B. Strong; former New York Secretary of State Francis Hugo. The list went on, 560 names in total. Some names were accompanied by addresses, phone numbers, and monetary figures. One of Bruckman's detectives reckoned that the numbers were debts and concluded that Gordon was a loan shark. He colorfully described her as "a female Arnold Rothstein," a phrase that later captured the imagination of the press. But Bruckman thought otherwise. Though they'd found some financial records among Gordon's documents, there wasn't enough to indicate a Rothstein-like operation. Bruckman suspected that the men listed in the black book were victims or perhaps targets in another kind of racket. According to his theory, Gordon wasn't a prostitute, not just a prostitute anyway; she was an extortionist who seduced rich men and then blackmailed them.[31]

In addition to the list of men, there was another list, or rather a catalog, of forty to fifty women. Instead of monetary figures, their names were accompanied by phone numbers, physical descriptions—height, weight, and complexion—and nude photographs. Apparently, in addition to her other occupations, Vivian Gordon operated an escort service.[32]

There were also letters and gifts, hundreds of them, mostly from men listed in her black book. Joseph Haan, the "candy Croessus," sent her a green leather glove box filled with sweets and a thank-you note. Samuel C. Herriman, millionaire patent lawyer, gifted her a bottle of Chicken Cock rye whiskey accompanied by a note, "from Sam to Vivian," inscribed on stationery from the exclusive University Club in Midtown. Some correspondence was encoded, notably a mysterious set of telegrams sent from Revere, Massachusetts, a suburb of Boston. And not all the letters were cordial. The detectives found threatening notes from anonymous sources, written in lead pencil on cheap paper. One accused her of being "a dirty stool pigeon," slang for a police informant. Another warned her to drop the suit against Teddy Schweinler. "You and that lawyer of yours had better watch your step or you'll be sorry if you don't," the writer threatened in hackneyed prose. "Watch your step and lay off, or it will be just too bad for you."[33]

Yet there was one letter that surpassed all the others in significance, a single typed page on the official letterhead of the Supreme Court of the State of New York, Appellate Division, dated February 17, 1931:

My dear Miss Gordon,
Your letter addressed to Mr. Kresel under the date of Feb. 7 has been turned over to me for attention. I should be glad to see you at the above address on Friday, Feb. 20, 1931, between the hours of 10 a.m. and 5 p.m.

Very truly yours,
Irving Ben Cooper[34]

Bruckman may not have recognized Cooper's name, but every cop on the force knew of Isidor Kresel, the former prosecutor turned grand inquisitor. His interrogations of police officers on the vice squad had received front-page coverage all winter. The vice beat was known to attract grifters who supplemented their salaries by shaking down gamblers and prostitutes, but Kresel's public exposure of police misconduct had brought shame on the entire department. The only man more reviled by the rank and file was Kresel's boss, Samuel Seabury, a former state judge who'd made it his mission to take down Tammany Hall. Governor Franklin Delano Roosevelt had originally authorized Seabury to investigate corruption in the magistrates' courts, city courts that handled petty crimes, but the crusading judge had expanded his inquiry to the vice squad. When he and Kresel uncovered a conspiracy between cops and prosecutors to frame innocent women as prostitutes, the press went wild.

In light of the scandal, a connection between Vivian Gordon's murder and Seabury's investigation was potentially explosive. If Gordon had accepted Irving Ben Cooper's invitation, it would mean that she'd met with him just five days before her murder. People would jump to the conclusion that she'd been killed for squealing to the investigators, and they'd blame the cops for her death. The newspapers, especially the crime-obsessed tabloids, would turn what was already a sensational case into a public inferno. Millions of people all over the city, the state, even the country would be watching Bruckman's progress and clamoring for him to find the killer. And if he failed, or if it turned out that the authorities were involved in the murder, the backlash could trigger an all-out war between Governor Roosevelt and Tammany Hall. After discovering the letter, Bruckman immediately notified Police Commissioner Edward Mulrooney. It would be a long night, the first of many.

CHAPTER 2
NOTHING TO BE CONCERNED ABOUT

River ice still clung to Manhattan's shores despite the mild weather in late February, encasing the long wooden piers that jutted into the Hudson River like outstretched fingers. Cargo ships, unable to dock properly, nestled up to the jagged ice and hoisted their freight precariously through the air with ropes and nets. Farther from shore, the broad, briny mouth of the Hudson flowed free. Freighters, ferries, fishing boats, liners, and tugs jostled among drifting ice floes, delivering people and goods to the world's busiest port throughout the winter.

But upstream from New York harbor, the Hudson's frozen shoulders converged toward the center, squeezing the ice floes until they fused into a solid plane north of the city. To the west, steep palisades towered over the ice like gnarled brown giants, capped and bearded by snowy forests. To the east, a wooded ridge rose more gently from the riverbank, interrupted here and there by fishing villages, mill towns, and majestic estates tucked into the hills. Past Poughkeepsie, where the river straightened and the wind barreled through the valley, sleek iceboats on steel runners skimmed the surface at 75 mph. Franklin Delano Roosevelt had raced this stretch when he was a young man in the early 1900s, competing with other wealthy men from the Hudson Valley aboard a 28-foot ice yacht named *Hawk*, a Christmas gift from his mother. His family home in Hyde Park overlooked the river, a handsome mansion of yellow-brown stucco and stone commanding a wooded estate that sloped down to the water. He spent his childhood in those woods and on that river—swimming, sailing, skating, fishing, and riding the horses that his father bred.[1]

Roosevelts had been breeding horses and raising crops in the Hudson Valley for generations. Blessed with wealth and pedigree handed down from Dutch settlers of New Amsterdam, FDR's paternal ancestors enjoyed quiet, dignified lives, content to leisurely steward their patrimonies from one generation to the next. His mother's family, the Delanos, were similarly pedigreed but more enterprising. Descendants of Pilgrims from Plymouth Rock, they built fortunes in whaling and shipping, lost everything, and rebuilt it all again, ultimately bequeathing a large inheritance to Franklin's mother, Sara.[2]

FDR chose a third path. His blue-blooded relations didn't consider politics to be a respectable occupation for a gentleman, but his distant cousin Theodore had broken decorum to lead a spectacular political career. Franklin was a sophomore at Harvard when "Cousin Ted" became president. After graduation, he married Theodore's niece, Eleanor Roosevelt, and followed her uncle's example by attending Columbia Law School. The practice of law wasn't his objective. An indifferent student, he managed to pass the bar and join a white-shoe firm in Manhattan but confided to a colleague that he hoped to enter politics at the first opportunity.

The career plan FDR proposed traced the exact course taken by Theodore—"first, a seat in the State Assembly, then an appointment as assistant secretary of the Navy . . . and finally the governorship of New York." The governor of the largest state in the union, he maintained, "has a good chance to be president."[3]

Twenty-four years later, in February 1931, Governor Franklin Delano Roosevelt was tantalizingly close to fulfilling his aspirations. He had followed the plan almost to the letter, substituting only the State Senate for the Assembly, and had already served two years as New York's governor. Though he publicly denied plans to seek higher office, his political advisers were quietly preparing a presidential campaign for the 1932 election. Yet he was no longer the swaggering, callow youth who had raced ice yachts and boasted of grandiose aspirations. Shallow ambition and gauzy idealism had given way to deeper appreciation for the suffering of America's working class and more sophisticated ideas about how to address the nation's ills. He had learned to temper his snobbery and employ his infectious grin to charm politicians and voters across the socioeconomic spectrum.

The transformation was physical as well as mental. He had turned forty-nine at the end of January. Wrinkles lined his high forehead, and white streaks tinged his hair. His shoulders and torso were stronger than ever, but his legs, paralyzed by polio—or possibly an autoimmune disease*—in 1921, had atrophied. Wearing heavy steel braces, with a cane in one hand and a sturdy companion clutching his other arm, he could create the illusion of walking for a few steps, enough to hide the severity of his disability from voters in an era when being seen as an "invalid" was a political liability, but he would never race an ice yacht up the Hudson again.

The mighty river is much reduced as it skirts Albany, 150 miles north of the mouth, a humble waterway fit for a provincial capital with a fraction of New York City's population. The governor's mansion stands on a low hill surrounded by unassuming row houses about a mile from the water. It was originally constructed in a simple Italianate style before the Civil War. Subsequent owners embellished it with Victorian Gothic flourishes, affixing turrets, balconies, wraparound porches, and sloping mansard roofs until it resembled "the classic house on haunted hill," as Franklin's son Elliot described it. Some of the building's staff members and residents, including at least one governor, believed it was actually haunted.[4]†

FDR occupied a large, sunny, second-floor bedroom in the corner of the building, which he often used as an auxiliary office. Propped up on pillows, he conversed with aides, signed papers, and even conducted interviews in his pajamas. He took breakfast in bed as well, reading the morning papers and smoking Camels though a slender cigarette holder while sunlight splashed through the big windows. "The newspapers are laid before him," recounted journalist Earle Looker, a frequent visitor. "He turns the pages with an impatience which quickly finds the headlines and the editorials he desires."

On the morning of February 27, 1931, the headline that caught Roosevelt's eye concerned a woman named Vivian Gordon whose body had been discovered in the Bronx. Ordinarily, local homicide investigations

---

* A peer-reviewed scientific study in 2003 concluded that Roosevelt might have suffered from Guillain–Barré syndrome, a rare autoimmune disease, rather than polio.

† According to legend, the house is haunted by the spirit of a groundskeeper who served its original owners in the 1800s. Former Governor David Paterson told the *New York Post* that he believed the story and had even participated in a late-night expedition to hunt down the ghost. His successor, Andrew Cuomo, dismissed the legend but allowed that "it gets creepy in that house, and there are a lot of noises that go on."

Governor Franklin D. Roosevelt at his desk in Albany, 1931.

were none of the governor's business. New York City officials resented interference from Albany, and state leaders usually avoided entanglement in city politics. "At such an unpleasant moment the traditional aloofness of the Governor of a State might be expected," Looker wrote. "Some gentlemen might withdraw into a sort of contemptuous isolation."[5]

But this was no ordinary homicide case. The papers reported that the victim might have met with an investigator from Samuel Seabury's anti-corruption commission days before her murder. Even the proud *New York Times*, which usually disdained sensational crime stories, elevated the explosive story to the top left column of its front page. Recognizing that the murder might precipitate political ramifications beyond New York City, FDR immediately resolved to apply the weight of the governor's office to the homicide investigation. "I was witness to Roosevelt's decision, the moment he had read the morning papers reporting the murder of Vivian Gordon, to build a fire under the authorities in New York City," Looker continued. "He did so immediately by telephone, with incisive comments and alert questions."[6]

Looker charitably ascribed the governor's urgency to his zeal for justice, but Roosevelt had other reasons to press for a swift resolution. New York City was awash in corruption and crime, both of which had exploded during Prohibition, and Manhattan's incompetent district attorney, Thomas C. T. Crain, had repeatedly failed to convict perpetrators in high-profile cases, starting with the unsolved murder of Arnold Rothstein. Though municipal justice was not technically the governor's purview, the scandals and murders had nonetheless tarnished FDR's reputation for effective leadership. A sensational news story about the murder of a beautiful extortionist threatened to draw even more national attention to the city's broken justice system, which would be especially damaging if the police turned out to be responsible for her death. The longer her killer remained free, the greater the threat to Roosevelt's presidential ambitions.

Yet he had to be cautious. If he pressed too hard on city officials, he risked antagonizing certain people whose support he'd need to win the Democratic presidential nomination. He knew, as everyone knew, that the center of power in New York City was not the mayor's office in City Hall. It was thirty blocks north in a smoky room on the top floor of a broad, four-story building that still stands at the northeast corner of Union Square. The building's façade is an homage to the founding of the republic. Massive columns and a triangular pediment evoke the neoclassical architecture of Federal Hall in downtown Manhattan, where George Washington swore the oath of office. The exterior walls were constructed with specially molded red bricks modeled on those Thomas Jefferson used to build Monticello. The building's interior has been remodeled since FDR's day, but there was once a ballroom on the third floor decorated with oil portraits and marble busts depicting former mayors, governors, and presidents, as well as other men, mostly forgotten, who wielded power more discreetly. An iron staircase spiraled up to a smaller chamber where rows of simple wooden chairs faced a large table. This was the inner sanctum where the Executive Committee of Tammany Hall convened. Thirty-five men representing every political district in New York City assembled here to select the officials responsible for running the municipal bureaucracy— prosecutors, judges, police commissioners, aldermen, and the mayor himself. Their influence radiated well beyond the five boroughs, though. They also selected New York City's delegates at Democratic Party conventions, a massive voting bloc that allowed them to dictate nominations for statewide offices and play kingmaker at national presidential conventions. The organization's mascot, a snarling tiger with coal-black eyes, was so

Tammany Hall headquarters was located in several previous locations in New York before moving to 44 Union Square at East 17th Street, in 1929. The building is shown here in 1929, just after its completion.

notorious that newspapers across the country often referred to Tammany Hall as "the Tiger."[7]

Officially, the Society of St. Tammany was a fraternal order like the Elks Lodge and the Rotary Club. Founded in the 1780s, the original members were ordinary citizens—craftsmen, mechanics, merchants, and lawyers—united in their enthusiasm for patriotism and pageantry. They invented secret handshakes and fetishized Native American culture, adopting a legendary seventeenth-century Delaware chief, known as Tamanend or Tammany, as their patron saint. In the early days, they were mainly known for marching in parades with war paint and tomahawks. They called their leaders *sachems* and their rank-and-file *braves*; the back room of a tavern where they held their rites was their *wigwam*. In 1812, the growing organization moved into a building of its own with a large banquet room that held 2,000 guests. Henceforth, the society's political wing and its headquarters were collectively known as Tammany Hall.[8]

Aaron Burr was the first to recognize Tammany's political potential. Though never a member himself, he cultivated its leaders and enlisted them to campaign for the Jefferson-Burr presidential ticket in 1800. On his instructions, they drew up a roster of every voter in the city, including financial profiles and voting records. A three-person committee was assigned to each of the city's ten election wards, overseen by a central steering committee, the precursor to the Executive Committee. Tammany's electioneering helped Burr win New York, and he nearly became president after tying Jefferson for electoral votes. The House of Representatives decided the tiebreak in Jefferson's favor, and Burr ultimately served one term as vice president before his duel with Alexander Hamilton ended his political career in 1804.[9]

One of Burr's protégés, Martin Van Buren, later took up the mantle. A shrewd political operator, Van Buren used Tammany Hall to orchestrate Andrew Jackson's presidential nomination in 1828. Politics was messy in the days before voter registration and secret ballots, but the elections in New York that year were exceptionally corrupt. Tammany braves towed cartloads of unnaturalized immigrants and underage boys from poll to poll, where they submitted pre-marked ballots. Others guarded polling stations and menaced opposition voters with hickory branches, a violent tribute to Jackson's nickname, "Old Hickory." The election was Tammany's first attempt at large-scale voter fraud, a strategy that it would continue to hone for decades as it developed more sophisticated ways to manipulate elections, such as issuing fraudulent naturalization papers, stuffing ballot boxes, and bribing vote counters.[10]

The election of 1828 was groundbreaking in other ways as well. To consolidate President Jackson's power and prepare the way for his own presidential campaign in 1836, Van Buren organized Jackson supporters from disparate cities and states into a cohesive national party. Tammany Hall represented the New York City chapter, the largest bloc in what soon became known as the Democratic Party. The new party brought novel methods to American politics. Victorious Democrats filled the government with party loyalists, a practice known as patronage. Rewarding supporters with administrative jobs wasn't unprecedented, but the early Democrats used patronage far more aggressively than their predecessors, dismissing officials at every level of government and replacing them with unqualified partisans. When Senator William Marcy of New York famously defended his party's practices by declaring, "to the victors belong the spoils of the enemy," he inadvertently coined both a proverb and a label for the politics of the era: the spoils system.[11]

The spoils system that the Democrats initiated took root in America's fertile soil and propagated like a weed—toxic, tenacious, and nearly indestructible. Leaders of the Whig Party denounced Democratic patronage but practiced it themselves when they came to power in the 1840s, as did the Republicans who supplanted the Whigs in the 1860s, starting with President Abraham Lincoln. It took Congress over half a century to enact civil-service laws to curb federal patronage, and the spoils system endured far longer in cities and states. Nowhere did the roots run deeper than on the island of Manhattan. A hundred years after Andrew Jackson's election, Tammany Hall still made the hiring decisions in city government. The top boss selected candidates for important offices, and the Executive Committee ratified his choices. Lesser positions were filled by lieutenants further down the chain.

The biggest problem with New York City's patronage system wasn't the incompetence of civil servants, though there was plenty of that. It was the graft. Tammany's sachems ruled a sprawling bureaucracy in one of the world's wealthiest cities. There were countless ways to skim the riches and no accountability because the comptrollers, police, prosecutors, and judges owed their jobs to Tammany Hall. William M. Tweed, the most notorious of Tammany's bosses, embezzled tens of millions of dollars from the city treasury in the 1860s. Other popular rackets included taking bribes and kickbacks from job applicants, contractors, and franchise seekers. Some Tammany bosses invested in real estate and then funneled public investment to the area to increase property values. The corruption started at the top, but it permeated all the way down. Building inspectors took bribes from developers. Beat cops shook down prostitutes. Under Tammany Hall, city workers answered to no one but their bosses, and their bosses were on the take.[12]

George Washington Plunkitt, a loquacious turn-of-the-century district boss, tried to excuse Tammany's corruption with a euphemism. He drew a distinction between "dishonest graft," under which he included blackmail and fraud, and "honest graft," which he regarded as smart business. "I seen my opportunities and I took 'em," he rationalized. As an example, he described an insider tip he'd received about a planned park project. "I got on to it, and went lookin' about for land in that neighborhood," he recounted. "I could get nothin' at a bargain but a big piece of swamp, but I took it fast enough and held on to it. What turned out was just what I counted on. They couldn't make the park complete without Plunkitt's swamp, and they had to pay a good price for it. Anything dishonest in that?"[13]

But many New Yorkers weren't so blasé about public servants profiting off the backs of the citizens or the fine line between legal and illegal corruption. Periodic Tammany scandals triggered waves of public outrage and inspired civic activists, known as "goo-goos," who campaigned for good government. In 1871, Samuel Tilden, a disaffected Tammany operative, organized a citizens group known as the Committee of Seventy to investigate Boss Tweed. Twenty years later, Presbyterian minister Charles Parkhurst, president of the New York Society for the Prevention of Crime, toured brothels and gambling joints in disguise to expose police corruption. In the 1890s, Good Government clubs, modeled on Tammany clubhouses, organized "Fusion Party" tickets that united Republicans, independents, and anti-Tammany Democrats.

The Fusion campaigns had some short-lived successes. After Dr. Parkhurst's exposure of police corruption outraged the city, New Yorkers elected a Republican mayor named William Strong, who ran on a Fusion ticket in 1894. As part of his effort to reform city government, Strong appointed Theodore Roosevelt police commissioner. Roosevelt had established a pugnacious reputation for battling the Tammany Tiger in the New York State Assembly, followed by six years taming federal patronage as a civil service commissioner in Washington, DC. Many hoped that he would clean up New York's notoriously corrupt police force. But two years later, the reform wave had already subsided. Strong lost the next election to a Tammany nominee, and Roosevelt returned to Washington with little to show for his work in New York. "The fact is that a reformer can't last in politics," scoffed George Plunkitt. "He can make a show for a while, but he always comes down like a rocket." The chief of police who served under Strong and Roosevelt lamented, "Tammany is not a wave; it's the sea itself."[14]

So it was when FDR began his political career. After winning his first legislative campaign in 1910, he and Eleanor rented a large brownstone near the capitol building in Albany. Unlike Theodore, Franklin was a Democrat, but he shared his cousin's contempt for the Tiger, and his goo-goo campaign theme won over his Republican-leaning district. Albany was a different matter, however. The governor and the majority of FDR's colleagues in the legislature were aligned with Tammany, which gave the New York City bosses effective control of state government.

The first order of business for the new session was to elect a United States senator. In those days, senators were chosen by state legislators rather than directly elected by citizens. Democrats controlled New York's legislature, and Tammany controlled the Democrats, which gave the top boss, Charles F. Murphy, the power to personally select New York's senator. He chose "Blue-eyed Billy" Sheehan, a corporate lawyer and former political boss who had amassed a dubious fortune over the course of his career. Though some questioned Sheehan's qualifications, the election was expected to be a formality. "No one denies that in the last analysis Mr. Murphy's wish will be the law of the caucus that decides who the Democrats in the legislature shall elect as Senator," declared the *New York Tribune*.[15]

But things didn't go quite as Murphy had planned. When the State Senate convened in January 1911, twenty-one Democratic senators absented themselves from the statehouse, denying Murphy a majority. They adjourned to the library of a nearby brownstone, the home of their ringleader, Franklin Delano Roosevelt. FDR was only twenty-nine years old and just two weeks into his first term in the State Senate, but he had a famous last name and a relish for confrontation. "There is nothing I love as much as a good fight," he proclaimed with a flash of his soon-to-be-famous grin. "I never had as much fun in my life as I am having right now." His panache reminded old-timers of his cousin Theodore. "If we've caught a Roosevelt, we'd better take him down and drop him off the dock," grumbled one Tammany regular. "Gee!" marveled another, "the other Roosevelt didn't lose much time in making trouble once he got here, but this fellow 'beat him' to it. His seat in the Senate wasn't even warm before he became a bolter. Ain't it fierce?"[16]

FDR and his band of insurgents held out for weeks, ultimately forcing Murphy to withdraw his candidate. They also introduced a bill expressing support for the proposed Seventeenth Amendment, which stipulated that US senators be directly elected by the voters in each state. Yet despite their bold resistance, the insurgency never amounted to more than a ripple in the Tammany sea. After dropping Sheehan, Murphy announced his second choice, Justice James O'Gorman, a former Tammany sachem. This time, a few insurgents broke ranks, and the boss got his senator. As the final vote got underway, a group of Tammany loyalists chanted,

Tam-ma-nee, Tam-ma-nee

Franklin D., like Uncle "The,"

Is no match for Tam-ma-nee[17]

FDR was undeterred. After his dramatic debut, he continued to attract headlines by assailing the Hall. "There is no question that the great majority of Democrats in this state are disgusted by the so-called State leadership of Charles F. Murphy," he proclaimed in December. "There is only one remedy. . . . Charles F. Murphy and his kind must, like the noxious weed, be plucked out root and branch." But his legislative career didn't last long enough to make a difference. In the spring of 1913, President Woodrow Wilson offered to appoint him assistant secretary of the Navy, and FDR, like his cousin before him, decamped for Washington.[18]

For all the parallels, there was a key difference between Franklin and Theodore that initially impeded the younger Roosevelt's career. As a Republican, Theodore had nothing to lose by attacking Tammany Hall, but Franklin's affiliation with the Democratic Party complicated matters. His goo-goo agenda appealed to voters in his upstate district, where Tammany's hold was tenuous, but winning statewide Democratic primaries was almost impossible without the Hall's support. Though election fraud was not as rampant as it had been in Boss Tweed's day, Tammany's ability to mobilize voters was formidable, especially among New York City's immigrant communities.

FDR soon discovered the limits of his insurgent posture when he ran for the United States Senate in 1914. The ratification of the Seventeenth Amendment the year before meant that Boss Murphy could no longer choose New York's senator by fiat, but FDR still had to win the Democratic primary in order to compete in the general election. To oppose him, Murphy recruited James W. Gerard, the US ambassador to Germany. Gerard conducted a languid, long-distance campaign from his residence in Berlin, while FDR feverishly crisscrossed New York State, but Tammany's get-out-the-vote efforts helped the distant ambassador trounce the upstart Roosevelt by nearly three to one.[19]

The humiliating defeat convinced FDR to change tack for the sake of his career. Gadfly no longer, he muted his denunciations of the bosses, made peace with Charles Murphy, and began publicly endorsing Tammany's candidates. So dramatic was his conversion that Murphy invited him to speak at the Hall's annual Independence Day celebration in 1917. He and the boss sat beside each other on the platform, posing for photos in matching straw hats as they chatted amiably. When it was FDR's turn to speak, he won a laugh from the audience when he quipped, "I am not entirely a stranger to Tammany Hall, and . . . our associations in the past have been more or less pleasant."[20]

Murphy, for his part, was receptive to Roosevelt's overtures. He was a different breed from his thuggish predecessors—mild-mannered, soft-spoken, and pragmatic. He was known as "Silent Charlie," but his reticence masked a brilliant political mind that enabled him to rise from poverty to become the most effective boss in Tammany's history. Having come to power at a time when the waves of reform were crashing hard and fast against Manhattan's shores, he perceived that the Tiger would have to reform its unsavory reputation in order to sustain its influence in the twentieth century. The "New Tammany" that Murphy cultivated was more competent, less corrupt, and committed to improving the lives of its poorest constituents. Though he himself had made a fortune through so-called honest graft, he cracked down on blackmail, prostitution, and other rackets that brought disrepute to the Hall. He also reversed Tammany's traditional subservience to corporate interests and embraced popular progressive causes like child labor laws and workplace safety regulations. Finally, he groomed smart, charismatic politicians with spotless reputations, such as Al Smith, one of New York's most popular governors.

Alfred Emanuel Smith grew up in a working-class tenement on the Lower East Side. His father descended from Italians and Germans, but Smith identified with the Irish Catholics on his mother's side. He attended Catholic school until he was fourteen, but after his father died, he dropped out and took a job at the Fulton Fish Market to support his mother and sister.

Charles F. Murphy, head of Tammany Hall from 1902–24, center, and Al Smith, future New York governor, right, at the 1916 Democratic National Convention in St. Louis, Missouri.

His introduction to politics was a local Irish saloon where he and other young men ran errands and performed political tasks for the saloon owner, "Big Tom" Foley, an influential Tammany leader. Foley took a liking to the confident, gregarious youth. He found Smith a patronage job in city government and later helped him win a seat in the State Assembly. The charismatic assemblyman soon caught the eye of Boss Murphy, who was looking for skillful young politicians with clean reputations to become the smiling faces of his "New Tammany." With Murphy's guidance and support, Smith was elected majority leader in 1911, speaker of the Assembly in 1913, and governor of New York in 1918.[21]

Smith had risen far from the fish market, but his ambitions reached higher still. New York's governors were perennially strong presidential contenders because their state accounted for nearly ten percent of the nation's total population. With Tammany's enthusiastic support, Al Smith stood a good chance of the winning the Democratic presidential nomination except for one problem: his religion. No major party had ever nominated a Catholic presidential candidate. Opposition to his candidacy at the 1924 Democratic National Convention was especially intense among Southern delegates, many of whom belonged to the Ku Klux Klan. To allay anti-Catholic prejudice, one of Smith's advisers suggested that he invite Franklin Roosevelt to deliver the nomination speech. "You're a Bowery mick," the adviser pointed out, "and he's a Protestant patrician and he'd take some of the curse off you."[22]

Roosevelt's own political career was on hold, derailed by the paralysis of his legs in 1921. Though he'd taken leave from politics while he recuperated, he hesitantly agreed to make the nomination speech for Smith. The most daunting task would be to reach the podium without a wheelchair. To prepare, Roosevelt had the distance from the convention floor to the podium measured. For hours a day, he practiced "walking" across his library at Hyde Park, a crutch under one arm and his sixteen-year-old son, James, supporting the other as he dragged his frozen legs across the floor. At the convention, he managed the feat with great difficulty. "Outwardly he was beaming, seemingly confident and unconcerned," James recalled, "but I could sense his inner tenseness. His fingers dug into my arm like pincers—I doubt that he knew how hard he was gripping me. His face was covered with perspiration."[23]

Frances Perkins, who would later become Roosevelt's labor secretary in the White House, remembered how frail he looked as he struggled to cross the stage. "There was a hush and everybody was holding their breath," she recalled. "Here was this terribly crippled person operating on a crutch and an arm and getting himself to the platform somehow, looking so pale, so thin, so delicate that it was a surprise to hear him begin to speak and see that his voice was strong and true and vigorous and that what he had to say had been not only well thought out but was delivered in a very convincing and dramatic kind of a way. While he stood there and while his voice was so vigorous and strong, he was literally trembling. The hand that was on the paper was literally shaking, because of the extreme pain and tenseness with which he held himself up to make that speech."[24]

Al Smith didn't win the nomination that year, but Roosevelt's nomination speech would be remembered, especially his rousing tribute to Smith, whom he dubbed "the 'Happy Warrior' of the political battlefield," in reference to a Wordsworth poem. Four years later, at the 1928 convention, a stronger and more confident Roosevelt once again praised the "the Happy Warrior, Alfred E. Smith." This time, Smith won the nomination on the first ballot.

The Happy Warrior faced a difficult path to the White House, though. The booming economy favored the incumbent Republican Party, and his opponent, Herbert Hoover, was widely admired. In addition, Smith continued to struggle against pervasive anti-Catholic prejudice, and his opposition to Prohibition was unpopular in rural areas. To have any chance of getting elected, he had to win New York State. His advisers urged him to recruit a popular gubernatorial candidate to bolster the ticket, and all agreed that Franklin Roosevelt was the most electable Democrat in the state.

Roosevelt wasn't ready, though. He wanted to run for governor, just not in 1928. He, too, believed that conditions were unfavorable for Democrats that year, and he needed more time to rehabilitate his legs, so he rebuffed Smith's repeated entreaties. The day before the state convention, Smith called him one last time and begged him to run "as a personal favor," but Roosevelt again declined.

"Frank, just one more question," Smith pressed. "If those fellows nominate you tomorrow and adjourn, will you refuse to run?"

Roosevelt said nothing for a few moments. Finally, he answered that he did not consent to being nominated but wasn't sure what he would do if the delegates nominated him anyway.

"Thanks, Frank. I won't ask you any more questions," Smith gleefully replied.[25]

The next day, the convention delegates nominated Franklin Delano Roosevelt by acclamation, and he reluctantly accepted, telling a friend, "When you're in politics you've got to play the game." Five weeks later, he narrowly won the gubernatorial election. Al Smith was less fortunate. Herbert Hoover crushed him in a landslide, winning forty of forty-eight states, including New York. After the humiliating defeat, Smith announced that he was "finished" with politics. "I certainly do not expect ever to run for public office again," he declared. "I have had all I can stand of it."[26]

Roosevelt, on the other hand, was back on the course that he'd set for himself at the beginning of his career, still following the footsteps of his cousin Theodore, which he hoped would lead him to the White House. But once again Tammany Hall complicated his plans.

After his rapprochement with Charles Murphy in 1917, Roosevelt had come to appreciate the boss's efforts to reform the Hall, and the two men had developed a cordial relationship. When Murphy died in 1924, FDR hailed his old nemesis as Tammany's "strongest and wisest leader . . . a genius who kept harmony, and at the same time recognized that the world moves on."[27]

But Murphy's successors lacked his vision. George W. Olvany, who took his place, was Tammany's first college-educated boss. He had a clean reputation before he came to power but exploited his position to funnel millions to his law firm while ignoring misconduct by his subordinates. His successor, John F. Curry, was even more retrogressive. Born in Ireland, he'd grown up among the gangs and tenement houses of Hell's Kitchen, where he worked his way up the Tammany ranks. He was fifty-five years old when he reached the organization's pinnacle in 1929, a gruff balding man with a square face and a bristly gray mustache. He smoked exactly three cigars a day, never drank, and spoke little. "It is a fiction, this New Tammany," he growled. "I will carry out the policies in which I grew up."[28]

Tammany's reversion wasn't only the fault of its leadership, though. The Roaring Twenties brought economic prosperity and population growth to the city, which fertilized a bloom of new factories, skyscrapers, bridges, and subway lines. The construction contracts, franchises, permits, and inspections presented numerous opportunities for venal civil servants to engage in "honest" graft. At the same time, Prohibition and the rise of organized crime fostered more nefarious schemes. The illegal bars, brothels, and gambling joints that proliferated in the 1920s were ripe targets for protection rackets and shakedowns by crooked police, prosecutors, and judges. Arnold Rothstein and other gangsters cultivated alliances with Tammany leaders for mutual profit.

Yet the resurgence of corruption failed to elicit much reaction from voters. New Yorkers were making too much money and having too much fun to worry about a little graft. Flush with cash, liberated from the starched collars and tight corsets of the Victorian era, they reveled all night at Gatsbyesque "whoopee" parties and glitzy nightclubs. "The whole golden boom was in the air," reminisced F. Scott Fitzgerald, "its splendid generosities, its outrageous corruptions and the tortuous death struggle of the old America in prohibition."[29]

The Volstead Act had done nothing to quench liquor consumption in Manhattan. No sooner did it go into effect at 12:01 a.m. on January 17, 1920, than illegal speakeasies began to sprout in basements and back rooms all over the city. By February, 15,000 speakeasies had replaced 10,000 saloons. "In the old days, you could wipe out a vicious saloon," groused Police Commissioner Grover Whalen. "Nowadays all you need is two bottles and a room and you have a speakeasy." Illegal bars could be found in apartments and brownstones, below banks and tailor shops, in the back rooms of butcher shops and grocery stores, above nightclubs, or in abandoned buildings. Some used secret passwords, padlocks, and spyholes to restrict entry; others distributed special cards made of metal or wood. The glassware and furnishings were expendable in case of raids, and many speakeasies employed electric dumbwaiters or drains in the floor to dispose of contraband in a hurry.[30]

Many nightclubs also served alcohol. Less discreet and more expensive to replace than the speakeasies, they tried to protect themselves from raids by bribing agents and officials. One nightclub owner, Larry Fay, even made a Tammany district leader a partner in the business. Fay was primarily a bootlegger who used the club to launder money and distribute alcohol, a common practice. Legs Diamond owned the Hotsy Totsy. Dutch Schultz ran the Embassy. Arnold Rothstein invested in dozens of nightclubs. The criminal connection didn't deter ordinary New Yorkers from patronizing such establishments. On the contrary, it added cachet by enhancing the thrill of illicit intoxication. Night after night, stockbrokers and socialites mingled with gangsters and con artists in smoky salons and swinging dance halls as they drank themselves into a collective stupor.[31]

Presiding over the debauchery was the mayor himself, the Honorable James J. Walker. Handsome and debonair, with sparkling blue eyes and an impish grin, he was New York's beloved cad. "Jimmy was the extrovert, the spontaneous eccentric, the sidewalk favorite, the beloved clown," wrote famed powerbroker Robert Moses. Frances Perkins recalled, "I don't think he ever took anything seriously. I don't think he took himself seriously. I don't think he took the City of New York seriously. The City of New York was like a pretty girl he took out for the evening to him." A 1957 biopic starring Bob Hope posthumously dubbed him "Beau James," but no one called him James in his day. He was always Jimmy. Born and raised in Greenwich Village, he had Tammany in his blood. His father, an Irish immigrant, had worked his way up the political hierarchy from alderman to state legislator to Manhattan's superintendent of public buildings, a lucrative office that allowed the family to live in style. As a young man, Jimmy Walker aspired to become a lyricist on Tin Pan Alley and even penned a hit single in 1906, "Will You Love Me in December as You Do in May?" But when his music career fizzled, his father pressured him to enroll at New York Law School. After graduation, he followed his father's footsteps into the state legislature and became a rising star in the Democratic Party.[32]

In 1925, Boss Olvany invited Walker to run for mayor. Politically, the popular state senator was an inspired choice. A gifted public speaker with an irreverent sense of humor, he peppered his speeches with one-liners and answered questions with wisecracks that delighted journalists, disarmed critics, and charmed voters. "He has a sixth sense for catching the mood, the atmosphere, the prevailing sentiment of any gathering and rendering it in felicitous sentences," wrote journalist Alva Johnston in *Vanity Fair*. He added that Walker seduced his audience with "impish leers and sly allusions which flatter the hearer into the belief that he and Jimmy understand each other; that they are two kindred souls; that they are two, and the only two members, of a secret mysterious order. Hundreds of thousands, if not millions of New Yorkers, firmly believe that they are among Jimmy's closest friends."[33]

George Olvany and John Curry valued Walker's common touch and popular appeal, but they also appreciated the mayor's loyalty to the not-so-secret order of St. Tammany. "I am the candidate of Tammany Hall," Walker proudly declared during his campaign, "and if elected I will be a Tammany Hall mayor." He was happy to let the bosses guide his policies

Franklin D. Roosevelt and James "Jimmy" Walker at the 1924 Democratic National Convention in New York City.

and appointments, and he expressed his gratitude to his benefactors with glowing tributes. "This was the only place where my immigrant father found welcome, help, and assistance when he landed in this country," he rhapsodized in a speech at the Hall. "Nearly all the humane measures that have been written into the statute books of the state in recent years emanated from this building." During another speech, he gushed, "I have never known a more attractive and finer character in political life than John F. Curry." Most significantly, Walker turned a blind eye to the corruption that metastasized during his tenure. "One thing about Jimmy," quipped one of his associates, "he may steal a dime, but he'll always let you take a penny." The comment was meant as a joke, but it wasn't far off the mark.[34]

Walker was not without talents or achievements. His mind was as sharp as his tongue, and he was quick to grasp complex issues. He presided over a number of significant projects, including an expansion of the subway system and the establishment of the Department of Sanitation. But he had a short attention span and a lax work ethic; he often arrived at work midday after partying all night. Administration bored him, and he made no effort to reign in the corruption that permeated the civil service. He much preferred ticker-tape parades, diplomatic junkets, and hosting dignitaries, including the queen of Romania, with whom he reportedly flirted. Though he'd given up his dream of becoming a lyricist, his attraction to show business endured. New Yorkers affectionately called him the "Night Mayor" in tribute to his fondness for theater and clubs; the dapper forty-nine-year-old mayor was often seen cavorting about town with his glamorous mistress, Betty Compton, a twenty-six-year-old Broadway star. His personal tailor helped him design his own ensembles, which he changed three times a day, twice during office hours and once more before he went out for the evening. The tailor also accompanied him on an official European tour in 1927, for which he packed forty-three suits, dozens of sports coats, and a hundred ties. Walker's wardrobe and lifestyle obviously outpaced his salary, even after he raised his own salary from $25,000 to $40,000, but no one paid much attention to that. His cheeky humor and roguish charm bewitched the public, and his evening revelries embodied the exuberance of the Roaring Twenties. Life was good, and Mayor Jimmy Walker lived an especially good life.[35]

Not everyone adored him, though. When he came up for reelection in 1929, he faced a spirited challenge from Representative Fiorello La Guardia, a Republican congressperson from lower Manhattan. La Guardia was an unlikely politician—a stubby, scruffy, cigar-puffing dynamo with a squeaky voice and thinning black hair. Like Walker, he hailed from Greenwich Village, but his father was Italian, his mother was Jewish, and he loathed the corruption of Tammany Hall. He had stunned the political establishment by winning his Tammany-friendly district in 1922. Now he sought to repeat the feat citywide in the mayoral race. All through the autumn of 1929, as the bloated stock markets began to tremble and heave, he crisscrossed the city, flinging charges of corruption and criminality at the mayor's office. He accused members of the administration of conspiring with Arnold Rothstein and alleged that the authorities had deliberately bungled the investigation of his murder to protect powerful politicians who had dealings with the legendary gangster. He even produced a promissory note for $20,000 to Arnold Rothstein signed by a city magistrate named Albert Vitale.[36]

But the attacks didn't leave a mark. Walker, true to form, laughed off the accusations. When La Guardia assailed him for raising his own salary, he quipped, "Why, that's cheap! Think what it would cost if I worked full time!" He ignored the Rothstein charges and dismissed the corruption allegations with a shrug. "Times have been altogether too good and opportunities too great during the last four years for the officials of this city to be annoyed with any petty graft," he scoffed. New Yorkers seemed to agree. Even as the mighty markets came tumbling down, they reelected Jimmy Walker by record margins. "He didn't have the proof," one of La Guardia's associates acknowledged. "What he said was probably true, but it didn't get under people's skin. They didn't believe him. They thought he was a little wild and reckless with his charges."[37]

But as the aftershocks from Wall Street's convulsions rattled across the country, the reality started to sink in. "Somebody had blundered," wrote F. Scott Fitzgerald, "and the most expensive orgy in history was over." Polly Adler, Manhattan's infamous madam, recalled New Yorkers' "stunned bewilderment" after the crash: "One minute you were kinging it on top of the world, and the next you were flat on your behind in the street, and that 'world' you had been on top of was a collapsed balloon." In the dreary dawn of the Great Depression, Jimmy Walker's quips seemed less amusing. The city was filthy, crime was rampant, and the cops were crooked. As the banks failed and the city coffers emptied out, people began to wonder where all the money had gone. "When the whole nation was living high off the hog, John Q. Public didn't give a damn how the Tammany boys were getting theirs," Adler observed. "But now it was a different story."[38]

The financial crisis furnished the conditions for a backlash against Tammany Hall, but the spark that triggered the firestorm was a bizarre scandal at a celebratory feast that went sideways. On December 7, 1929, one month after the election and a few weeks into the financial crisis, sixty men gathered in the upstairs banquet hall of the Roman Gardens restaurant in the Bronx. They sat around a long, horseshoe-shaped table, sipping coffee and smoking cigars past midnight while a five-piece band played jazz, and a series of speakers toasted the guest of honor, Magistrate Albert H. Vitale. Vitale was a favorite son in the Bronx's Little Italy. A second-generation immigrant, he had risen from poverty to become a judge on the Magistrates' Court, which handled everything from divorce to petty crime. The Tammany bosses appreciated the way he followed orders and drummed up support among Italian-American voters, and he seemed poised to rise even higher. The guests who gathered at the Roman Gardens to celebrate Vitale were optimistic. They didn't worry about the scandals that trailed him—his social interactions with mafiosos or the $20,000 loan from Arnold Rothstein that La Guardia had revealed. If they recognized Ciro Terranova, the Artichoke King, at the banquet, they didn't draw attention to him. Speaker after speaker praised Vitale's achievements and prophesied a golden political future for the forty-three-year-old magistrate.

When the toasts and tributes concluded, around one in the morning, Vitale rose to thank his supporters. But as he cleared his throat, four well-dressed men quietly entered the room from the stairwell. Three more sauntered behind him from the kitchen. They fanned out across the room, brandished revolvers, and ordered the guests to place their hands on the tables. Vitale hesitated, unsure what to make of the interruption. "Come on, now, judge," admonished one of the gunmen. "This is no joke. Sit down." Vitale sat, and the intruders worked the room, demanding money and jewelry from each guest. When one encountered an off-duty detective reaching for his holster, he pushed a gun in his face. "Oh, so you're a cop eh?" he snarled. "Sit right down, Mr. Cop, and don't make a move, or you'll be a dead cop."

Vitale attempted to defuse the situation. "Gentlemen, obey all orders," he called out. "Let them take what we have." He stared fiercely at the detective, willing him to comply. But even as the officer relinquished his weapon, Vitale slipped off his own four-and-a-half caret diamond ring. Pretending to fix his belt, he slid it into the waistband of his trousers.

Ten minutes later, the intruders calmly departed with bags of loot, leaving one man at the stairwell to cover their escape. "Stay right where you are for three minutes," he ordered before following his comrades down the stairs. The roar of two cars racing off could be heard through the windows.

When the news broke the next day, journalists reported the story with an air of incredulity. Even in the crime-ridden 1920s, a seven-man holdup at a fundraiser for a prominent magistrate seemed absurd. The story soon grew stranger still. Instead of immediately reporting the theft to the police, Vitale rushed back to his office. After a few phone calls, he arranged for the stolen valuables to be returned to his guests, including the detective's revolver. Yet the thieves, who had not even bothered to disguise their faces, remained at large. Commissioner Whalen advanced the theory that the holdup was an elaborate ruse arranged by Ciro Terranova. According to Whalen, Terranova had staged the robbery to recover an incriminating murder contract from another guest who had threatened to send it to the police over a financial dispute. Once Terranova's gangsters had retrieved the evidence, they returned the loot. Detectives had even discovered a note in possession of a Terranova lieutenant that said, "Tell Vitale not to worry."

But these revelations and accusations only produced more confusion and dismay. Why didn't Vitale or the off-duty detective report the crime immediately? How had the magistrate arranged for the stolen valuables to be returned to his guests? And why were Terranova and other gangsters invited to the banquet in the first place? Even jaded New Yorkers accustomed to malfeasance by Tammany officials shook their heads in astonishment and disgust.[39]

An investigation ensued, and Vitale was ultimately removed in March 1930 by the Appellate Division of the State Supreme Court, but the scandals kept coming. In May, County Judge W. Bernard Vause was charged with taking a $250,000 bribe from a steamship company seeking a pier lease from the city. In June, William F. Doyle, a horse veterinarian turned real estate lobbyist, was indicted for bribing building regulators to obtain variances for his clients. In July, Magistrate George Ewald, whom Mayor Walker had appointed to replace Vitale, was charged with fraudulently selling worthless stock in a mining company.[40]

The duty of prosecuting these cases fell to the new district attorney of Manhattan, Thomas C. T. Crain. A personal friend of Boss Curry, Crain had served Tammany Hall in various capacities since 1887, including twenty-four years as a judge. As he approached the mandatory judicial retirement age of seventy, Curry saw fit to nominate him for district attorney. Unlike most Tammany leaders, Crain came from old money. Courtly and mild-mannered with an aquiline nose and a cleft chin, he traced his ancestors to the *Mayflower* and lived in an old mansion on the Upper West Side with two sisters and several servants. Though his reputation was perfectly respectable, he was ill-suited for the job of chief prosecutor. Even in his younger days, he wasn't known for his dynamism or his work ethic. At seventy, wizened and frail, he lacked the vigor to run a district attorney's office, especially in the teeming, rough-and-tumble borough of Manhattan, which was precisely why Curry selected him.[41]

After the scandals broke, Crain promised to pursue an "impartial investigation" that would expose incompetent officials "if such there be" and punish lawbreakers "if there be any dishonesty" but insinuated that he didn't expect to find much of either. His priority, rather, was to exonerate honest officials and "lift any unjust stigma" produced by the scandals. He promptly dismissed the charges against Judge Vause, and his half-hearted prosecutions of Vitale, Doyle, and Ewald did not inspire confidence. Meanwhile, the hapless investigation of Arnold Rothstein's murder, which he had promised to solve, continued to founder.[42]

The snowballing scandals and lack of legal accountability finally drew a reaction from shell-shocked New Yorkers as they reeled from the deepening financial crisis. Long-dormant civic reformers spoke up to denounce the district attorney and the Walker administration. Republican legislators in Albany demanded an independent investigation of the city magistrates. But Jimmy Walker shrugged off the ripples of protest. "If there are any irregularities in the city among civil employees, I am more anxious than anyone else to find out about them," he assured the press. "Of course, I know the boys in Albany must play politics, but that's nothing to be disturbed about."[43]

Governor Roosevelt was not so sanguine. He had long maintained a studied silence on Tammany's affairs. During the mayoral campaign, he escaped to his country estate in Warm Springs, Georgia, and rebuffed reporters' inquiries with the excuse that he was on vacation. He didn't endorse Walker, a fellow Democrat, but he also ignored La Guardia's demands to launch a state investigation into alleged corruption and election misconduct. When he returned to Albany, he continued to avoid entanglement in city affairs on the grounds that the governor's office should not interfere with "the principle of home rule," a convenient excuse for inaction. "Governor Roosevelt's declaration that he lacks the power to investigate the affairs of New York City and the scandals—too numerous to mention—that are featured daily on the front page of every city paper is in the highest degree disingenuous," protested Republican State Chairman William J. Maier.[44]

But Tammany's scandals were becoming a political liability, and though the Republicans were powerless to act without a legislative majority, their public demands for an investigation put Roosevelt in a bind. On one hand, he feared antagonizing the Tammany bosses, whose support he'd need to win the presidential nomination. On the other, he couldn't be seen to ignore rampant corruption in his home state if he hoped to win the general election. "I had to do a lot of hard thinking over that . . . demand," he confessed to a friend. He eventually found a way out of the predicament by quietly pressuring Mayor Walker to launch an internal probe of municipal corruption. Walker dutifully ordered the inquiry, and Roosevelt pledged to guarantee its integrity. "I shall stand ready to send the Attorney-General," he promised, "whenever it becomes apparent that an investigation is not as complete and as searching as it should be." But critics derided the choreographed routine as a "smoke screen" designed to avoid a serious corruption probe. "The average citizen understands that the Governor is not going out of his way to embarrass Tammany Hall," retorted one Republican leader.[45]

Before Walker's internal investigation even got off the ground, however, another scandal broke. During the inquiry into Magistrate Ewald's mining stocks, it came out that his wife had personally delivered $10,000 of her father's money to a Bronx Tammany boss named Martin Healy on the very same day that Mayor Walker appointed her husband to the bench. Under District Attorney Crain's gentle questioning, she testified to a grand jury that the money was a friendly loan to help Healy build a house in Long Island and that he had given her a promissory note, which she couldn't produce, unfortunately, because she had lost it. Jimmy Walker also took the stand to deny any undue influence in the appointment. "If Ewald voluntarily contributed any money for that appointment, he might just as well have thrown it in the sewer," he scoffed. The grand jury, evidently persuaded, dismissed the charges.[46]

The collapse of the second Ewald case provoked a swift and furious public response, not only from the usual Republican critics but also from some of Roosevelt's Democratic allies. Stephen Wise, a renowned Reform rabbi, was a close friend of Al Smith's and had campaigned for him in 1928. After the grand jury's verdict, Wise sent Roosevelt a strident telegram decrying "the breakdown of justice in the city of New York" and exhorting him to "act with the vigor and directness which the people expect." The rabbi subsequently shared his message with city papers, many of which printed it in full on their front pages and echoed his demands in their editorials.[47]

Facing broad public outrage over the Ewald verdict and other scandals, Roosevelt finally conceded that state intervention would be necessary. Still hoping to avoid a "general fishing expedition" that might ensnare top Tammany officials, he ordered New York Attorney General Hamilton Ward Jr. to investigate the accusations against Ewald but forbid him from expanding the investigation beyond the bribery case. Ward, a Republican, chafed under the restriction but reluctantly agreed to Roosevelt's terms. "I am a fisherman," he complained to the press. "You know it is difficult for a fisherman to be told where to fish."[48]

But Mayor Jimmy Walker wasn't about to let a tiresome state investigation hamper his fun. The day after Roosevelt's order, he invited Betty Compton to sail with him aboard a friend's yacht. "I read in the papers," he said to her, "something about fishing. If the Attorney General fishes, why can't we?"

They didn't catch much though. A storm from the north brought fierce winds that rocked the boat and made Walker seasick, so they docked at Montauk at the eastern tip of Long Island. After disembarking, Compton persuaded Walker to escort her to the Star Island Casino, a not-so-secret gambling house that catered to rich New Yorkers vacationing in the Hamptons. When the couple entered the gaming room through a hidden door in the kitchen, the manager greeted the mayor discretely: "Good evening, Mr. W. What is your pleasure?"

"I haven't any pleasure," Walker replied. "I'm still seasick. But Miss C. would be pleased to play hazard.*"

The dice favored Compton that night, and she accumulated about $2,000 in chips, but her streak was interrupted by the unwelcome arrival of the vice squad. "Stand where you are!" an officer shouted as he burst through the door, "This is a raid!"

Amid the chaos, Walker managed to slip away into the kitchen. Compton was less fortunate. As the police led her outside, she saw her lover sitting at a table in a waiter's apron calmly eating a plate of beans. After her release a few hours later, she furiously accosted him at the yacht. "Why did you desert me?" she shouted. "You and your beans!"

"Monk," he answered, "I knew you'd get out all right. But as for me, Governor Roosevelt has decided to keep that investigation within reasonable bounds. It might be a good idea if I didn't tempt fate at this moment by showing up in a rural hoosegow."[49]

The story came out anyway a few days later when a deputy sheriff who had participated in the raid revealed that he had spoken with the mayor at the casino and let him off. "He called me to one side and said he was Mayor Walker," the officer told the press. "He asked me to let him go to the boat. I did."[50]

But Walker pooh-poohed the deputy sheriff's account, claiming that he'd eaten at the restaurant but never entered the gambling room. "If I had been at the casino and someone had asked me if I were Mayor Walker, I would not have identified myself as the mayor," he scoffed.

The local district attorney accepted Walker's excuse at face value. "That satisfies me," he said. "I see the mayor admits he was around there when the raids occurred. I'm willing to let it go at that."[51]

Governor Roosevelt wasn't particularly bothered about Walker's Montauk adventure. New Yorkers expected a bit of misbehavior from their mayor, and recreational gambling wasn't considered a terrible sin. The bribery in the Magistrates' Courts was much more objectionable, though, and it quickly became clear that investigating Ewald wasn't enough to appease Rabbi Wise and others who had demanded action from the state.

---

* Hazard: A dice game related to craps.

Roosevelt recognized that he had to open a wider investigation of the magistrates, but he was loathe to extend the authority of Attorney General Ward. Authorizing a Republican politician like Ward to investigate Democratic officials would infuriate Boss Curry and risk an expansive inquiry that might spiral out of control. Yet whoever led the investigation had to be credible. Roosevelt needed a politically independent Democrat with legal acumen and unimpeachable integrity who would command respect across the political spectrum. One candidate stood out from the rest, a former judge from the New York State Court of Appeals. Samuel Seabury was a lifelong Democrat and had even been nominated for governor in 1916, but he was a staunch advocate of good government and no friend of Tammany Hall. Though he'd long since retired from politics, his name was still famous, and his reputation was impeccable.[52]

Roosevelt was solely responsible for initiating the investigation and selecting Seabury to lead it, but he took pains to hide his fingerprints by quietly pressing the Appellate Division of the State Supreme Court

Samuel Seabury, c. 1920s.

to launch the inquiry. The presiding judge was skeptical but changed his mind during a private luncheon with Roosevelts at his Hyde Park estate. The next day, the court ordered "that Hon. Samuel Seabury be and he hereby appointed referee* to conduct an investigation of the magistrates' courts in the First Judicial Department and the magistrates thereof." When reporters asked FDR to comment, he praised the decision as if he had nothing to do with it, declaring that he was "very happy that the investigation will be made as suggested by the Appellate Division."[53]

Good government advocates also applauded the choice, but the Tiger was sullen. "No one welcomes such an investigation more than myself," Walker insisted with feigned nonchalance. "If I didn't, I would have been out long ago." But the usually voluble mayor said little more about the inquiry and did not comment on Judge Seabury. Boss Curry said simply, "Tammany Hall stands just where it did when I came into office, for clean government." Then he quietly ordered his minions to resist the investigation. Even Al Smith, who epitomized the New Tammany, was troubled by Roosevelt's choice.[54]

"That's an awful thing to do," he grumbled to Frances Perkins. "Why did he appoint a commissioner?"

"He had to do something," she replied. "After all, information about Walker is coming out. Walker is not too on the straight. There have been lots of things wrong."

"Sure, that's right. But why did he appoint a man like Seabury?"

"Well, he's a well-known Democrat and an honorable Democrat."

"Yes, but he's a Democrat without any heart and he's crazy about himself," Smith countered. "He'll promote himself out of this. There are plenty of other Democrats that he should have appointed. Why didn't he appoint Jerry O'Connor? He's a sharp, shrewd lawyer, but he's practical. He won't go too far."[55]

But like his Tammany allies, Smith refrained from public comment and waited uneasily to see what would happen next.

---

* In legal terms, referees are court officials who are authorized to hold hearings, examine witnesses, and make recommendations to judges but not to pass judgment themselves.

CHAPTER 3

OLD HEADS FOR COUNSEL, YOUNG HEADS FOR WAR

SAMUEL SEABURY'S APPOINTMENT WAS ARRANGED SO HASTILY THAT NO one even informed him before the announcement went to press. He was in London at the time, enjoying an extended summer vacation with his wife, Maud. Far removed from New York and only vaguely aware of the scandals that rattled the city that summer, he spent his days in the cramped aisles of fusty British bookstores. Fourteen years had passed since he'd resigned from the bench and resumed his law practice in Manhattan. His fastidiously combed hair had gone silver, and the high, pale cheeks of his youth had sagged into ruddy jowls as he coasted gently toward retirement. The flames of political aspiration had long since cooled, and he'd made peace with the fact that his life would not be extraordinary. Well-compensated but unfulfilled by private practice, he channeled most of his energy into collecting rare books and documenting his illustrious family tree.

He'd grown up under the gaze of his distinguished ancestors, a long line of Samuel Seaburys dating back to the Plymouth Colony. Their glossy eyes had glared down at him from the walls of his father's library as if admonishing him to live up to his name and fulfill the motto emblazoned on the family crest, *Supera Alta Tenere*, Hold to the Most High. Those other Samuel Seaburys were men of God—rectors and deacons and doctors of theology—all the way up the chain. His great-great-grandfather, the Right Reverend Samuel Seabury, had been America's first Episcopalian bishop.* But young Samuel Seabury—the last Samuel Seabury, for he and Maud had no children—chose a more worldly path. By the time he came of age, the family fortune had diminished. His father, the rector of a struggling church in Greenwich Village, couldn't afford to give

---

* The Right Reverend Samuel Seabury is popularly remembered as a prominent Loyalist before the American Revolution and a rival of Alexander Hamilton.

Samuel Seabury as a young man in the early 1900s.

him an Ivy League education like his ancestors. Instead, Seabury applied to New York Law School at age seventeen and paid his own way by clerking and tutoring. He often worked and studied until 3:00 a.m., woke at 7:00, and arrived at class red-eyed and bleary. After graduation, he set about building a law practice and soon established himself as a formidable trial lawyer.[1]

Though he'd forsaken the cloth, Seabury had inherited his ancestors' sense of virtue and decorum. His appearance was always immaculate—clean-shaven, hair slicked, hat brushed, collar starched, tie straight, suit dark and dignified. He expressed himself eloquently with perfect grammar, and he never cursed. His ideals were lofty: he championed the poor, confronted the powerful, and denounced the wicked. His integrity was unimpeachable. Supporters lauded his rectitude, but detractors criticized his sanctimony. "His dignity was Jove-like and a little appalling," wrote journalist Milton MacKaye. "There was a half-credited conviction among his associates that anyone who called him Sam, chucked him in the ribs, and offered him a cigar would be promptly dealt with by a heaven-sent bolt of lightning." A *New Yorker* profile quipped, "When he says, 'It is raining,' there is a sonorous majesty to his voice that gives the observation the solemnity of a Papal bull." Behind his back, people sarcastically called him "the Bishop."[2]

Though high-minded, Seabury wasn't prudish. He didn't strive to save souls or extirpate sins; ordinary vices didn't concern him. What provoked his ire were corruption and inequality. He criticized the abuse of power and excesses of free-market capitalism, which had magnified economic and political disparities during the Gilded Age, and he admired the radical ideas of economist Henry George, whose proposed "single tax" on land value promised to alleviate poverty and establish a more just society. Seabury's devotion to improving the world wasn't merely philosophical. After passing the bar, he could have traded on his family name to gain a position at a white-shoe law firm. Instead, he became a criminal defense attorney and often took on indigent clients, though he had little money himself. He also represented unions fighting for safe workplaces and eight-hour workdays. In his twenties, he joined a Good Government Club and delivered fiery orations at political events, ignoring the jeers and occasional stones hurled by Tammany thugs who tried to drown him out.[3]

There are obvious parallels between Seabury and FDR, both ambitious, blue-blooded Democrats who championed good government and repudiated Tammany Hall. But they had different natures and inverted trajectories. Roosevelt entered politics as an opportunistic moderate with few ideological convictions but moved left over the course of his career. Seabury started out as an earnest idealist with radical ideas but grew more pragmatic as he aged. To Roosevelt, law school was a springboard for his political aspirations. To Seabury, it was the training ground for a legal career. When he ran for office in 1899, it was to be a city judge. In Manhattan, where the Tiger reigned, his only hope was to join a Fusion ticket with Republicans and other anti-Tammany Democrats. The first campaign met with defeat, but two years later, he caught a reform wave that swept him into office along with a Republican mayor. Only twenty-eight years old, he became the youngest judge in the city's history.[4]

Unlike his Tammany-backed colleagues on the bench, Seabury was brilliant, hard-working, and honest, and he soon established a reputation as a superb trial judge. Such traits weren't necessarily advantageous for judicial advancement in New York, but he also had a knack for attracting powerful patrons. The first of these was newspaper magnate William Randolph Hearst. A pioneer of "yellow journalism," Hearst made a fortune by acquiring newspapers and boosting circulation with lurid stories about sex, crime, and corruption. After he'd assembled a media empire, the megalomaniacal tycoon embarked on an audacious political career, using his newspapers to flog his populist campaigns. When he ran for governor in 1906, Seabury joined the ticket as a candidate for the State Supreme Court, which in New York's counterintuitive nomenclature is a trial court, not the state's highest court. Aided by ringing endorsements from Hearst's newspapers, Seabury won his judicial election even as Hearst lost his gubernatorial bid.[5]

While serving on the Supreme Court, Seabury attracted an even more powerful patron. In the summer of 1914, former president Theodore Roosevelt invited him to dine at his estate at Oyster Bay on Long Island Sound. Though retired from public service, the elder Roosevelt remained wildly popular and politically influential.* He saw in Seabury a fellow aristocrat and progressive champion who could clean up New York. "By George, it does me good to come in contact with a man who is not afraid, and whose blows count!" Roosevelt gushed in a letter after their meeting. "I want you on the Court of Appeals, or as Senator, or as Governor!" Though he had no direct influence over Democratic primaries, his endorsement convinced Charles Murphy that Samuel Seabury could win a competitive election, and the pragmatic boss agreed to nominate him for the Court of Appeals in 1914. With Roosevelt's backing and Tammany's blessing, Seabury was one of the few Democrats to win statewide elections that year.[6]

As a justice on New York's highest court, with a fourteen-year term, Seabury had attained a position of influence and prestige from which he could advance his ideals. If he'd wished, he might have remained on the bench for the rest of his career. But those ancient Samuel Seaburys kept whispering, urging him to reach higher still. They weren't the only ones stoking his ambition. After Seabury joined the Court of Appeals, Theodore Roosevelt invited him back to Oyster Bay to discuss the upcoming gubernatorial election. At the meeting, he criticized the Republican incumbent, Charles Whitman, and urged Seabury to run against him, pledging his "open and aggressive support" for a gubernatorial campaign.

The opportunity was tantalizing. As governor of New York, Seabury could implement his ideas to protect workers and reduce economic inequality. Though the term was only two years, he would gain a national reputation that might lead to higher office—the Senate, the Supreme Court, perhaps the White House. He might even eclipse his most famous

* In 1912, Theodore Roosevelt founded the Progressive Party, popularly known as the Bull Moose Party in reference to his famous boast that he felt "as strong as a bull moose." Though short-lived, the party actively competed in US elections from 1912 to 1920. In New York State, the Progressives often played kingmaker by nominating Democratic or Republican candidates.

ancestor, the Right Reverend Seabury. Yet his initial response was guarded. "I do not see how you could support me, since I would support Wilson again for President," he demurred, knowing that Roosevelt despised Woodrow Wilson, who had trounced him in the 1912 presidential race.

But Theodore Roosevelt pressed on with characteristic exuberance. "I have considered the problem from every angle," he insisted. "I will support the Republican candidate for the Presidency, but that will in no way interfere with my giving you my support for the governorship. . . . If you secure the Democratic nomination, my support will insure your election."[7]

Elated by Roosevelt's assurance, Seabury yielded to his ambition and jumped into the governor's race in 1916. As the primary season commenced, his supporters touted his qualifications and boasted of his support from Roosevelt and Hearst. His candidacy had broad support upstate, but Tammany Hall was hostile. Though Charles Murphy had acquiesced to Seabury's judicial bid in 1914, he was loath to back such a renowned reformer for governor. Fortunately for Seabury, he failed to find a suitable alternative with sufficient popular support. "Murphy and his allies are as strongly opposed to the nomination of Judge Seabury tonight as ever," reported the *Tribune* on the eve of the state convention, "but they have been unable to find a candidate of sufficient calibre to beat him. They have hunted high and low, only to see each Democrat suggested by one of their group for the nomination bowled out in jig time."[8]

Lacking a primary opponent, Seabury was nominated by acclamation. He promptly resigned from the Court of Appeals and launched his campaign with a promise to purge government agencies of "the political rings that now control and infest them," which rankled Boss Murphy. No sooner had he committed himself than his patrons began to forsake him. Hearst was the first to go. The day after the nomination, he enjoined his supporters to reelect Governor Whitman. Editorials in Hearst papers soon started attacking Seabury as "chameleonic" and "the tool of Murphy." Theodore Roosevelt was next. Despite his promises to Seabury, Roosevelt also endorsed Whitman, explaining that he "cannot support Justice Seabury" because "it is out of the question for me to support any man who is supporting Mr. Wilson in this campaign."[9]

After Roosevelt's statement, Seabury stormed to Oyster Bay and confronted the former president, calling him a "blatherskite" to his face—about as close as he ever came to profanity. But it was no use. Opposed by both Hearst and Roosevelt and with only half-hearted support from Murphy, he had no shot. He ran a hard campaign, but when it was over, he retired from public service and returned to his private law practice, dispirited and disillusioned. He kept a framed copy of Roosevelt's flattering letter on his wall as a sardonic testament to political perfidy. His legal work at least brought him wealth, if not prestige. In 1927, he bought a magnificent six-story town house on the Upper East Side and hung portraits of his ancestors on the walls of the library, where they could console themselves with his fine European furnishings and rows of walnut bookcases stuffed with rare books.[10]

But he wasn't fulfilled. In search of purpose, he buried himself in genealogy and book collection. He and Maud spent their summers in Europe, but he cared little for Italian delicacies or Parisian cabarets. His favorite destination was Britain, where he spent weeks combing through rural church archives for records of his ancestors. In London, he haunted art galleries and bookstores to collect paintings of bewigged British lords and ancient legal treatises. In August 1930, he was delighted to discover an exceedingly rare first edition of *The Just Lawyer*, a 300-year-old exposé of judicial malfeasance in Elizabethan criminal courts. He carried the treasure back to his suite at the luxurious Carlton Hotel and was examining the find when a phone call interrupted his perusal at 11:00 p.m. An American reporter on the line asked for a statement about the new anti-corruption commission he was to lead. Dumbfounded, Seabury replied that he had no comment. "If I am to be referee, as the press reports, I obviously do not want to judge the case before it is tried," he added. As he hung up the phone, thoughts of rare books slipped away, and the dormant embers of ambition began to smolder again.[11]

The official cable from the Appellate Division of the New York State Supreme Court arrived the next day. There was no question of declining the appointment. The Seaburys promptly cut short their vacation and booked passage home on a transatlantic liner. During the six-day voyage, wireless news bulletins reported yet another scandal from Manhattan. New York State Supreme Court Justice Joseph F. Crater had gone missing. He was last seen around 9:00 p.m. on August 6 as he hailed a taxi on Times Square, dressed for the evening in a pinstripe suit with a panama hat cocked at a rakish angle. According to his law clerk, he had spent the afternoon destroying

DETECTIVE DIVISION CIRCULAR No. 11 SEPTEMBER 17, 1930	POLICE DEPARTMENT CITY OF NEW YORK	BE SURE TO FILE THIS CIRCULAR FOR REFERENCE

Police Authorities are Requested to Post this Circular for the Information of Police Officers and File a Copy of it for Future Reference.

$5,000.00 REWARD

The CITY of NEW YORK offers $5,000 reward to any person or persons furnishing this Department with information resulting in locating Joseph Force Crater

Any information should be forwarded to the Detective Division of the Police Department of the City of New York, 240 Centre Street, Phone Spring 3100.

JOSEPH FORCE CRATER
JUSTICE OF THE SUPREME COURT, STATE OF NEW YORK

DESCRIPTION—Born in the United States—Age, 41 years; height, 6 feet; weight, 185 pounds; mixed grey hair, originally dark brown, thin at top, parted in middle "slicked" down; complexion, medium dark, considerably tanned; brown eyes; false teeth, upper and lower jaw, good physical and mental condition at time of disappearance. Tip of right index finger somewhat mutilated, due to having been recently crushed.

Wore brown sack coat and trousers, narrow green stripe, no vest; either a Panama or soft brown hat worn at rakish angle, size 6⅞s, unusual size for his height and weight. Clothes made by Vroom. Affected colored shirts, size 14 collar, probably bow tie. Wore tortoise-shell glasses for reading. Yellow gold Masonic ring, somewhat worn; may be wearing a yellow gold, square-shaped wrist watch with leather strap.

EDWARD P. MULROONEY,

Phone Spring 3100.   Police Commissioner

An NYPD wanted poster offering a $5,000 reward for any information regarding the disappearance of Justice Joseph Force Crater, September 17, 1930.

documents and cashing two large checks. He also happened to be a close associate of Tammany boss Martin Healy, who had taken the $10,000 bribe from Magistrate Ewald's wife, prompting speculation that his disappearance was connected to the case. An investigation later uncovered a long list of mistresses and underworld connections as well as evidence that Crater had bribed his way onto the bench, but the detectives found no solid clues about what had become of him, and the mystery has still never been cracked.[12]*

* Crater's case is still open. In 2005, NYPD cold-case detectives dug out the case files after receiving a tip that Crater had been murdered by a cop and buried in Coney Island, but they were unable to validate the information.

Seabury received scant information about the Crater case during his voyage, and his only knowledge of the scandals that he was tasked to investigate came from brief news reports that had filtered into the European press, so he wasn't prepared for the clutch of reporters who met him at the Hudson River pier. They asked the judge to pose for photos and peppered him with questions about the new commission. Which magistrates would he investigate? What was his opinion on the Crater case? What about reports that some members of the bar doubted his statutory authority? Did he intend to investigate City Hall? Seabury only smiled and said simply, "Well, we will see."[13]

He set to work the next morning, embracing his return to public service with heroic zeal. Within weeks, he'd assembled a small team of investigators at the New York County Courthouse on Foley Square near the entrance to the Brooklyn Bridge. The building was only a few years old, but it had already become a New York icon, destined to be featured in future courthouse scenes from *The Godfather* and *Law & Order*. The colonnaded portico, triangular pediment, and majestic dome evoked an ancient Roman temple that some mischievous deity had transplanted to downtown Manhattan. Granite goddesses representing Law, Equity, and Truth gazed down at the passerby from atop the pediment. At their feet, ten-foot-high letters proclaimed, "THE TRUE ADMINISTRATION OF JUSTICE IS THE FIRMEST PILLAR OF GOOD GOVERNMENT," a slight misquote from George Washington, who had written about "the *due* administration of justice" in 1789.[14]

Seabury and his team occupied a suite on the fifth floor, room 542. He laid out his strategy at the first full staff meeting in early September. Though they would employ prosecutorial methods and hear testimony in a courtroom, he emphasized that their work was ultimately political; the public would be the jury. "It is only by humanizing this inquiry that we can translate our findings into a language the great mass of the people can understand," he contended. "The public will not be aroused to an awareness of conditions as they actually are in the magistrates' courts through graphs, charts and reports. We must divorce it as far as possible from legalistic machinery. There is more eloquence in the testimony of an illiterate witness telling of oppression suffered, than in the greatest sermon or editorial or address ever written."[15]

bondsmen who operated at the Women's Court in Greenwich Village, where all the prostitution cases in Manhattan were tried. The red-brick Victorian Gothic courthouse and its castle-turret clock tower still stand at the corner of Sixth Avenue and West Tenth Street, though the building has been converted to a public library and the adjoining jail has long since been demolished. In contrast to the picturesque exterior, the cells were dark, dirty, and cramped—barely wide enough to fit a narrow iron cot with no mattress—and two inmates often had to share a cell, due to overcrowding. Across the street from the prison, a row of two-story buildings with plate-glass storefronts housed the offices of the bondsmen, who waited like spiders for accused women to fall into the web of New York's justice system. After gouging them for bail fees, they'd refer the women to defense attorneys who occupied back offices in the same row of buildings. The lawyers had relationships with police detectives, prosecutors, and magistrates. A cop could be bribed to skip a hearing. A prosecutor could be suborned to drop a case. A magistrate could be induced to dismiss the charges. Everyone involved in the scheme, including the bondsmen, would receive kickbacks from the defense lawyers' exorbitant fees.[24]

Guilt or innocence didn't matter; a woman's fate was bound to her bank account. For those with means, the scheme amounted to an expensive and humiliating shakedown, but they emerged with their reputations intact. Brothel owners like Polly Adler paid for their more valuable sex workers to go free. But the unfortunate women who couldn't afford the fees were almost always convicted on the strength of police testimony, no matter how dubious the evidence or inconsistent the story. The magistrates of the Women's Court rarely disputed the vice officers, and they were not known for leniency.

The treatment of Black people was particularly heinous. Acuna told Seabury that whenever vice cops needed arrests to meet their quotas, they "swooped down upon the Negro section of Harlem, 'crashed flats,' and made arrests at random." They accused any women they found of prostitution. The men, they would beat savagely and arrest as pimps. The cops knew that their victims had no hope of fair hearings in the Magistrates' Courts.[25]

Acuna was unsparing as he confessed his participation in these schemes. He had been living a double life—lying to his wife and gambling away his earnings as he helped crooked cops and lawyers destroy women's lives. Guilt haunted him, but he was too dependent on the money and too scared to quit the business. The single time he defied his employers by telling the truth about an innocent woman in court, they retaliated by planting marked bills on him and sending him to prison. He saw the Seabury investigation as a way to escape the trap.[26]

As he spilled out his story to Cooper, he recited names, dates, addresses, and other details.

"Are you sure of these things, absolutely certain of your figures?" Cooper probed.

Acuna laughed self-consciously. He explained that he had a "trick memory" that enabled him to remember minutiae for years. Cooper was skeptical, but court records substantiated Acuna's account. The investigators also subpoenaed bank records for the people he named and discovered numerous deposits that far exceeded the account holders' incomes. Under questioning, John Weston, a former prosecutor in the district attorney's office, broke down and confessed that he had accepted $20,000 in bribes from lawyers, bondsmen, and vice cops. He corroborated Acuna's allegations and named defense lawyers, bondsmen, and vice cops who had colluded in the shakedown racket.[27]

Acuna also proved brilliant and unflappable in the courtroom. Effortlessly recalling vivid and specific details, he described nineteen cases in which he'd played the stool pigeon, resulting in the arrests of thirty-two women. Overall, he estimated that he'd been responsible for the arrests of 150 women, thirty or forty of whom had been sent to trial without evidence. He accused twenty-eight cops that he'd worked with of participating in the vice racket. When Seabury brought fifty police officers into the courtroom and lined them up, double file, against the wall, Acuna walked down the line and picked out all but one of the twenty-eight by name, tapping them on their shoulders as they scowled. His only mistake was to confuse one officer with his partner.[28]

Acuna seemed to enjoy sparring with his cross-examiners and had a knack for provoking their anger or duping them into asking questions he wanted to answer. His most formidable interlocutor was a balding, thirty-seven-year-old attorney from Brooklyn named Samuel Leibowitz, who repeatedly lost his temper. "I will not tolerate this stool pigeon making

Defense attorney Samuel Leibowitz in the courtroom at the Chile Acuna trial in New York, January 1931.

side remarks and grimaces at me," he shouted at one hearing. "I'll punch him in the nose."[29]

Leibowitz was one of the most renowned and successful criminal defense lawyers of the era. He'd won acquittals for numerous murderers and gangsters, including Al Capone, and boasted that he'd never lost a client to the electric chair. As a defense lawyer, he was more accustomed to vilifying police officers than defending them, but he also craved publicity,

and the Seabury hearings were making headlines, so he offered to represent several of the vice cops that Acuna had accused.

Leibowitz had a genius for impeaching witnesses. He often employed
private agents to dig up dirt on his clients' accusers, which he then shared
with his contacts at the *Daily News* to impugn a witness's credibility
before they met in the courtroom. On January 4, 1931, he arrived at a
police station with a young Puerto Rican woman named Pilaro Rios,
who claimed that Acuna had been her pimp. She told the police that
Acuna had seduced her soon after she immigrated to New York with her
husband. "I fell in love with him," she said. "I left my husband and did
whatever Chile told me to. It was at this time that I became a prostitute.
All the money I earned I turned over to Chile." She claimed that she'd
worked at various brothels operated by Acuna and was arrested during a
police raid.

The story was scooped by *News* reporter John O'Donnell, whom Leibowitz had tipped off ahead of time. "I will prove that Acuna is a felon
and that his testimony regarding so-called frameups by the police is mere
revenge against officers who raided his own immoral dens and seized his
women," Leibowitz told O'Donnell. He promised to bring Rios to the
Seabury hearings to confront Acuna in person.[30]

There was some trouble with the dates, though. Chile Acuna wasn't
in New York during the period Rios described. After the *News* published
allegations, Acuna led a delegation of journalists down to Washington,
DC, where he'd lived and worked from 1925 to 1927. He took them on
a nostalgia tour of his time there, unearthing payroll reports, apartment
leases, and election rolls as he reconnected with old acquaintances who
testified to his character. After the press reported Acuna's alibi, Pilaro Rios
disappeared. Leibowitz didn't give up though. He found two more women
who accused Acuna of procuring prostitutes and shared their stories with
the *News*. Unlike Rios, the new witnesses actually testified at the hearings,
but within a year, they'd both recanted.[31]

Acuna was Seabury's star witness, but his testimony was corroborated by
many others. John Weston, the former prosecutor, publicly confessed to taking bribes from twenty-one defense lawyers, three bondsmen, and two vice
cops to fix more than six hundred cases. A number of the arresting officers in
these cases were among the twenty-eight vice cops that Acuna had accused.

Seabury also invited many victims of the Women's Court conspiracy to testify about their experiences. Their sorrowful accounts of unlawful arrests and fixed trials corroborated Acuna's account and outraged the public.[32]

Finally, Seabury called the officers themselves to the stand and confronted them with records for bank deposits that far exceeded their salaries. The witnesses offered various explanations for their wealth, usually involving gambling winnings and the largesse of wealthy relatives. Detective Robert Morris claimed to have received $40,000 from his Uncle George, which he initially kept at home and later deposited in installments. "In a box?" asked Isidore Kresel, recalling the son-in-law broker with no bank account.

"In a box," Morris confirmed.

"A tin box, of course—a little tin box?" Judge Seabury interjected.[33]

When Officer William O'Connor took the stand, Kresel asked him, "Did you inherit any money from an uncle?"

"I did," O'Connor replied.

"I thought so," said Kresel. "Now I suppose you are going to tell me that the O'Connor fortune was kept in a little tin box?"

"Yes. My wife kept the money, and she kept it in a tin box," O'Connor answered.[34]

Officer James Quinlivan claimed that he'd won $10,000 from poker, pinochle, and a lucky bet on a horse named Florabell. He added that he'd entrusted the money to his mother for safekeeping.

"Did she keep it in a little tin box?" asked Kresel, eliciting snickers from the courtroom.

"No, in a trunk," Quinlivan replied.[35]

Though the hearings were occasionally amusing, even the most jaded New Yorkers were shaken by the evidence that predatory attorneys and police officers had conspired to fleece innocent women, often destroying their lives in the process. Police Commissioner Edward Mulrooney suspended the accused policemen and assigned fifteen officers to round-the-clock security for Chile Acuna. In a public letter addressed to Judge Seabury, Governor Roosevelt declared that he had been "deeply disturbed and greatly incensed by the unearthing by the investigation being conducted by you showing framing up of women by some members of the so-called police vice squad," and he promised to pardon any woman who had been wrongfully framed. For once, Mayor Walker left off his wisecracking. "I will confess," he declared, "I have been more or less shocked by the reports of the framing of innocent women." His chief concern, however, seemed to be the "harmful publicity from the reports," some of which, he added, "have been exaggerated."[36]

Meanwhile, Tammany Hall launched its counteroffensive. In December, the city's chief counsel refused to pay the modest salaries of Seabury's staff. According to the state law that authorized the investigation, the city was obligated to cover the commission's "reasonable expenses." But the statute said nothing about paying a team of lawyers, the counsel argued, and he did not think their salaries constituted a reasonable expense. Mayor Walker coyly played along, expressing his sincere desire to assist the investigation but insisting that he had to abide by the chief counsel's findings. "The city officials must obey the law," he shrugged. "Maybe Judge Seabury does not have to." In response, Seabury appealed to the State Supreme Court, which promptly ordered the mayor to obey the law by paying the salaries.[37]

But Tammany's next salvo hit its mark. Before joining the Seabury commission, Isidor Kresel had been general counsel for the Bank of the United States. Gutted by the stock market crash of 1929, the bank staggered along for another year before going bankrupt in December 1930. Auditors found evidence that the CEO had been manipulating the books to hide its precarious financial state. In January, the district attorney appointed a lawyer named Max D. Steuer to investigate. Steuer was a Tammany loyalist, and he loathed Isidor Kresel, who had nearly gotten him disbarred for coaching a witness a few years earlier. On February 10, he indicted Kresel along with the bank's other directors. The move was transparently political, but Kresel chose to resign in order to avoid tainting the commission.[38]

"The investigation is going right ahead," Seabury assured the press after he regretfully accepted Kresel's resignation. "I am going ahead with the staff I now have and in which I have the greatest confidence." But while the junior attorneys on his staff were talented and driven, they lacked Kresel's experience. When he'd hired them, Seabury had shared his philosophy with the team, "Old heads for counsel—young heads for war." The loss of Kresel meant that Judge Seabury was the only old head left in the office.[39]

By that time, public interest in the investigation was also begin-ning to wane. A train of court officials, policemen, stool pigeons, and falsely accused women continued to take turns on the witness stand, but the public had already absorbed the most shocking revelations, and the press accounts of Seabury's hearings no longer made the front pages. The investigation had succeeded in exposing corruption in the city courts and ousted some of the perpetrators, but as it neared its conclusion, it seemed unlikely to reach high officials or threaten the Tiger's dominion.

On the morning of February 26, 1931, two weeks after Kresel's resigna-tion, Samuel Seabury began his day as usual. His driver pulled up to the town house at 8:25 in a dark green Lincoln luxury car with personalized plates. Seabury settled into the back seat, lit his pipe, and read the *Times*. The only news about his investigation was a page-three story on Magis-trate Jean H. Norris, New York's first female judge, who was due to testify in his hearing room that afternoon. They reached the courthouse shortly before 9:00, and Seabury got to work.[40]

The first witness that morning was a vice officer named Richard Ganley. A Russian ballet instructor had accused him and his partner, Andrew McLaughlin, of framing her for prostitution. She'd previously testified that an "unknown man" had come into her studio offering her $10 for a lesson. When she turned her back to wind up the Victrola, the man suddenly stripped down. "I wanted to shriek," she recalled. "I was terrorized." As she stood before the naked stranger in speechless shock, Ganley and McLaughlin burst through the door. "So this is the kind of place you are conducting," Ganley sneered, "a disorderly place." They arrested her, and she testified that she'd paid $345 to a bailiff and a lawyer to avoid conviction. When Seabury subpoenaed Ganley's bank state-ments, he discovered deposits of $13,128.36, of which only $727.09 came from the vice officer's $3,000 annual salary. At the hearing that morning, Ganley looked nervous. When Seabury pressed him about the deposits, he refused to testify on grounds of self-incrimination and demanded to see his lawyer.[41]

During a lunchtime recess from the hearings, several newspaper reporters approached Seabury. They informed him that the body of a woman named Vivian Gordon had just been found in Van Cortlandt

Park in the Bronx, apparently strangled to death. According to police records, she'd been arrested for prostitution in 1923 by Andrew McLaughlin, one of the two officers now under investigation for framing the ballet instructor. The journalists had received information that Gordon had made contact with Seabury's commission before her murder, and they wanted to know whether she was connected to the anticorruption inquiry.[42]

Seabury didn't recognize the woman's name, but he directed his staff to look into the records. Sure enough, they found a letter signed by a Vivian Gordon residing at 156 East 37th Street. The handwriting was flowery, with circles dotting the *i*'s and other playful embellishments, but the subject of the letter was grave:

Dear Mr. Kresel,
I have some information in connection with a "frame-up" by a police officer and others which I believe will be of great aid to your committee in its work.

   I would appreciate an interview at your earliest convenience.

Very truly yours,
Vivian Gordon[43]

The letter was dated February 7, three days before Isidor Kresel's resignation. According to Seabury's records, the letter had been passed along to Irving Ben Cooper, who invited Gordon to come for an interview on February 20 between 10:00 a.m. and 5:00 p.m. There the paper trail ended. Seabury summoned Cooper to his office, but the lawyer had little to add. He remembered replying to the letter, but as far as he knew, the woman never accepted his invitation.[44]

Seabury was alarmed. Tammany Hall had previously resisted his investigation using legal methods. The murder of a witness would signify a very dark turn in the case. To confirm the identity of the woman who sent the letter, he instructed Cooper to obtain a handwriting specimen from the police for comparison. The lawyer departed immediately and soon returned with a sample of Vivian Gordon's handwriting and a grainy photograph of a woman with short, wavy hair. The distinctive handwriting matched perfectly, but neither Cooper nor anyone else recognized the woman in the photograph.[45]

Feeling that the case required more scrutiny, Seabury composed a letter to Police Commissioner Edward Mulrooney. "Dear Mr. Commissioner," he wrote, "During the recess in the hearing conducted before me today I was informed that a certain Vivian Gordon was found murdered early this morning." He confirmed that his office had received a letter from "the deceased" and noted that she had failed to appear the previous Friday as scheduled. Enclosing a copy of her letter, he concluded, "May I ask you to be good enough to apprise me of the circumstances surrounding the death of Vivian Gordon?"[46]

That evening at home, Seabury received a surprise visit around 11:00 p.m. When he answered the door, Irving Ben Cooper rushed in, with a newspaper under his arm. Its front-page headline blared, "GIRL VICE WITNESS IS MURDERED." The article included the letter Vivian Gordon had written to the commission, along with graphic details about the crime scene. There was also a picture of her, much clearer than the grainy photograph Cooper had received from the police. The new photo jogged his memory. She *had* come to the office the week before, but she didn't mention the original letter, and he hadn't connected the two until he saw her photo in the paper. During the interview, she claimed that she'd been framed in 1923 by Officer Andrew McLaughlin at the instigation of her ex-husband, who sought custody of their daughter. Cooper had promised to look into the case and urged the woman to collect any documents that would corroborate her story. That was the last he'd heard from her.[47]

Cooper's revelation was stunning. If it turned out that a cop had killed Gordon in order to silence her testimony, the ramifications would be enormous. Seabury ordered Cooper to prepare an affidavit detailing his interactions with the victim and dispatched him to the Bronx morgue to identify the body, despite the late hour. Then he called he called Bronx District Attorney Charles B. McLaughlin to inform him of the new developments.

Cooper was bleary-eyed when he appeared at the office the next morning. He'd only had a few hours of sleep. But he presented Seabury with a signed affidavit confirming that the murder victim was the same woman he'd met with the week before.

"At about 1 a.m. February 27, 1931, I examined the body of the said Vivian Gordon at the Fordham morgue," he attested. "This examination removed the slightest doubt which remained in my mind as to the identity of the Vivian Gordon whom I interviewed last Friday.

"When I interviewed Vivian Gordon . . . she stated to me that she wished me to help her right what she termed was a wrong inflicted on her by reason of the charge of prostitution which had been preferred against her in March 1923.

"She also stated to me that she was convinced that such an arrest was the result of a plot concocted between the arresting officers and her former husband, who was anxious to obtain complete custody of their infant daughter.

"Her statement with regard to the events leading up to her arrest in March, 1923, was that she was residing at a hotel in New York City; that she had some mail which she had turned over to some man other than her husband with the understanding that she was to call at his residence later in the day and obtain such mail from him; that while on her way to this man's residence (which was not far from the hotel) she was accosted by another man who was a total stranger to her and who later turned out to be one of the arresting officers.

"This stranger asked her whether she was going to see the man (naming him, but I do not recall the name) and, upon her responding in the affirmative, the stranger stated to her that he was a roommate of that man, and was told to take her to the apartment to await his arrival, which would be in a few minutes; that shortly after her entering the apartment she was arrested and charged with prostitution; that she gave the name of Benita Bischoff, and upon her plea of guilty was sentenced to Bedford Reformatory.

"Our understanding when she left me at the conclusion of the interview was that she was to obtain such documentary or other proof as she could, to corroborate her story, and that she would call me as soon as she made such discovery, and in any event, within a week or two. She left me with her telephone number, Caledonia 6856,* which she stated was an unlisted one.

---

* Early phone numbers included the names of telephone exchanges that were distributed around the city. Callers would dial the first two letters of the exchange name followed by four digits.

"During the course of her interview with me I learned that that she was an actress and that her husband was connected in some way with the stage. She added that at the present time she was doing some painting.

"She emphasized the fact that if she could establish her innocence of the charge preferred against her in 1923 she could regain the custody of her daughter, whom she had not been permitted to see over a long period of time since past."[48]

Seabury pondered Cooper's affidavit. The story about the stranger and the mail was odd, but Gordon wasn't the only witness to accuse McLaughlin of framing women, and the timing of her murder, five days after she met with Cooper, was suspicious. Whether or not McLaughlin had anything to do with her death, the sensational mystery was bound to attract tremendous public attention, which would make it politically difficult for Tammany to resist his investigation and might even provoke the governor to expand his mandate. Perhaps this poor woman's death would serve a greater purpose.

Seabury immediately composed a second letter to Commissioner Mulrooney. "Since writing to you yesterday afternoon," he wrote, "certain facts have developed which I desire to call to your attention. Mr. Cooper of my staff informed me that he had examined the various photographs of the slain woman, Vivian Gordon, as published and that he recognized her as a person who called at the investigation headquarters and whom he interviewed last Friday, February 20. . . . I have asked Mr. Cooper to make an affidavit incorporating therein whatever information he has with regard to his interview with Vivian Gordon and I herewith inclose [sic] a copy thereof."[49]

Naturally, he sent copies of the letter and affidavit to the press.

CHAPTER 4
DON'T WORRY, LITTLE GIRL

COMMISSIONER EDWARD MULROONEY WAS USUALLY SOFT-SPOKEN AND slow to anger, but when he read Seabury's letter, his eyes flashed and his ruddy cheeks turned pale. He paced across the thick mulberry rug on the floor of his office, craning his head back and fixing his eyes on the ceiling as he struggled to control his fury. He'd held his tongue for months, quietly seething while Seabury's investigators shredded the reputation of his department. Almost every day, the press headlined some new scandal uncovered by the "vice quiz," as the tabloids dubbed the inquiry. And then, just when the newspapers had begun to shift the story to the back pages, a sensational homicide returned it to the banners. The morning papers were already braying about the "GIRL VICE QUIZ WITNESS FOUND MURDERED IN PARK," and the *Daily News* even breached journalistic propriety by printing a photo of her corpse in the woods. In Mulrooney's opinion, Vivian Gordon was a low-life criminal, but the press was reimagining her as some kind of tragic heroine. The Seabury connection, and the judge's artfully leaked letters, only heightened the drama—and intensified Mulrooney's exasperation.[1]

He didn't fear for his own reputation. Though many of his friends and relatives were Tammany stalwarts, Mulrooney was honest and capable. Like Inspector Bruckman, he avoided politics, advancing through the ranks on the strength of his ability rather than his loyalty. "I know of no man in the Police Department with a finer, stronger or cleaner character," Mayor Walker had rhapsodized at his inauguration. "Your devotion to duty has led you away from spectacle and sensation, and yet there is romance in it." The appointment of such a straight shooter had come as a surprise to the political establishment. Some speculated that Walker had selected him to mollify FDR and Republican critics in Albany. Others surmised that the flamboyant mayor preferred a self-effacing police chief who wouldn't upstage him.[2]

If the latter, there was no better candidate. Unlike his flashier predecessors, Mulrooney detested speeches and press conferences. "He is primarily a 'cop's cop,' without frills, fads or any desire for publicity," the *Times* reported. Mulrooney had joined the force in 1896 after reading Commissioner Theodore Roosevelt's recruiting advertisements for "men of brawn and brains," and he spent thirty-four years climbing the ranks before his promotion to commissioner. He looked the part, too, with pronounced features, heavy-lidded eyes, and a formidable jaw. "He is like a cop in a play," pronounced the *New Yorker*, "even to his husky voice and the way he talks out of the corner of his mouth."[3]

But it had become impossible to avoid politics once Seabury began digging into the affairs of the vice squad. Mulrooney wasn't naïve or complacent. He knew there were dirty cops on the force, and he tried to remove or sideline them when he could. But he felt that the extensive coverage of a few bad apples had unfairly tarred the entire force. To preserve the department's fraying reputation, he would have to persuade the public that "New York's finest" were worthy of the moniker by fully and openly cooperating with investigators. In the Vivian Gordon case in particular, he would commit the full force and weight of the New York Police Department until the killer was brought to justice. He assigned every available detective and numerous patrolmen to the case, a gargantuan task force that grew to include more than a hundred officers. Every cop who'd ever interacted with Vivian Gordon would be interrogated, starting with Andrew McLaughlin, the plainclothes vice officer who had arrested her in 1923. Mulrooney also planned to coordinate with the police in Philadelphia to question Gordon's ex-husband. Finally, he would establish headquarters at the very center of the investigation—Gordon's apartment on East 37th Street.[4]

By late morning, Gordon's three-room apartment was jammed with more than twenty detectives. Bronx District Attorney Charles McLaughlin—no relation to Officer Andrew McLaughlin—soon arrived with two assistants and joined the detectives scouring for clues. Adding to the chaos, Mulrooney allowed in members of the press, who proceeded to barrage him with questions about the progress of the investigation. "There are absolutely no new developments in the case," he replied gruffly. The DA chimed in, adding that the two suspects mentioned in Gordon's diaries, John Radeloff and Samuel Cohen, had been arrested and were being held as material witnesses on $50,000 bail.[5]

"Have you any evidence linking Harris, alias Cohen, and Radeloff to the crime other than the diaries of Miss Gordon?" queried a correspondent from the *Times*. McLaughlin refused to comment, so the reporter reframed the question. "Does the act of holding Radeloff and Cohen in high bail indicate that you know who the slayer is?"

"No," the DA replied. "I will say this—I would not have felt right about having the bail fixed at any lower sum."[6]

The questions then turned to the theory that cops were behind the homicide, given Gordon's accusations against a vice officer. Mulrooney pointed out that Andrew McLaughlin had a solid alibi; he was currently on an ocean cruise returning from Bermuda. There were no charges against him, and he would "report for duty when he returns on a liner tomorrow noon." But the journalists would not be put off so easily. There had been reports of a threatening letter found in Gordon's apartment. Mulrooney admitted that the detectives had discovered a letter accusing her of being "a dirty stool pigeon" but noted that there was no indication that the sender was a cop; it may well have been sent by one of Gordon's criminal associates. Vivian Gordon had been "running around with some pretty tough babies," he added.[7]

Standing by his side, Inspector Henry Bruckman underscored the point. "From the information we have at present, it certainly does not seem that she made her money at any lawful trade," he said. "She was evidently a woman of many acquaintances." DA McLaughlin also chimed in. "I think this woman was a shake-down artist, a blackmailer. I don't think she was one of the regular vice girls," he declared, adding, "I do not anticipate the slightest lack of cooperation on the part of the police. In the past the Police Department has always cooperated loyally with any investigation in which the police appeared in any way involved. There is nothing to involve the police in this matter, in fact the indications are the opposite."[8]

As the newsmen and detectives talked over each other and jostled for space amid the boudoir dolls and orchid-colored walls, a petite woman with a long, pale face and tilted dark eyes discreetly examined the double-framed photographs of Vivian Gordon and her daughter. She noticed the worn edge of a piece of paper poking out from behind the girl's picture and gently teased it from its hiding place. It was a handwritten letter dated March 14, 1923—five days after Vivian Gordon's arrest by Officer McLaughlin. The meticulous curves and loops of the letters appeared to be the work of a child practicing her cursive penmanship.

Dear Mama,

I am very sorry you are sick. I hope you will be better very soon. Daddy will bring me to see you as soon as you are better.

Please write me as soon as you can as I miss you very much.

I am going to see Dr. Gibson tomorrow while daddy is in New York.

He saw Lois and Marion at the hotel last night.

I learned how to make a new B. How do you like it?

I am very lonesome without you.

All my love & kisses,
from your Baby
and Daddy

After reading the letter, the woman passed it to her photographer, who snapped a picture. Then she handed it over to the authorities.[9]

Her name was Grace Robinson, crime correspondent for the *News*. A demure, mild-mannered woman of thirty-six, she was an anomaly in the masculine milieu of newspaper journalism. Her colleagues described her as "mouselike and sweet." Yet Robinson was New York City's premier crime reporter. Born in Omaha, Nebraska, she'd dropped out of college to support her family after her father died, earning $10 a week as a telegraph editor at the *Omaha Bee*. Nebraska law prohibited women from working at night, but she received special dispensation because of World War I.[10]

She was twenty-five when she moved to New York City, a wide-eyed midwesterner without a friend or a job. She had her first cocktail at the Brevoort Hotel in Greenwich Village and her first cigarette at the Port Arthur tearoom in Chinatown. She found a room for $3 a week and worked various clerical jobs until she landed an editorial position on the woman's page at the *New York Evening Mail*. Three years later, in 1922, the *News* hired her to report for the society pages under the pen name "Debutante."[11]

Daily News crime correspondent Grace Robinson in an undated photo at an outdoor café.

The *Daily News* was America's first tabloid. The pages were half the size of standard broadsheets and filled with photos, comics, contests, and ads. The front pages had no articles at all, only gargantuan headlines, photos, and captions. The stories fixated on crime and sex, and the writing was breezy and unsophisticated. "Try and get in a couple of crime pictures every day," publisher Joseph Patterson urged his managing editor. "You can get direct action pictures showing how the crime was committed, or at least get in pictures of people connected with crime either as victim or criminal." Professional journalists scoffed at the upstart paper when the first issue rolled off the press in 1919, but the tabloid size was ideal for reading on the subway, and its working-class readers appreciated the photos, simple language, and voyeuristic stories, as well as the price of two cents per copy compared to the nickel price of the *Times*. By 1925, the *News* was selling a million copies a day and had the largest circulation in the country. Three years later, Patterson ordered the construction of the Daily News Building, a thirty-six-story Art Deco skyscraper striped by alternating bands of white brick and slender tiers of windows. Completed in 1930, the iconic building on 42nd Street housed the *News* for the next sixty-five years.[12]

Female journalists of the era rarely received the same respect accorded to their male colleagues. Routinely dismissed as "sob sisters," they were expected to write sentimental, human-interest stories, not hard news. But Grace Robinson's ambitions were too big for the society pages. While covering rich New Yorkers vacationing in Palm Beach in 1925, she noticed flames rising from the roof of the Breakers Hotel. After alerting the fire department, she rushed to the entrance to interview the high-society guests as they scrambled from the hotel in pajamas and bathrobes, clutching whatever cash and jewels they'd managed to grab as they fled. Then she raced across the golf course through clouds of smoke to file her story at the nearest Western Union office, beating out the Associated Press and all other competitors. Joseph Patterson, who held relatively enlightened views on female reporters, celebrated her scoop and promoted her to the crime desk, where she quickly proved her mettle. Victims and criminals alike responded to Robinson's empathetic demeanor by opening up to her, yet her writing was trenchant and powerful. She worked eighteen-hour days interviewing politicians, celebrities, gangsters, and prostitutes, and was even arrested while chasing a story.[13]

Unbeknownst to Commissioner Murphy, Robinson had already managed to obtain a brief interview with John Radeloff just before his arrest. "I've been Miss Gordon's lawyer for two years," he told her. "At the time she was sent to Bedford, I recall that she said that Detroit was her home town. Her husband and she had separated, she told me, and she had sued him for divorce in Pennsylvania." He informed Robinson about the Schweinler affair and the Radlow case, and he related an incident in which Gordon asked him for a large quantity of carbolic acid, claiming that she needed it for a lotion mixture. When he called her bluff, she confessed, "I want it to throw in the face of a fellow named Jimmy." Radeloff said that he had no idea who "Jimmy" was. "She used to associate with the best and the worst elements in town," he explained. He also revealed that he'd spoken to Gordon several hours before her murder. "I talked to her at 5:30 last night over the phone, and I was to call her today," he said, though he did not elaborate on what they'd discussed.[14]

Robinson had also paid a visit "the musty old Women's Court" in Greenwich Village, where she obtained Vivian Gordon's court records. The magistrate who adjudicated the case, Henry Stanley Renaud, was a prim little Tammany judge with gold-rimmed glasses who favored bow ties with winged collars. His courtroom policies were unwavering. Whenever police officers testified, he accepted their testimony without question. "They were sworn officers of the law, and also were sworn to tell the truth in court," he later explained to the Seabury commission. On the other hand, whenever police officers missed a hearing, Renaud immediately dismissed the case. These policies made his courtroom the perfect venue for shakedown schemes. If the accused paid a bribe, the arresting officer would absent the hearing, and the case would be dismissed. Otherwise, the officer would testify, and the suspect would invariably be convicted.[15]

Vivian Gordon evidently didn't have money for a bribe, and her lawyer advised her to plead guilty to soliciting Officer McLaughlin. The minutes of her hearing had been destroyed, leaving only a brief plea delivered by the attorney: "The defendant pleads guilty and throws herself on the mercy of the court. She was in a desperate situation when she made the offer to the officer." But Magistrate Renaud was merciless. Ordinarily, first offenders were given probation, especially if they had children or families, so Gordon's lawyer was astonished when Renaud sent her to Bedford, as he subsequently told Robinson in an interview. "I was barred from an appeal because she'd pleaded guilty," he added. When Judge Seabury later asked Renaud why he'd sentenced her to the reformatory, the magistrate became flushed and nervous. "She was sent to, perhaps, Bedford, because it is one of the best schools in the country," he said, as if incarceration were a privilege. "If they took off the 'reformatory' name, it would be full of girls coming of their own volition. It is a wonderful school."[16]

Tragically, Gordon had only confessed her guilt in order to win a light sentence that she didn't receive. Grace Robinson also found Gordon's probation records at the Women's Court, which revealed that a few days after her sentencing, she contradicted her lawyer and swore her innocence to her probation officer.

"I am an actress and a model. I have been earning $100 a week," she told Officer Myra Hughes. "Of late, though, I've been working as a movie extra, and modeling in a fashion parade. My money had all gone, this night, and I was feeling pretty low. I was expecting an engagement at the Hippodrome for my little girl, 7 years old, who is a clever dancer. But it hadn't come through, and I was stony broke.

"This night I went up to West 100th St. to visit a couple friends who were actresses. They offered to loan me money, but I wouldn't take it. I knew they couldn't afford it.

"When I reached 68th St., on my way home, a man in a car picked me up. I told him my hard luck story, and he said, 'Don't worry, little girl. I'll help you out.' Then he put $20 in my stocking. He said that he had plenty of money—that he was rich, in fact. I took him to Al Marks' apartment—he was my boyfriend—in West 64th Street. I had a key. Then this man told me he was a police officer and put me under arrest. I did nothing illegal. I merely took his gift of money. Nothing happened that could constitute a basis for a prostitution charge. This officer turned out to be Andrew McLaughlin, vice officer."[17]

Curiously, this account of the incident differed materially from the version that Gordon told Irving Ben Cooper eight years later. The boyfriend, Al Marks, was certainly the mysterious "man other than her husband," she described to Cooper, but in her account to her probation officer, she said nothing about collecting her mail from him. Nor did she mention that McLaughlin claimed to be his roommate and led her into the apartment. She said that she had a key.

Yet, even back then, years before the Seabury investigation revealed the corruption that permeated the vice squad, Gordon suspected a setup. According to the probation records, she told Officer Hughes her theory that her husband, John Bischoff, had framed her in order to win custody of their daughter, Benita, who shared her name. The records also included a letter from Bischoff denying Gordon's allegations. "I believe you know this is not true," he wrote to Hughes, "and as I would like to have some record which might be of value to me in years to come when my little girl reaches womanhood, I would be grateful for a letter from you stating that I did everything possible to assist my wife."[18]

There were only two witnesses to Vivian Gordon's arrest in 1923, the suspect and the arresting officer. The former was dead, so Grace Robinson turned her attention to the latter. Officer Andrew McLaughlin had a reputation within the police department. Handsome and cocksure, with thick, black curly hair, he dressed like a dandy and was known for boozing and gambling. At parties, he made himself the center of attention by cracking off-color jokes and belting out songs in a rich baritone voice. Plainclothes vice officers usually worked in pairs, but McLaughlin liked to stroll the streets on his own during off-hours to pick up prostitutes; his colleagues called him "the Lone Wolf of Broadway" and the "the Sheik of the Vice Squad."* He'd amassed a remarkable record during his time in the vice squad—over 1,000 arrests in eleven years. In addition to busting prostitutes, he had a penchant for staging dramatic raids on dance halls, cabarets, and spirit seances. He once arrested world-famous dancer Gilda Gray and her troupe of hula dancers mid-performance. At the subsequent hearing, he quarreled with the incredulous magistrate over whether the women's "writhing abdominal motions" should be considered "indecent and immoral." But McLaughlin's crusade against indecency had little to do with his moral standards. He was one of the vice officers implicated by John Weston, the prosecutor who had confessed to the Seabury commission about the shakedown racket at the Women's Court.[19]

After leaving Vivian Gordon's apartment, Grace Robinson traveled up to Washington Heights at the north end of Manhattan, where McLaughlin lived with his family. The building itself was unpretentious, but Robinson was astonished by what she saw when his wife let her inside the apartment. "Only a finished interior decorator with an eye for the exotic, the bizarre, and with plenty of money at his disposal, could have done it," she wrote. "The place might well be a temperamental movie star's retreat. The big living room is done in yellow silk and old rose. Yellow damask and primrose hangings cover the windows. Against a wall is a small upright piano, with

---

* "Sheik" was slang for a lady's man, inspired by Rudolf Valentino's 1921 blockbuster film, *The Sheik*.

hand-carved woodwork, across which is a gorgeous embroidered Spanish shawl." She admired the wrought-iron lamps, luxuriant Persian rug, and hand-worked pillows. "The large bedroom breathes soft seductiveness," she gushed. "Half a dozen or more dress dolls play peek-a-boo from their toy thrones upon mahogany dressers and a boudoir table. Upon the latter table with its three beveled mirrors is a staggering array of perfumes, cold creams, and other appurtenances of the toilette, all in cut crystal. Walls of both rooms are covered with costly paintings and etchings in Japanese crystal frames."[20]

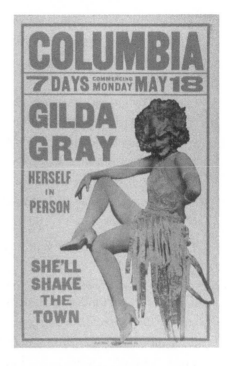

A poster advertising a Gilda Gray show on May 18, 1925, at the Columbia, a burlesque theater on Times Square in New York.

Edna McLaughlin, Andrew's wife, was a "strikingly pretty brunette of 27," fashionably attired in a chic fur-lined "sports coat" that showed off her figure. Standing with her two young children, she told Robinson that her husband was on vacation in Bermuda; she expected him back the next day. "He just made up his mind to go all of a sudden," she said. "He goes on trips frequently and I never ask any questions." Then she suddenly became defensive. "He never discussed his police affairs with me," she insisted, "but his record is absolutely clean. And this investigation will prove it."[21]

Robinson doubted that Officer McLaughlin was "absolutely clean." An honest cop on a $3,000 annual salary couldn't afford such opulent furnishings, not to mention spontaneous solo cruises to Bermuda. After the interview, she returned to the News Building to complete the five thousand–word story she would file that afternoon. Her opening was vivid and theatrical, delivered in the breathless tone of a town gossip whispering explosive secrets to her confidantes:

A red-haired woman, found strangled to death in Van Cortlandt park, yesterday became the center of the seething fires of graft, bribery, frameups, shakedowns and judicial corruption which have agitated New York.

The victim, Mrs. Benita Bischoff, 32, who also was known to New York's night life as Vivian Gordon, was being awaited anxiously at the Seabury investigation into police crookedness, even while her brutal assailant strangled her with clothesline.

She had promised to reveal "a frameup by a police officer." It was Plainclothesman Andrew J. McLaughlin who was responsible for her being sent upstate to Bedford Reformatory, for prostitution, back in 1923. McLaughlin, a vice cop, is under suspension, under charges of "framing" innocent women.[22]

The riveting synthesis of murder, sex, and scandal was perfectly crafted to thrill tabloid readers, and *News* publisher Joseph Patterson never squandered an opportunity to boost circulation. The next day, the front page featured a gruesome photo of the garroted corpse lying in the woods. Just below it, a large glamour shot of the beautiful murder victim was captioned, "Red-headed and vivacious Vivian Gordon, strangled into silence." In addition to the front-page headlines and photos, the paper devoted three full pages to Robinson's story and related photos, including portraits of Officer McLaughlin, Judge Seabury, Commissioner Mulrooney, and John Bischoff; a policeman's hand holding the murder rope; a picture of Gordon's building; a photocopy of the letter she wrote to Isidor Kresel; and the poignant portrait of her daughter Benita posing in a ballet costume. Patterson subsequently assigned a whole team of journalists to cover the story, which would dominate the paper's headlines for weeks to come.

The *News* wasn't the only paper to capitalize on Vivian Gordon's murder. Its tabloid rivals, the *Daily Mirror* and the *Evening Graphic*, also covered the case extensively. Even highbrow papers like the *Times* devoted considerable space to the murder, using the Seabury connection to justify extensive coverage of a lurid crime story. Meanwhile, the AP and UPI wire services exported the story to thousands of newspapers across the country and around the world.

While Robinson was interviewing Edna McLaughlin in Washington Heights, an AP correspondent based in Philadelphia traveled across the river to the suburb of Audubon, New Jersey, where Gordon's ex-husband, John Bischoff, lived. He'd remarried and had a fourteen-year-old stepdaughter in addition to Benita, who was sixteen. His wife, Eunice, told the reporter that her husband was out of town. He worked at a correctional facility near Washington, DC, and only came home on weekends. She refused to answer questions, but the reporter had better luck with a local police officer who'd interviewed her that morning. Eunice had told him that Vivian Gordon was around forty years old, not thirty-two, as had been previously reported. Her maiden name was Benita Franklin. She said that Gordon had been educated at a convent in Michigan City, Indiana, and had been employed as an actress for several years before she met John Bischoff in 1912. After their divorce, Eunice said that Gordon had pestered the family with frequent letters and attempts to visit their daughter. "She bothered my husband so much that we were forced to move from our former residence," she added. "Several times she came here and created scenes."[23]

She also furnished the police officer with the most recent letter from Gordon. It was dated January 19 and was posted from the office of John Radeloff three weeks before she contacted the Seabury commission.

Dear Mr. Bischoff:

You have probably heard about the vice investigation now going on in New York City, which is growing day by day, that a number of convicted girls have been framed by the police and others.

You know that I am one of those girls and that my conviction was caused by a frame-up between you and Detective McLaughlin. You may think that you have had the last laugh, but get this—I am going before the investigation committee this week and intend to tell the whole story of this dirty frame-up.

When I am through it will be just too bad for you. Little Benita is old enough now to realize that a dirty trick has been played on me. I intend to go the limit and you know as well as I do that this will mean your finish.

Although I am not interested in hearing from you, if you have anything to say you can write me in care of my attorney, John A. Radeloff,
66 Court St., Brooklyn, N. Y., and mark the letter personal.

> Yours truly,
> B. F. B.[24]

Following disclosure of this bombshell, the reporter reached John
Bischoff by telephone at his office in Lorton, Virginia. Bischoff's manner
was brusque and disdainful. He seemed indignant that a man of his station, superintendent of industries at the Occoquan Workhouse, should be
called upon to answer such scurrilous accusations. He claimed that he had
never read Gordon's letter and dismissed the allegations as "too silly even
to countenance with a denial," adding, "I have not seen nor heard from my
wife for ten years and cannot understand her reason for writing that letter.
I was informed of her death yesterday by persons who knew us both and I
was greatly shocked."[25]

The Occoquan Workhouse had a notorious history. In 1917, a prominent
group of suffragists known as the Silent Sentinels were incarcerated there
after being arrested during a protest outside the White House. Shocked by
the fetid condition of the facility and the brutality of the guards, they staged
hunger strikes and refused to work. On November 14, the prison superintendent ordered a crackdown, which became known as the "Night of Terror." Prison guards beat, kicked, and choked the defiant inmates, strung one
up by her wrists, and smashed another into an iron bed, knocking her out.[26]

These events had occurred before Bischoff joined the staff, but the
conditions in 1931 weren't much better. As superintendent of industries,
he oversaw the work facilities at Occoquan. Inmates under his supervision
made clothes and stamped license plates for the District of Columbia. In
addition to his salary from the federal government, he earned income by
consulting for companies that supplied industrial machinery to Occoquan,
a conflict of interest that would later become the subject of a federal investigation and to which he would respond with similar haughty disdain.[27]

The wages and consulting fees allowed Bischoff and his family to live
more comfortably than when he had first met a young actress named Benita
Franklin in 1912. He was less important then, too, as a twenty-four-year-old

college dropout from the mechanical engineering program at Clemson College who had spent his whole life in Charleston, South Carolina. Benita was nineteen, beautiful, sophisticated, and wild. She'd traveled across the country on the vaudeville circuit, performing musical comedy under the stage name Vivian Gordon. Smitten by the vibrant young woman, Bischoff accompanied her up the coast as she toured the eastern seaboard. They lived like vagabonds, feral and free, until she became pregnant in 1915. Then she retired from the stage, and he took a job as a mechanical engineer at a small factory that produced custom printing machinery in Philadelphia. There was no wedding ceremony, but she took his last name, and they named their daughter Benita, after her mother.[28]

John Bischoff quickly settled into domesticity. Benita Bischoff,* his common-law wife, did not. Speaking later to Grace Robinson, he portrayed her as a volatile, abusive spouse who beat him and hurled crockery during their frequent fights. According to Bischoff, the greatest source of friction was the child, who had inherited her mother's theatrical talent. "My wife wanted to bring up our daughter to follow in her footsteps on the musical comedy stage simply because of the child's marvelous talent," Bischoff said. "I objected strenuously to our daughter becoming a stage dancer when still a child and the disagreement brought endless quarrels."[29]

Eventually, she left him and took seven-year-old Benita to New York City. Bischoff accused her of living with "various men" in New York, including Al Marks, and filed for divorce in December 1922, charging abandonment and "cruel and barbarous treatment." But before the hearing date, she was arrested for vagrancy, leaving Benita alone at the residential hotel where they lived at that time. "It is just a coincidence that before my divorce was granted, I called on long-distance telephone to New York and the night clerk at the hotel there told me my wife had been arrested and he had taken the child to his home in Long Island," he said. "I hurried to New York, obtained the child from him, and my former wife never regained possession of her after that, although she tried many times."[30]

---

* To avoid confusion with her daughter, I'll henceforth mainly refer to Benita Franklin Bischoff as Vivian Gordon even when describing the time before she adopted the alias. This usage is consistent with how her friends and family referred to her after her death, including those who originally knew her as Benita.

When the divorce was granted in 1924, Bischoff received full custody of Benita. He claimed that the criminal charges against his wife had no influence at the divorce hearing, though the court records noted that she did not appear because she was incarcerated. Bischoff also insisted that he had done everything he could to help her. "I sent her $50 for counsel fees," he said. "I arranged with Myra Hughes, probation officer, to release her in custody of her uncle in Detroit. When my wife came to trial she made a scene and said she didn't want to go into her uncle's custody. She preferred to be in the custody of Al Marks. As a result, Vivian went to Bedford Reformatory."[31]

Bischoff's casual reference to Bedford seemed to imply that the sentence was a reasonable consequence for the crime. He said that he attended the trial and observed nothing to indicate that Gordon had been framed. "Even if she had been," he added, "she had been guilty previously of misconduct with men." Yet Gordon had no prior arrests. She pleaded guilty and begged for mercy, and she had a young child. Under the circumstances, her sentence was extraordinary, even if she were guilty of the crime.[32]

The New York police were also quite anxious to hear John Bischoff's story. When he returned home to Audubon for the weekend, he was visited by Detective Donald Carey from Inspector Bruckman's staff, who escorted him to New York for questioning. Bischoff wore a dark suit and a light fedora, smart yet conservative attire befitting a prominent federal official. He was a tall, stern-faced man with dark, receding hair slicked tight to his scalp. Protruding ears, sunken cheeks, and a sharp chin gave his face a triangular shape. At 2:30 on Sunday afternoon, March 1, they reached the old Bronx County Courthouse, a square granite Beaux Arts edifice guarded by a massive statue of Justice whose vacant eyes gazed blankly at the horizon as she fingered the hilt of her broadsword. For the next three hours, the top officials of the investigation, including DA McLaughlin, Commissioner Mulrooney, and Inspector Bruckman, grilled Bischoff about the life and death of Vivian Gordon.[33]

"I know nothing of my former wife's murder," he insisted. "I cannot even offer a clue. I did not even know she was alive or dead. As for the allegation that I framed her and sent her to prison on a vice charge, that is ridiculous. However, it is no more ridiculous than other attempts she has made in the past to embarrass me, my wife, and obtain my child."

While the police were interviewing Bischoff, another drama was unfolding just offshore. That morning, the SS *California* had steamed into New York Harbor and dropped anchor near Staten Island. The captain hoisted a yellow flag, dull beneath overcast skies, to signal for routine quarantine inspection. A federal cutter sidled up beside the cruise ship, and crew members dropped a gangplank between the vessels to allow passengers from the cutter to board. The boarding party included quarantine physicians, customs officials, and the ubiquitous crime reporter for the *News*.

As soon as Grace Robinson stepped gingerly from the bobbing gangplank onto the deck of the cruise ship, she began making inquiries about Officer Andrew McLaughlin. The passengers she encountered praised "the pleasing young fellow" with a wonderful singing voice who had been "the life of the party" on their voyage. When she located McLaughlin, suntanned and jaunty in a suit and a white linen golf cap, she introduced herself and proceeded to ply him with questions while the ship cleared quarantine and progressed toward the South Street Seaport.[34]

"Do you know this dead woman Gordon?" she asked.

"I think I do," he answered breezily. "I recollect a very ritzy, well-kept woman whom I arrested once—she impressed me because she was snooty and unlike the common run of women of that class."

But when Robinson filled him in on the details of the arrest and the letter she sent to her ex-husband, he backpedaled.

"Well, that can't be the woman I'm thinking of. Because that snooty woman bragged to me that she was a 'kept lady' and never pretended to being married. As true as there's a God in heaven as truly as I'm now on my way to meet my wife and children (if I ever get there), I don't remember the Gordon woman at all."

"She claims she wrote you some time ago," Robinson pressed him. "Did you receive her letter?"

"Yes, I did. I received a letter about a month ago," he admitted. "It was a well-written letter—sounded as if it was from a person of education. This Gordon woman explained that at last she was going to have revenge on me. She said she was going before Judge Seabury and tell how I framed her in 1923, and at last she was going to square up with me. I just laughed. Because if she claimed framing in 1923, neither Seabury—nor anybody else can do anything now. It's outlawed after five years. So she had no legal comeback. And I didn't fear anything the police department might do, because my record," he drew himself up proudly, "my record is an open book. I invite anybody that's interested to look it over. I am a citizen of New York. I have a wife and two children and I'm helping to make this city a cleaner city and a better place for my children to live. I studied for the priesthood under the Jesuit fathers. I feel proud of that also.

Officer Andrew McLaughlin in New York after he was picked up by detectives upon his return from a cruise to Bermuda, March 1, 1931.

"Well, I took this Gordon letter and stuck it in my pocket and paid no more attention to it. If I'd been worried about it, I could easily have gone over the records and found the case. But I wasn't that much interested. I tossed it in a drawer at home, and so far as I know, it's still there."[35]

When they arrived at the pier, McLaughlin was greeted by a barrage of blazing flashbulbs and raucous questions from reporters at other papers who had missed the opportunity for an exclusive interview. "I wouldn't know her from Eve," he hollered back. "It's all Greek to me. The first I knew she'd implicated me in her framing charges was when I began to get radiograms from newspapers and the news was posted on the ship's bulletin board."

There were detectives waiting for him, too. As they guided him through the swarm of journalists and into a waiting squad car, his fellow passengers called out their goodbyes. "Half a hundred snappy-looking women, companions on the whoopee cruise to Bermuda, chorused 'good luck' and 'happy days,'" Grace Robinson reported, as McLaughlin climbed into the car and sped off toward the Bronx.[36]

When he arrived at the courthouse at 4:00 p.m., John Bischoff was still being interrogated. Neither man showed any indication that they knew one another. Bischoff was dismissed at 5:00 and headed back to Audubon with Detective Carey to collect documentation. McLaughlin walked out twenty minutes later and announced that he'd be going back on the beat. "I was never worried for a second," he said with a grin as the cameras flashed. Later that evening, he submitted the letter he'd received from Vivian Gordon to the police. Like the one addressed to Bischoff, it was dated January 19.

Mr. McLaughlin:

You no doubt recall how you framed Benita Bischoff on March 9, 1923, causing her conviction for vagrancy. She is now writing to tell you she is going to appear before the vice committee and tell the whole story.

She leaves the rest to your imagination, which she hopes is as good now as it was when you concocted those lies about her in court.

Yours truly,
B.F.B.[37]

Meanwhile, Grace Robinson had one more witness to interview that day. Vivian Gordon's ex-boyfriend, Al Marks, had been summoned by the police but had not yet turned himself him. Robinson found him first and got him to agree to an interview. He fit the mold of the other men that had attracted Vivian Gordon. Smartly dressed in a blue suit and spats, he was handsome, dark-haired, and suave, and he spoke with a low, seductive voice. Robinson worked her journalistic charm, and he opened up about his relationship with Gordon and her arrest in 1923.

He was on parole when he met her, he said, following a two-year stint at Sing Sing for grand larceny. He'd never dated a woman like Gordon before. "Vivian was a lovely creature in those days, before that Bedford experience," he recalled fondly. "She was a talented, highly intelligent girl. She played the piano beautifully. She was far above the ordinary run of women.

"She was getting $50 a week from her husband. It wasn't enough to live on. I helped her out. We lived together at the Hotel Langwell, and Benita was with us. Her husband kicked about the child growing up with me around. He tried to take the kid away. But she was crazy about me. She told Bischoff she was in love with me."

The affair turned rocky after a few months, however, and Marks moved out. On the day of Gordon's arrest, he said she'd telephoned to say that she had to see him urgently. He invited her to come over but had to step out and wasn't home when she arrived. He told Robinson that he'd left the door unlocked for her—yet another discrepancy in the varied accounts of Gordon's arrest. When he returned to the apartment, he found her with Officer McLaughlin, already in custody.[38]

Grace Robinson had heard reports that Marks was employed as a stool pigeon for the vice squad. He denied the accusation and insisted that he had no role in framing Vivian Gordon. As proof, he explained that he, too, was arrested that day and charged with "keeping a disorderly house"—a catchall legal term that included running a brothel or a casino. Since he was on parole, the magistrate sent him back to Sing Sing for another eleven months.[39]

He also had an alibi on the night of Gordon's murder. He and his wife had spent the evening with friends at the Lenox Club in Harlem, a Black-owned jazz club where Louis Armstrong and Duke Ellington once played.

At 2:30 a.m., they migrated to a late-night supper club on Broadway. He said that his friends and the proprietors of both establishments could attest to his presence.[40]

He told Robinson that he saw Vivian Gordon only once more after her arrest. "The last time I saw her—three and a half years ago—she threatened me and tried to get money out of me," he recalled. "'I need money,' she cried. 'I want $250. If you don't come across, I'll go to the District Attorney about you.' I had no money, then, and couldn't help her out."

Before parting, Robinson asked Marks if he planned to visit Gordon's body in the morgue. "Go to the morgue?" he replied, taken aback. "Why should I go there? What use would that be?"[41]

His account did little to unravel the mystery of Gordon's arrest. On one hand, the shifting explanations of why and how she ended up in Marks's apartment with Andrew McLaughlin suggest that she may indeed have intended to exchange sex for money, with Marks possibly acting as a pimp or at least a facilitator. That theory would also be consistent with her desperate need for money and her later criminal activity. On the other hand, Andrew McLaughlin's unexplained wealth and the other framing allegations that Seabury uncovered indicate that he was hardly an honest cop, so it wouldn't be surprising for him to have framed Gordon as well. Finally, while there was no evidence tying John Bischoff to his wife's arrest, he had an obvious motive, and the opportune timing of the divorce proceedings was suspicious.

Yet, even if Gordon had been framed in 1923, the police had uncovered nothing besides her threatening letters that tied Andrew McLaughlin or John Bischoff to her murder in 1931. The other question that occupied Grace Robinson concerned Gordon's activities after her arrest. If Marks's story about her demand for $250 were true, it would suggest that she did not have the fortune that was attributed to her, at least not when he encountered her in 1927. The next stage in Robinson's inquiry would aim to answer the question, *Who was Vivian Gordon?*

CHAPTER 5
A WOMAN OF MANY ACQUAINTANCES

On Saturday, February 28, two days after Vivian Gordon's murder, a letter arrived at room 542 of the County Courthouse, addressed to Irving Ben Cooper. The brief note, scrawled in pencil on a yellow Western Union telegraph slip, warned:

> Well, there is one squealer that won't talk, and we've just started. You ain't heard nothing yet.
>
> We are sorry to see three nice young men go wrong, but we gave you a chance to go easy and lay down. We could have made you all big shots, but it's too late now.
>
> We broke Kresel and we will break Seabury and you youngsters too.
>
> We are taking things into our own hands now. Our big stiffs haven't got no guts. We'll show them and you too. You thought we didn't know what was going on in your office. We know every move you make, so don't go too far.
>
> Dr. X———

A second letter, in the same hand on another yellow slip, addressed two of Cooper's colleagues more succinctly, as if the author couldn't be bothered to compose a second threat. "See my letter to Cooper," the note said. "It goes for all three and old Seabury, too."[1]

Judge Seabury made no public comment on the letters. He simply shared copies with Commissioner Mulrooney and the press, then carried on with his investigation. In light of Vivian Gordon's murder, he had ordered Irving Ben Cooper to try to discover what she had intended to reveal to the commission. "Please understand that I am not investigating the murder of Vivian Gordon," he told reporters. "That is not within my jurisdiction, and I have not the facilities necessary for such an investigation. I am interested only in what Miss Gordon could have told us in connection with illegal activities of police or magistrates."[2]

The first person that Cooper interviewed concerning the Gordon case was Ann Tomkins Gibson, a fifty-one-year-old physician from Philadelphia. She was the "Dr. Gibson" to whom seven-year-old Benita had referred in her letter to her mother. Gibson had befriended the Bischoffs after Benita was born and maintained ties with both husband and wife after the divorce. She was one of the only people who had been close to Vivian Gordon both before and after her arrest. "I knew her and treated her when she lived here, and we were good friends," she later told the press. "In fact, I guess I am one of the few friends Vivian had during her hectic life."[3]

Dr. Gibson was the picture of respectability. She dressed conservatively and wore oval, wire-frame glasses. Her long, somber face and thoughtful dark eyes conveyed seriousness and intelligence. In addition to her successful obstetrics practice, she also dabbled in the emerging field of social psychology, which she hoped would provide "the key to the solution of the criminal problem." Though she had no children of her own, she directed a summer camp for girls in New Hampshire and delivered speeches on child-rearing to various organizations in Philadelphia. Impressed by the work of Harvard psychologist William McDougall,* she promoted his theory that "every human being is but the complex of a variety of instincts" and advised parents to monitor and mold their children's instincts in order to achieve a healthy balance. These ideas also informed her attitude toward her friend Vivian Gordon. Her descriptions of the younger woman tended to be clinical and patronizing. "She was a good girl who tried to rise above her early environment," she said, "but she was attracted by bright lights and the easy ways of life which had been her heritage."[4]

Gordon's "heritage" is somewhat mysterious, and Gibson's account left many gaps, but her childhood certainly wasn't a happy one. Benita Franklin was born in 1891, the fourth of five children in a middle-class family from Michigan City, Indiana, a charming seaport nestled between

---

* In addition to his theory of instincts, William McDougall promoted eugenics and racist theories of intelligence. There is no evidence that Dr. Gibson endorsed these views.

the sand dunes on the southern rim of Lake Michigan. Her father, a Canadian immigrant, had been the superintendent of a chair factory when the children were young but later became a prison warden at the Illinois State Penitentiary in Joliet, a suburb of Chicago seventy miles from Michigan City. Dr. Gibson described Benita as a troubled child, clever and talented but "wild and stubborn" and "helpless from protecting herself." She blamed the girl's misbehavior on self-destructive tendencies and poor parenting, but she either didn't know or didn't appreciate how difficult Benita's childhood had been and how that might have affected her development.[5]

According to the federal census, eight-year-old Benita and her siblings were separated from their parents and living in Catholic orphanages in Chicago in 1900, the three girls in one, the two boys in another. Their mother, Maggie Franklin, lived in a Chicago boardinghouse at that time; their father, John W. A. Franklin, was unlisted. It wasn't uncommon for parents in financial distress to send their children to orphanages, but it's not clear that money was the issue in this case. Four years later, John obtained a divorce, alleging that Maggie had laced his food with morphine. It seems likely that she suffered from substance abuse or psychiatric problems and that John, unable to care for five young children while working at the penitentiary, temporarily placed them in orphanages in nearby Chicago. In a subsequent press interview, Gordon's eldest sister, Lillian Thurston, suggested that the Franklin children had been deprived of "a mother's love and a real home." She didn't mention the orphanage but told reporters, "My father and mother separated when we were young and, we all more or less had to shift for ourselves. I was adopted by Mr. and Mrs. Douglas Thurston, but Vivian was not so fortunate and did not find a home with such fine people."[6]

In 1906, John Franklin sent Benita to the Ladies of Loretto convent in Ontario, close to his family. She impressed the nuns with her musical talent on the violin, clarinet, and piano, but she was traumatized by her family life and miserable at the strict Catholic convent. She twice attempted suicide by slitting her wrists, and the Ladies of Loretto soon expelled her. At that point, she disappeared from the record until the 1910 census, which places eighteen-year-old Benita at the Home of the Good Shepherd, a reformatory for delinquent girls in Denver, indicating that her troubles continued through her teenage years. Afterward, she briefly moved in with her father and Lillian, who had relocated to Detroit. "It was in 1912 in Detroit that Vivian Gordon—since she is better known by that name—left our family circle," Lillian recalled. "When she went East, she severed all but a casual connection with us."[7]

"East" wasn't a specific place. Benita became a traveling stage performer, touring up and down the East Coast. The newspapers would later describe her as a chorus girl, but her true vocation was musical comedy. Though the early twentieth century is often associated with risqué dance revues featuring bare-legged women, late-night cabarets attracted a relatively small audience. America's dominant genre, by far, was vaudeville. Every self-respecting town had at least one opera house where traveling troupes entertained local crowds with wholesome variety shows that featured comedy routines, dance performances, musical theater, magicians, and circus animals. The theatrical pieces were shallow, sappy affairs, stuffed with songs, dances, and frantic costume changes. When assessing a potential hit, producers tried to gauge its mainstream appeal by pondering, "Will it play in Peoria?" Even in New York City, home of erotic revues like the *Ziegfeld Follies* and *George White's Scandals*, family-friendly musical spectacles ruled the theater district. One block west of the New Amsterdam Theatre, where the Ziegfeld Girls bared their legs at midnight, the colossal Hippodrome, where Gordon's daughter would later audition, staged extravagant productions with hundreds of singers and dancers performing for audiences of 5,000 or more.[8]

But Vivian Gordon never played the Hippodrome or any other famous theater. She was one of thousands of itinerant vaudevillians who traveled from town to town, performing at two-bit venues for less than $10 a day. The work was neither steady nor glamorous. Unruly spectators tossed coins on the stage when they enjoyed the show and hurled vegetables at performers when they didn't. When an act bombed, the stage manager often cut it on the spot, leaving the players stranded and penniless in whichever remote town they'd landed. Occasionally, bankrupt managers absconded in the middle of the night without paying the hotel bill, depriving the cast members not only of their jobs but also their belongings, held as recompense by furious innkeepers. Yet there was also camaraderie and romance on the road. Most of the performers were young and gregarious. They drank, gambled, flirted, fought, and played pranks on each other, savoring freedom and

Patrons line up outside the Hippodrome on West 43rd Street and Sixth Avenue to see a show, c. 1920.

dreaming of stardom. There was sex, too, one-night stands and long-term relationships. Above all, there was the stage itself. However ramshackle the theater or vulgar the crowd, when they stood on those wooden stages, Vivian Gordon and the other vaudevillians feasted on the attention from those strangers in the dark and pined for it after the curtain fell.[9]

Gordon's stage career did not last long, however. While performing in Charleston, South Carolina, in 1912, she met John Bischoff and fell in love. They made a striking pair. She was witty and vivacious, five-foot-two with full cheeks and teasing eyes. He towered over her, his manner brusque and his face severe. Relationships came difficult to Benita. Having grown up in a dysfunctional home, separated from her parents when she was eight years old, she struggled with agonizing insecurity and had difficulty trusting others. Her relationship with Bischoff was tempestuous, characterized by "brief moments of passionate happiness and bitter interludes of discord," as Grace Robinson put it. But they stayed together, and after two years, she became pregnant. They rented an apartment on the first floor of a row house on Walnut Street in Philadelphia and settled down to raise a family.[10]

In Philadelphia, Gordon befriended Dr. Gibson, who treated her before and after her pregnancy. "She was extremely beautiful, and everyone who knew her loved her," the doctor recalled. For a time, Gordon seemed to have overcome the demons of her youth. Setting aside her theatrical ambitions and nomadic lifestyle, she embraced the role of middle-class housewife and devoted herself to raising her daughter. "She loved the little girl, better than anything in her life," Gibson said. "I have known few women in my medical career with greater mother love than hers."[11]

Yet Broadway continued to beckon, like a distant searchlight grasping at the clouds. Her bitter quarrels with her husband intensified as she flailed against the confines of domesticity. Bored and frustrated, she transferred her unfulfilled ambitions to her daughter, who had inherited her theatrical talent. Unable to afford dancing school, Gordon taught her what she knew. "Her mother was very proud of the child's talent," Gibson recalled. "When Benita was only five, the two visited me in my home in Frankfort. Her mother put on a phonograph record, 'The Dying Swan,' and the child executed the dance of that name with marvelous grace. Later she appeared on the stage in Philadelphia, dancing in a large mid-town theatre."[12]

The opportunities in Philadelphia were limited, however. New York, two hours away by train, was the place for aspiring actors and dancers, an Emerald City where bow-tied wizards in boater hats made dreams come true. More than seventy theaters and scores of nightclubs crowded around Broadway as the famed thoroughfare elbowed through Midtown Manhattan, heedless of the grid that ruled lesser avenues. By night, a tangled canopy of streetlamps, billboards, and theater marquees bathed the neighborhood with electric light as pleasure seekers migrated along "the Great White Way" like herds of wildebeests in search of watering holes.[13]

New York City had long been the center of American theater, but before the Jazz Age, Broadway's influence was mainly domestic. That changed after Black composers Eubie Blake and Noble Sissle introduced white audiences to jazz music and tap dance in a trailblazing musical called *Shuffle Along*. The show's success in 1921 inspired other Broadway composers to incorporate jazz into their work, including George Gershwin, whose synthesis of jazz and classical styles revolutionized musical theater. In 1923, another all-Black Broadway revue, *Runnin' Wild*, popularized a new dance style named for Charleston, South Carolina, where it originated. Derived from African American folk dances, the Charleston became a national craze, followed by the Black Bottom and Lindy Hop, which swept America and Europe in swift succession. As jazz and jazz-inspired music and dance styles spread around the world, Broadway became a cultural juggernaut, setting global trends and drawing the world's top musicians, actors, and dancers—as famous in their day as rock stars and Hollywood celebrities today.[14]

Vivian Gordon dreamed that her daughter, Benita, would one day be among them. Many Broadway stars, including Mae West, Josephine Baker, Marilyn Miller, Fred Astaire, and Bill "Bojangles" Robinson, had begun their theatrical careers as children. Hoping to emulate their success, Gordon brought seven-year-old Benita to Manhattan to try to make it on Broadway. They rented a room at the Hotel Langwell near Times Square. In its heyday, the thirteen-story, salmon-colored residential hotel had drawn millionaires and foreign dignitaries, and it remained popular among the theater set into the 1920s, but it had become seedier. In 1921, a music industry executive was robbed at gunpoint in his room. Two years later, a couple of convicted bank robbers shot each other in the corridor. The rent was affordable, though, and the location was ideal for Benita's auditions.[15]

Gordon found sporadic acting and modeling work but depended on begrudging support from her husband to make ends meet. She started dating other men. "Vivian had taken up the ways of a demimondaine," Gibson said disapprovingly. "Benita was taken to eat in restaurants by strange men, and many men called upon her mother."[16]

Then Gordon was arrested by Officer McLaughlin, and her life changed forever. Sentenced to a minimum six months at the reformatory, she was recommitted twice for parole violations and only obtained her freedom in November 1926, two and half years after her arrest.

The New York State Reformatory for Women at Bedford Hills had been established in 1901 with the best of intentions. Rather than send convicts to the workhouse or county jails, which would "deepen their degradation," Bedford was designed "to prevent young folks from becoming delinquents at all." Most inmates were young women convicted of minor crimes: petty larceny, disorderly conduct, and vagrancy—that is, prostitution. The official age limit was thirty, though Gordon was thirty-one when she arrived, and some prisoners were in their fifties. The staff was almost entirely female. Instead of jail cells, inmates were housed in residential buildings overseen by matrons who were supposed to guide their charges along the path of rehabilitation. Instructors taught them practical skills like cooking, sewing, gardening, laundry, and housework to help them find employment after their release. Sunday chapel was obligatory.[17]

The Hotel Langwell near Times Square, where Gordon stayed with her daughter, Benita, during her Broadway auditions, and where was Gordon was later arrested by Officer Andrew McLaughlin in 1923 (see page 96).

But Bedford wasn't the "wonderful school" that Magistrate Henry Stanley Renaud praised. For all the founders' high ideals, it was still a prison and not a pleasant one. "Discipline is maintained by brutal despotism, tyranny, threats and corporal punishment," Grace Robinson recorded in a memo. "Inmates have been kept in straightjackets for as long as four weeks. There are cages used for punishment in use nearly all the time. . . . Short rations are another form of punishment. Dr. Palmer the superintendent has choked and beaten the inmates himself." The worst part of the Bedford experience, however, was the aftermath. Former inmates were permanently branded as "Bedford Girls," which precluded respectable employment no matter what the matrons taught them. Vivian Gordon certainly didn't profit from the education extolled by the magistrate who sentenced her. She did, however, gain some practical skills that helped her earn a living on the outside.[18]

"You can't imagine what I learned at Bedford," she wrote to her sister, Arnolda Franklin, after her release. "The class of women there was awful. They showed me and told me how to do everything in the underworld. Dope fiends, blackmail—oh, Arnolda, you wouldn't understand that I got thoroughly educated in vice by living among these women. And you know, Arnolda, I am not slow to learn. In my case, the reformatory reformed me from innocence to vice—just contrary to its purpose. Oh, this is a terrible thing! Once branded, they fall deeper and deeper. I know full well the horror of my way of living, but it is the only way I know now, after that terrible experience."[19]

The time Vivian spent at the Bedford reformatory transformed her. The hopeful, doting mother who entered in the spring of 1923 emerged a cynical, embittered courtesan in the fall of 1926. She'd lost everything—her reputation, her dreams, and her daughter. "Before she went to the reformatory, she and the child were inseparable and she was happy," Dr. Gibson said. "When she came out, she was cold and bitter and calculating. She wanted to be good, she told me, but it seemed impossible to her after her sentence at New Bedford."[20]

Gibson believed that Gordon's suspicions of her ex-husband had festered into an irrational obsession during her incarceration. "When she returned from Bedford, she came to see me in Philadelphia and told me how she'd been framed by her husband," she said. "A brilliant woman, with powers that might have taken her far in useful accomplishment, she had become a maniac on the subject of vindication and vengeance. Her one purpose in life was to get possession of her daughter, of whom she was deprived when she was branded a scarlet woman by her sentence to Bedford."[21]

But what Dr. Gibson failed to appreciate, perhaps because she had no children herself, was that Gordon had not simply lost custody of her child. Benita had been cut out of her life entirely. John Bischoff didn't permit her to visit or even to communicate with her daughter. In the eight years between her arrest and her death, Vivian Gordon saw her child only once.

"Two years ago, her mother came to me and told me she wanted to see Benita and arrange for the leaving of money for Benita's education," Gibson recalled. "She then went to the Audubon public school where Benita was in her classroom. In the corridor, Benita repulsed her mother, and did not want to talk. The child became so upset that she was taken home by a school nurse. Her mother returned to my home here, very much enraged. She swore the child's mind had been poisoned against her. She blamed Mr. Bischoff."

Gibson didn't express much compassion for her friend as she casually recounted this anecdote, describing Gordon's anger but not her anguish after being rejected by her only child whom she hadn't been permitted to see or communicate with for years. Even John Radeloff, who later described the episode in a press interview, exhibited more sympathy, noting that Gordon was so distraught that she collapsed at the scene and was violently ill during her return to New York.[22]

Not only did Dr. Gibson lack empathy for her friend's despair, she actively discouraged her from trying to contact her daughter. As a result, Gordon's only link to Benita was Gibson herself, which likely explains why their relationship endured. "On my advice, except for the one occasion when she visited Benita at the Audubon school, Vivian never attempted to communicate with her daughter or see her," she said. "No letters were ever passed between them. Benita had no desire to communicate with her mother. I told Vivian she could not be a mother and a courtesan too and for that reason she had to take herself away from Benita as far as possible. She agreed with me in this, and it was followed. I informed Vivian from time to time about Benita, and Vivian was perfectly satisfied. She only held that one thought that the child's mind had been poisoned against her. She felt a false vengeance toward her former husband."[23]

Gibson was certain that Bischoff had nothing to do with Gordon's arrest. "The stories that Mr. Bischoff may possibly have framed Vivian are utterly untrue, although it's true Vivian believed that very thing," she declared. "It was a psychosis with her, one subject on which she was mentally unbalanced. She wanted to vindicate herself to the child, yet she continued to live the way of a common prostitute. Was that reasonable? She could not be a mother and a woman of the street also. Mr. Bischoff was always the gentleman with Vivian Gordon. He even gave money to her when he knew she was receiving money from men. He is an upright honest man and Vivian Gordon, while generous and brilliant, was a woman without character."[24]

Dr. Gibson was a cooperative and informative witness but ultimately disappointing to Irving Ben Cooper, for she knew little of her friend's activities in New York. Gordon had spoken to her only vaguely about "friends" who gave her money, $30,000 in total. She had shared an ominous prediction with the doctor just before her death, however. "Two weeks ago, without the slightest bit of seriousness or any premonition," Gibson recalled, "she told me one day she would meet a gentleman who would tie a stocking around her neck."[25]

After interviewing Dr. Gibson, Judge Seabury received a letter from another friend of Gordon's, Cassie Clayton of Erie, Pennsylvania. Clayton stated that she'd been Gordon's roommate in New York. She volunteered to speak with the investigators and included a letter that Gordon had sent to her on February 19, the day before she met with Cooper:

Cassie Dear:

Just a line to say I'm glad to locate you. I haven't time to write now cause I must be up early tomorrow as I appear before the Vice Commission to state how I was framed up & railroaded—in 1923—by my ex-husband & N.Y. police.

I reckon you've noticed the investigation that's going on in N. Y. for the last few months. (It's about time) Anyhow I wrote them a letter & they answered, asking me to appear in Supreme Court tomorrow. Boy I'll be glad to get that cleaned up if it takes my last breath. To be

Cassie Clayton, a friend of Vivian Gordon's from Erie, Pennsylvania, at the New York County Courthouse to meet with Judge Seabury, March 2, 1931.

vindicated, vindicated, vindicated. And then when folks feel mean &
nasty they can't say "Why, she this, she that & the other thing."

Yes, Cassie, that's been done. Oh! You don't know what trouble
is. Material trouble, maybe, but real mental anguish—No! And God
forbid that you ever know it. I know it's tough to be up against it, but
at least you have your boy to share your joys as well as adversity, and
that's a lot . . .

Pardon my haste will write you at greater length as soon as possible. Let me hear from you.

BONNIE[26]

Upon receiving the letter, Seabury dispatched one of his process servers, Edmund Perry, to escort Cassie Clayton to New York. She returned
with him by train the next day, a willowy brunette with flapper-short
hair and round, wide-set eyes, smartly dressed in a fur coat and a black-
and-white dotted blouse. She was skittish about returning to the city and
told friends in Erie that she feared for her life. Perry was also on edge
and later divulged to Grace Robinson that several "mysterious persons"
had approached them during the trip. But they reached the steps of the
New York County Courthouse without incident, and Perry ushered her
between the towering columns under the gaze of the granite goddesses on
the portico. Her heels clicked against the marble floor as they crossed the
domed atrium and took an elevator to the fifth floor.[27]

When they arrived, Judge Seabury welcomed Clayton into his office.
He introduced himself and his assistant, Irving Ben Cooper, and invited
her to share what she knew about the murder victim. She told them that
she'd met Gordon soon after her release from Bedford, when she still
went by the name Benita. "Bonnie," as Clayton called her, was living in a
squalid tenement on the Lower East Side, earning a meager living at the
city's brothels, where she might charge $20 a night, splitting half with
the madam.[28]

Her fortunes improved after she met Joseph Radlow at the Roosevelt Hotel in 1927. He wasn't the tall, dark, and handsome type that she
usually preferred. Stocky and balding, he had a round, fleshy face with a
double chin that spilled over his collar, and he wore small, round glasses
that accentuated his pudgy features. But he knew how to make a buck.

Radlow inhabited the netherworld of corporate finance where shady bro-kerages known as bucket shops preyed on small investors who had more greed than prudence. The markets were surging, and everyone thirsted to drink from the fountain of money flooding down Wall Street. Those who couldn't afford to invest bought on margin, borrowing from their brokerage and repaying the loan when the stock rose. But most bucket shops refused to make margin calls.* If the stock fell, the client forfeited the whole investment.[29]

Many bucketers traded penny stocks on curb markets—unregulated outdoor marketplaces on streets adjacent to reputable stock exchanges. Some peddled worthless blue-sky stocks that promised to revolutionize emerging industries like aviation. One fraudulent enterprise claimed to have designed an airplane that seated 1,000 people and stopped dead in the air at the push of a lever. Exploiting the rapid expansion of telephone networks, bucketers also purchased sucker lists with phone numbers for people who had recently come into money. They rented back-office boiler rooms with banks of telephones and hired salespeople known as dyna-miters who employed high-pressure sales techniques to take advantage of credulous investors.[30]

Radlow's specialty was reloading. He obtained lists of people who had been swindled in stock frauds and proceeded to swindle them again. In one scam, he recruited investors to collaborate in a scheme to manipulate a Boston curb stock for mutual profit. Each participant was required to make a substantial deposit and sign an agreement promising not to sell any shares until the maneuver was complete, with the deposit as guaran-tee. Then Radlow simply absconded with the deposits, knowing that the suckers wouldn't report the theft since he held evidence of their collusion in an illegal stock-manipulation scheme. When he was later arrested for another crime, a parole officer estimated that his scams had netted as much as $200,000 in a year—nearly four million in today's dollars. The officer described him as a "plausible, ingratiating individual who frankly

---

* When buying on margin, the investor is required to guarantee the loan by maintaining a minimum ratio of equity to debt. When falling share prices reduce the equity, brokers typically execute margin calls, meaning that clients must invest more money to maintain the minimum ratio.

admits that moral principles have no place in a man's business career." Perversely, even as he worked his rackets, Radlow served as a paid informant for the state attorney general.[31]

Gordon's relationship with Radlow was more collaborative than romantic. In the parlance of the business, she played the role of a "bird dog," whose job it was to bring prospects to Radlow. Dressed in finery, she lingered in the lobbies of luxury hotels, where she might catch the eye of a rich sucker and reel him into their scheme. A month after she and Radlow met, they moved into the fashionable Drake Hotel, registering as "Mr. and Mrs. V. Gordon." After the Drake, they migrated to the charming Pickwick Arms in Greenwich, Connecticut, and then to the glamorous Waldorf-Astoria in New York. Their relationship eventually went sour over a financial dispute. When Radlow was arrested in 1928, Gordon testified that he'd cheated her out of $50,000. It was through Radlow that Gordon met the two men featured so prominently in her diaries—Samuel Cohen and John Radeloff. Cohen was another accomplice in the securities racket; he, too, would be arrested in 1928, and his confession led to Radlow's conviction. Radeloff acted as their defense lawyer in the case.[32]

Unlike his cousin Radlow, Radeloff was exactly Gordon's type—slender, handsome, and debonair. Like her ex-husband, he radiated confidence and treated her with contempt. He was also manipulative, repeatedly pushing her away and drawing her back in, frightening her with threats of violence only to declare his love the next day. "Whatever Bonnie was to other men, make no mistake she fell for Radeloff hard," Cassie Clayton said. "I was living with her when she first met him. She told me she had a new boyfriend and that he was a peach. She described him to me as tall and handsome and a devil with women. When I met him, I wasn't terribly impressed, but he was good to her at first. He used to take her candy and flowers, and shower her with all kinds of attention. I used to go out when he arrived. Bonnie would say: 'Cassie, dear, run along, like a good girl, the boyfriend is coming,' and I didn't need a second invitation."[33]

Vivian Gordon could be a difficult roommate, prone to mood swings and heavy drinking, but Clayton tolerated her intemperance and accorded her more empathy than Dr. Gibson ever did. "Sometimes I used to quarrel with her and tell her I didn't quite like the way she was doing things, but I don't know as I blame her so much," she explained. "She had a terrible life and was embittered. Bonnie didn't care about anything after they took her child away. She went the limit and you can't blame her for anything she did."[34]

Vivian and Cassie lived at the brand-new Park Central Hotel on Seventh Avenue and 56th Street, kitty-corner to Carnegie Hall. Billing itself as "the world's finest apartment hotel," the Park Central offered tenants the latest amenities: electric refrigerators, radio outlets, and running ice water in every room, a requisite among high-end hotels of the era.* Residents and guests could enjoy food and entertainment on the panoramic roof garden on the 32nd floor or downstairs in any of the five "period" salons, each decorated in a unique style—Gothic, Arabian, Louis XV, Italian Baroque, and American Colonial. A gymnasium, swimming pool, and Turkish baths in the basement were supplied by artesian water pumped through bedrock. The hotel accommodated many celebrities over the years, including Mae West, Jackie Gleason, and Eleanor Roosevelt.† But it also attracted unsavory characters like Arnold Rothstein, who operated a "floating" craps game that migrated between various hotels to avoid detection. It was after one such game, in room 349 of the Park Central on November 4, 1928, that he received a fatal bullet in the gut.[35]

Clayton told Seabury and Cooper that Gordon became acquainted with Rothstein at the hotel but moved out before his murder. After the Park Central, Vivian briefly lived in an apartment on 51st Street but was evicted for throwing rowdy parties. Finally, she rented the apartment at 156 East 37th Street where she would spend the remaining two years of her life. Meanwhile, Cassie got married and left New York. They corresponded infrequently after that, and Clayton knew little of her friend's subsequent activities, much to the disappointment of Judge Seabury and Irving Ben Cooper, who had reached another dead end. After the interview, Seabury passed Clayton on to Commissioner Mulrooney for further questioning. He revealed nothing to reporters about what she'd said, at least not on the

---

* The ice water was stored in an elevated tank and circulated through pipes to bathroom taps.

† The iconic Mermaid Room, built in the 1940s, originally featured a painted ceiling with bare-breasted mermaids. At Eleanor Roosevelt's insistence, the mermaids received fish-net brassieres in the 1950s.

record, but someone in his office leaked Clayton's reference to the Roth-stein connection, a sensational tidbit guaranteed to excite the press.[36]

Not that the press needed prodding. The *News* had assigned a whole team of reporters to hunt for dirt on Vivian Gordon. The obvious place to seek information about a "Bedford girl" was a brothel. In the nineteenth century, New York City's "bawdy houses" had operated in the open. Pros-titutes beckoned from the doorways and windows of brownstones. Pimps and madams distributed business cards, placed newspapers ads, and hosted monthly balls. Guidebooks for "sporting men" rated various establishments. But the culture changed at the turn of century. The same puritanical cur-rents that drove passage of the Eighteenth Amendment prompted a crack-down on the sex industry, and New York's brothels went underground. Discreet apartments in large residential buildings replaced the brownstone parlors that had been visible from the street. Instead of buying advertise-ments, madams paid off cops to avoid raids. Yet, as with speakeasies, secrecy increased the attraction. The brothels became exclusive, available only to those in the know. They also took on symbolic importance. Visiting a bor-dello was more than a means of sexual gratification; it was also a rollicking act of defiance against the moralists. Many patrons, women as well as men, came for the drinks rather than the prostitutes. In short, brothels became cool, and the coolest of them all was the house of Polly Adler.[37]

Adler operated a number of establishments over the course of her career, but the ritziest was located at 201 West 54th Street, a block from the *Ziegfeld Follies*. Gilded mirrors and French baroque reproductions graced the walls of the bedrooms, and the salon featured deep-pile Persian rugs and a Gobelin tapestry depicting Vulcan and Venus "having a tender moment," as Adler put it. The bar paid homage to the recently discovered tomb of King Tut, which had inspired a craze for Egyptian ornamentation, and the Chinese-themed gambling room hosted mah-jongg, another con-temporary fad. A chef prepared late-night meals, and a bartender served up a steady stream of cocktails for the stiff price of a dollar a drink.[38]

But what made Adler's establishments stand out wasn't the amenities, it was the women. They were beautiful, of course, but also gracious and refined. Adler often dispatched them to nightclubs to drum up business or hired them out as private escorts. "To qualify as one of my girls, a candidate either had to know how to dress and behave like a lady or be willing to learn," she related in her memoir. "I stressed to them that the man who paid a couple of hundred to take a girl out for the evening didn't care to be seen with a painted slut. . . . As for the girls' conduct in the house, the rule was: Be a lady in the parlor and a whore in the bedroom." She refused to hire drug addicts, and her employees weren't permitted to drink on the job. Whenever customers bought them cocktails, the drinks still cost a dollar, but the bartender secretly substituted iced tea for whiskey.[39]*

The reputation of Adler's house attracted a higher class of clientele. Journalists, socialites, politicians, marketing executives, college boys, and Broadway stars fraternized in her salon. Jimmy Walker allegedly visited Adler's place before he ran for mayor. High-rolling gangsters came, too, and Dutch Schultz paid handsomely to use one of her places as a hideout during his war with Mad Dog Coll. But the coolest of Adler's patrons were the famed members of the Algonquin Round Table, a group of playwrights, producers, actors, and theater critics who gathered for lunch every day at the Algonquin Hotel in Midtown. They engaged in spectacular wordplay, bombarding one another and anyone they disdained with fusillades of bon mots and barbs of sarcasm. They often met up again in the evenings as they progressed from Broadway shows to trendy speakeasies, a rolling party that frequently terminated in Polly Adler's salon after midnight. Some came for sex. Some came to party. Some just came to eat. Years later, old-timers still spoke "wistfully of the many evenings they climbed those hallowed stairs . . . for a midnight omelet at Polly's club. Polly kept an accomplished chef, and the drinks were a dollar, and gossip ran like bathtub gin, alternating with the champagne of cultured discourse."[40]

The star of the party was Adler herself. The Algonquin wags adored her self-deprecating wit, sly double entendres, and unintentional malapropisms. Barely five feet tall in high heels, with a moon face, bulging eyes, and gap teeth, she spoke "pure New Yorkese" with a gruff, smoke-coarsened voice and a strong Yiddish accent. She'd come alone to the United States

---

* Adler's trick was revealed one night when a gangster named "The Lug" mistakenly swigged a glass of tea, made a choking noise, and hurled it against the wall. After a moment of tense silence, The Lug relaxed and said, "Okay, Polly, so you got to make a living. Well, fix me another drink." But he took revenge the following night by slipping Mickey Finns into some of the tea glasses.

when she was only thirteen, leaving her family in the tiny Russian village where she was born. She stumbled into the sex trade almost by accident. A minor gangster with whom she'd become acquainted recruited her to manage a "house of assignation" in Morningside Heights, near Columbia University, where a few prostitutes he managed could turn tricks. Soon she was recruiting customers from nearby speakeasies and clearing $100 a week. By 1927, she was operating multiple establishments with profits of $60,000 a year—more than a million in today's dollars—all while keeping her business a secret from her parents, who eventually followed her to New York.[41]

A clever, cultured woman like Vivian Gordon was a natural fit for Adler's establishment, so Grace Robinson wasn't surprised when her junior colleague, Jack Miley, turned up a connection. "The strangulation victim is an old pal of Polly Adler," he recorded in a memo that he shared with Robinson, "She has known Polly and been on her call house books, at least two years and probably much longer. My informant is an employed chorine* who herself works for Polly when show business is lousy, which in her case is most of the time.

"Gordon and Adler were on more friendly terms than Polly was with any of her other girls, according to my informant. Polly treated her more as an equal than an employee," he continued. "She seemed to have heavy dough and patronized the less fortunate kids who were trying to make an easy saw-buck† on the Ostermoor.‡ The dead girl constantly boasted to the others of her rich boyfriends, said she didn't have to go to Adler's and just worked to keep her mind occupied, or words to that effect. In most instances, she brought her own men to the place, and they seemed to run the middle-aged business type."

But Miley's source also described Gordon as a "trouble maker" who often tangled with the madam. In the fall of 1930, she and Adler had "a helluva quarrel" that permanently severed their relationship. "This hairpulling bee took place at Polly's last stand, an apartment at 255 West 88th St.," Miley wrote. "Their fight was over some middle-aged spender

---

* Chorine: A woman who dances in a chorus line.
† Saw-buck: A ten-dollar bill. Traditional $10 banknotes featured the Roman numeral X, which resembles a wooden sawhorse.
‡ Ostermoor & Co.: A luxury mattress manufacturer, originally based in Manhattan's Little Italy neighborhood.

"Vice Queen" Polly Adler, seen here at the Atlantic City boardwalk, 1935.

whom the Gordon gal brought to Adler's. Polly ordered her from the place in this guy's presence one night, and told other girls who were friends of hers: 'She'll never come in my house again!'"[42]

Grace Robinson incorporated Miley's scoop in her three-page spread the next day, describing her as "a kind of high lieutenant in the Adler organization." The madam herself wasn't available to comment on the story, though. According to Miley's source, she was hiding out in Miami, "where she plays around in the Roman baths," a reference to the famous Roman Pools Casino.[43]

Adler had skipped town in November after receiving a tip that Judge Seabury's process servers were coming for her. She knew plenty about the shakedown schemes of the Women's Court, having spent a fortune on police protection and payoffs. She'd learned her lesson early when her apartment was raided by a certain Officer Andrew McLaughlin in January 1921. But unlike Benita Bischoff, Adler had money for bribes, and the charges were dismissed. She was arrested a number of times after that—faithless vice cops tended to violate protection agreements when they needed to make quota—but she and anyone who worked for her always went free. She had no interest in discussing these activities with Judge Seabury, however. "Personally, I had nothing to fear from Judge Seabury," she recounted in her memoir. "The investigators were interested in me only because they knew I had entertained many members of the Magistrates' Courts and vice squad and numerous other city officials, and because I had paid out thousands of dollars in bribes to keep my house running smoothly and my girls and myself out of jail. But I had to get out of town because I wasn't going to talk. In the first place, I am not an informer. In the second place, even though I knew I wasn't going to squeal, if I accepted service of a subpoena a lot of people might be dubious about my ability to keep clammed up and decide to insure my silence in ways I didn't care to dwell on."[44]

Adler also discussed Vivian Gordon in her memoir, but she discounted reports of their friendship. "I knew her only as an attractive brunette in the same business as I, out to feather her nest quickly," she claimed. "There was nothing unusual in her having my address since we operated in the same circles, yet even though our acquaintance was of the slightest, the papers alleged that she had worked for me and that there had been a hair-pulling contest between us, and much bad feeling." Yet Adler's friend and ghostwriter, Virginia Faulkner, was skeptical. She recorded in her notes that the usually unflappable madam, who breezily described interactions with dangerous mobsters, seemed nervous when discussing Gordon, and her evolving descriptions of their relationship were inconsistent. At first, Adler spoke openly of her friendship with "Viv" but later suggested that she barely knew her.[45]

On Sunday morning, the day after the *News* ran the Adler story, an eight-cylinder Cord Phaeton luxury car with three passengers zigzagged down Hudson Boulevard in Jersey City. As it careened past a crowd of churchgoers, a patrolman stepped into the road and thrust his palm out. When the vehicle halted barely six inches in front of him, he leapt onto the running board and accosted the driver, a small, stocky man with blue eyes and reddish-blond hair. "What do you think you're doing, young fellow?" the officer shouted.

"Say," the driver slurred, "maybe you don't know who I am."

The patrolman assured him that he did not and demanded to see his license. When he failed to provide one, the cop ordered him out of the car and arrested him with the assistance of a couple more officers who arrived by motorcycle.[46]

The driver, Charles "Vannie" Higgins, was the biggest bootlegger in Brooklyn. He may not have been as infamous as his rival, Legs Diamond, but he was more successful and equally ferocious. To facilitate his massive smuggling operation, he'd acquired two airplanes, a fleet of trucks, and several speedboats, including one called the *Cigarette*, the fastest rum-boat in New York Harbor. Fearless and scrappy, he often personally led his gang into combat and was blamed for numerous murders and assaults, including the hit on Diamond, though nothing ever stuck.[47]

But after carousing all night at a roadhouse party in New Jersey, he was in no shape to take on Jersey City's finest. He spat at one cop and took a wild swing at another before they knocked him senseless, and he toppled, conveniently, into the sidecar of the motorcycle. During the melee, his passengers, two well-dressed blond women, jumped out of the Phaeton and ran over to another car that had been following them. The other car raced away as soon as they climbed aboard.

Several hours later, a *News* correspondent found Higgins sobering up in a jail cell. The journalist hadn't come all the way from New York to report on a gangster's drunk-driving arrest; he wanted to find out whether Higgins knew Vivian Gordon.

"Sure I knew her," Higgins replied.

"When did you last see her?"

"Say, I haven't seen that dame for more than a month," he snapped.

"What did she tell you when she last saw you?"

Higgins glowered at the reporter disdainfully. "Say, you don't think I'm sap enough to tell you anything about her, do you?" he retorted and refused to say anything more.

After his arraignment, the owner of the roadhouse where he'd been partying posted $1,750 bail on his behalf. Ten minutes after Higgins left the courtroom, three New York detectives arrived to question him about Vivian Gordon, but he was already gone.[48]

Grace Robinson colorfully described the bootlegger's arrest in her next Vivian Gordon piece on March 2, despite his reticence on the topic. Having failed to get any useful information from Higgins himself, she and her colleagues then tried to locate his ex-girlfriend, Jean Stoneham, the woman that Gordon had accused of stealing clothes. Stoneham's last known address was the Monticello Hotel, where Legs Diamond was shot. Described in the brochure as a quiet hotel near Central Park that catered to "ladies alone or families," the Monticello was favored by married gangsters seeking discreet accommodation for their lovers. Legs also kept a mistress there; he was hiding out in her suite when Higgins's hit men attempted to assassinate him.[49]

But Stoneham no longer lived at the Monticello. She'd left town in the summer of 1930 after she and Higgins broke up. Grace Robinson's colleague, Louis Davidson, had covered the story in October. "The girl who received the love notes and left hooks of Vannie Higgins, as gallant a gangster as ever beat up the girl friend, was identified last night when her story of events leading up to the shooting of Jack (Legs) Diamond . . . was revealed exclusively to the *News*," he wrote. "Gallant Vannie beat the girl unmercifully in a spat in their suite. Then he sent her to Boston where he left her stranded without money. Broke and friendless, the girl fell into the hands of the police." When they took her in, the cops found letters from

Higgins that implicated him in the attack on Diamond and other crimes. But Legs wasn't talking, and there wasn't enough evidence to prosecute Higgins. Jean Stoneham went temporarily into police protection and then disappeared.[50]

Four months later, Vivian Gordon's murder returned Stoneham to the spotlight, and the *News* was desperate to find her. On March 3, Davidson finally tracked her down in Detroit, where she was building a new life. "I'm on the up and up now," she told him. "None of those Broadway guerillas are going to knock me off." She confirmed that she'd lived with Gordon in New York, though their friendship had ended in acrimony, and said that she knew Radeloff, too. According to Stoneham, Gordon's relationship with the handsome lawyer had been tempestuous. She often threatened to have him disbarred if he left her, and she predicted that he would someday have her killed. "But she loved that man more dearly than life itself," Stoneham said, "and she'd have gone to hell for him if he said the word." Asked whether she believed that Radeloff murdered Gordon, Stoneham demurred. "Vivian was due to get the business. I know a dozen reasons why she might have been rubbed out."[51]

They'd met in 1929, soon after Stoneham arrived in New York from Nova Scotia, where she'd grown up. Gordon took the nineteen-year-old Canadian under her wing and taught her how a young woman with beauty and brains could make a killing in the big city. The Roaring Twenties had unleashed a cultural explosion of hedonism and excess. Even prominent citizens indulged in the debauchery, especially rich men. "Speakeasies and theatres, nightclubs and bordellos swarmed with the boys who had hit it big and were busting to throw it around," Polly Adler related in her memoir. "Every other guy was a Champagne Charlie, a Diamond Jim, a Bender the Spender, ready to shoot the wad on such necessities as Corona-Coronas, Veuve Clicquot, Cartier knickknacks, Cadillacs, yachts, and fancy ladies."[52]

All those eager men wandering up and down Broadway with swollen wallets and ravenous libidos presented an opportunity, and Vivian Gordon seized it. For graying businessmen who coveted the glamour and debauchery of Manhattan's nightclub scene, she was an irresistible companion. Chic, sophisticated, and sexy, with an acid wit, she escorted her dates to the city's most exclusive speakeasies and later invited them back to her room. Her "sugar daddies" included some of the city's wealthiest men. "She loved to talk of her friendship with the late Draper Daugherty, Harry Thaw, John Hoagland, Jeff Livingston, the racing man, and other celebrities," Stoneham said.[53]

So long as her paramour lavished her with generous gifts, she would allow their romance to continue, but the biggest payoff often came at the end of the affair. When a man tired of her, she would threaten to sue him or to create a scene that would attract authorities unless he paid up. She chose her marks carefully—rich men with reputations to protect who would pay to avoid a scandal—and kept a notebook with names and biographical information for hundreds of potential targets. John Radeloff also participated in these schemes, offering a gloss of professionalism and underscoring the threat of litigation. "She was always threatening to sue some wealthy man," Stoneham said, "and they always paid when her lawyer, Radeloff, came around to see them. If they were smart and didn't, she and Radeloff usually let 'em go."[54]

Gordon's other black notebook, the one with women's names, related to another racket of hers. The book was a catalog of "party girls," a euphemism for prostitutes hired by business executives to entertain clients and prospective customers. Many businessmen who came to New York on corporate junkets wished to savor the delights of the famously sinful city, and Manhattan's dealmakers were eager to oblige them, using sex to facilitate commerce. The visitors often didn't even realize that their flirtatious companions were prostitutes, paid for by companies seeking their business. A number of madams profited from the lucrative business, but Polly Adler was New York's premier provider, and Gordon was a partner in the operation, according to Stoneham. "Polly could tell those New York cops plenty about Vivian Gordon and their party girl racket," she said. "Why don't they ask her about Vivian?"[55]

For Adler, the party girl racket was just another channel for her brothel business, but Gordon had other plans. She taught her "young forty-niners," as she called the women she employed, the art of mining gold from rich men, ordering them to document their trysts and ferret out information that could be useful for extortion. "We're not in this business for our health," she told them. "We're in it for every cent we can get. Make the men pay. They'll give phony names, but when they go to sleep, look for letters, cards, etc. or get their names from tailor's labels in clothes." Gold-digging and blackmail were far more lucrative than prostitution, netting as much as $1,000 per man or even $10,000 from a heavy spender. The proceeds were usually split three ways, a third for the woman, a third for Gordon, and a third for John Radeloff.[56]

Gordon also sought to emulate Adler's brothel business, but she was late to the game. In 1930, she arranged to rent an upscale apartment on the Upper West Side and engaged a police lieutenant to provide protection, but her plans went awry when the vice cop was targeted by the Seabury commission. "There goes my place," she groused. "I had it all fixed, but the fixer couldn't even save himself."[57]

Even as she expanded her operations, Gordon was not above turning tricks herself to bring in extra revenue. She had a small network of cabbies and busboys whom she paid to deliver drunk men to her, and her rates were high. "She was the greatest little check-hiker you ever met," Stoneham said. "She always raised 'em. Usually she boosted 'em from $100 to $1000, or something like that. She had a sweetie who was a cashier in one of those Broadway bootleggers' banks, and he used to shove those hot checks through for her before the chumps could come out of the ether and raise a yell. Then he would come over to our apartment and play around himself."[58]

Gordon also earned income from her rental properties, loans, and stock market investments, but her greatest sources of revenue were her sugar daddies, and the sweetest daddy of them all was a sixty-eight-year-old widower name Henry Joralmon. Having earned tens of millions as a banker and president of a chemical company in Denver, Joralmon devoted his retirement to distributing his fortune to beautiful young women in Manhattan. After his wife died in 1923, he immediately embarked on a long-term affair with a very young woman, Annette Franco, who worked at the souvenir counter at the Biltmore Hotel, where he lived. Promising to marry her, he installed Franco and her parents in a luxury suite at the hotel. But that didn't prevent him from pursuing other dalliances. When he went out on the town, he usually wore a money belt stuffed with $100 and $1,000 bills, which he handed out to whomever caught his fancy.[59]

Vivian Gordon met the philandering multimillionaire while she lived at the Park Central Hotel in 1927. A friend of hers who remained anonymous, likely Cassie Clayton, recalled the fortune she reaped from her evenings with Joralmon. "Night after night she would come home to the Park Central, half-plastered, and throw sometimes $800, sometimes $700, on the bed and tell Radeloff, Cohen, and me—'that's all the old guy had tonight.'" At first, she kept the identity of her mysterious benefactor a secret. "Radeloff, night after night, tried to get Vivian to reveal the identity of Joralmon," the friend continued, "but Vivian was wise and held out on Radeloff. This was her private source of income and she didn't want Radeloff to cut in on it. . . . Then one night she revealed the name to Radeloff and I suppose the lawyer cut himself in. Vivian told me later, 'I would give my right arm if I had been able to keep Joralmon's name a secret from Radeloff.'"[60]

Not all of Joralmon's gifts were monetary. He often accompanied Gordon to fashionable clothing stores and sat near the door, reading a newspaper, while she gathered as much as $1,200 worth of lace, nightgowns, silk negligees, and smart Parisian clothes. Then he cheerfully paid the bill. He also paid for the $2,000 mink coat, $2,500 diamond ring, and $900 Swiss watch that the elevator operator saw her wearing on the night of her murder. The ring was originally meant for Joralmon's girlfriend, Annette Franco, but he broke off the relationship in 1928. When Franco subsequently sued him for what she claimed was a broken engagement, Gordon helped him out by digging up dirt on the young woman, and he gave her the ring in gratitude.[61]

Fine clothing, jewels, and lingerie were especially valuable to Gordon, not merely as ornaments of vanity but as tools of her trade. When men met her in luxury hotels and upscale nightclubs, they saw a sophisticated, well-to-do lady, not a prostitute. She also worked the finery into her extortion schemes. "Vivian was paid for that coat and ring a thousand times," Stoneham said. "She would get a John in her flat. She'd hide the coat and ring in a bag that covered her mattress. Then she'd say they'd been stolen and threaten to go to the police. The sucker would always pay for them, rather than get implicated in a larceny case."[62]

She employed a similar ruse to punish forty-niners who double-crossed her. "Why, Vivian framed me herself," Stoneham declared. "She put one of her dresses and some clothes in my bag after I quarreled with her and left her apartment." This was the incident described in Gordon's diary.

She eventually dropped the charges against Stoneham, but other women weren't so lucky. "I know at least six girls whom Vivian Gordon framed and sent to Bedford," Stoneham claimed. "She boasted about it when she was drunk. They were girls who had crossed her in money matters, who held out money they got from men to whom she introduced them."[63]

Unlike her treatment of her other marks, Gordon never tried to extort money from Joralmon. After their affair ended, she introduced him to one of her forty-niners, twenty-five-year-old Helen Dorf. The apple-cheeked brunette was much more reserved than Jean Stoneham. Gordon described her as a "sweet kid" from the Bronx but complained in her diary that Radeloff was "racing around" with her. Dorf also proved willing to talk about Gordon and Radeloff when Doris Fleeson, another *News* correspondent, visited her home in the Bronx and interviewed her with her mother and sister at her side. "I never knew Vivian Gordon was a notorious woman," Dorf said. "All that's come out about her and her dealings with Radeloff simply stun me. I thought them both nice friends of mine."[64]

But she did have some notion of Gordon's schemes. "When I first met Vivian, she tried to interest me in getting money from wealthy men," she elaborated. "'Helen,' she said, 'there isn't a chance of exposure. And you don't have to give up much. When these men get good and drunk, they forget why they wanted to meet you in the first place and they pay plenty. You don't have to pick them up on the streets and run the risk of arrest by a vice cop. I have connections with taxi-drivers who make a specialty of taking out rich rounders. As soon as they are fairly drunk, I get a call and meet them. The taxi boy gets a small split; he never knows what I get, and if he does, what's the difference? It's a safe and profitable racket. It's much better than wasting your time at a party where the most you get is drunk on bum liquor.'"[65]

By the time Gordon introduced Dorf to Joralmon, he was legally blind and terminally ill. Imminent mortality seemed to have buoyed his generous spirit, for he gifted the young woman $30,000—over half a million in today's dollars. Astonished by the size of the gift, Radeloff and Gordon decided to help themselves to their shares. "When I told Vivian about it, she said for me to keep five thousand and give the other twenty-five thousand to her to invest," Dorf claimed. "She said Mr. Radeloff would invest it safely, and give me a weekly payment out of the earnings. He gave me sixty-five dollars a week for a little while, and then stopped, and I never heard of the money again."[66]

Helen Dorf didn't name Joralmon during the interview, but she didn't deny her sister's frequent interjections that Joralmon had indeed been her benefactor. Her mother, an old-fashioned Russian-Jewish immigrant, seemed satisfied by her daughter's explanation that the money had been given to her by a philanthropic friend. "Who is Joralman, honey?" she asked innocently. Then turning to the reporter, she said proudly, "Helen won the San Francisco Exposition prize as the most beautiful child in New York City. She was nine years old then. There was never a sweeter, lovelier little girl than Helen was then."

Returning to the topic, Fleeson asked Helen, "Did he ever make love to you?"

"I've got nothing to say!" the young woman shouted hysterically. Then, turning to her sister, she added, "Don't you say nothing either. You talk too much."[67]

Helen Dorf and Jean Stoneham were reliable witnesses, and their stories were corroborated by Gordon's diary and court records, but not all of the *News*'s sources were trustworthy. The day after publishing interviews with Stoneham and Dorf, the paper ran a sensational story by Martin McEvilly, normally the news photographer, which claimed that Gordon and Legs Diamond were partners in an extortion scheme targeting stockbrokers.

"Vivian and Jack had been taking the boys right and left. They were the envy of every racket mob on Broadway," declared an anonymous source, described only as "a girlfriend of the pair." She dropped names that had clearly been pulled from newspaper reports and recounted conversations in preposterously vivid detail, replete with caricatured gangster lingo. In one exchange, she described a dispute between the pair over a $2,000 roll of bills that Diamond tossed at Gordon.

> Vivian said: "What? Is that all? That's a lousy little cut for such a soft touch. And if it hadn't been for me you wouldn't have got a dime!'"
>
> Diamond said: "Don't you like it? Aren't you satisfied, kid?"
>
> Vivian told him: "You know I'm not, you piker. Where is the rest on my end? Come on, get it up, big boy!"

Diamond's thin face grew livid. His eyes snapped. Half rising from the table, he snapped at Vivian: "Well, that's all you're going to get, you dirty little bum. So take it and shut up—if you don't want to get hurt!"[68]

The story was soon discredited. Though Vivian Gordon was acquainted with Legs Diamond, there's no evidence they ever collaborated. Yet that didn't stop the *News*'s headline editors from inserting Diamond's name at every opportunity.

The reporting did lead, indirectly, to a police raid on Diamond's compound in the Catskill Mountains, where he was still convalescing from the 1930 assassination attempt at the Monticello. Fifteen state troopers, reportedly dispatched by Governor Roosevelt, searched the property for two unidentified men wanted for questioning in the Gordon case, but neither Commissioner Mulrooney nor Inspector Bruckman had any clue who they were searching for. Two days later, it came out that the raid had been instigated by a newspaper reporter posing as a federal agent who had tricked the troopers. Diamond subsequently complained that the officers had entered without a warrant and taken valuable personal papers.[69]

Accurate or not, the headlines served their purpose. The depiction of Vivian Gordon as a femme fatale and underworld mastermind, with connections to New York's most notorious gangsters and secrets that would blow apart the Seabury investigation, enthralled the public. Newspapers as far away as Sydney and Singapore covered the story. Day after day, the New York papers clanged out prurient revelations about the "titian-haired Broadway butterfly" on their front pages, none more shrilly than the *News*, which had devoted full-cover photo spreads followed by three to four pages of reporting every day since the murder.

For most readers, the story was a form of salacious and suspenseful entertainment, but two readers were significantly affected by the reporting. One was Governor Franklin Roosevelt, who was concerned about the political implications of the metastasizing story and the lack of progress in the investigation. "So startling were the revelations made yesterday, that Gov. Roosevelt speeded his plans to take a personal hand in probing the mystery," Grace Robinson wrote. A bundle of documents, believed to include a copy of Vivian Gordon's diary, was sent to the governor's mansion. Roosevelt also demanded updates from District Attorney Charles McLaughlin, sternly informed Commissioner Mulrooney that the police were "on trial," and summoned Judge Seabury to a "secret parley," though he slyly told the press that the judge "simply paid me a social call."[70]

Yet the reader most profoundly affected by the sensational reporting on Vivian Gordon was not anyone of political importance, just a sixteen-year-old girl. John Bischoff had never told his daughter, Benita, the truth about her mother. He had done everything in his power to prevent any relationship between them, to the point of relocating so that Gordon couldn't find them. He told Benita that her mother was a successful Broadway dancer whom, for some unexplained reason, she would never be allowed to see. That myth exploded in spectacular fashion on Thursday, February 26, as news of Vivian Gordon's murder poured from the pages of every newspaper in the country.

On Friday, Benita set off to school as usual, but she turned back after thinking that she saw someone point at her. She kept to her room all weekend, refused to eat, and slept fitfully. "Several times I went up to her room and found her stretched across the bed, crying as though her heart would break," said her stepmother, Eunice Bischoff. "She would smile, wipe away the tears and pretend that she had gained control of herself, but it was no use. The poor child couldn't tear her thoughts away from the murder of her mother and the rest of it."[71]

"I'll never be able to face my friends," Benita told her stepmother. "I guess that it's time for me to change my name now, mother. I think I'll adopt my middle name, Fredericka, because of this trouble in New York."[72]

She didn't attend school on Monday either but did visit the ice rink for hockey practice in the afternoon. "Benita came into the rink with her skates, but none of the girls went over to talk to her," said a boy who knew her. "I don't think they snubbed her; they acted as though they didn't know exactly what to do. I watched Benita, and she put on her skates, and tried to act as though nothing was out of the way. But after she skated around by herself for a while, she took off her skates and left, and when she walked down the pike, she had her head down and was crying and sobbing."[73]

On Tuesday, Benita returned her schoolbooks to her teacher, explaining that her family was moving away. "The poor child's grief was written on her face," the teacher said. "I asked her to keep her books until she actually left school. I told her that all of us loved her and wanted to help her and be her friends, and asked her to come back to her classes. When I told her that, all of the grief vanished from her face, and she smiled a warm smile that lighted her face. She seemed immensely cheered and lighter of heart, and so did I. I watched her as she crossed the grounds, and she was walking briskly, her head up and her books under her arm."[74]

Benita also kept a diary, bound in purple leather, a Christmas gift from her stepmother. In its pages, she recorded her growing despair as the horrifying news about her mother screamed from the presses.

> *February 28: What an awful mess mother got herself into. She has been found dead in New York and they are saying terrible things.*
>
> *March 1: Everyone is so nice to me, especially mother (referring to her step-mother). I guess I'll change my name from Benita to Fredericka.*
>
> *March 2: They are saying so many things. It is awful.*
>
> *March 3: All my bad luck comes at one time. This time it started the day I was born and has not stopped yet, except for a little recess now and then that's just long and frequent enough to make me dissatisfied, to know what I am missing. I've quite decided to turn on the gas.*[75]

Eunice Bischoff had gone to work on Tuesday. "All day long, I kept thinking of her, until I was almost frantic," she cried, halting between sobs. "I hadn't the faintest idea that she would do anything to herself, but I was frantic to get home, just to see that she was all-right. I hurried home, and was just about to call as I opened the door, but then I . . ." She faltered again, then continued. "I smelled gas . . . and then I found her gone."[76]

She rushed into the house and pushed open the kitchen door, dreading what she would find. Benita lay on the floor in a brown polka-dot dress and tennis shoes. "I clasped her to me and called her, but she did not respond," Eunice wept. "I called the police, after opening the windows. While they worked over her, I prayed that she would live. Then the doctor came and ordered her taken to the hospital in Camden. I prayed all the way up and hoped she would survive, but God willed otherwise."[77]

John Bischoff was back at work in Lorton, Virginia, when he received the message. "I saw Benita this morning," he said slowly. "I was afraid something of the sort would happen. She was heartbroken and ashamed. She wouldn't go to school or go out of the house. No one could console her. She's the innocent victim of the whole thing. She did not know anything about her mother's past until this case broke. I would have given anything if only her name could have been kept out of this. That is what killed her."[78]

PART II

NOTHING BUT THE TRUTH

CHAPTER 6
EVERYBODY IN NEW YORK

THE FIRST TIME INSPECTOR HENRY BRUCKMAN PAGED THROUGH VIVIAN Gordon's diary, as he sat in her orchid-hued apartment the day her body was found, the solution to the case had seemed obvious. "He is not to be trusted," she wrote. "He would stoop to anything." The death threats, lovers' quarrels, manipulations, and criminal acts recorded in the diary pointed to one man, John A. Radeloff. Bruckman had ordered his arrest the same afternoon, along with his henchman Samuel Cohen, the "loft thief" that Vivian Gordon mentioned in her diary. Bruckman and Commissioner Mulrooney spent the whole night interrogating the two men at the Bathgate Station in the Bronx.[1]

John Radeloff was a smooth operator—smartly dressed, slender, and handsome, with a cleft chin and slicked brown hair that narrowed to a slight widow's peak. At the station, he smiled and laughed as if he enjoyed being interrogated about the murder of his ex-lover. Freely admitting their relationship, he spoke at length about Vivian Gordon's gold-digging schemes, telling the detectives all about Henry Joralmon, the generous widower, and Frederick "Teddy" Schweinler, the magazine printer. He admitted that Gordon had informed him of her plan to contact the Seabury commission and claimed that he'd tried to discourage her. "I don't see what you can do," he told her. "Your case is eight years old." But he said that she ignored his counsel, insisting, "I'll give Mr. McLaughlin the needle and make some trouble for him."[2]

Radeloff denied any knowledge of Gordon's murder, though. When Bruckman confronted him with the menacing warnings from the diary, he shrugged and dismissed her fears as paranoia induced by her addiction to alcohol and sleeping pills. He also had an alibi. He'd stayed home on the night of February 25 to play bridge, he said, adding that the other

OPPOSITE: John Radeloff, left, is seen leaving the Bronx County courthouse, where he appeared before a grand jury in the Gordon case, March 1, 1931.

participants—his wife, his brother, his sister-in-law, and a neighbor—would confirm that he'd been home all evening.[3]

Next, Bruckman turned his attention to Sam Cohen. The physical contrast between the two suspects was striking, like that of the comedy duo Laurel and Hardy. Cohen was a hulk of man, perhaps 300 pounds, with a wide, pear-shaped face nestled over a bulbous double chin. His clothes were shabby and unkempt, and he looked as if he hadn't shaved for days. He also had a lengthy rap sheet. Sam Cohen, alias Chowderhead Cohen, alias Sam Goldberg, alias Charles Harris, had been arrested thirteen times for grand larceny, burglary, receiving stolen goods, and impersonating a Prohibition agent. He'd served time in three different prisons, including Sing Sing. But at the station house, he insisted that he'd gone straight and pleaded with the police not to publicize the Charles Harris pseudonym, which he said he'd been using to put his past behind him.[4]

Cohen had none of Radeloff's suave composure. Attempts to rattle a confession from him only made him hysterical. When Mulrooney warned, "Sam, you're going to burn for this," Cohen jumped up and shouted frantically, "I'm not going to burn for you or anyone else!" To calm him down, Bruckman brought in another officer who had established a rapport with him during previous arrests. Once he relaxed, Cohen proved to be a likable, good-natured fellow despite his criminal record. He didn't know Gordon as well as Radeloff did, but he spoke frankly about their interactions. He said that she had occasionally hired him as a bodyguard at $150 a week and once paid him to accompany her to Philadelphia in a scheme to force her ex-husband to pay "alimony." According to Cohen, she'd laughed and said, "We'll put the arm on him." But when they arrived in Philadelphia, John Bischoff was out of town, and they returned to New York empty-handed.[5]

Cohen also had an alibi. He claimed that he was playing cards at a club in the Bronx until 12:30 a.m., when a taxi driver friend picked him up and drove him home. The only person who could testify to his whereabouts after that was his wife.[6]

When Bruckman finally concluded his examinations early the next morning, he was no closer to solving the case. Though suspicious of both men, especially the glib lawyer, the only evidence he had on them was in the diary. So he turned them over to Bronx District Attorney Charles

McLaughlin, who arranged to hold them as material witnesses with a $50,000 bond assigned to each.

While Bruckman was interrogating Radeloff and Cohen, a taxi driver who'd read about the case in the papers had called the station to relate an alarming incident he'd witnessed on the night of the murder. The cabbie, Frank Ryan, said that he'd been waiting for a fare at a taxi stand in the Bronx around 2:30 a.m. when another yellow Checker cab stopped beside him at a traffic light. Through the window, he heard a woman screaming and saw two men appear to strike her inside the vehicle. Ryan called out to two other drivers waiting at the stand, but as they approached the car together, it sped off through the red light. Ryan leapt into his own cab and gave chase, followed by the other two cabbies. An off-duty patrolman also heard the commotion and jumped onto the sideboard of one of the other cabs, clinging to the chassis as it careened around corners.

The three taxis pursued the yellow Checker through the dark streets. After a few blocks, the others lost the trail, but Ryan followed close and pulled up next to the mysterious cab when it stopped at another light. Peering through the glass, he saw the woman sitting upright in the right corner of the rear seat. She was no longer screaming and looked unharmed. Then the other driver noticed him looking and drove away in the direction of Van Cortlandt Park. Ryan's own engine stalled, and he watched helplessly as the Checker raced away. Squinting at the license plate, he made out the last three digits, 8-1-0.[7]

Bruckman sent a detective to try to track down the Checker while he interviewed the cabbies and patrolman. But no sooner had he taken down their stories when he received another lead that pointed in a quite different direction. A woman who said that she worked for Vivian Gordon claimed to have seen her on the night of the murder. When Bruckman brought her in to the Bathgate Station, she told the detectives a strange story.

Her name was Leonora Halsey. She'd emigrated from Cuba and had previously worked as a nightclub dancer in Harlem but now lived with her husband in Mount Vernon, a suburb just north of the Bronx, not far from Van Cortlandt Park. Two weeks ago, she said, she'd fallen into conversation with a red-haired woman on the subway. The woman introduced herself as Mrs. Biddle and offered to employ her as a maid for $25 a week. Halsey accepted the offer and went the next day to Mrs. Biddle's home at 156 East

37th Street, Apartment 3C. She said that she worked for Mrs. Biddle twice more that week and on Tuesday and Wednesday of the following week. Before she left on Wednesday evening, February 25, she said that Mrs. Biddle asked her to go out to buy a pair of stockings and offered to pick her up on the corner of 45th Street and Broadway. "I'm going up Westchester way for dinner," she said, "and I'll be glad to drive you home."[8]

Halsey did as she was told. At 11:00 p.m., a car pulled up to the corner, as promised, but in addition to the chauffeur, Mrs. Biddle was accompanied by two men in evening dress sitting on either side of her in the back seat. One of the men opened up a folding seat on the left side for Halsey to sit. Mrs. Biddle and the two men bantered and laughed as they drove through the Bronx, and Halsey heard them discuss plans to visit a restaurant. They dropped her off at her home in Mount Vernon around midnight, and that was the last she saw of Mrs. Biddle.

The next day, she said, a man that she didn't recognize came to her home and told her that Mrs. Biddle no longer required her services. Later that day, she discovered Mrs. Biddle's true identity when she recognized Vivian Gordon's photo and address in the newspapers, and she alerted the police.[9]

While Bruckman's detectives interviewed witnesses, the police department's forensic pathologists employed scientific methods to reconstruct Vivian Gordon's murder. Their field was still in its infancy. Until the 1920s, forensics had been an amateurish business. As in most cities, the coroners of New York were neither required nor expected to be doctors. They were ordinary elected officials, nominated by Tammany bosses on the basis of political loyalty rather than technical expertise. The motley crowd of coroners who served in the five boroughs between 1898 and 1915 included nineteen well-connected physicians, eight undertakers, seven politicians, six real estate agents, two saloonkeepers, two plumbers, a musician, a dentist, and a butcher.[10]

But as forensic science matured, progressive reformers began to introduce the new scientific methods into detective work. In 1918, the New York State legislature replaced the old coroner's office with a new chief medical examiner who was required to be a physician and to have passed a civil service exam. New York's first permanent chief medical examiner was a pathologist named Charles Norris. When he took over the new

Dr. Alexander Gettler, a noted forensic chemist with the New York City Office of Chief Medical Examiner, working in the toxicology laboratory of the city morgue at Bellevue Hospital, c.1920.

department, he hired a team of accomplished scientists, including chemist Alexander Gettler, regarded as the founding father of American forensic toxicology.[11]

It was Gettler who analyzed Vivian Gordon's neural tissue the day after her murder and concluded that she was mildly inebriated at the time of her death—"half drunk," as he put it. He also analyzed the contents of her stomach, which indicated that she'd recently eaten an unusual meal that included celery, onions, cabbage, sauerkraut, eggs, and raisins. "Was she a vegetarian?" queried the editor of the *Brooklyn Daily Eagle*. "Was she known to have been dieting?" While Gettler's report shed no light on the cause of death, it did prompt detectives to inquire at speakeasies and nightclubs where Gordon might have imbibed alcohol on the night of her murder.[12]

Dr. Louis Lefkowitz, assistant medical examiner at Fordham Hospital in the Bronx, performed the autopsy. He confirmed that Gordon had been killed by "asphyxia due to strangulation by cord" but also reported a 3½-inch contusion on her chin and a second contusion on her temple, which suggested that she'd been beaten and perhaps knocked unconscious before she was garroted. There also were numerous scratches on her skin, but these were likely inflicted after death when her body was dragged through the underbrush. Lefkowitz additionally noted two thin scars that traced her hairline on either side of her face, evidence of plastic surgery.[13]

"The rope was wound around the neck as follows," the report continued. "Situated in the middle of the back of the neck was a slip knot, through which slip knot the rope was inserted. The very end of this proximal portion of the rope was knotted by a single knot which prevented the slipping of the slip knot. The first loop around the neck made by this slip knot was extremely tight and indented the skin. The rope was then wound twice around the neck from right to left, coming from behind, anteriorly, making three loops in all."[14]

The rope itself was also subject to scientific examination. The weather-beaten cord was 8' long and 7/32" thick. Detectives initially suspected that it had been used as a clothesline, but when the district attorney sent it to a chemistry lab at Columbia University for analysis, the chemists found no clothing fibers embedded in the material. "The rope is impregnated with a considerable quantity of animal fat, which is not apparent to the eye or to the sense of touch," the chemists reported. "A guess is made that the animal fat in the rope came from a kitchen but that is frankly a guess."[15]

Every day, packs of journalists hung about the Bathgate Station and the Bronx County Courthouse. They recorded the comings and goings of grand jury witnesses, devoured forensic reports, and shadowed the detectives like hungry dogs, snapping up any morsels tossed their way or carelessly dropped. As usual, Grace Robinson outpaced the rest. In addition to nabbing exclusive interviews with John Radeloff, Al Marks, and Andrew McLaughlin, she had a source inside the Bronx DA's office, Assistant District Attorney Sam Foley, who informed her that "despite d. a. mclaughlin's denial, there ARE name of prominent persons and of MORE THAN

ONE policeman in Vivian's diaries," according to her notes. She also had eyes on Bruckman when he escorted Leonora Halsey, the housemaid, from the station after her interrogation. "Another probably significant witness was a dark, plump Spanish woman who, after being closeted for a couple of hours with Inspector Henry Bruckman was driven away from the Bronx in a police car with three detectives," she recorded in an internal memo. "One of the men was overheard asking her, 'When did you see her last?' She replied, 'Wednesday.' V. G. was killed Thursday."[16]

On Tuesday, March 3, Robinson teased readers with another explosive scoop. "Police of every precinct in the metropolitan district received an alarm to search for a Ford coupe, believed to be the murder car," she wrote. "The alarm read: 'Search all garages and places where autos are stored for Ford coupe No. N-88-19 which is wanted in 50th precinct for homicide. This car is wanted in connection with the murder of Vivian Gordon. The owner is Harold Doman of 203 West 117th St.'"[17]

The next morning, Inspector Bruckman and District Attorney McLaughlin abruptly departed the grand jury hearing on an unspecified errand. On their way out, McLaughlin told reporters that Harold Doman, the man referenced in the broadcast, was a key witness. "The alarm for the coupe was in order to pick up Doman," he stated. "I assure you I will interrogate him this afternoon. His name appeared in the papers we found in Vivian Gordon's apartment. I consider this a very important development in this investigation." Asked whether he suspected Doman of the murder, he hesitated before answering, "Well, I cannot say at this time whether I do or do not."[18]

Robinson was waiting outside the station with the other journalists when McLaughlin and Bruckman returned in the afternoon with two men in custody. One was "a well-dressed scowling blonde of Dutch extraction with the build of a wrestler" and the other "a slinky, sleek Porto-Rican with the snapping black eyes of a snake," as Robinson put it. They hid their faces behind their hats while the flashbulbs crackled.[19]

After the witnesses entered the station, McLaughlin lingered outside and opened up to the press about the arrests. He named the two witnesses as Harold Worthington Doman and Louis Zeno, describing them as "procurers" who once ran a brothel at 851 West End Avenue that catered to wealthy men in Morningside Heights. He said that Vivian Gordon had mentioned the two men in her diary and reported visiting the brothel several times the previous winter. She later quarreled with the two men and feared that they might hurt her.[20]

"Hal" Doman was already known to the police, but McLaughlin said that they had trouble locating him after Gordon's murder. They confirmed that he'd rented the West End flat under his middle name, Worthington, but the lease had ended some time ago. They also discovered another apartment that he'd rented more recently in a residential hotel at 203 West 117th Street in Harlem, but that lease had expired in September. The hotel clerk said that he continued to receive mail at the address, though, and came every so often to pick it up, most recently on February 23, two days before the murder.[21]

The clerk also mentioned that Doman owned a black Ford coupe, a helpful tip. Inspector Bruckman located the vehicle registration and broadcast the alarm to all the city precincts and surrounding suburbs. A patrolman who'd heard the message stopped the car on the street at 110th and Central Park West. Doman wasn't in it, but the driver, a garage attendant, claimed that Doman had lent him the coupe, and he provided addresses for both men. Doman was living at the Hotel Breslin in

A police officer examines the Ford coupe with the license plate No. N-88-19, after it was seized in connection with the Gordon homicide investigation, March 4, 1931.

Midtown, where detectives found him "sidling about the sportsmen in the lobby," as Robinson put it. Zeno was arrested at his apartment in Harlem, she added, "snappily dressed in a green suit and grooming his black hair with handfuls of pomade."[22]

The usually stern-faced district attorney seemed almost buoyant as he described the capture of the two men. "We are much nearer a solution of the crime now than we were this time last night," he boasted. To the journalists' delight, he also released the diary entries that described Gordon's interactions with Doman and Zeno, which were duly printed in all the papers.[23]

> *February 1, 1930: Hal Dolman, alias Worthington—Taylor & Louis Zeno 851 West End Ave. were to dinner. H. D. stole a bottle of perfume from me—when questioned denied it—H. D. claims they have an apt. at 80th and Park (?) also—but are hiding.*
> *February 3, 1930: 7 P. M. have gone to 851 West End— 4th floor in case anything happens.*
> *February 19, 1930: L. Z. dinner. J. A. R.*
> *February 25, 1930: 851 West End. Dinner.*

In the next entry, Gordon described the brutal assault that she'd suffered in the company of Teddy Schweinler, the publisher. After the beating, she sought shelter at the West End brothel, where she was treated by a doctor and sent home in the care of a woman she called Vernon Rapez:

> *Officer Terufera gave me a $ for taxi. I went 851 West End—Zeno— about 10:15 Saturday A. M. Dr. came—ye Gods—concussion brain—2 broken ribs—bruises from head to foot—851 West End— Terrible place—Ran into Doman Feb 28 after 4 years—he is with Zeno—who looks shady—a Porto Rican—however I left there with Dr. on this date—Vernon Rapez a girl from there came with me— Dr. said either she come or I have nurse.*

A few days later, Doman and Zeno, displeased that Gordon had enlisted one of their prostitutes as her nurse, called her at home to complain. The diary continued:

*March 6, 1930: 851 West End Ave. got nasty on phone—sore
because their girl Vernon Rapez was here taking care of me—she left
yesterday—So I slammed up the phone receiver—its best—I find
they are "?" Zeno is a Porto Rican—ye Gods! where'd he get that
Spanish stuff?* [24]

The next day, while the detectives were questioning the new suspects,
Inspector Bruckman received a tip from the police in Newark, New Jersey. Doman and Zeno had rented an apartment there on February 1, 1931.
Though they'd committed to rent for three months, they terminated the
lease at the end of February, right after Gordon's murder. According to the
Newark police, they shipped their furniture to a friend in Hillside, New
Jersey, not far from the newly constructed Newark Airport. Bruckman
immediately dispatched detectives to search the man's home, where they
discovered two trunks bound with rope similar to the cord used to strangle
Vivian Gordon. Bruckman ordered them to cut a sample and deliver it to
the lab at Columbia University that had been analyzing the murder rope.[25]

In the meantime, the police searched for the woman from 851 West
End who had nursed Gordon after her ordeal. But Grace Robinson found
her first. Her name was Vernon Repez, spelled slightly differently from the
way Vivian Gordon had recorded it. A pretty, petite twenty-four-year-old
with a round face and dark hair, she told Robinson that she had lived with
Doman for a time but denied being a prostitute.

"Vivian Gordon, who didn't look more than half her 37 years when
she was dressed for a party, began coming into the place at odd hours,"
Repez said. "She came there with John Radeloff. But she didn't seem to
be very afraid of Radeloff at that time. In fact I never thought Radeloff was anything more than a friend of hers. I didn't even know he was
her lawyer."

According to Repez, Gordon tried to recruit her into her schemes.
"Vivian told me I was a fool for working," she recounted, "and told me she
could teach me how to get 'plenty of dough and that's the only thing that
counts,' as she would say. She offered to introduce me to rich men and told
me she'd show me how to get 'money in chunks' from them.

"I never accepted Vivian's offers. But she kept after me. Doman got
sore about that several times. He told Vivian to leave me alone and they

had some bitter quarrels. Radeloff never took any part in these although he came there with Vivian.

"Finally I left in March of 1929. That was after Vivian was hurt, and I nursed her until she was well—a thing any woman would do for another. She kept telling me that I should meet the men she would get for me. But I didn't like her way of living and left her."

Though Vernon Repez's account corroborated Gordon's diary, she had little to offer the homicide investigation except her own speculations. "I don't think that Vivian could have been murdered for her money," she surmised. "That's hardly possible because when she went out she seldom took more than $1 with her."[26]

Hal Doman and Louis Zeno weren't much help with the investigation either. Both men spoke willingly to the police about their interactions with Vivian Gordon, but they revealed nothing about her murder. On March 4, the Columbia chemistry lab completed its analysis of the rope sample from the chest found in New Jersey. Though the size was similar to the murder rope, the texture differed. When the lab report came back, Bruckman reluctantly released the two material witnesses; he had no basis for holding them any longer.[27]

After their release, Robinson's colleague, John O'Donnell, obtained an exclusive interview from Louis Zeno. According to Zeno, Gordon first met Doman in 1925 while she was out on parole from Bedford. Doman was running a speakeasy on West 74th Street and he used to give a cut when her dates ordered drinks at the bar. They also slept together a few times, Zeno said, but their relationship ended after a few months when Doman lost his speakeasy, and Gordon went back to Bedford for violating parole.

"Then in January 1930, Vivian ran into Doman in West 34th Street," Zeno continued. "They spoke to one another and Doman brought her up to our apartment for a drink. That was the first time I ever saw her. The following Sunday we were invited to her apartment for dinner. She was an excellent cook, by the way, and was very proud of her 'potatoes à la Gordon'—candied sweets.

"Then, a month after I had first met her came the episode or the beating up in the Palace Hotel. She was in terrible condition that morning when she arrived in the apartment. Both eyes were blackened, her lips split and driven into her teeth. Her breasts and ribs were a mass of bruises.

Louis Zeno leaves the Bronx district attorney's office after being questioned regarding the murder of Gordon, March 5, 1931.

We couldn't imagine what kind of a weapon had been used on her. From her waist down to her knees, back and front were stripes, her calves were scratched across."

Gordon told Zeno and Doman that she'd spent the night drinking champagne in Greenwich Village with Teddy Schweinler and a few friends. The group eventually migrated uptown and visited the Palace Hotel for a final drink at 5:30 a.m. "She was alone in one of the two rooms with one of the men—not Schweinler—when he tried to throw her on the bed and she resisted," Zeno said. "Then the beating up started, with all three men joining in. She was finally knocked across the bed, fell out the other side and crawled underneath. They aimed kicks at her from each side, and she tried to protect herself by grasping the springs of the bed and lifting herself from the floor. Then she became unconscious and woke to find herself on top of the bed, her dress ripped off and a man attempting unnatural intercourse. She, finally climbed down the fire-escape and called a cop."

Zeno told O'Donnell that he suspected John Radeloff, Joseph Radlow, and Chowderhead Cohen of orchestrating the assault as well as Gordon's murder. "They had the strongest motive," he contended. "In the first place her death would benefit Radeloff financially—he wouldn't have to account for the loss of her money that she was complaining about. Radlow would be freed from the obligation of defending the suit she had started against him for causing her arrest last summer." Zeno added that the last time he'd spoken to Gordon, two weeks before her death, she'd expressed foreboding about the three men, telling him, "I'm expecting trouble from this trio."[28]

District Attorney Charles McLaughlin wasn't known for congeniality. He was a short, gruff martinet with no patience for chitchat or drama. He kept his back straight, his mustache clipped, and his black hair cropped in a crew cut. At 9:00 a.m., he often stationed himself at the office entrance, watch in hand, to check arrivals. One of the assistant district attorneys, Frank Martin, recalled being scolded by "the Chief" for showing up at 9:05 after working all night on a case. "Taking half a day off, I see," McLaughlin said snidely. He later apologized after learning about Martin's late night but added, "If you can get in at five minutes after nine, you can be here at nine." The only times McLaughlin loosened up in front of his staff were at weekly team dinners when he treated everyone to mounds of pasta at a nearby Italian joint. For a few hours, he indulged in banter and shoptalk with his assistants. "Invariably at nine the next morning," Martin recounted, "the Chief would again be wearing his refrigerated office personality, as if the preceding night's conviviality had never taken place."[29]

Though an honest and effective prosecutor, McLaughlin's debut as district attorney of Bronx County had been rocky. He was elected in 1929 on the same ballot as Mayor Walker. A month later, gangsters held up

Magistrate Albert Vitale and his guests at the Roman Gardens restaurant. The highly publicized robbery was a baptism of fire for the new district attorney as he struggled to make a case out of the accusations that former police commissioner Grover Whalen leveled at Ciro Terranova, the Artichoke King. Even if Whalen were right and Terranova had faked the robbery to recover an incriminating murder contract, the police didn't have enough evidence to take him to trial, so McLaughlin was helpless to prosecute. In the end, Vitale was disbarred, but no one was indicted.

The murder of Vivian Gordon was McLaughlin's second high-profile case, and the stakes were far higher. After the victim's connection to the Seabury commission became public, everyone assumed that the cops were behind the killing, and many suspected that Tammany chiefs had ordered Gordon's execution. Civic do-gooders screamed for justice and demanded accountability. One of the loudest critics was Rabbi Stephen Wise, the reformed rabbi who'd previously urged Roosevelt to investigate the magistrates. He and Unitarian minister John Haynes Holmes had cofounded a civic organization called the City Affairs Committee. After Gordon's murder, Wise and Holmes exploited the sensational crime by publicly demanding an investigation of the entire city government, including the mayor's office.

"The murder of Vivian Gordon lights up our city's life as with a lightning flash. In no more sinister and dramatic way could the alliance between 'the forces of law' and the forces of lawlessness have been exposed," they wrote. "How shall we meet the challenge . . . with a merry quip to a press super-tolerant of Mayoral wise-cracking, or with a mock-serious homily to his faithful underlings? Shall we meet it with some faltering and paltry ineptitude of a District Attorney pitiably fumbling about in a place of law . . . ?

"Or shall that challenge be met as if we were citizens resolute and unafraid. Governor Roosevelt, after some prodding, took one vigorous step and by that step made possible the Seabury investigation. That is a beginning—but it is not enough. The affairs of New York cry for investigation from top to bottom, either beginning or ending with the office of the Mayor."[30]

All the agitation seemed to have influenced Governor Roosevelt, who was leaning hard on McLaughlin and demanding regular updates on the progress of the investigation. Normally, a district attorney would wait for

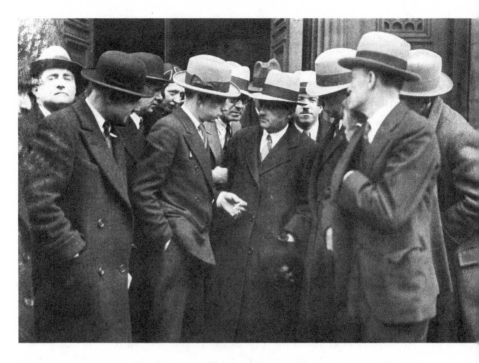

Bronx district attorney Charles McLaughlin (center, with hand in pocket) fields questions from reporters about the Gordon case at the Bronx County courthouse, March 4, 1931.

the police to build a case—or at least to name a suspect—before becoming actively involved, but McLaughlin was determined to avoid another ill-famed fiasco. After the Seabury connection was discovered, he immediately convened an unusual grand jury to assist the investigation. Grand juries were designed to gather and weigh evidence for criminal indictments, but the detectives hadn't named any suspects in Gordon's murder, so there was no one to indict. Yet a grand jury was needed to compel testimony from reluctant witnesses, so McLaughlin opened an inquiry with an unidentified defendant, officially named "The People of the State of New York against John Doe."[31]

Every day, a fresh parade of witnesses came before the grand jury to answer McLaughlin's questions: John Radeloff, Sam Cohen, Joseph Radlow, Andrew McLaughlin, John Bischoff, Al Marks, Irving Ben Cooper, Dr. Ann Gibson, Cassie Clayton, Helen Dorf, Vannie Higgins, Teddy Schweinler, Leonora Halsey, Hal Doman, Louis Zeno, and Vernon Repez, as well as Emanuel Kamna, who found the body; Louis Lefkowitz, the medical examiner; the taxi drivers who saw the screaming woman; a cabbie whose plates ended in 810; John Weir, the lawyer who represented Gordon when she was sent to Bedford; Myra Hughes, her probation officer; Lewis Corey, who had borrowed $10,000 from her; a bellhop who referred men to her; the owner of a nightclub that she frequented; Radeloff's wife; McLaughlin's brother; and on and on. When a reporter asked McLaughlin whether he suspected anyone of committing the murder, he answered with a rueful smile, "Yes, everybody in New York."[32]

A few nuggets of interesting information came out of the grand jury testimony. Ralph Dellevie, president of National Tours, Inc., revealed that his company had offered Officer McLaughlin free passage to Bermuda in return for entertaining the other passengers—especially unattached women—a common practice on luxury cruises. Eric Seibers, the superintendent of Gordon's building, testified that he witnessed Sam Cohen attempt to abduct Gordon from her apartment in early February, a few days after she sent the letter to Kresel. According to Seibers, Cohen "dragged her violently into the elevator" and tried to force her into a taxi waiting outside, but Gordon broke free, slammed the taxi door on him, and ran back to her apartment.[33]

But most of the witnesses were useless. Vannie Higgins denied knowing Gordon, even though he'd admitted it to the press a week before. Others were more forthcoming about Gordon herself but provided no pertinent information about her murder.[34]

One by one, the leads dried up, too. Cabdriver Frank Ryan recanted his story about chasing a taxi through the Bronx, claiming that he never left the taxi stand. The other two cabbies and the off-duty cop stood by their accounts, but their description of the screaming woman was a poor match for Vivian Gordon. Still, detectives thought they'd made a break in the case when the Bureau for Motor Vehicles reported that a taxi driver had applied for a new license for his vehicle, which he'd converted into a private sedan the day after the murder. The car and plates were similar to the fleeing taxi, but under questioning, the owner denied that there had been any assault in his vehicle that night. And when Bruckman brought in the two cabbies, they failed to identify him as the driver of the mystery cab.[35]

In desperation, Mulrooney distributed a circular to every taxi company in the city, asking for information to "assist the Police in tracing

DETECTIVE DIVISION
CIRCULAR No. 3
MARCH 6, 1931

POLICE DEPARTMENT
CITY OF NEW YORK

POST IN CONSPICUOUS
PLACE

CHAUFFEURS' CO=OPERATION

IS REQUESTED BY THE

POLICE DEPARTMENT, CITY OF NEW YORK

Information wanted that may further assist the Police in tracing the movements of

VIVIAN GORDON

An appeal is made to all chauffeur's that might have driven the person whose photographs appear on this circular, at any time. This information will be treated STRICTLY CONFIDENTIAL and the Chauffeur furnishing same will not be inconvenienced.

THE DESCRIPTION OF VIVIAN GORDON IS AS FOLLOWS:

VIVIAN GORDON also used the name of BENITA BISCHOFF—Age, 38 Years; Height, 5 feet, 2 inches; Weight, 130 pounds; light auburn hair reaching to shoulders, heavy and bushy; gray eyes; fair complexion and full face.

At the time she was last seen she wore black velvet dress, collar and cuffs trimmed with cream colored lace. Cheap ornamental bar-pin 2½ inches long with imitation green jade circle size of 10-cent piece near each end, with a flare of rhinestones protruding from each circle at each end, pinned to dress in center of breast; black pliable straw hat, close fitting, black and white bow on front; gun metal silk stockings, black suede pumps, with square steel buckles.

Brown Mink Fur Coat, 42 inches long, shawl collar, bell sleeves, two-tone brown lining effect, may have label marked "Maison Simone" valued at $1800. White kid gloves wrist length.

Choker of imitation pearls, small size.

Lady's platinum ring, fancy design, one round diamond in center, 2 karats, 9 points; 14 diamonds around large diamond, weight 95 points; 6 diamonds in shank, 3 on each side, weight, 10 points. Scratch No. 26249 on ring, and valued at $2,000.

Lady's rectangular shaped diamond wrist watch, number of diamonds unknown; Meylan movement, Number 41519, Case Number 50865, Scratch No. C-602; Stock No. 8986, made by Black, Starr & Frost, valued at $665.

Post in a conspicuous place where it may be read by your chauffeurs.

PHONE SPRING 6-3100.

PHONE: HACK BUREAU, BARCLAY 7-5720.

EDWARD P. MULROONEY,
POLICE COMMISSIONER

An NYPD circular distributed to taxi companies on March 6, 1931, asking any drivers, or "chauffeurs," who "might have driven the person whose photographs appear on this circular, at any time" to confidentially contact the police.

the movements of Vivian Gordon." The circular included two photos of Gordon, a mug shot and a glamour portrait. It described her appearance in detail and catalogued her clothing and accessories, which ranged from tawdry ("Cheap ornamental bar-pin 2½ inches long with imitation green jade") to opulent ("Brown mink fur coat, 42 inches long, shawl collar, bell sleeves, two-tone brown lining effect, may have label marked 'Maison Simone' valued at $1800"). Crime reporters were thrilled by the detailed inventory, but the circular drew no credible leads.[36]

Leonora Halsey outside the Bronx DA's office after questioning, March 1931.

The Cuban housemaid's story was even more dubious than the taxi drivers' accounts. For one thing, Leonora Halsey's description of Mrs. Biddle differed in some ways from Vivian Gordon. And though Halsey insisted that Biddle's address was the same as Gordon's, she described the apartment as having five rooms and facing the street when it had three and faced the courtyard. None of the building staff recognized her either. Her account of purchasing stockings at 11:00 p.m. was also implausible, especially since Gordon's dresser held a drawer full of stockings.[37]

Two days after her interview at the Bathgate Station, Halsey's story took an even stranger turn. On the morning of March 4, she called the Mount Vernon police to report that she'd been attacked. She claimed that two men purporting to be New York City police officers had come to her house in the middle of the night and announced that her grand jury appearance had been postponed. When she started asking questions, she said, one of them jerked his hand from his pocket and threw acid in her face. Halsey slammed the door, ran screaming into her house, and called for a doctor.[38]

But this tale was also full of holes. "The Mount Vernon police tell me that they could not find footprints in the snow where the two men had visited or left the house," McLaughlin told the press afterward. "The stuff thrown at her was apparently a very weak solution of Lysol, which did little, if any harm. This particular incident is closed, as far as we are concerned."[39]

There was nothing left of McLaughlin's swagger when reporters asked him about the progress of the investigation. "We have opened up many lines of investigation," he answered, "but so far as concerns any real progress along any of them I must say, no we have not."

When one of the reporters reminded him of his earlier boast that the investigators were close to solving the crime, he retorted, "I would be a fool if I said anything of the kind. We have opened forty new angles in the case since yesterday."[40]

As the investigation faltered, McLaughlin started to panic. Governor Roosevelt had warned Commissioner Mulrooney that the police were on trial, but McLaughlin knew that his career also hung in the balance. A district attorney might win hundreds of convictions, yet one infamous debacle could ruin him. The bungled Rothstein investigation had already ended the political career of Manhattan's previous district attorney, Joab Banton, and civic leaders were now demanding the dismissal of Banton's successor, Thomas Crain, after he too failed to solve the case.[41]

McLaughlin was determined to avoid the same fate, but the Gordon investigation wasn't going his way. Once the most promising leads came up dry, there was nothing left but to interrogate the "500 sugar daddies" named in Vivian Gordon's black books and scour the pawnshops for her missing diamond ring and mink coat. "We are up against a stone wall," he admitted to Grace Robinson, "but we shall not omit a single clue, no matter how trivial, nor overlook a single person, no matter how slight his acquaintance with the dead girl or her activities, in an effort to solve this murder."[42]

Such a broad investigation would require considerable manpower and time, which would certainly try the patience of the public, not to mention the governor. Despite his professed confidence in the police, McLaughlin didn't actually trust them to solve the murder in a timely manner, even with 200 officers on the case. Moreover, the investigation wouldn't be restricted to the five boroughs. Many of the sugar daddies lived in far-flung cities, and Gordon's valuables might have been pawned anywhere in the region.

So one week into the investigation, McLaughlin made a radical decision to outsource parts of the inquiry to a private company: the Pinkerton National Detective Agency. Founded in Chicago in 1850, the storied agency had made a name for itself by foiling a plot to assassinate Abraham Lincoln before his inauguration. After the Civil War, Pinkerton agents were often employed by railroad companies and banks to guard trains and hunt outlaws in the Wild West, including a failed pursuit of Billy the Kid. Later, the agency developed a lucrative strikebreaking operation to serve industrialists like Andrew Carnegie. But even as Pinkerton expanded into new markets and opened branch offices across the United States and Europe, the agency continued to provide criminal detective services, and it had the manpower, the distribution, and the credibility that McLaughlin sought.[43]

"The Pinkertons have offices in forty cities in the United States, and have better facilities and more direct communications than the New York police," he told the press when he announced his decision on March 6. "If the New York police wanted out of town information, they would have to communicate with the police department of that town, and it would take more time than we think necessary. We have found that the Pinkerton men will go directly to the place or person indicated, do what we want done immediately and report at once."[44]

Their first assignments would include tracking down Polly Adler in Miami and investigating the mysterious bank job in Oslo that Vivian Gordon had mentioned in her diary. McLaughlin also wanted the "Pinks" to question Gordon's paramours in Chicago and other cities. He was so eager to start that he committed to paying Pinkertons' fee out of his own pocket. "Should the bill go to the board of estimate and not be honored, I would have to pay it," he admitted.[45]

His enthusiasm was not shared by Commissioner Mulrooney, however, who'd been blindsided by the decision. The use of private detectives in New York City police investigations wasn't unprecedented, but outside agents had never been employed to solve a homicide, nor so conspicuously in such a high-profile case. McLaughlin's decision to go public about the Pinkertons covered his own backside while humiliating the police department. The evening after his announcement, Mulrooney, Bruckman, and several other detectives stormed into the district attorney's office. Reporters eavesdropping at the door heard angry shouting that lasted three hours. Shortly before midnight, the participants finally emerged, glum and tight-lipped. As they rushed into the elevator, the officers tried to shoulder out reporters, but the journalists, anticipating resistance, formed a flying wedge and managed to shove a couple of their colleagues into the cage.

"Is this the first time you know where Pinkerton detectives have worked with the New York police?" one asked Mulrooney on the way down.

"The Pinkertons always have worked with the New York police," he replied curtly.

Meanwhile, the other reporters scrambled down the five flights of stairs and intercepted him on the sidewalk as he was getting into his car. Asked whether the Pinks were taking over the investigation, Mulrooney barked, "See Mr. McLaughlin!" Then he slammed the door and drove off.[46]

The next day, after the morning papers made public the extraordinary rift between the police commissioner and the district attorney, the mayor summoned Mulrooney to his office. After their conference, he spoke to the press with Mulrooney at his side and tried to paper over the dispute. "I am told that the retaining of the Pinkertons by the Bronx district attorney was the result of a conference between him and the police commissioner," he said. Asked his opinion of the decision, he demurred, "That is policing, and it is not my business to interpret the motives of the police department."[47]

Mulrooney tepidly repeated the official line. "One phase of this investigation, which I can't explain, lies far away, and the Pinkertons were hired because it was thought that they could handle it faster than we could," he said, passive voice. He didn't contradict Walker's statement that he'd participated in the decision, despite denying it the day before.[48]

At a separate press conference, McLaughlin was also conciliatory as he played down the Pinkertons' role in the investigation. "They are not working in New York City," he repeated emphatically. "The New York police are taking care of all the local angles of the investigation."[49]

The journalists dutifully recorded the official return of harmony. Only Grace Robinson bothered to interview the third party to the dispute. Herbert S. Mosher, manager of Pinkerton's New York City criminal division, had no time for niceties. When Robinson asked him whether his agents would work under Commissioner Mulrooney's supervision, he snapped, "Absolutely not." Backtracking slightly, he spoke vaguely about cooperating with the police but then barked, "But we don't take a case to follow 'suggestions' from others. We take it for thorough investigation. We have pulled our best men from far corners of the country. No politics interfere with us. We are a commercial organization. In our business, we either produce, or we cease to exist."[50]

Despite the proclamations of solidarity and promises of cooperation, Mosher's bluster underscored the fact that there were now three

The casket of Vivian Gordon's daughter, Benita Bischoff, is carried out of Foster's Funeral Parlor in Collingswood, New Jersey, March 6, 1931.

autonomous teams of investigators pursuing Vivian Gordon's murderers: Bruckman's detectives, McLaughlin's prosecutors, and the Pinkertons. And none of them were close to solving the case.

While the investigators squabbled, a somber scene unfolded a hundred miles away in Collingswood, New Jersey. In a hushed room banked with flowers and perfumed by the scent of numerous floral bouquets, the body of young Benita Bischoff lay in a white, satin-lined casket. She was dressed in a beige silk gown, and her hair had been waved and combed back from her face. Occasional sobs burst from the pews while the pastor intoned the funeral rites. Benita's stepmother, Eunice, fainted during the service and had to be revived. After the ceremony, eight girls from Benita's school wept silently as they bore her casket to the hearse waiting outside.[51]

The scene on the street was far more chaotic. Hundreds of spectators and journalists crammed the sidewalks, craning to see the casket as it passed. Three state troopers and ten local police officers held back the crowd and ushered the mourners to their automobiles. The officers then mounted motorcycles and escorted the five-car procession through the suburban streets and over the Benjamin Franklin Bridge, where they were relieved by Philadelphia police officers, who guided the procession to a grassy cemetery west of the city. After the casket was laid in the ground, Eunice Bischoff, weeping bitterly, tossed a rose into the grave, and was followed by Benita's stepsister and the pallbearers, who scattered petals over the casket.[52]

The press coverage and outpourings of affection at Benita's funeral contrasted with another burial that took place a few hours later. There were no floral bouquets at the Fordham morgue where Vivian Gordon's body lay in a closed silvered casket. Only two mourners came to escort her coffin to the cemetery, each bearing a small floral wreath. One was Gordon's older brother, Pierre Moorehead Franklin, who had come to New York to bury his sister and settle her estate. His round face was pale and haggard as he shambled out of a limousine, aided by a woman who traveled with him, Mable McCabe. She didn't know Vivian Gordon. She was just a kindhearted nurse employed by the Lincoln Hotel, where Franklin was staying, who had come to support him in his sorrow.[53]

The casket was loaded into the hearse, and the two-car procession traveled north, passing within blocks of the thicket where Gordon's body had been found. Once they arrived at Mount Hope Cemetery in Westchester, an undertaker delivered the funeral rites at the grave site. While he spoke, Franklin broke down sobbing and begged for a last look at his late sister. When the casket was opened, he fell to his knees, weeping bitterly, and kissed her cold lips. The nurse drew him away as the casket was closed and slowly lowered into the grave.[54]

Pierre Franklin was a traveling car salesman based in Montreal. He hadn't seen his younger sister in several years, though he'd sent unanswered letters begging her to get in touch. He was conducting business in New Brunswick at the end of February when he saw her photograph on the front page of a Canadian newspaper. Stunned by her murder and descriptions of her life in New York, he spent two days in a state of shock. When he finally gathered himself together, he wired the New York City police and set off on a 700-mile road trip to the city. Upon arrival, detectives took him to the Fordham morgue to claim the body. He burst into tears when he saw his sister laid out on the stone autopsy table, exclaiming, "Poor girl, poor girl."[55]

After the ordeal, Franklin drove to Manhattan and checked into the Lincoln Hotel near Times Square. Alone with his grief in a strange city, he spent hours in his room sifting through newspaper reports about his sister's scandalous life and tragic death. In the evening, he finally ventured out for dinner at Silver's restaurant on 42nd Street near the hotel. As he sat staring at his food, he suddenly had an idea to call his niece, Benita, to offer her some comfort. But on his way back to the hotel, he visited a newsstand to purchase more papers and saw a headline from one of the late editions: "STRANGLED WOMAN'S DAUGHTER COMMITS SUICIDE BY GAS." He bought the papers that covered the story and shuffled back to the restaurant.[56]

Jack Hanley, correspondent for the *News*, had received a tip that Vivian Gordon's brother was dining at Silver's. He found him there later that evening, sitting at the same table, "a set look on his strong and rather flat features, a pile of the latest papers before him, the food on the table growing cold, unnoticed as he read story after story of Benita's suicide." Aggrieved by scandalous press reports about his sister, Franklin had thus far refused to speak with journalists, but he was desperate for a sympathetic ear. Hanley struck up a conversation with him and gained his trust.[57]

"From the restaurant we went to his hotel room," Hanley reported in an internal memo to Grace Robinson, "where he paced up and down the floor alternately speaking bitterly of the 'way they run that girl to the ground,' and how he would say nothing to reporters." Franklin was agitated and often incoherent; his state of mind seemed to mirror the state of his room, which was "filled with papers from many cities, overflowing on bed, chairs and desk, all turned to the story of his sister's death." While ranting, he picked up offending articles and held them out to Hanley, as if submitting court's evidence. "It says here that I am going to take her body to Montreal for the funeral," he exclaimed, pressing his hands against his head. "I haven't told a soul of my plans for the funeral—it won't be in Montreal—why do they print that?"[58]

Hanley didn't obtain much useful material from Franklin that evening, but he won the promise of another interview. Yet when they met again for dinner the next night, Franklin said little. "The stories on the case deepened his resentful suspicions of the press—his refusal to talk was a fear of being grossly misquoted," Hanley wrote. "But to the writer, he felt a sympathetic attitude and was confident that his remarks were not to be violated or twisted. Nor shall they be. An appointment was made for the following day in which he offered to tell the story of Vivian Gordon's life as he knew it—the contributing factors and events leading up to her marriage."[59]

The next day was the funeral, though, and Franklin felt too depressed to go through with the interview. He postponed again the day after that but promised to speak with Hanley the following evening. That meeting never took place. At 5:00 a.m., hotel staff found Franklin wandering the hallways in nothing but an undershirt, wringing his hands and calling out his sister's name—her real name, Benita. Martha McCabe, the hotel nurse, tried to coax him back to his room, but he resisted. He was a relatively large man, and it took five security guards to subdue him. He continued to shout and struggle after they got him back to the room, which was now littered with newspaper clippings. Photographs of Vivian Gordon lined the walls, along with the picture of little Benita in dancing costume that her mother had treasured.[60]

When the police arrived at 9:45 a.m., they found Franklin gibbering on the floor of the bathroom. They strapped him to a stretcher and sent him by ambulance to the psychiatric ward at Bellevue Hospital. Under doctors' care, he recovered his senses and was released the next day.[61]

Hanley never got his interview, though. Franklin returned to Canada and tried to put the tragedy behind him. In the end, he gave only one brief interview to a newspaper in Montreal. "I have come here to rest and get away from it all," he told the reporter. "I can be quiet and forget a little. In New York, that was impossible." All the same, he paced his hotel room restlessly, and when he spoke of the allegations against his sister, his voice turned shrill, "like the cry of a wounded animal."

"She was a remarkable woman," he insisted. "In everything she did there was that touch of distinction. She played the piano, the clarinet and the violin; she painted rather well and made her own clothes. I know too that she loved her daughter.

"I have gone back to New York and seen again the paintings from her own brush that adorn her walls. I have seen the instruments she played so often in my hearing. Why, even the sewing machine in her workroom had in it a half-finished dress. I ask you, could my sister who did all these things, be bad the way they say she is?"[62]

Before Vivian Gordon's funeral, Pierre Franklin had paid a visit to the Surrogate Court to inquire about his sister's estate, rumored to be worth tens of thousands of dollars. The county surrogate informed him that according to state law, the inheritance belonged to Gordon's daughter, Benita. When she committed suicide, the property transferred to John Bischoff.[63]

It would have been a strange twist of fate if Gordon's riches had ended up in the hands of the man she sought to punish, but there wasn't much left by the time she died. In her clover days, she used to play the stock market and loaned thousands to friends and associates. John Radeloff set up a holding company for her called the Vivigo Corp., listing himself and Chowderhead as officers. On his recommendation, Gordon used the company to purchase sixteen lots in Brooklyn for $75,000 in 1929. But property was grossly overpriced, and the value plummeted further when the stock market crashed. After Gordon berated Radeloff about the "rotten deal," he helped her unload the Brooklyn lots in exchange for four two-family houses in Queens. Each house was worth $18,000 but carried a mortgage of $11,000, so Gordon's total equity after the trade was only $28,000, a tremendous loss.[64]

The financial crisis also wiped out Gordon's stock market investments, and her income dwindled as the men on whose largesse she depended held tighter to their wallets. The Queens properties at least provided some rental income, and she squeezed every penny she was owed from her tenants, counting the money five times before putting it in her purse and summarily evicting anyone late on their payments. The superintendent of the properties described her as "a hell of a landlady, who used to come around and drink."[65]

The rental income wasn't enough to cover her costs though. In the autumn of 1930, she took out a second mortgage on the Queens property, but when she failed to make the payments, the mortgage owner took control of the houses, and her remaining income evaporated. She closed her checking account and stashed her dwindling cash reserves under her mattress. At the beginning of February 1931, weeks before her death, she recorded in her diary that she was broke. By then, all she had left of value were the mink coat, Swiss watch, and diamond ring, and even these were taken from her on the night of her murder.[66]

After she died, the New York County Surrogate's Office assessed the value of her estate at $200.[67]

CHAPTER 7
A MATTER FOR JUDICIAL CONSIDERATION

THE CITY CLUB OF NEW YORK WASN'T MANHATTAN'S RITZIEST CLUB. Wealthy industrialists favored the opulent Metropolitan Club on Park Avenue, bedecked in marble and gilt, while bluebloods gathered at the more tasteful Union and Knickerbocker clubs on Fifth Avenue. The City Club, by contrast, occupied a staid seven-and-a-half-story elevator building on 44th Street, a block west of Times Square. It offered the usual clubhouse amenities: lounge, library, dining room, reading room, billiards room, roof garden, and forty-four guest rooms "regarded by the members as among the most comfortable in clubdom."[1]

There was plenty of competition. Four other clubhouses occupied the same block—the Harvard Club, Yale Club, Penn Club, and New York Yacht Club—and there were more than sixty such clubhouses citywide. In addition to providing opportunities to network and socialize, club membership also signified status—wealth, class, prestige, or power. The most exclusive gentlemen's clubs catered to old-money elites and dated back to the mid-nineteenth century, but the majority had emerged during the Gilded Age to satisfy the nouveau riche's desire for the trappings and privileges of the upper class. Most were men-only, though some allowed female guests in designated dining rooms. Women's clubs also began to appear in the early twentieth century, including the Women's City Club, founded in 1915, which featured Eleanor Roosevelt on its board of trustees.[2]

The original City Club was a little different from the other gentlemen's clubs. It had been established in 1892 with a specific mission to "promote social intercourse among persons specially interested in the good government of the City of New York." In keeping with their mission, the founders hoped the club would provide a virtuous alternative to Tammany Hall where men from diverse economic classes could meet and collaborate to improve the city. To make the club accessible to all, membership dues were kept low, only $25 a year in 1904, compared to $1,000 at the Metropolitan. But despite the democratic positioning, the majority of City Club members were affluent lawyers and businessmen, and the ethos was paternalistic. After one club dinner, three earnest members dressed in white tuxedos ventured out to the tenement houses by the East River and proceeded to lecture the locals from the back of a truck. They were rewarded for their efforts by a volley of eggs and vegetables, which soiled their dinner jackets so thoroughly that they were refused entry when they retreated to the club.[3]

The City Club was more effective when it focused on lobbying local and state officials, and it played influential roles in mass transit expansion, historic building preservation, and public safety initiatives. Yet, in its first forty years, the club had made frustratingly little progress toward its core mission to improve city government. In election after election, the City Club backed Fusion candidates who challenged Tammany Hall. Some campaigns were successful, but the reforms never lasted. "They were mornin' glories," jeered Tammany district boss George Plunkitt, "looked lovely in the mornin' and withered up in a short time, while the regular machines went on flourishin' forever, like fine old oaks. Say, that's the first poetry I ever worked off. Ain't it great?"[4]

But in the spring of 1931, Tammany's grip on the city seemed more tenuous than it had been for years. The crime wave and economic slump had eroded the mayor's popularity. One of the City Club's own members, Judge Samuel Seabury, had roused New Yorkers from their apathetic daze by exposing the rot that permeated the justice system. Finally, the unsolved murder of a "fiery titian-haired vice quiz witness" had captured the public's imagination and driven the collective outrage to new heights. The City Club's leaders were not especially concerned by the Gordon case per se, but they saw an opportunity to expand the scope of Seabury's investigation by capitalizing on the scandalous crime. Some members advocated for a citywide investigation, but club president Richard Childs and board chairman Joseph Price argued that a more incremental approach had a better chance of success. They proposed to focus on Tammany's most vulnerable official, District Attorney Thomas Crain, whose inept leadership of Manhattan prosecutors had drawn nearly universal scorn. On March 6, nine days after Vivian Gordon's murder, the trustees assembled in the executive room on the top floor of the clubhouse and voted in favor of their leaders' proposal to seek Crain's ouster.[5]*

Following the vote, Childs and Price composed a formal petition to Governor Roosevelt demanding the district attorney's removal. "He has failed properly to conduct prosecutions for crimes and offenses cognizable by the courts of New York County," they charged. "He has initiated many investigations but has conducted them inadequately and ineffectively. His conduct of the office of District Attorney since he took office January 1, 1930, has been incompetent, inefficient and futile, with the result that the local machinery of prosecution has failed to function properly and the administration of the criminal law in New York County has been brought into disrepute." To support their accusations, Childs and Price enumerated Crain's many failures, including the Rothstein murder he had pledged to solve, the disappearance of Justice Crater, and the scandals in the magistrates' courts, among others. One case they did not mention was the murder of Vivian Gordon, which was outside the Manhattan district attorney's jurisdiction. Though her killing had provided the impetus for their action, it was Thomas Crain, far more than Bronx District Attorney Charles McLaughlin, who embodied the prosecutorial failings of the Walker administration.[6]

This wasn't the City Club's first attempt to oust a public official. Its members had filed such charges several times before but only once succeeded in getting someone removed from office, and that had been thirty years earlier when Theodore Roosevelt was governor. In the case of Crain, however, their timing was exquisite. The Vivian Gordon case had become the political liability that Franklin Roosevelt had feared, infuriating New Yorkers and exposing the degradation of the city's justice system to the entire nation. Republicans in Albany were already attempting to exploit the case by preparing a new bill to authorize a full citywide investigation. Removing Crain would serve a dual purpose by demonstrating FDR's resolve to address the crisis while defusing Republican demands for a "fishing expedition" that could expose even more damaging conduct by

---

* Seabury wasn't present at this meeting, and there is no evidence that he had any direct role in the planning, but according to Grace Robinson, he privately told club members that if the law were respected in New York, Vivian Gordon wouldn't have died.

city officials. There were even rumors that Roosevelt had orchestrated the City Club's action himself.[7]

Whether by chance or design, Roosevelt was in Manhattan when the club made its move. Though he preferred his estate in Hyde Park, he also owned an elegant town house on East 65th Street near Central Park, a gift from his mother, where he stayed whenever business brought him to the city. After receiving the petition from Childs and Price, he summoned District Attorney Crain and Boss Curry to his home and presented the City Club's accusations to them. He gave Crain a stark choice: resign immediately or face a state-authorized inquiry into his performance. Roosevelt would have preferred to avoid another politically damaging inquiry, and he even offered to have the City Club's petition suppressed if Crain would agree to step down on the grounds of "ill health," but the elderly district attorney refused.[8]

And so, seven months after initiating the investigation of the magistrates' courts, Roosevelt again found himself in need of an investigator with sterling credentials and unimpeachable integrity. And once again, he turned to Judge Samuel Seabury, whose renown had ascended even higher during the magistrates' investigation. "I have decided to appoint you commissioner under Section 34 of the public officers' law to hear and investigate formal charges which have been filed with me against the district attorney of the County of New York," he wrote to Seabury. "I am very confident that your fine reputation for fairness and justice peculiarly qualifies you." At the conclusion of the letter, Roosevelt qualified the scope of the inquiry by adding, "You will, of course, note that the charges made do not in any way involve the personal integrity of Justice Crain, but relate solely to his competency to fulfill the office which he holds." At least, that's what he hoped Seabury would conclude. Incompetence was not as scandalous as corruption.[9]

As with the magistrates' investigation, Seabury first learned of his appointment from reporters, who accosted him when he returned to the courthouse after the lunch recess. "I have no comment to make," he replied gruffly. In truth, he was less enthusiastic about the second appointment than he had been about the first. He was still busy with the magistrates' investigation, and he agreed with Roosevelt that Crain was incompetent but probably not corrupt. There was more glory in exposing crooked cops and judges than in rebuking a weak district attorney, especially one who had been targeted for political reasons. Nonetheless, Roosevelt prevailed on him to take on the new appointment. "I accept the mandate of the governor designating me as commissioner in the matter of the charges filed against District Attorney Crain," he declared after receiving the formal offer.[10]

When Roosevelt first chose Seabury to investigate the courts, Tammany leaders had been wary but calm, unsure how aggressively or effectively the former judge would pursue his mandate. But six months of devastating hearings had removed any doubt about the mortal threat he posed to the organization. "Intense resentment against Governor Roosevelt is felt among the members of the District Attorney's staff and in Tammany over the appointment of Mr. Seabury as commissioner," reported the *New York Times*. "A frequent comment in the Criminal Court Building on the selection of Mr. Seabury was that the accuser had been made the judge."[11]

Yet in public, at least, Tammany leaders held their tongues. Like Roosevelt, they hoped the Crain probe would satisfy the critics, so they lay low and avoided provocation. "The scope of the inquiry is of great interest to Tammany, which so far has averted a general inquiry," the *Times* piece continued, "and the hope of some Tammany officials is that the Crain investigation may help prevent such an inquiry." Neither Boss Curry nor District Attorney Crain commented publicly on the Seabury appointment. One of the only city officials willing to speak on the record was Commissioner Mulrooney. Still determined to redeem the reputation of the scandal-plagued police force, he promised to "very willingly cooperate with any investigating body that may investigate the Police Department."[12]

Even Mayor Walker seemed to have surrendered his panache. He'd previously arranged to take a monthlong vacation in California—for health reasons, he claimed, though he didn't disclose the nature of his ailment. Samuel Untermyer, a wealthy New York lawyer, had invited him to recuperate at his estate in Palm Springs. "I feel that the climate and quiet will do me more good than any other place I can think of," Walker told the press. "Mr. Untermyer has told me that he felt that his own recent rest at Palm Springs after his illness had probably saved his life."[13]

Ordinarily, the mayor's departures from New York were well-publicized, theatrical affairs, but not this time. On the same day that Seabury accepted his new appointment, Walker and a small entourage drove unannounced through the Holland Tunnel to the train station in Jersey City, hoping to avoid the press. To Walker's dismay, he found that journalists had already staked out the station. "Just one picture, boys," he said with weary resignation. But when one of the reporters asked him whether he had any comment on the new Seabury investigation, he snapped, "No I haven't. That's the reason I'm taking this vacation, to get away from all that stuff." With that, he and his guests boarded a luxurious private railcar on loan from the vice president of the B&O Railroad.[14]

By the time the train reached Chicago the next day, Walker had recovered his aplomb. A crowd of reporters greeted him at the station, and he spent ten minutes posing for pictures and bantering with photographers as they shouted, "Hey, Jimmy! Turn your head this way!" "Take off your hat, Jim!" "Lift your head and smile, Mr. Mayor!"

"Say, when you fellows get through with this head of mine, I'll have a crick in my neck," he retorted.[15]

He kept up the repartee as he descended from the platform for a brief stop to freshen up at a hotel. "I'm told the sunlight out at Mr. Untermyer's ranch is high in percentage of violet rays," he said. "I'm told it never blisters, so I'm going out there to soak myself in it for a couple of weeks." Even the inevitable request for his thoughts on the investigations in New York didn't dampen his spirits. "Nothing," he answered with a grin, "Nothing but the broad smile on my face."[16]

His allies back home didn't share his sangfroid, however. The City Club's petition had failed to appease Tammany's critics. On the contrary, its success emboldened other reformers. Every day, another civic organization or concerned citizen's group hurled new accusations at the mayor and Tammany Hall. On Tuesday, the day after Walker's departure, the Society for the Prevention of Crime issued a strident letter to the governor and members of the state legislature denouncing the mayor's "wise-cracking remarks" and "flippant attitude" toward corruption and imploring state leaders "to give full power to Hon. Samuel Seabury to make a city-wide investigation." On Wednesday, the Socialist Party Committee on Public Affairs sent its own letter to the governor and legislators urging them to investigate "every branch of the government of New York City—legislative, executive and judicial." On Thursday, the floodgates opened as the Citizens Union, the New York Society of the Methodist Episcopal Church, the Greater New York Federation of Churches, the chancellor of New York University, the president of the Teacher's Union, and famed philosopher John Dewey each issued separate demands for citywide investigations.[17]

"The day's response to the movement for a city-wide inquiry was described as 'amazing' by those who have been sponsoring it with very little popular support," reported the *Times*. "In their opinion the filing of the charges against Mr. Crain furnished the definite starting point for the movement for the extension of the investigations, but many attributed the signs of the awakening of public opinion to the murder of Vivian Gordon, who had given information to Mr. Seabury, and to the suicide of her 16-year-old daughter, Benita Bischoff."[18]

The editors of the *New York Herald Tribune* were similarly struck by how Seabury's investigation and Gordon's murder had brought New Yorkers' simmering resentments to a furious boil and channeled the outrage into a direct assault on Tammany Hall. "While Mayor Walker smiles his way westward the mood of the city becomes grimmer by the hour," they opined. "Time and reiteration have always been requisite to the development of strong public sentiment. The truth must be personified in striking cases—as in the appalling Gordon murder, with its chain of inevitable corruption and catastrophe. There must be leadership—strong, effective, upright—as in the labors of Judge Seabury. A democracy should properly be slow to anger, but it can and should be merciless when convinced that its faith has been abused."[19]

The *Daily News* was even more emphatic. "In her wildest dreams of vengeance against the cop and the court who sent her to prison for immorality, Vivian Gordon never hoped for anything like the forces let loose by the circumstances of her murder," wrote *News* journalist Bertha Bartlett. "Removal of Mayor James J. Walker, a final day of accounting for District Attorney Thomas C. T. Crain—demands for the executive ax to be laid right and left in the New York City administration, are beating upon Gov. Franklin D. Roosevelt as a sequel to the finding of a beautiful, red-haired vice witness strangled before she could tell all she knew."[20]

Yet Mayor Jimmy Walker continued to shrug off the turmoil as he made his way to California. "They can find me in the desert if they want to investigate me," he taunted his critics at a layover in Kansas City. "I'll be back in a couple of weeks and they may investigate me all they want.

"This mayoring is going to get me down if I'm not careful," he added. "I've been working long hours. Right now, I'm going to rest and I expect to finish out this second term as mayor, and that doesn't end until 1933."[21]

In Dallas, he mocked the Society for the Prevention of Crime's criticism of his wisecracks. "If laughing is a crime, I am a criminal all right," he scoffed. "Because I certainly intend to keep it up." Then, as if to prove the Society's point about his flippant attitude, he pooh-poohed the corruption in the Women's Court. "What is strange is that six or eight policemen out of thousands have been found to be crooked," he continued. "We are glad they are found out and we want to be rid of all such as soon as possible, but it is nothing to get excited about."[22]

He found a receptive audience out west. The residents of Palm Springs treated the scandals in New York with more curiosity than disapproval, and they welcomed the mayor with gusto. Palm Springs was a city on the make. A decade earlier, it had been a remote desert town with a couple hotels and a few scattered ranch houses, but its fortunes improved dramatically after a paved highway linked it to Los Angeles in 1924. Wealthy Angelenos and Hollywood stars began making the four-hour road trip to the desert oasis to savor the balmy winter climate, therapeutic hot springs, and spectacular scenery, which included gorges lined by majestic palm trees and desert vistas backed by snow-capped mountains. Physicians recommended fresh air and low humidity to treat tuberculosis and other ailments, which made Palm Springs a popular winter destination for wealthy convalescents from across the country. In 1930, Samuel Untermyer bought The Willows, a magnificent Spanish-style villa on four acres of property graced by orchards, cactus gardens, and a cascading waterfall. Touting the restorative powers of the desert, he often invited dignitaries and intellectuals to stay for weeks during the winter. Mayor Walker was the latest luminary to accept the wealthy lawyer's invitation, and Palm Springs officials were eager to fete his arrival in hopes that his celebrity would boost the town's prestige—and its property values.[23]

As his train approached the city, two masked cowboys brandishing enormous six-shooters flagged it down and leapt aboard. They made their way to the mayor's private car and escorted him outside at gunpoint, his hands in the air and a grin on his face. A newsreel camera documented his arrival as he stepped out into the blazing sunshine and 103-degree heat wearing a russet brown suit, tan fedora, tan shirt, tan gloves, tan oxford shoes, and a tan and blue tie. He gamely clambered down the embankment, ignoring the sand that worked its way into his oxfords, and spoke a few words into the microphone about his impressions of the beautiful countryside and "peaceful" atmosphere before returning to his railcar for the final leg of the journey.[24]

But the spectacle was only beginning. Samuel Untermyer's automobile was waiting at the train station along with an entourage of six mounted cowboys wearing silk shirts, kerchiefs, and Stetson hats. They escorted the mayor toward a hotel on the outskirts of town, where he planned to stay until his suite at the villa was ready for him—the same suite that Albert and Elsa Einstein had recently vacated. Three minutes into the trip, however, a horde of yipping cowgirls and Cahuilla Indians on horseback raced out from a side street and surrounded the car. They abducted Walker at gunpoint for the second time and forced him into an antique stagecoach, which they conducted back through town, firing revolvers in the air and "whooping like crazy." As the cavalcade approached the train station, forty more cowboys hurtled from another side street and halted in front of the stagecoach. "Here you are, Mayor!" bellowed one of the newcomers, plucking the fedora from Walker's head and replacing it with a huge ten-gallon hat. "We don't go in for derbies or silk toppers on the desert."[25]

Thus attired, the mayor was paraded through the streets while locals cheered and reporters snapped photos. After several loops, the group at last veered off and led the rattling stagecoach to the hotel, with Walker clinging to his new hat with one hand and the rail of the seat with the other. When he finally reached his destination, still jaunty but disheveled, two little girls presented him with a bouquet of desert flowers. Then another member of the welcome party brought forth a little burro and urged Walker to "ride the Democratic donkey."

"Okay," he agreed. "Bring him on. I'll ride him." The burro did not share his complaisance, however. Eying the mayor distrustfully, the animal hung back and resisted its owner's pulling and prodding. The standoff continued until another round of celebratory gunshots spooked the little donkey and sent it cantering off into the desert. After a few final questions from journalists, the mayor was also permitted to take his leave. "I'm not talking politics," he told them. "I came for sunshine and mud baths. I'll take care of the situation in New York when I return."[26]

One person missing from the spectacle was Walker's host, Samuel Untermyer. After spending most of the winter in Palm Springs, the seventy-three-year-old lawyer had returned to Manhattan at the beginning of March. The clean desert air had done wonders for his health, he claimed, allowing him to resume his typical fourteen- to sixteen-hour workday. A chronic insomniac, he often awoke at 4:00 a.m., worked until breakfast,

Prominent lawyer Samuel Untermyer sporting a lady slipper orchid in his lapel, 1932.

and traveled to his office with a secretary, so he could dictate during the commute. His long, lucrative legal career was legendary. He'd started college at thirteen and begun arguing cases in court as a sixteen-year-old law student at Columbia University. When he was young, he grew a beard to make himself seem older; he later replaced the beard with a bushy mustache that, together with his prodigious nose, gave him a distinctive if slightly comical appearance. At twenty-five, he was earning $50,000 a year as a corporate lawyer; by his early thirties, he was a multimillionaire. His work ethic, intellect, and audacity had made him one of the most sought-after and highest-paid attorneys in the country, the first in history to charge a million-dollar legal fee. In addition to his Palm Springs villa, he owned a majestic 171-acre estate overlooking the Hudson River just north of the city where he bred show-dog collies and exotic flowers. At court, he always wore a lady slipper orchid in his lapel and had his chauffeur bring a fresh one from the greenhouse at lunchtime.[27]

Though he never ran for office himself, Untermyer was deeply involved in politics and frequently offered pro-bono counsel to city, state, and federal officers. His political orientation was difficult to categorize. He'd made a fortune in the service of corporate trusts but later helped Congress investigate monopolistic practices and craft antitrust legislation. He supported good government and disapproved of corruption, but he was a lifelong member of Tammany Hall and a close friend of Jimmy Walker. When Governor Roosevelt appointed Seabury to investigate Thomas Crain, Untermyer leapt into the fray, volunteering to represent the embattled district attorney free of charge.

Crain enthusiastically accepted the offer, but Samuel Untermyer may not have been the best man for the job. Though his legal genius and court-room prowess were renowned, the case would not be decided by judge or jury but rather by the governor, whose guiding principle was political expe-diency. Thus, the only court that mattered was the court of public opinion. Untermyer understood that, but he lacked the charm and subtlety required for the task, and his political talents were far inferior to Roosevelt's. His first move was to draft a snide, sarcastic letter, nominally addressed to Crain but intended for the newspapers, in which he mocked the "self-righteous and self-appointed guardians of the people" who had lodged such "flimsy charges" against his client. "Notwithstanding your present robust health and your unusually alert mental and physical energy and activity," he wrote to Crain, "the damning fact remains that you have been guilty of the hei-nous crime of having reached the biblical age of threescore and ten years." After disparaging the accusations of incompetence, he proceeded to attack Seabury's impartiality and impugn Roosevelt's motives with barely dis-guised contempt. "In appointing Judge Seabury," he continued, "the Gov-ernor, due probably to the overwhelming pressure of work, was ignorant of or overlooked the close relation of Judge Seabury to those charges which could not but create, to put it mildly, an unconscious or subconscious bias, however impartial he might otherwise have been disposed."[28]

If Untermyer hoped to pressure the Governor into dropping the inves-tigation or replacing the lead investigator by publishing a belligerent letter in the papers, he failed. Roosevelt made no comment directly to the press but communicated through unnamed friends that he resented Unter-myer's insinuations. Citing Seabury's accomplishments and distinguished reputation, he expressed confidence that the former judge would conduct "a fair and impartial inquiry." He also reiterated that Seabury's task was "to gather evidence, not to make a judgment," and that he, the governor, would make the final decision about Crain in accordance with the New York State constitution.[29]

Untermyer's grandstanding was the least of Roosevelt's troubles. He'd spent the week batting away demands by various civic organizations that he investigate Jimmy Walker. Again, he refrained from direct comment but let it be known through intermediaries that he found the various accusations too vague to merit serious consideration. Well-aware of Walker's opulent lifestyle and fondness for "wine, women and song," as one of his advisors put it, Roosevelt's attitude toward the "little mayor" was patronizing but not accusatory, as though he were a wayward child in need of discipline. "Our little Mayor can save much trouble in the future by getting on the job, cleaning his own house and stopping wisecracks," he wrote to a friend. "If he does not do all this he can have only himself to blame if he gets into trouble." By "trouble," he meant political, not legal, trouble. Despite the mayor's peccadillos, Roosevelt doubted that he was guilty of any serious offenses that warranted investigation. "Walker's no fool," he told Frances Perkins. "He's been around a lot. He certainly hasn't gotten himself involved in things that are really doubtful."[30]

Yet, regardless of his personal views on Walker, Roosevelt was acutely sensitive to the public sentiment aroused by Seabury's revelations and the unsolved Vivian Gordon case. In addition to the flood of petitions from good-government advocates in New York City, Republican legislators in Albany were pushing a new resolution to authorize a citywide investigation. The measure was a few votes shy of a majority due to opposition from the Republican boss of Westchester County, who had instructed local legislators to vote against it. Some journalists speculated that he hoped to trade Westchester's support for infrastructure projects; others, that he'd cut a deal with Tammany.[31]

As the political tension escalated, Roosevelt became uncharacteristically prickly and ill-tempered. On Saturday, March 14, he escaped to Hyde Park for the weekend, far from nagging reporters and grandstanding politicians, but even that respite was marred by a visit from Boss Curry. Roosevelt refused to reveal what they'd discussed, but newspapers reported that Tammany leaders had warned him that they would consider

Tammany chief John F. Curry (right), grand marshal of the 1931 New York City St. Patrick's Day parade, tips his hat as he rides down Fifth Avenue with Roderick J. Kennedy, longtime chairman of the parade committee, March 17, 1931.

an investigation of the mayor to be an "unfriendly act" and that they threatened to oppose his presidential nomination.[32]

Tammany's power was on full display in Manhattan the following Tuesday as 20,000 New Yorkers, many in military uniform, marched up Fifth Avenue to celebrate St. Patrick's Day. Trumpets blared, snare drums rattled, and bagpipes wailed as 200,000 cheering onlookers waved Irish and American flags. A light green car trimmed with nickel led the slow procession from Midtown to East Harlem. In the back seat sat the grand marshal of the parade, John F. Curry, looking slightly less dour than usual. A cold wind tugged on the handles of his gray mustache and snatched at wisps of white hair whenever he tipped his top hat to the crowd. Governor Roosevelt wasn't present in the reviewing stand as Curry rumbled past, but later that evening, he paid tribute to the patron saint of Ireland at a charitable dinner. In an anodyne speech, he lauded New York's Irish American leaders, including his predecessor, Al Smith. He neglected to mention the city's proudly Irish mayor, however.[33]

When Roosevelt returned to his Manhattan residence on East 65th Street at 10:30 p.m., he found two unwelcome visitors waiting in his study. Rabbi Stephen Wise and Rev. John Haynes Holmes had come to present him with yet another petition to investigate the mayor, which they'd drafted on behalf of their organization, the City Affairs Committee. FDR accepted it curtly and promised to read it, but as they turned to leave, his pent-up temper boiled over. "I have listened to you," he snapped. "Now you sit down and listen to me." Then he proceeded to lecture the stunned civic leaders for half an hour about an unrelated affair before finally sending them off.[34]

After venting his spleen at Wise and Holmes, Roosevelt caught a midnight train to Albany, but he found no peace when he returned to work at the Capitol on Wednesday. Reporters crowded the Executive Chamber and clamored to know how he intended to respond to the City Affairs petition. On edge and in need of sleep, he responded testily, refusing to answer their questions and admonishing them for politicizing what he described as "a matter for judicial consideration," though he was not a judge. He even threatened to charge the correspondents with contempt of court if they speculated about his decision, a threat that the *Times* described as "wholly without precedent."[35]

"Will you give Mayor Walker an opportunity to answer the charges before you decide to investigate him?" one reporter asked.

"That is a matter for judicial consideration," Roosevelt replied.

"Have you notified Walker that the charges are now in your hands?" asked a second.

"That is another matter for judicial consideration," he answered.

"When do you expect to decide whether or not you will order an investigation of Walker on these charges?"

"That also is a matter for judicial consideration," he repeated, "and I cannot give out any information on the point until I have reached a decision."[36]

It took him another week to make up his mind. He couldn't ignore the new petition as he had the others. Wise and Holmes were respected public advocates, and the document was cleverly crafted. In rejecting previous demands to investigate the mayor, Roosevelt had cited the vagueness of the allegations, which he'd contrasted with the City Club's "far more specific" charges against Crain. So Wise and Holmes studiously modeled their charges on the Crain petition, using Roosevelt's own standard to force his hand.

"He has ignored conditions of inefficiency and corruption," they wrote. "He has appointed unworthy men to public office and kept in office unworthy men subject by law to his removal." Much of the text was lifted directly from the Crain letter and modified for Walker. "His conduct of the office of Mayor since he took office on January 1, 1930, has been incompetent, inefficient and futile," they charged, "with the result that the local machinery of government has failed to function properly and the administration of the city has been brought into disrepute." To address Roosevelt's concern about specificity, they enumerated the corruption scandals that had plagued Walker's administration and documented his failure to dismiss or prosecute the implicated officials.[37]

Trapped by his own words, Roosevelt concluded that he couldn't afford to dismiss the charges outright. To stall for time, he decided to request an official response from the absent mayor. "My Dear Mr. Mayor, in accordance with the usual procedure in such matters, I am transmitting to you a copy of charges filed by the 'City Affairs Committee,'" he wrote to Walker, "I should like to receive such answer thereto as you may desire to make as soon after your return to New York City as possible. I understand that you are planning to come in about ten days."[38]

Tammany's reaction to Roosevelt's decision was mixed. Rank-and-file loyalists who had hoped that the governor would dismiss the petition were furious, but wiser political veterans saw cause for optimism. If the governor had wanted an investigation, they reasoned, he would have opened one straightaway. By requesting a response from the mayor, he had given Walker an opportunity to defend himself and set himself up with a pretext to reject the charges.[39]

They may have had the governor pegged, but they hadn't reckoned with the state legislature. While Roosevelt was mulling over how to respond to the City Affairs petition, Senate Majority Leader John Knight quietly reached out to Judge Seabury. Intense pressure had been brought to bear on the Westchester Republicans who had blocked the resolution for a citywide investigation. Fierce lobbying by Republican leaders and a barrage of letters and telegrams from constituents had induced the dissidents to cut a deal. They agreed to drop their objections to a broad investigation if Seabury were chosen to lead it.

Knight showed Seabury a draft of the proposed resolution, which would establish a special legislative committee "with full power and authority to investigate, inquire into and examine the administration and conduct of the various departments of the government of the City of New York." Unlike the previous investigations, the scope of the inquiry was nearly unlimited, granting the new committee the authority to investigate any city official, from dogcatcher to mayor, as well as those who did business with the city.

After reviewing the text, Seabury proposed changes to enhance the committee's subpoena power and agreed to serve as chief counsel on the condition that he be given a free hand to conduct the investigation. Three days later, following the news of Roosevelt's decision to send the City Affairs charges to Walker, the Senate majority leader introduced the new resolution during a late-night session at the Capitol. Pandemonium broke out as the Westchester rebels voted for the resolution while Tammany stalwarts howled in dismay.[40]

"I would like to know what kind of deal the two Republicans made to change their votes," shouted one irate Democratic senator, red in the face.

Senator Walter Westall of Westchester leapt to his feet. "If you will step out into the hall, I'll tell you," he hurled back.

"Come on out!" retorted his challenger.

After the other senators intervened to prevent a fistfight, another Democrat shook his fist at his colleagues.

"Go ahead," he raged. "Go ahead and investigate if you dare. But remember, there will come a day when the people rise in their might and show what they think of these attacks on Mayor Walker, just as they did in the last mayoralty election."

But they couldn't stop the roll call. The resolution passed the Senate 26 to 24. In the Assembly, a Democratic filibuster delayed the count until 3:30 a.m., but the measure passed 76 to 70.[41]

The resolution was structured in such a way that the governor's signature wasn't required, avoiding the risk of another veto. That suited Roosevelt well enough. Though he'd have preferred to avoid a citywide inquiry altogether, the legislature's end run around the executive branch alleviated the pressure on him to open his own investigation, which would have created a permanent rift with Tammany Hall.[42]

Tammany leaders, on the other hand, were furious. Caught off guard by the surprise defection of the Westchester legislators, they huddled with their legal team to plot tactics for resisting the investigation. As usual, city officials refused to comment except for Commissioner Mulrooney, who once again promised, "We will help in every way."[43]

Samuel Untermyer, who didn't work for the city or the organization but seemed to be positioning himself as Tammany's unofficial spokesman, was more loquacious. Declaring that the mayor and police commissioner shouldn't be held responsible for "the framing of women . . . by a few men who betray their uniform," he railed against "the cruelty and injustice of mob psychology that has been stimulated, whipped into action and goaded and magnified by the ambitions of faithless public officials and that section of the reckless irresponsible press that lives on sensations."[44]

Back in Palm Springs, Jimmy Walker kept informed of political developments by telephone. He'd been making the most of his desert getaway and diligently complying with doctors' orders to avoid work, go to bed early, and take "sun-baths" twice a day. He rose every morning between nine and ten o'clock, rubbed Russian mineral oil into his skin, and trudged out to Untermyer's flower garden wearing only a white sheet and a navy-blue beret. As the yellow sun blazed from a cloudless sky and the bees hummed to themselves as they worked the flowers, he lay down on the ground in a small enclosure with green canvas walls, unwrapped the sheet, and bathed his bare skin in sunlight. After the sunbath, he usually held a press conference on the veranda, clad in black, orange, or yellow-polka-dot silk pajamas, depending on his mood. His skin was sunburn-red and his cheeks covered with stubble, but reporters noted a fresh glint in his eye as he parried their questions. "No matter how many statements are issued in New York, I will positively make no reply until I return home," he answered. "Politics is out. Weather is great."[45]

He spent most of his time at the villa, occasionally venturing out to tour the desert landscape or throw a ceremonial pitch at a local baseball game. He declined an offer for a thermal mud bath at the Cahuilla Indian reservation, however. "Thank you, no," he quipped. "I've been in one constantly during the past eighteen months." In the afternoons and evenings, he indulged his showbiz infatuation by mingling with Hollywood starlets and movie moguls. His frequent meetings with film executives sparked rumors that he was laying plans for a career in the film industry, which he repeatedly denied. "I'm satisfied to be mayor of New York, and I'm not going into motion pictures—yet," he told one persistent journalist. Then, after posing for newsreel cameras by running around a cactus and jumping over a ditch, he called out to the reporter, "Hey you, doesn't this look like I'm in motion pictures?"[46]

But the revelry came to an end when the state legislature voted to open a citywide investigation. After the news broke, Walker swaggered out to the veranda for his daily press conference wearing a knee-length purple silk dressing gown and sage-green pants. "Where is that horse that was going to kick me in the chest?" he joked, but the little burro was nowhere to be found. Instead, he was joined by Dr. Silas Lewis, who had come up from Los Angeles to examine him.

"Doctor," said Walker, grinning and rocking on his heels with his hands stuffed in the pockets of his gown, "will you announce the verdict?"

"Do you want me to tell you exactly what I think?" Dr. Lewis asked.

"Let everyone know the worst."

"When Mayor Walker arrived here, he was suffering from physical exhaustion and general fatigue . . ."

"You see," Walker interrupted, "I fatigue myself as well as others."

The doctor, a slightly gray and serious man, smiled pleasantly and continued. "I now find his heart action greatly improved, his muscle tone and color better, indicating an increase in red corpuscles," he said, "but I think he should remain in California another month and complete the restoration of his health. The Mayor should move to higher altitudes as his improvement progresses. He should finish his course of treatment at an altitude of about 5,000 feet."[47]

Walker had no intention of remaining in California at any elevation, though. He had originally hoped to lie low until the uproar in New York subsided, heeding the advice of Tammany strategists to avoid discussing politics (while ignoring their complaints about conducting press conferences in pajamas). But the political crisis had come to a head in his absence, and he now needed to address it directly. "Seriously, though," he said after a couple more wisecracks, "I could spend another month here with satisfaction. But I am now in fighting trim and must return."[48]

The crowd that gathered to welcome Walker home when he arrived at Grand Central Station at 8:30 on Easter morning was subdued compared to previous receptions. Tammany leaders were determined to avoid the optics of a big spectacle, and the formal welcoming committee included only two city officials and Commissioner Mulrooney, who shook Walker's hand as

Mayor Jimmy Walker, escorted by city officials, shakes hands with an admirer upon his return from his trip to the West Coast, April 5, 1931.

he disembarked from his private car. A couple hundred curious commuters, applauded his arrival, but there were no cheers. Walker gave them a smile and doffed his hat, then drew his face into a serious expression in keeping with Tammany's instructions.

The greatest commotion came from the staccato bursts of flashbulbs and occasional shrieks by startled spectators who stood too close to the news cameras. Reporters shouted out questions, but for the first time in his history of homecomings, Walker declined to hold a press conference, and he answered only one question concerning the charges against him. "What charges?" he scoffed. "It doesn't seem to me that there are any charges." Then, feeling that he had to make some statement, he added, "I am happy to return to the city of my birth, the city which has honored me. I return with renewed health and vigor to the cleanest and best city in the world." He moved his jaw as if to speak again but thought better of it and made his way through the crowd.[49]

Walker continued to shun publicity when he resumed work the next day. Hundreds of supporters had gathered in front of City Hall to celebrate his return, but he ordered his car to drop him off at the rear of the building and bounded up the stairs two at a time. His office was decked in colorful flowers—tulips, lilies, and more—arrayed on windowsills, desks, chairs, and walls. After shaking hands with his aides and speaking briefly with reporters, he settled down to work. For the first time in his mayoral career, he spent a full eight hours in his office, breaking only briefly for a lunch of soft-boiled eggs.[50]

At the end of the day, he called the reporters in and laid out his plan of action regarding the City Affairs charges, explaining that he had turned down offers from Samuel Untermyer and other Tammany lawyers to help him craft a response. "I am going to write my response myself," he exclaimed, slamming his fist on the table. "What would a lawyer know about it? It is my answer and no one else's."[51]

Though he presented this approach as a matter of personal honor, it was also strategic. Like the Crain inquiry, the decision over whether to investigate his conduct was a political one, and Walker was far more skillful at politics than the lawyers. He was also much more popular than John Curry and other Tammany leaders. By publicly spurning Tammany support, he hoped to make it easier for Roosevelt to dismiss the charges.[52]

It took two weeks of long workdays (by Walker's standards) for the mayor to complete his response to the charges, a letter of 15,000 words that his secretary hand-delivered to Roosevelt in Albany. Defensive and indignant in tone, the letter was an exercise in obfuscation. Walker successively belittled the corruption scandals, exaggerated his responses to charges of malfeasance, celebrated his administration's accomplishments, denigrated his accusers, and ultimately threw up his hands, declaring that he had taken all measures "humanly possible over the personnel of a vast machine of government which numbers more than 130,000 employees." Newspapers at the time treated the letter charitably. Historians have not, including Roosevelt biographer Kenneth Davis, who criticized the response for "its lack of logical organization, its glaring omissions, its failure to address in any meaningful way the specific charges, and for the malicious aspersions it cast upon the character and motives of his accusers."[53]

But it didn't matter. Since the state legislature had authorized a city-wide inquiry, Roosevelt no longer felt pressure to investigate the mayor. "I have given the charges and the reply my most earnest consideration," he declared at the end of April. "I do not find sufficient justification in these documents as submitted to remove the Mayor of the City of New York or to proceed further in the matter of these charges." His brief statement did not mention any of the City Affairs Committee's enumerated allegations or Walker's rebuttals. The only explanation he offered for his decision was a single sweeping criticism that the charges were not "sufficiently specific." In truth, they were no less specific than the charges against Thomas Crain. Notwithstanding Roosevelt's insistence that the question was "a matter for judicial consideration," the cardinal difference between the two cases was political: the district attorney was expendable; the mayor was not.[54]

Walker was presiding over a board meeting at City Hall when a reporter stepped behind his chair and whispered the news to him, loudly enough for all to hear. The mayor's face betrayed no reaction. "I have no comment to make at this moment," he replied, "but this does not preclude me from making a comment at some other time and place." The crowd burst into applause, and one of the attendees exclaimed, "Mr. Mayor, we congratulate you!" Walker nodded his thanks but admonished the well-wisher for speaking off-topic and rapped his hammer to proceed with business.[55]

Tammany leaders were also meeting when the news broke. The spacious second floor of the clubhouse overlooking Union Square was crowded with district leaders and captains seeking favors from Boss Curry. "The decision was inevitable," Curry gloated. "It is only another vindication of Mayor Walker's splendid and unparalleled record." Murmurs filled the chamber as the assembled Tammany chiefs discussed the implications of the news. Though pleased with Roosevelt's decision, they hadn't forgiven him for considering the charges in the first place, nor for his action against Crain. And they were worried about the looming citywide investigation that Roosevelt had not initiated but which he had done little to prevent and which they feared might prove far more perilous to Tammany Hall than any of the others.[56]

CHAPTER 8
PASSAGE TO OSLO

A MILE AND A HALF PAST THE SOUTHERN TIP OF MANHATTAN, WHERE THE cold Hudson currents bled into the Atlantic Ocean, the Statue of Liberty gazed serenely across the harbor, oblivious to the drama that had engulfed her adopted city. She'd stood sentinel on that rocky islet for nearly half a century while her golden-orange skin faded to a dreary brown before brightening into the iconic verdigris for which she is known today. Millions of hopeful immigrants had sailed below her upraised arm in search of freedom and prosperity; many chose to settle on nearby shores. In the early twentieth century, nearly three-fourths of New York's citizens were either foreign-born or children of immigrants. Henry Bruckman's parents were German. Andrew McLaughlin's were Scottish. Fiorello La Guardia's were Italian. Edward Mulrooney's, Charles McLaughlin's, and Jimmy Walker's were Irish.[1]

Most new immigrants moved into squalid tenements and eked out subsistence wages on factory floors, striving for better lives for their children. A few fortunate ones achieved some degree of prosperity in their own lifetimes. John Radeloff's father, Meyer, was one of these. In 1891, he and his young bride, Ida, left their little village at western edge of the Russian Empire, crossed the Atlantic, and settled in the Jewish immigrant enclave of Williamsburg, Brooklyn. Meyer became a local soda water distributor and sold life insurance on the side until he'd saved enough money to send himself to New York Law School while supporting a wife and three children. He graduated in 1910 at the age of forty and went on to build a successful legal practice. He also founded a construction company, invested in real estate, and participated in anti-Tammany political campaigns. To his Yiddish-speaking compatriots, he was a *macher*, an important person, and a *mensch*, an honorable man.[2]

John, the eldest son, seemed destined for even greater success. A charming, self-assured young man and an excellent student, he won a scholarship to Cornell University, where he "sailed through college with the stiff wind of his personality blowing," according to his senior year-book. After graduation, he attended Columbia Law School and joined his father's firm, which handled everything from criminal defense to divorce suits. When Meyer died in 1928, John and his brother, Sam, relocated the office to the twenty-seventh floor of a brand-new skyscraper in downtown Brooklyn. One of the other tenants in the building was Samuel Leibowitz, the criminal defense lawyer who tangled with Chile Acuna during the magistrates' investigation. Leibowitz and Radeloff had been classmates at Cornell. When Radeloff came under suspicion in the Vivian Gordon case, Leibowitz publicly vouched for his character. "After knowing Radeloff for 20 years, I would say that he was one of the cleanest-cut chaps I know," he told the *Brooklyn Daily Eagle*.[3]

In those days, "clean cut" had a more flattering connotation than it does today, but the modern usage, which emphasizes the *appearance* of respectability, would have been more appropriate. On the surface, Rade-loff was a prosperous attorney and a doting family man, a *macher* and a *mensch* like his father. But Vivian Gordon's diary painted a different pic-ture. Her scathing accounts of his behavior exposed him as a dishonest and dishonorable man who callously exploited others to support a debauched, self-indulgent lifestyle—not a *mensch* but a *schmuck*.

In addition to the death threats recorded in the diary, Gordon also accused Radeloff of absconding with the rent payments from her prop-erties in Queens. "J. A. Radeloff had collected some of the rents on June 4—cash—has not turned it over to me," she charged, "has been on a drunk since Wednesday making himself big shot with my $'s." Three days later, she added, "Just as I thought he used my 'rents' (which he collected) to go on a 'bat.' I demanded the rents at once—got $50—of it the balance to be here tomorrow before noon—when I insisted on putting the screws to him he gave one of his usual threats."[4]

She also accused Radeloff of welching on a $500 loan. When the debt came due, he avoided her for days until she cornered him. Then he wrote her a bad check. Despite this breach of trust, she continued to lend him money in ever smaller amounts—$170, $50, $25—and had to badger him for repayment. "J. A. R. borrowed 25," she wrote on February 14, 1931, her final diary entry, "to be returned Monday, 2/16/31."[5]

She also portrayed Radeloff as an inveterate womanizer. He cheated on his wife with her, and he cheated on both of them with other women. "Found that while I was in hospital he was racing around with T—D— whom I introduced to him last June," she vented in March 1929. "Fickle person he is. No wonder he had no time to see me. Men are all beasts. He was also running with B—C—, sweetheart of a singer at Dizzy." A few months later, she laced into him for romancing her protégé Helen Dorf. "T'was a year ago I introduced J. A. R. to H. D.—maybe he still is running with her—who cares? Any 'skirt' will do for him."[6]

What particularly drew Gordon's ire, however, was one of Radeloff's legal shenanigans that cut too close to home. He often represented men embroiled in divorce suits, but his services weren't limited to legal counsel. To bolster his clients' cases, he also helped them frame their wives for adultery. "J. A. R. is an out and out crook," Gordon raged on August 24, 1929. "He's been mixed up in phony divorces—one of which a man named C—. (I think it is spelt that way) J. A. R. would stoop to anything."[7]

Gordon may have read about the "phony divorce" in the *News*, which reported that a man named Walter McCurley had hired Radeloff to represent him in a divorce case in 1927. McCurley claimed that his wife, Gertrude, had cheated on him with an insurance salesman named Joseph Cappucci. In light of her infidelity, Radeloff persuaded the judge to limit her alimony to a mere $15 a week for care of their disabled ten-year-old son.

But the alleged affair was a setup. After separating from Walter, Gertrude purchased fire and life insurance from Cappucci. The insurance agent expressed his appreciation by taking her to dinner, where he pretended to become severely intoxicated. In order to avoid a scene at the restaurant, Gertrude allowed him to escort her home and sleep on the couch. Later that night, Walter burst into the apartment with witnesses in tow and accused Gertrude of cheating on him. Cappucci, feigning ignorance of the plot, comforted Gertrude after Walter left and referred her to a divorce lawyer he knew, a certain John A. Radeloff. What he didn't mention was that Radeloff was already representing her husband. Radeloff didn't mention this pertinent fact either when he charged her $1,500 and then dropped her case.[8]

That might have been the end of the business, had not Gertrude read in the paper about a strikingly similar divorce case in which a woman was accused of cheating with the same insurance salesman, Joseph Cappucci, and whose husband was represented by the same attorney, John Radeloff. When Gertrude appealed the ruling, a New York Supreme Court justice decided in her favor. Calling the case "the most diabolical plot to ruin women's reputations that I have heard of," he referred the matter to the district attorney for criminal prosecution. But Cappucci skipped town, Radeloff denied taking Gertrude's money, and neither faced charges.[9]

Radeloff also escaped punishment when his cousin, Joseph Radlow, and Chowderhead Cohen were convicted of receiving stolen securities—the same case in which Vivian Gordon testified that Radlow owed her $50,000. The investigation had begun with a raid by federal agents on the Cosmopolitan Fiscal Corporation, one of Radlow's bucket shops. As a co-owner of the corporation, Radeloff was sought for questioning, but the prosecutor decided not to pursue charges against him.[10]

In fact, his only known conviction was a reckless driving charge in 1924, when he was stopped while zigzagging drunkenly across the road with one arm around a young woman. Unable to produce the $100 bail, Radeloff persuaded his escort to bail the two of them out with her platinum wristwatch.[11]

His luck with law enforcement finally ran out after the police found Vivian Gordon's diaries. Yet, even then, the police lacked sufficient evidence to name him as a murder suspect. To keep him in custody, District Attorney McLaughlin was obliged to hold him as a material witness along with Chowderhead. This legal maneuver wasn't uncommon. New York State law allowed crime witnesses to be detained indefinitely as long as a judge deemed their incarceration necessary to secure important testimony, and prosecutors often abused the statute to hold material witnesses for weeks or months. Still, the grounds for holding Radeloff and Cohen were "rather scanty," as the judge put it when he reluctantly upheld McLaughlin's petition to set bail at $50,000—equivalent to nearly a million dollars today. After four weeks of legal wrangling, Radeloff's lawyer managed to cut his client's bail amount to a more reasonable $5,000, but Radeloff still didn't pay. "I want absolute freedom or nothing. I am being illegally detained," he loftily proclaimed to the press. In truth, given the state of his finances, he likely couldn't afford even the reduced amount.[12]

Nonetheless, McLaughlin feared that he wouldn't be able to hold his material witness much longer. To keep Radeloff in jail, he arranged to remand him into the custody of District Attorney Thomas Crain on an unrelated charge of extorting money from a tailor in Manhattan. "The release of Radeloff was done purely as a gesture to the New York County District Attorney," he told incredulous reporters after the lawyer was shipped off to Manhattan. The gambit failed, however, when bail for the extortion charge was set at a more affordable $2,500, which Radeloff posted immediately. (Chowderhead Cohen remained in McLaughlin's custody subject to a $40,000 bail, due perhaps to his prison record or to the ineffectiveness of his lawyer.)[13]

Radeloff said nothing to the press the day he finally walked free after four weeks in jail. He was saving his story for an exclusive interview with the *Daily News*, for which he was likely paid handsomely. When *News* correspondent Martin Sommers met him at his office the next day, he was as poised and self-assured as he had been under questioning at the Bathgate Station. "Radeloff, alert, keen and soft-spoken, is far from the semi-racketeering type of attorney he had been painted in police descriptions," Sommers gushed in a March 26 article. "He is a much superior type of counsellor, intelligent, strictly open-minded in dealing with facts in a rational manner, and exhibits an unusual degree of penetration."[14]

While incarcerated, Radeloff had consumed the voluminous reporting on the Gordon case, and he was well-informed about the status of the investigation. When he spoke to Sommers, he adopted a sleuth-like tone as he enumerated the list of suspects:

> I do not believe that the police killed her. Patrolman Andrew J. McLaughlin, the only policeman she threatened and the only one against whom she proposed to testify at the Seabury inquiry, did not have a sufficient motive. McLaughlin had arrested her and sent her to Bedford almost eight years ago. She pleaded guilty. And anyway the case was outlawed through the statute of limitations. There were other charges against McLaughlin before Seabury. He didn't regard Vivian's complaint as of great importance.
>
> Joseph Radlow, who once had her arrested for extortion, had no reason to kill Vivian Gordon and besides he's not the killing kind.

Radlow uses his head to accomplish his purposes. I have never known him to be engaged in a quarrel of violence. He is not a man who would kill if he could.

The story that Jack (Legs) Diamond's friends or enemies might have killed Vivian Gordon will not hold water. Vivian knew Diamond casually, if at all. She did know Diamond's wife, Alice Schiffer Diamond, but only socially.

Vannie Higgins, too, had no reason whatever to kill Vivian Gordon or get her killed. Higgins knew Miss Gordon only through Jean Stoneham. Jean went from her association with Vivian Gordon, to her friendship with Higgins. Miss Stoneham's connection with Vivian Gordon and Higgins did not overlap to any extent.

Poor Sam Cohen, the ex-convict, proved a perfect alibi. So, too, did Vivian Gordon's husband, John E. C. Bischoff. Cohen knew Vivian. He accompanied her to Philadelphia as her bodyguard when Vivian went there to argue with her husband over money and the custody of their child, Benita, who committed suicide. But Cohen had no motive for killing her. The only suspicion against either Cohen or myself arose out of entries in Vivian's diaries, and I shall show conclusively that these could not have any bearing whatsoever on the crime, committed two years later.

"I shall next consider my own case," Radeloff told Sommers. "I talked to Vivian Gordon last on 5:30 p.m. on the day before she was killed. I telephoned her and asked her to send me checks to cover rent and coal on her Jamaica Ave. property. She told me I should have the checks in the morning and that concluded the conversation.

"I went home and had dinner with Mrs. Radeloff. That night, for the first time, I listened to a track meet over the radio, and commented upon it to Samuel Radeloff, my brother, when he arrived with his wife for an evening of bridge. A neighbor joined us and I remained at home throughout that night. These facts have all been checked and re-checked by the police."[15]

Next, Radeloff turned to the incriminating diary entry in which Gordon claimed that he told her that Cohen had threatened to "take her out somewhere no one will know what happened to her." No longer the sleuth, he recast himself as a psychologist and proceeded to diagnose Vivian Gordon's mental state.

"We must not lose sight of the fact that she was a woman haunted by numberless fears, even though she was one of the most recklessly brave persons who ever lived. She always was in the shadow of countless enemies," he posited. "In order to reach a fair conclusion one must also remember that she was a person strongly addicted to alcoholic beverages and sleeping pills—to such a degree that they acted upon her as a drug . . .

"What have you, then, except a situation where a person, obsessed by the fears mentioned, would conceive of a possible attempt to harm her?" he continued. "Consider the exact text of the entry. We find nothing in it to indicate that I had ever threatened her with harm, or even hinted at such conduct. We see a fear, born of introspective hallucination, gnawing at her mind, a mere consciousness that I was able to harm her."[16]

Having thus dispatched the suspicions against Cohen and himself, Radeloff returned to his detective work. "It is inconceivable to me, from what else I knew of her affairs, that any of her rich acquaintances wished her dead," he asserted. "She quarreled with some of the men she knew quite seriously. She even threatened some of them, and attempted to carry her threats into execution. But I do not believe her victims took her threats as seriously as she did.

"It must be remembered that Vivian dealt with men of the world, men whose wives were completely disillusioned as to their fidelity; and such men as these are often threatened by women such as Vivian. Sometimes they temporize. Sometimes they pay. Sometimes they laugh and do nothing. But it is rare, indeed, that a man of any real importance puts himself in the shadow of the electric chair to silence a courtesan's tongue."[17]

Finally, Radeloff advanced his own theory about who killed Vivian Gordon, which he introduced with an anecdote. "At least a dozen times I sat in Vivian Gordon's apartment at 156 East 37th St. when the phone rang, and she would answer," he recounted. "Her end of the conversation went something like this: 'What do you want? You got your bit! That's all you get, see? Sure I got mine. But you got yours and that's all . . . You're a liar! He didn't give me that! He spent that on me while we were out. You don't get any cut on that! Yes, listen! I'll get you before you get me!'

The *News* cover of March 26, 1931, featuring a pointing John Radeloff. After his release on March 24, Radeloff shared his theories on the case with *News* correspondent Martin Sommers. The exclusive interview was featured in a three-part series from March 26 to March 28.

"And about this point the receiver would go bang," Radeloff continued. "It was almost always some taxicab driver who had helped Vivian get a man the night before or had helped her in getting money out of some man in some way. I am convinced that one of these men murdered her. Vivian drove hard bargains and she was absolutely fearless in enforcing them."

At one point, Radeloff casually reconstructed the brutal murder of his former lover and client. "I believe Vivian had dinner at home," he began. "She kept liquor always in her apartment and I believe she had a few drinks there on the night she died. This would explain the alcohol in her stomach.

"Then, in all probability, the taxicab driver who had been associated with her as a procurer phoned her. The driver probably told her he had a heavy-spending prospect in town and she probably agreed to a date. I believe the driver told her he would take her to the meeting place in a cab. Such a rendezvous is borne out by the fact that Vivian wore her best clothes, including her mink coat and her diamond ring and wristwatch.

"When the taxicab called for her, I believe the man who murdered her was riding in it. Perhaps he even posed as the man of wealth with whom she was to spend the evening.

"I believe that Vivian was rendered unconscious almost immediately by a blow she was dealt on the jaw. The blow was hard enough to break the skin, the autopsy revealed. When she was unconscious, I think she was stripped of her coat and valuables. Then, when she had been stripped, I believe the rope was pulled tight around her neck until death took her."[18]

The day after the interview, giant headlines on the front page of the *News* proclaimed, "RADELOFF POINTS TO SLAYER OF VIVIAN GORDON." A full-length portrait of the dapper lawyer in a dark suit pensively holding his index finger in the air occupied most of the space below the headline, followed by a two-page spread devoted to his theories about the murder. Another two-page spread extended coverage of the interview into a second day, and in subsequent articles, the *News* continued to quote Radeloff as an authority on the murder investigation.[19]

Inspector Henry Bruckman did his best to ignore the yowling headlines. He was happy to leave the press conferences to the police commissioner and the district attorney while he focused on detective work. Between the

Pinkertons and the legions of police officers that Mulrooney had assigned to the case, there was no shortage of manpower, but grilling sugar daddies and poking around pawnshops had yet to uncover a single clue. So Bruckman turned his attention back to the only solid evidence in police possession, the three black datebooks in which Vivian Gordon documented the final twenty-six months of her life. His team had already identified and interrogated most of the people mentioned in the diaries, including Radeloff, Cohen, Radlow, Doman, Zeno, Schweinler, Stoneham, Dorf, and others, but one key individual still eluded them. Who was Harry A. Saunders, the man who'd borrowed $1,500 from Gordon to "clean up a bank" in Oslo?

Bruckman had posed this question repeatedly to John Radeloff at the Bathgate Station, but the loquacious lawyer was tight-lipped on the subject of Saunders and the Norwegian bank job. He'd admitted receiving telegrams from Oslo but insisted that he was just a passive middleman and had no clue who Saunders was or what he and Gordon were planning. "I was curious and asked her what they were about," he said, "but she just put me off by saying it was just a business deal she happened to be interested in."[20]

The diaries suggested otherwise. In ten entries over seven weeks, Gordon described the Oslo job as Radeloff's deal and stated that he repeatedly solicited money from her to fund the operation, $1,500 initially and another $500 after Saunders burned through the cash.

The first mention appeared in the summer of 1929, three months before the stock market crashed:

July 20, 1929: H. S. sailed for Oslo "?"

August 6, 1929: Radiogram to J. A. R. office from H. S. Oslo, letter follow. J. A. R. left here. He is to phone me first thing in the morning about 500. Phoned his home 1 A. M.

August 12, 1929: H. S. $1,500 (?) J. A. R. That awful headache again. Sold 100 Congo 23 ⅛.

August 13, 1929: J. A. R. brought me letter he got from H. S. about wanting 500 more from me. J. A. R. here again hinted about my getting killed—saying "I'd better get my collar and shirt out of here. If you should get killed they'd look for me." There is $18,000 in mortgages of mine in his office.

August 16, 1929: J. A. Radeloff check for $500 came back. J. A. R. another radiogram from H. S. giving address. Foenix Hotel, care Larson, his confederate over there.

August 17, 1929: Supposed to get money from Norway today—another one of J. A. R.'s rotten deals. I gave him $1,500 (on his say so)—to H. Saunders for passage to Oslo, Norway, for himself and two others to clean up a bank there. The money was supposed to be cabled to my bank on this date (for safe keeping) until their return.

August 22, 1929: H. T. R., Ill., Athletic Club, Chi. Mrs. R—here. Cable from Harry Saunders alias Chas. Rubin, Oslo, wanting 500 to be sent to Hotel Foenix, Oslo.

August 26, 1929: Ha ha. J's friend W—gave him a "rubber" 200 check his friend. J. A. R. here about 500 for Sweden. Maybe we'll see if another cable comes tomorrow. J. A. R. very hard pressed for money. Nat (from J. A. R.'s office) came up here with letter from J. A. R. saying for me give the check for 500 (to go to Sweden) to Nat also stating that Harry Saunder's sister had phoned—saying she had a cable from H. S. asking why his cable and letter to J. A. R. cable to me had not been answered, also giving me quotations on my stocks. Nat refused to leave the letters so I refused check "something shady there."

August 28, 1929: Phoned J. A. R. and in no few words told him what I thought of Nat's actions yesterday no! I did not agree to give another 500 for H. S. in Oslo and send plenty. If they think they are going to double cross me they are crazy and I told him so. M—G—phoned. Why?? Such sudden solicitude for my welfare. More of J. A. R.'s work.

September 5, 1929: J. A. Radeloff here today about $500 to be cabled to Harry Saunders.[21]

If Gordon's datebooks could be believed—and it was hard to imagine why she would have recorded lies in her private diary—it would mean that Radeloff had perjured himself when he denied knowing about the Oslo business before a grand jury. But why? Was he just avoiding implicating himself in an attempted bank heist, or did Saunders have something to do with Gordon's murder? Bruckman had interviewed Nathan Pietkowsky, the clerk from Radeloff's office whom Gordon called "Nat," but he had nothing to add, insisting that he had only delivered Radeloff's letter to Gordon and knew nothing of its contents. Neither Sam Cohen nor anyone else connected to Radeloff admitted knowing Saunders.

The name was all too common, but the New York police and Pinkertons had nonetheless questioned every Harry, Henry, Harold, Harrison, Harvey, Saunders, Sanders in the city directory. One of the diary entries also mentioned an alias, "Chas. Rubin," so the detectives had questioned men named Charles, Charlie, Chas, Rubin, and Reuben as well. But they failed to turn up anyone who might have traveled to Norway to rob a bank.[22]

Other than the man's name, the diary contained only one pertinent piece of information about the mysterious Saunders. On July 20, 1929, he had apparently sailed to Oslo. Obtaining and combing through handwritten, unalphabetized ships' logs was painful work. Multiple transatlantic liners, each carrying hundreds or even thousands of passengers, departed daily from New York harbor, the world's busiest port. There was no guarantee that Saunders had sailed directly to Norway or that he'd left on the date Gordon had recorded, given that she'd appended a question mark to the diary entry.

But Bruckman finally caught a break this time. The passenger log for the Norwegian liner SS *Bergensfjord*, which departed New York City on

The SS *Bergensfjord*, c. late 1920s, docked in Oslo, Norway.

July 20, 1929, listed a "Charles Rubin." He'd occupied a stateroom with two other passengers, which squared with Gordon's comment that her $1,500 had paid for two unnamed accomplices to travel with him. According to the passenger log, their names were James Cotter and, intriguingly, Sam Cohen. The log contained little information about the three passengers, but it did include passport numbers, which enabled Bruckman to requisition their passport applications from the State Department.[23]

Passports were not difficult to falsify in those days. Birth certificates could be counterfeited, acquired from dead people, or stolen from municipal archives. But the applications were handwritten, so Bruckman brought in a graphologist to compare the writing from the passport applications to that of convicted criminals from New York City. The handwriting expert quickly determined that the "Sam Cohen" who had applied for a passport was not Chowderhead Cohen, who, in any case, was known to be in New York at the time of the voyage. But he was able to link "Charles Rubin" to another convicted felon known to the police as Harry Stein.[24]

Harry Stein was a hard man, unburdened by conscience or devotion. He had no children or enduring relationships, save with his mother and siblings. Though he'd acquired a fiancé after his last prison term, the wedding was indefinitely delayed, and the woman knew nothing of his life or even his real name. Names, like people, were mere instruments to Stein. He sluffed them off as easily as a snake sheds its skin.

He was born Schmerl Norstein, but his parents gave him a more American name, Harry Stein, after the family emigrated from Russia to Philadelphia when he was six. At seventeen, he joined the army under a name of his own invention, Alexander B. Norse. His military career was brief. After abandoning his post in Arizona during the Pancho Villa expedition, he was sent to Leavenworth, where he served one year and received a medical discharge. Still going by Alexander Norse, he moved to New York, found a job as a messenger for a contracting company, and promptly absconded with $774.66 from the company payroll along with some loans that he'd finagled from his coworkers. He skipped town and returned to Leavenworth, where he hid out with a young woman he'd met while in the service. The escape was foiled, however, when cops discovered the couple's correspondence at Norse's abandoned apartment in New York.

They alerted the authorities in Leavenworth, who arrested and extradited him. The local paper noted that he refused to answer officers' questions and did not seem afraid of being returned to New York.[25]

Alexander Norse spent a year at the Elmira Reformatory in upstate New York. After his parole, he reconnected with a friend from childhood, Mary Glicksman, and her husband, William. The couple welcomed him into their home in the Bronx and helped him find a job. One evening, Alexander

Harry Stein, aka Charles Rubin, aka Harry Saunders, April 1931.

and his younger brother, Louis, visited Mary while William was away. She entertained them with phonograph records and fed them Welsh rabbit for dinner, but when she turned her back to do the dishes, she heard one of the brothers say, "Aw what's the use of waiting for Bill to come home . . . Let's grab it while the grabbing's good." They seized her, gagged her with a napkin, bound her to a chair, and fled with her diamond ring and some cash.[26]

A few days later, Alexander called William at home. "How's the missus?" he asked nonchalantly, "All right, eh?"

Furious and flabbergasted, Glicksman retorted, "What's the idea, anyhow? What you calling me up for, I'd like to know?"

"Say, Bill, you ain't sore, are you?" Norse replied, "You haven't gone and tipped off a friend o' yours to the bulls, have you, huh?"

"You'll find out fast enough," Glicksman rejoined angrily. "You'll get the idea when you're in jail." He hung up and dialed the police, who traced Norse's call to an empty telephone booth.

The brothers fled to Atlantic City, but Alexander once again betrayed himself by communicating with a young woman. Police intercepted his cable asking her for $50. This time, he was sentenced to ten years at Sing Sing.[27]

After his release in 1927, he dropped Alexander Norse in favor of the name he'd grown up with, Harry Stein, but continued to use aliases whenever the need arose. He told his new girlfriend that he was a salesman named Harry Stone and that he hoped one day to become a civil engineer. He kept up the ruse even after they became engaged, but the only merchandise he sold was stolen loot to pawnshops and dope to drug addicts.[28]

These were small crimes, though; there wasn't much money in them. Then, in 1929, Stein was invited to participate in what promised to be the biggest heist of his career with a potential million-dollar payoff. While at Sing Sing, he had befriended a Norwegian burglar named Karl Larsen. Larsen later returned to Norway and scouted an opportunity to hold up the Bank of Oslo. He told Stein that he needed three accomplices to do the job, so Stein recruited two petermen—safecrackers—from his prison network.[29]

The fare for a transatlantic voyage wasn't cheap, and the gang would need money for operations, so Stein turned to yet another Sing Sing pal, Chowderhead Cohen, to help him fundraise. Cohen introduced Stein to his lawyer friend, John Radeloff. Radeloff didn't have the capital, but Vivian Gordon did. At his urging, she loaned Stein $1,500 to fund the operation.[30]

When the three Americans arrived in Norway, they rented a quaint cottage in a forest across the fjord from Oslo. To avoid suspicion, they adopted a cover story, purporting to be wealthy businessmen—a railroad heir, a Hollywood mogul, and a doctor—who had come to the remote spot to collaborate with Karl Larsen on a secret invention. The local villagers were nonplussed by the Americans' "modest grooming" but declared the foreigners to be courteous and amiable, noting that they "diligently courted the many young ladies of the place." Visitors to the cottage often found the inventors fiddling with their contraption, which had electrical wires coming out of it. Yet, every afternoon, the men drove to Oslo on mysterious errands, returning late at night.

Their stay at the cottage was brief. After two weeks, "Mr. Harry," as Stein styled himself, informed the landlady that they would have to depart immediately to film a movie in the north. In fact, the bank robbery had been indefinitely delayed.* Deprived of their main objective, the three

---

* The reason for the delay is unclear. Larsen later attempted the heist by himself, armed with a club and a revolver, but he was caught and imprisoned.

Americans tried to salvage the trip by scouting out diamond-smuggling opportunities in Paris and Berlin until they ran out of money. Stein returned home in September, empty-handed and indebted to Gordon for $1,500 plus interest.[31]

The identification of the mysterious Harry Saunders sent a ripple of excitement up the chain of command. Commissioner Mulrooney and District Attorney McLaughlin agreed to keep the new lead under wraps until they had collected more evidence, but they didn't hide their enthusiasm from the press. "There have been new developments, but their nature and importance cannot be disclosed at this time," McLaughlin teased. "Many entanglements have been untangled," Mulrooney added cryptically.[32]

A round-the-clock surveillance team was assigned to Harry Stein. He lived with his mother and two sisters on Park Avenue, not in the swank section but uptown among the tenements and railroad tracks in a burgeoning Puerto Rican enclave that some had begun to call Spanish Harlem. The police noted that he seldom left the apartment before noon. In the afternoons, he usually sauntered downtown through Central Park and spent the day hanging about the theater district.[33]

Times Square was as bustling then as it is today, but seedier. "The sharpies have always liked the Square for easy picking," wrote Abel Green, editor of *Variety* magazine. "Every gimmick imaginable goes on the Big Street, from fake auction rooms to shell game, dame-baited speaks operating openly, creepers and badger workers with improved methods, undercover rendezvous of intermediate sex luring Freudian students, and everything else." The sidewalks were crammed with "sightseers, theatre patrons, unemployed actors and actresses making the rounds seeking employment; street fakers offering their wares and watching for cops; handbook men, three-card monte boys, touts, tipsters and steerers for speaks."[34]

Stein didn't engage in any illicit activity during his afternoon strolls, though. He had no evident occupation and seemed content to wander the streets, offering occasional nods to other racketeers and criminals he knew. He was well-dressed for an unemployed ex-con, tall and slim, with a receding hairline and a cleft chin. Bushy beetle-brows, bisected by a pair of deep furrows above the bridge of his nose, accentuated his habitual scowl. The undercover cops had no trouble trailing him unseen in that

A bustling but "seedier" Times Square at night, November 1932.

crowd. Whenever he ducked into a restaurant or speakeasy, one or two followed him inside and took a table within view.[35]

One of his regular hangouts was a seedy Romanian teahouse* on Sixth Avenue near Bryant Park, where the patrons were invited to play cards for sandwiches, getting free food if they won but paying double if they lost. Stein usually dined alone, but he was joined one evening by a husky, reptilian fellow who greeted him warmly. The man had two distinctive moles on his right cheek, one large and bulbous, the other small and dark, like a moon orbiting a planet. The detectives who witnessed the

---

* Teahouses enjoyed a surge of popularity during the 1920s. Though tea was on the menu at these establishments, they usually offered lunch menus and were more akin to what we might now call a luncheonette or a café.

meeting couldn't make out the conversation, but they recognized Stein's companion as Samuel "Greenie" Greenberg, a forty-four-year-old professional burglar and six-time convicted felon who had overlapped with Stein at Sing Sing. Moreover, when the graphologist later compared Greenberg's handwriting to the Norwegian passport applications, he was able to identify him as the man who had traveled with Stein using the name Sam Cohen. Police also determined that Greenberg had submitted Chowderhead's birth certificate with the application, another link to Radeloff's circle.[36]

A second surveillance team was assigned to Greenie, who lived on Rivington Street on the Lower East Side. When he ducked into a phone booth a few days later, his tail took the booth next to it and overheard Greenberg asking to speak to "Harry." But Harry apparently wasn't home because Greenberg hung up immediately. Afterward, the police traced the call to an apartment near Times Square. It turned out that the "Harry" that Greenberg was trying to reach wasn't Stein but another man, Harry Harvey, who had rented a room in the apartment. He, too, was placed under surveillance.[37]

Harry Harvey had the physique of a thug—thick neck, barrel chest, hulking shoulders. His face was plain and broad, with an undershot jaw and shaggy eyebrows fixed to a receding forehead. His looked younger than the other two, and his manner was furtive and awkward. None of the cops recognized him, and he didn't appear to have a criminal record. Nor were they able to connect him to Vivian Gordon or the Oslo expedition. The trail seemed like a dead end, but the cops tapped his phone just in case.[38]

For the next couple weeks, the investigators made little headway. They kept up the surveillance on Stein and the others, but they still lacked concrete evidence tying any of the men to Vivian Gordon's murder. Then, in late March, Commissioner Mulrooney received a tip from a mysterious source, whose name he never divulged. "It so happened that during my personal work on the case I made contact with a person who could give me information," he later told the press. "This person was 'smart' in the ways of the world, and he knew the value of his information."[39]

The value of that information turned out to be $15,000—more than the police commissioner's annual salary. "I accordingly took the matter up with the Mayor," he continued, "and we discussed the advisability of obtaining the necessary money from the Board of Estimate, but decided against that course on the ground that it would result in publicity which would have interfered with our work." Mulrooney wanted to keep his information under wraps to avoid spooking any suspects before the police were ready to move, so he quietly reached out to leaders of the Patrolmen's Benevolent Association, who agreed to cover the cost.[40]

The only information ever revealed about Mulrooney's source was later unearthed by Grace Robinson. According to her own "underworld source," the person who collected the reward was a private detective who worked with paid informants. One of his contacts was a fence named David Butterman, who specialized in stolen furs. A few weeks after Gordon's murder, Butterman approached the detective with some particularly valuable information and asked for assistance in seeking a reward from the police. The detective agreed to assist, but instead of helping Butterman, he took the information directly to Mulrooney and claimed the reward for himself.[41]

In addition to Butterman, Mulrooney's source named several people who could corroborate the story. One was a man named William Vigdor, who owned a thrift shop in Revere, Massachusetts, a suburb of Boston. The name of the town rang a bell: the coded telegram found in Gordon's apartment had come from Revere. Unwilling to trust anyone else with his discovery, Mulrooney turned over his commissioner duties to his deputy and secretly traveled to Massachusetts.[42]

Vigdor spoke freely with Mulrooney. He said that he and Butterman were relatives and sometimes did business together. They had both known Vivian Gordon and had employed her as an intermediary in some of their more sensitive communications. He admitted to being the author of the coded telegram found in Gordon's apartment and showed Mulrooney a cable he'd received from her on February 13, twelve days before her murder. Decoded, it read, "Unable to get you on phone. Is that matter of which I spoke several weeks ago all right? Answer." Gordon had sent the telegram, but she wasn't the author. It was signed, "Dave," whom Vigdor identified as Butterman. The telegram that the police found in Gordon's apartment after her murder was Vigdor's answer to Butterman's question: "Everything all right. Call me any time."[43]

Vigdor claimed that his acquaintance with Gordon was slight and insisted that he knew nothing of her murder, but the confirmation of a link between Butterman and Gordon was sufficient for Mulrooney to take action. He returned to New York and assembled a team of thirty detectives whom he trusted. Assuming the role of lead detective, he assigned tasks to the officers and ordered them to report back when they'd completed their work.[44]

Early in the morning on April 5, six officers from Mulrooney's team raided Butterman's apartment in Washington Heights, rousing him and his family from bed. His wife, Anna, a pretty, petite woman of thirty-two, came clean immediately. She told the police that Harry Stein had called them at home between 2:00 and 2:30 a.m. on the night of Vivian Gordon's murder and insisted that she wake her husband. "I was pretty sore that we should be waked up like that," she added.[45]

David Butterman, a short, uneasy man with square features, confirmed his wife's account and said that Stein asked to see him in the morning. They met for breakfast at a restaurant on 96th and Broadway. Then Stein led him uptown to a boardinghouse on Riverside Drive.

"The landlady, Mrs. Madeline Tully, let us in and we went to the kitchen," Butterman continued. "Stein showed me a lady's diamond wristwatch. I asked him how much he wanted for it and he said, 'The boys are asking $100.' I told him it was worth only $50 to me. He would let me know, he said. He showed me a full-length mink coat and when I asked his price he said, 'The boys would like $400 for it.' I cut out the lining, spread the coat on a couch, and tried to obliterate some factory marks by rubbing ink on them. I spilled some of the ink on the couch cover. I asked him if he had anything else—that this was cheap merchandise. He said he had nothing, but somebody else had a diamond ring downtown."[46]

After he left the boardinghouse, Butterman took the wristwatch to his brother-in-law, William "Doc" Rosenfeldt, who sold jewelry on the street in Times Square. Rosenfeldt wasn't interested in the watch, but he was curious about the ring, so Butterman contacted Stein and invited him to bring it to Rosenfeldt's apartment. Stein soon arrived with what appeared to be a platinum engagement ring with one large diamond ornamented with four side stones and six accent stones. Stein claimed that the center diamond was more than two carats and offered to sell the ring for $1,000. But Rosenfeldt, after examining the stone, declared that it was smaller than Stein claimed and that the price was too high. They argued about the size of the diamond and haggled over the price but couldn't come to an agreement. Stein finally left with the ring and watch.[47]

That evening, David and Anna Butterman took the mink coat to a dressmaker for appraisal. By that time, the newsboys were already shouting from streetcorners about the murder of a "Girl Vice Witness," but the details about Gordon's missing ring, watch, and coat didn't make the papers until the following morning. When David Butterman read the news, he connected the dots and decided to cut the mink loose immediately, stashing it in a coat check in Times Square. Anna Butterman later delivered the claim check to Stein. "Harry, why did you ever give a thing like that to my husband?" she demanded.

"What do you want from me?" he replied chastely. "I have nothing to do with it. Someone gave it to me. If there'd been anything wrong about it, I'd never have given it to you."[48]

The Buttermans' confessions represented a stunning break in the case. Mulrooney's team now had evidence tying Harry Stein directly to the murder. They spent the next two days corroborating the testimony with Rosenfeldt and the dressmaker. Madeline Tully, the landlady, was hostile to the police and denied everything, but they found the ink stain on the couch that Butterman had described. They were unable to discover the whereabouts of any of the stolen items, however, which would have strengthened the case against Stein.[49]

Meanwhile, Detective Raymond Henshaw reported another breakthrough. He'd been responsible for monitoring the phone line to the apartment where the mysterious Harry Harvey had rented a room. At 6:15 p.m. on April 7, the landlady answered a phone call from a man who asked for "Harry." After she passed the phone to Harvey, Henshaw heard the caller say, "Harry, this is Harry. I've got something. It isn't much. But it's something. Can I come over? How do they feel about it over there?"

"Well, that's all right," Harvey replied.

"I'm at Second Avenue now," the caller continued. "I'll be over in fifteen minutes. I'll take the bus over."

A few minutes later, Henshaw saw Harry Stein arrive at Harvey's building. The two men had a conversation in the foyer. Then Stein pulled something from his pocket and handed it to Harvey.[50]

Two days later, Mulrooney made his move. On the morning of April 9, his detectives fanned out across the city and began rounding up suspects and witnesses, starting with Harry Stein, who was picked up at 88th Street and West End Avenue on the Upper West Side. Nearly thirty others were arrested that day. To avoid attracting attention while the roundup was ongoing, Mulrooney had the detainees taken to a holding area at the Police Academy, across the street from police headquarters. All but four were questioned and released, including Harry Harvey. The remaining four were Stein, David Butterman, Samuel Greenberg, and Morris "Doc" Levine, who had been identified as the third member of the Oslo gang. Of the four, only Butterman was willing to talk, but he had little to add to his previous statements. Greenberg and Levine maintained that the Oslo expedition had been a pleasure trip. Stein claimed that they'd been scouting a bootlegging opportunity. All three denied knowing anything about Vivian Gordon except what they'd read in the papers.[51]

After eighteen hours of fruitless interrogation, Mulrooney dispatched his prisoners to the Bronx—Stein to be arraigned as a murder suspect, the others to be held as material witnesses. News of the arrests had gotten out, and hundreds of people gathered outside the county courthouse to see the man alleged to have killed Vivian Gordon. Stein looked dapper, if bedraggled, in a brown suit and dark blue overcoat with a velvet collar. He covered his face with his hat as he was led through the crowd. No counsel accompanied him in the courtroom, and he said nothing when the judge ordered him held without bail.[52]

In another courtroom, Butterman, Greenberg, and Levine covered theirs faces with handkerchiefs as the cameras flashed. Judge Harry Stackell, the same judge who had previously approved $50,000 bail for Radeloff and Cohen, now considered an identical request to hold three new material witnesses. He called out Butterman's name first, but the only response was a muffled voice.

"Which is Butterman?" the judge asked quizzically.

Butterman held up his hand.

"Better take that handkerchief away from your face," Stackell admonished him.

"I refuse to do so," Butterman answered through the handkerchief.

"Have you anything to say?" asked the exasperated judge.

"Yes," Butterman replied. "I have this to say. I think that the bail of $50,000 is too high and should be reduced lower."

Judge Stackell did not agree. He approved the prosecutor's request, and all three witnesses went to jail.[53]

Two individuals were conspicuously excluded from Mulrooney's grand roundup: John Radeloff and Chowderhead Cohen, who had been released from jail two days before Stein's arrest. Their absence from the arrest list was notable, since the police had learned that both men were well-acquainted with Harry Stein. Yet they were not summoned. Radeloff even contacted Bruckman to ask whether he was wanted for questioning, but the Bronx inspector declined.[54]

Grace Robinson, on the other hand, was eager to speak with them about their acquaintance with Harry Stein. "I knew him under the name Simmons or Symons," Radeloff told her. "He and Cohen came into my office together a couple of years ago. We never had any business dealings. I did not dream that he had ever heard of Vivian Gordon. Still less did I imagine that he knew her. Vivian never mentioned his name. If he had been an intimate friend of hers, I think she would have told me of him." He professed ignorance about the Oslo operation. "Letters and cables came from Oslo to Vivian at my Brooklyn office," he said. "I was curious and asked her what they were about. But she just put me off by saying it was just a business deal she happened to be interested in."[55]

Chowderhead Cohen told Robinson that he knew all four of the arrested men. "When Stein and I were in Sing Sing together we ate at the same table," he said, "but I never knew until today that he knew Vivian. I knew Doc Levine, Greenberg and Butterman pretty well but they never cracked to me about knowing Vivian although they must have known that I knew her pretty well."[56]

And yet, one of Grace Robinson's sources in either the police department or the DA's office gave her information that, if true, meant that

Radeloff and Cohen had lied to her. According to the source, one of the detainees claimed to have witnessed a heated meeting between Radeloff, Gordon, Stein, and a friend of Cohen's named Max Rudolph in Radeloff's office two weeks before the murder. Radeloff and Gordon were quarreling about the Queens properties when the lawyer allegedly menaced her. "Do you see these two men here?" he asked, gesturing at Stein and Rudolph, "They'll take care of you. You'll be out of this world soon!"

To which Gordon calmly responded, "I know that."[57]

CHAPTER 9
A DAMNABLE CONSPIRACY

MAYOR JIMMY WALKER, HARD AT WORK ON HIS RESPONSE TO THE CITY Affairs Committee, took a break to celebrate the arrest of Harry Stein. "This was Mulrooney's own case and he ran it down and broke it himself—alone," he crowed to the press. "It was really a most remarkably dramatic incident. There was Mulrooney, a cop whom I placed at the head of the cops, strolling up and down a corridor, and suddenly stopping to point a finger at Stein with the words: 'You are charged with the murder of Vivian Gordon.' . . . It was a splendid piece of work for which the Commissioner is entitled to all the credit."[1]

Walker's jubilation was understandable, given the political toll the case had taken on his administration, but it was also premature. The evidence against Harry Stein was circumstantial. No witnesses claimed to have seen him commit the crime or even heard him confess it. The motive was unknown. The police didn't have the murder weapon and hadn't recovered the missing ring, coat, or watch. They didn't know where Gordon had been killed or if it even happened within the court's jurisdiction—a point emphasized by Harry Stein's new lawyer, Samuel Leibowitz.

"How does anybody know Vivian Gordon was murdered in the Bronx?" he declaimed to the press. "The spot where her body was found is only a two-minute automobile ride from the Westchester County line. Physicians said she had been dead six to nine hours when her body was discovered at 8:30 in the morning. In that time, she could have been carried from Utica, from Richmond, Va., from Boston, or from a point forty miles out in the Atlantic Ocean before she was deposited in Van Cortlandt Park."[2]

Leibowitz was one of New York's hottest criminal defense lawyers. His meticulous research, courtroom histrionics, and unconventional tactics seemed to have a magical effect on juries. Born in Romania, his last name was originally Lebeau, but his father, Isaac, changed it on the advice of a fellow immigrant who told him that Leibowitz sounded more American.

Isaac peddled dry goods from a pushcart on Orchard Street until he'd saved enough money to open a small shop in Harlem, then a larger one in downtown Brooklyn. His prosperity eventually enabled him to purchase a house in Brooklyn and send his only son to Cornell University, though Sam helped pay his own way by waiting tables and washing dishes.[3]

At Cornell, Sam distinguished himself by his work ethic. In addition to excelling in his studies, he was a gifted actor and debater, talents that would serve him well in his future legal career. He graduated with a law degree in 1915—in the same class as his fellow Brooklynite, John Radeloff. After acing the bar exam, Leibowitz decided to become a defense lawyer, not for idealistic reasons but because he doubted that corporate firms would hire a Jewish Romanian immigrant. It was a fortuitous choice because he was an extraordinary defense counsel. His arguments weren't always legally sound, but he had an intuitive grasp of human psychology that enabled him to persuade juries to acquit his clients, much to the dismay of outraged prosecutors and judges. He demonstrated his ingenuity at the trial of his first paying client, a notorious pickpocket known as Izzy the Goniff.* Leibowitz didn't deny that Izzy was a professional pickpocket. On the contrary, he argued that Izzy was so proficient and experienced that he couldn't possibly have been caught on the Coney Island boardwalk with his fingers in someone's pocket. The jury acquitted.[4]

Not all of his methods were entirely kosher. When defending a butcher accused of burning down his shop for insurance money, Leibowitz asked a chemist to prepare vials of kerosene, gasoline, and water. When firefighters who claimed to have found kerosene-soaked rags on the premises took the stand, Leibowitz asked them to identify each vial, always starting with the pungent kerosene, which saturated their nasal sensors and caused them to identify all three as kerosene. Then he asked the jurors to smell the three vials but presented them in the reverse order. The butcher was acquitted.[5]

Between 1919 and 1923, Leibowitz handled nearly 1,000 criminal cases and won acquittals in 800 of them. As his reputation grew, so did his ambition. He began offering his services to defendants in sensational

---

* *Goniff* is Yiddish for a thief or scoundrel.

cases, especially homicides. Tabloid readers knew him as the crack lawyer who defended the Gigolo Murder Widow, the Mother Honor Slayer, the Breadknife Murderess, the Vendetta Woman, the Razor Slayer, the Pants Murderer, and the Insurance Death Plotter.[6]

He also represented several notorious gangsters, including Al Capone. When Capone visited his native Brooklyn in December 1925, he took the opportunity to settle a score with the White Hand, an Irish gang that had chased him out of New York several years earlier. After midnight of Christmas Day, he and eight Italian mobsters ambushed the White Handers at a social club, leaving three dead and one wounded. Samuel Leibowitz later visited the survivor in the hospital and prevailed on him to sign an affidavit stating that he didn't recognize any of the shooters. Then he persuaded the judge to release his clients. When the district attorney subsequently dropped the charges for want of evidence, Capone and the mafiosos invited Leibowitz to a lavish banquet where they joyfully clinked champaign glasses and shouted, "Viva Leibowitz!"[7]

Leibowitz had yet to gain widespread renown outside the city at the time of Vivian Gordon's murder. The infamy of the case presented an opportunity to put his name in every newspaper in the country. He also had a personal connection with his old classmate, John Radeloff, whose law office was in the same building as his own. So even though his client list was overflowing, and Harry Stein couldn't afford his fee, he offered to represent him. Then he plunged in with typical truculence. "The case will collapse. It's another dud," he declared to the press. "There is no evidence that Stein and the Gordon woman were together that night, simply because they were not together. The police have not established the scene of the murder, not even the county. And unless they do no grand jury will return an indictment. Stein isn't worrying."[8]

In such a high-profile case, Leibowitz knew that jurors might come to trial with preconceived opinions, so he proceeded to make his argument to the public before the trial began. First, he had to humanize his client, no easy task given Stein's criminal history and sullen demeanor. Since Stein hadn't uttered a word in public, Leibowitz reported what his client had told him in private: "I didn't kill Vivian Gordon. I'm not the least worried. I don't know who did kill her. I had absolutely nothing to do with the murder. And if I had, do you think I'd be such a fool as to stay within the New York City limits?" Or at least, that's what he said Stein told him, though the sentiment sounded suspiciously like Leibowitz's own pronouncements.[9]

He also enlisted Stein's sister, Lee Norris, a vaudeville actress, to speak on her brother's behalf. "I've just visited Harry in jail," she told the press. "The idea of arresting him for such a crime is preposterous. He finds himself in this situation because of the flimsiest circumstantial evidence and through sheer coincidence. He's the most devoted brother two girls ever had." She described how he had supported the family when she and her sister were out of work, how he had even gone without food so that the others could eat. "Why, Harry wouldn't hurt a soul," she exclaimed, recounting a time when he had become so incensed by a man beating a horse that he seized the whip and beat the man. "That's the sort of person Harry is," she concluded without irony.

"The idea of his being Vivian Gordon's sweetheart is too ridiculous for words," she continued. "He's too devoted to his own little sweetheart, whom we are all so fond of. He's a one-woman man." To underscore her point, she shared the private message that Stein had supposedly entrusted her to pass to his fiancée, but which sounded oddly wooden: "I love you. I am innocent. Have faith in me. Don't believe any false and exaggerated statements you may see about me. My case is being handled by an excellent lawyer and I am not worried."[10]

The charm campaign took a hit the next day, though, when a middle-aged dressmaker named Lola Baker marched into the Bathgate Station and fingered Stein as the rogue who had assaulted and robbed her the year before. "My God, I know that man," she told Inspector Bruckman. When they'd met the previous spring, he'd told her that his name was Charlie Brooks. They went on a couple of dates and seemed to be enjoying one another's company, but after she invited him back to her Midtown apartment, he attacked her. "He tried to chloroform me, and strangle me with a handkerchief," she exclaimed. "He hit me in the jaw and broke two of my ribs. I'm a pretty strong woman. I defended myself, and he didn't succeed in knocking me unconscious. But he got away with my two diamond rings." She reported the crime to the police but had no way to identify her attacker until she saw his picture in the *Daily News* after his arrest in the Gordon case. When Bruckman put Stein in a lineup, Baker picked him out immediately. "That's the man. I could never forget him," she declared, staring him in the eye.[11]

The crime occurred outside Bruckman's jurisdiction, so he referred Lola Baker to the authorities in Manhattan. "Well, even if we don't hold him for murdering the Gordon woman, he'll get a forty-year rap on this new charge, anyway," he told the press afterward. "This certainly shows he's a natural, born strangler."[12]

Samuel Leibowitz countered immediately. "It never fails," he declared. "Every sensational murder case always brings a retinue of cranks, usually persons of social obscurity, who see an opportunity of getting their names in the papers."[13]

Yet, the fact that Lola Baker had reported the crime to the police a year earlier suggested that she hadn't simply fabricated the story for the sake of publicity. Her accusations were similar to Stein's assault and robbery of his friend Mary Glicksman in 1921, which, according to the press, had also involved strangling. Accurate or not, these stories contributed to the public perception that Stein was a "natural born strangler," as Bruckman put it. As long as the police lacked stronger evidence tying Stein to the Gordon murder, Leibowitz wasn't overly concerned, but he began preparing a defense strategy just in case.

As usual, he focused on human psychology. The stories that Judge Seabury told about venal police officers preying on innocent women, followed by months of lurid reporting on the death of Vivian Gordon and of her daughter, had exerted a powerful influence on the city's collective psyche. The same outrage that drove the expanding investigations could be harnessed to protect Leibowitz's client. Many New Yorkers were already convinced that Vivian Gordon was the victim of a grand conspiracy. Leibowitz decided to feed and exploit these suspicions by portraying Harry Stein as the patsy in a police coverup. This narrative would appeal to jurors already conditioned to the abuse of power in the justice system. It would also enable Leibowitz to turn his client's regrettable criminal history into an advantage by arguing that Stein had been targeted precisely because he was such an obvious suspect.

The irony that he had just spent the last few months defending police officers exposed by Seabury's inquiry did not give him any pause. His job, as he saw it, was to provide each client the best possible representation, regardless of his own personal beliefs.

One of his ideas was to link Vivian Gordon's murder to the other great enigma on everyone's minds, the disappearance of Justice Joseph Force Crater. Both mysteries had aroused New Yorkers' suspicions, and there were already rumors that the cases were connected. If he could link them, they would amplify each other, sowing further doubt in the jurors' minds. To this end, he hired private detectives to tease out any connections between Gordon and Crater.[14]

In addition to the Crater angle, Leibowitz also instructed his agents to sniff out the mysterious source who had informed Commissioner Mulrooney about David Butterman and William Vigdor. In the underworld, Butterman had an unsavory reputation as a "squealer," suspected of tipping off the authorities after he received stolen goods. He reputedly had a liaison in the police department and also sold information to private detectives, including legendary sleuth Noel C. Scaffa. The Scaffa Detective Agency was steeped in mystery and intrigue. Employing secretive, possibly illegal methods and a network of informants, Scaffa was credited with recovering millions of dollars' worth of stolen jewelry for his clients. The prospect that his name might be connected to the Gordon case opened yet another fertile opportunity for Leibowitz to exploit.[15]

What his agents uncovered might not be admissible in court, but the newspapers' standards of evidence were less stringent. Leibowitz had a relationship with Harvey Duell, city editor for the *News*. If the sleuths turned up anything, he could easily turn the story over to the press.[16]

Sure enough, Grace Robinson published her story about Mulrooney's source a couple weeks later. "It was Butterman's cupidity that precipitated the squeal that landed Stein behind bars," she wrote. "From an underworld source, the *News* learned that Butterman, itching for a possible reward, called up a private detective and informed him of the whereabouts of the valuables. The detective, instead of fretting about . . . the reward which Butterman expected, merely communicated with the police."[17]

Robinson's article didn't name the private eye, but the story provided Leibowitz with a convenient vehicle to speculate about Noel Scaffa, who was known to trade in information gleaned from paid informers like Butterman. Even more helpful was the Justice Crater bombshell that the *News* published two weeks later, unusually with no byline.

"A new and lurid light was cast on the strange joining of Justice Joseph Force Crater's disappearance and the Vivian Gordon murder mystery yesterday," the story began, "when Sam Cohen told the *News* that the dead courtesan was a night club pal of the missing jurist, and that she apparently had marked him for her next and biggest blackmail victim." According to Chowderhead, Gordon met Crater at the Club Abbey, a notorious Midtown nightclub owned by Dutch Schultz. The *New Yorker* nightlife columnist described the club as "one of those ominous places in which Everybody suddenly finds himself late at night, much against his will." It was one of Crater's favorite haunts and prime hunting grounds for Gordon.[18]

Gordon didn't know who Crater was when she saw him at the Abbey, Cohen said, but she'd heard he was a big shot, so she bribed the host to seat her and a companion at a table next to his. When her companion found an excuse to leave, Crater invited the beautiful woman sitting by herself to join his party, introducing himself as Joe Crane.

According to Cohen, they became well-acquainted and saw each other many times afterward. Gordon tried to dig up information about the mysterious Mr. Crane that she might use as leverage, but she didn't learn his true identity until she read about his disappearance in the papers. "Why, that's my friend, Joe Crane," she told Cohen. "That's the fellow I've been trying to get information about. If I'd dreamed he was Judge Crater, I'd have used different tactics."[19]

Chowderhead was the only source named in the article, so its veracity is questionable. Crater and Gordon both frequented the Abbey, and it's quite possible that they met there, but it's also possible that Cohen invented their relationship, perhaps in return for payment from Leibowitz's agents.

In any case, this story was eclipsed by yet another *News* scoop involving Justice Crater. This one probably was not Leibowitz's handiwork, as it didn't reflect well on his client. It was also one of the oddest stories of the whole case. The central figure was a convict at Sing Sing named Joseph Lesser, who claimed that Justice Crater had secretly visited the prison under an assumed name after his disappearance in August. "I happened to be in the common room where visitors are received. Crater stopped and spoke to me," he said. "I knew him well. I could not be mistaken about his identity. Before I went to jail, I had seen him several times about my case."

Then the story turned even stranger. Lesser, a Brooklyn real estate broker, had been convicted of forging mortgages worth nearly $300,000 in 1929. He claimed that during his trial, Harry Stein and John Radeloff had tried to help him influence the judge. It was through them that he met Crater before his appointment to the Supreme Court. Lesser told the *News*:

> Stein . . . came to me and said that he would be able to fix the case for me if I was willing to put up enough money. . . . I said I was interested and Stein, who introduced himself under the name of Stone, a few days later brought John Radeloff into my Manhattan office. They told me that they would be able to reach Judge Donnellan, whom I didn't know. Radeloff said he was a great friend of Crater's and that Crater was Donnellan's most intimate pal. In this way the contact would be made.
>
> Then, later, I was introduced to Crater. Crater told me he would have to have $10,000 cash to help me out. I talked with Crater several times, frequently going down to the Libby hotel to see him. I said the price was all right but that I wanted to put the money in escrow to be turned over to Crater as soon as my case was fixed for me. This Crater refused to do. He said the money must be placed on the line. I refused to do this and the deal flopped. I cancelled the checks that I had given Radeloff for expenses.[20]

To corroborate his account, Lesser presented the voided checks made out to Radeloff.

Lesser initially reported his sighting of the missing justice in a letter to Crater's wife, who was desperate for information about her husband's whereabouts. When word of his allegations later reached the governor's office, Roosevelt took them so seriously that he secretly dispatched his personal legal adviser to Sing Sing to investigate. The results of his inquiry were never revealed, but the prison warden concluded that Lesser's claims were without foundation. "We made an exhaustive investigation," he told the *News*. "We compared visitors' signatures with the handwriting of

Judge Joseph Force Crater and his wife, Stella, relaxing at their Maine cabin in the summer of 1930, before his disappearance on August 6 of that year.

Crater, and we checked up on every 'Rosen,' the name Crater is supposed to have used. But I would bet all the tea in China that Crater has never been behind Sing Sing walls after he vanished from New York."[21]

There was still the matter of the voided checks, though. When Radeloff was confronted with the information, he admitted that at least part of Lesser's story was true. "This Stein, or Stone, called me up one day and said that he had a case for me," Radeloff said. "The case subsequently turned out to be Lesser's. With Stein, who made the appointment, I met Lesser in uptown Manhattan and he told me of his difficulties. I agreed to take his case and see what I could do for him and he gave me a check—this was one on which he subsequently stopped payment and the stub of which was located in his files."

He said that Lesser never mentioned Crater but spoke of seeking help from "a certain prominent politician connected with the biggest hotel on the Lower East Side." This was likely the Libby Hotel, which had been placed in receivership* under Crater's supervision.

---

* A court-ordered remedy to protect financially distressed assets, such as hotels. The receiver is a neutral party who stewards the assets until they can be sold or restructured.

"At any rate, I told Lesser I didn't care to handle a case in which so many different individuals would be active," Radeloff continued, "and I asked to be relieved from further participation. I never heard from him again and he stopped payment on the $100 check."[22]

Years later, Lesser admitted that he'd invented the story of Crater's prison visits but said that their business dealings were real. He'd concocted the prison story in hopes of recovering $2,150 that he'd paid to Crater to fix his case. Radeloff and Stein's involvement was also likely true, since Radeloff himself confirmed it. That meant that his relationship with Stein went deeper than he'd intimated when he said that they'd never had any business dealings.[23]

Still, the police did not summon him.

After Stein's arrest, the homicide investigation went quiet. Commissioner Mulrooney returned to his administrative duties. Inspector Bruckman continued to focus on the case but did not speak with the press. At the end of April, there was a brief flurry of excitement about a report that a man matching Harry Stein's description had tried to exchange a diamond ring for an automobile in the suburb of New Rochelle, but nothing came of it. None of Vivian Gordon's stolen valuables were recovered. The material witnesses in custody provided no additional information. As for Radeloff and Cohen, their bail dropped from $50,000 to $5,000, and then they were released. By mid-May, Harry Stein was the only person connected with the case still in custody.[24]

But sometime between Stein's arrest on April 9 and late May, the detectives learned that Harry Harvey's real name was Harry Schlitten. The way they made this discovery was never revealed, but they'd continued to tap his phone and likely overheard him reveal his name. At first, the name meant little, for Schlitten had no criminal record. Digging into his background, they identified him as a minor thug who earned a living in various mob-related activities—strikebreaking, poker dealing, and protection rackets. The breakthrough came when they searched for his name in the records of automobile rental companies. They discovered that a man named Harry Schlitten had rented a black, seven-seat Cadillac Imperial sedan from the K & S Auto Renting Company on the Lower East Side at

8:00 p.m. on February 25, the night of the murder. And he had returned it around one in the morning.[25]

Armed with this information, the police rearrested Schlitten on May 23 and brought him back to the Police Academy for questioning. Commissioner Mulrooney, Inspector Bruckman, District Attorney McLaughlin, and others took turns working him all night. They tempted him with offers of immunity and threatened that he'd end up in the electric chair if another witness broke first. In early hours of the morning, the exhausted prisoner's resolve crumbled, and he agreed to confess in exchange for criminal immunity.[26]

Schlitten told the investigators that he and Harry Stein ran in the same circles and had worked together in the past. In February, Stein had approached Schlitten at the Romanian teahouse on Sixth Avenue and said that he needed a driver. He was cagey about the job but hinted that he needed to put someone "out of the way" and promised Schlitten a share of the take—$1,000, maybe $2,000.[27]

Schlitten had a chauffeur's license but no car, so he asked an associate, Isadore Lewis, to hooked him up with a cheap rental. "On the night of February 25, Lewis and I went to the K & S Auto Renting Company at 123 Suffolk Street and hired a Cadillac car," he said. "We drove uptown to 38th Street and Third Avenue, right near Miss Gordon's apartment." Harry Stein was waiting at the corner, accompanied by another man, Samuel Greenberg. They both climbed into the car, and Stein ordered Schlitten to drive uptown. They dropped Lewis at 49th Street and continued up to 100th and Park so that Stein could pick up something from his apartment. He returned a few minutes later with a rope and told Schlitten to drive to the Bronx to "look for a spot." They selected a dark street corner on Grand Avenue in Morris Heights, a hilly residential neighborhood where the streets wriggle free from the city's relentless grid.[28]

"Then we drove Stein back to 38th Street and Third Avenue," Schlitten continued, "and returned to the Bronx, waiting at Grand Avenue for Stein to return." While they waited, Schlitten asked Greenberg about the job.

"I know as much about it as you do," Greenie replied. "The funny part of this is that I'm supposed to have $250,000 worth of diamonds on me and a party is coming here to try and get them." He explained that

Stein had concocted this ruse to lure the victim to the Bronx by promising her a share of the supposed booty. He'd arranged to pick her up in a taxi and take her to meet Greenberg at a secluded location. Once they were all in the Cadillac, her role in the robbery was to "play up to" Greenberg and distract him. Then Stein would beat him and take the stones.[29]

Sure enough, a cab with two passengers soon arrived at the meeting spot. "When the taxi with Stein and Vivian found us," Schlitten said, "Stein persuaded her to get out and get into our car. She thought everything was set for taking the rocks off Greenberg.

"I drove around on Sedgwick Avenue while Stein made the rope noose and she talked to Greenberg," he continued. "Stein took the rope and threw it around the girl's neck, making a noose. Then he pulled—tight. She was trying to fight back—trying to free herself from the noose. Stein tightened the rope again."

Her last desperate gasp for air produced a staccato screech that Schlitten described as a cackle. "She cackled just once," he murmured. And then she was dead.

"Stein wanted to throw her body out right there. He was getting scared," Schlitten continued. "But Greenberg wouldn't agree. They had an argument about it. All this time Vivian was lying limp in the back of the car. Greenberg said they should find a more secluded place. This was near the Harlem River, a lonely enough spot, but it didn't suit Greenberg. So I drove to Mosholu Avenue and into Van Cortlandt Park. Greenburg picked out a place. It was 500 feet northwest of the Jerome Avenue entrance. When Greenberg was satisfied, he and Stein lifted Vivian out. She was limp and sagging. One carried her by the shoulders, the other by the ankles. They tossed her into the bushes.

"Then I started back downtown. We'd gone only about 200 feet when somebody discovered one of her slippers was still lying in the back of the car. Stein picked it up and threw it out on the road.

"Then we went to 48th Street and Eighth Avenue. We picked Lewis up there. Later I drove the car back, with Lewis, to the Suffolk St. garage, and paid the $10 rental. Stein had given me $25. After I paid the rental charges, I kept the $15 change. Later he gave me $210 on account and still later my balance of $50. I returned the car at 1 a.m., February 26. We'd taken it out at eight the night before. The whole job took only five hours."[30]

* * *

After Harry Schlitten confessed, the police immediately arrested Isadore Lewis and Samuel Greenberg. Lewis was known as Izzy English, though he was Russian like the others. When the detectives told him that Schlitten had confessed, he admitted his own minor role in the crime and corroborated the details about the automobile rental. Though he hadn't witnessed the murder, he confirmed that they'd rented the car at Stein's behest and that Greenberg was with him on the night of February 25.

He also claimed that Stein met him a few days later at the teahouse and asked him to retrieve a mink coat from the coat check in Times Square. But Lewis had read about the crime in the papers and wanted nothing more to do with it. "I told him no and that he was a dirty louse," he exclaimed. "I told him that he was trying to get me to pick up the coat that belonged to Vivian Gordon. He told me not to talk so loud because people might hear me."[31]

Greenberg, on the other hand, refused to cooperate. Like Stein, he was born in Russia and had spent much of his life behind bars. "I don't know anything about this murder," he told Assistant Chief Inspector John J. Sullivan.

"You know Stein, don't you?" asked Sullivan.

"Yea. I know him. I met him two years ago in Sing Sing," Greenberg admitted, but he refused to say anything about the homicide allegations. "I'm sticking to my story," he repeated. "I don't know anything about it."

"You're going to have a hard time convincing twelve men of that," Sullivan taunted.

"That's just what I'll do, though," Greenberg retorted.[32]

Yet the case was far stronger than it had been when Mulrooney's team had rounded up Stein and Greenberg the month before. With Schlitten's confession, the police now had an eyewitness account of the crime, corroborated by Lewis and Butterman.

"The detective work reflects the highest credit on the department," boasted Mulrooney at a press conference. "It is one of the most intelligent, persistent efforts that has been carried out by detectives in many, many years."[33]

Mayor Walker, beaming at Mulrooney's side, was almost giddy. "I am here to congratulate Commissioner Mulrooney and his men on this splendid detective work which illustrates the efficiency of the whole force," he gushed. But then he pivoted, exploiting an opportunity to lash out against the Seabury investigations.

"Commissioner, have you any papers here for the first few days after the murder?" he asked.

Mulrooney shook his head.

"It might be interesting to look them up or republish certain portions of them," Walker mused. "Wasn't there something said by some Mr. Cooper about the police having done away with this woman because she might be an unpleasant witness?"

The commissioner acknowledged that he had seen "some such intimation."

"Wasn't it more than an intimation?" the mayor went on. "I think there were some rather strong statements for which, perhaps, no one was directly responsible. But I think, injustice to the commissioner and the department, that these statements made either by certain newspapers themselves or inspired by other persons, that the police had done away with this woman should be pointed out to have been proved false."[34]

Yet reporters weren't convinced that the case was as cut-and-dried as Walker insinuated. Sources within the police department had revealed that investigators were seeking a "higher up" who might have ordered the killing and that Radeloff was still under surveillance. Mulrooney did little to dispel the rumors. He told reporters that "robbery might be one motive," which implied other possibilities. Nor did he deny that investigators were scrutinizing a "third man," though he claimed it wasn't Radeloff.[35]

"Wasn't Radeloff once exonerated?" Grace Robinson asked.

"I refuse to discuss that," he replied. "The police department is not exonerating anybody. All such information must come from District Attorney McLaughlin."

When she pressed him about the allegation that Radeloff had threatened Gordon in front of Stein at his law office, Mulrooney did not dispute it. "Yes, I remember that incident very well," he admitted.

"Will there be more arrests?" she asked,

"Yes."

"Will you rearrest Radeloff?"

"I advise you to have patience," he answered, concluding the interview.[36]

* * *

Sam Leibowitz laughed when Grace Robinson asked him about the rumors. Doubts about the killers' motives and talk of unnamed "higher ups" played into his legal strategy by giving him an opportunity to promote his conspiracy theory. "Before this case is over, the lid will be blown off, and a lot of prominent men in this town will be taking trains for the hinterland," he promised. "The whole thing is a frame-up against Harry Stein. The real killer is simply trying to get out by hanging the guilt on Stein."[37]

District Attorney McLaughlin, realizing the peril, tried to smother such talk. "I am not looking for a higher-up," he stated emphatically. "I am ready to take Stein and Greenberg to trial on Monday, with Schlitten, driver of the murder car, as my star witness. Radeloff is not concerned in this trial. The case is 100 per cent perfect as it stands now. Vivian Gordon's murder was actuated by robbery pure and simple. There are no other persons in it so far as my evidence shows. If any others are involved, it will be on evidence of which I have no inkling.

"In addition to the robbery motive," he added, "Stein may have been additionally spurred by Vivian's eternal trailing after him, with demands for the $1,500 which she advanced for the Oslo bank-robbing expedition, and for other sums she loaned him. They totaled more than $2,000."[38]

Leibowitz, who'd mainly represented defendants in Brooklyn and Manhattan, had never faced McLaughlin in court. "What sort of guy is McLaughlin?" he asked another attorney. "Don't cross that toy bulldog," the lawyer answered. "If you do, he'll sink his teeth into the seat of your pants and never let go." But Leibowitz didn't heed the advice. During jury selection, he turned to McLaughlin and demanded, "I want you to behave yourself during the trial."

McLaughlin jumped up, flushed and quivering. "Your Honor, Your Honor," he spluttered to Justice Albert Cohn,* who had been his colleague

---

* Albert Cohn's son, Roy Cohn, was an infamous attorney known for his flamboyant style, ruthless tactics, and unethical methods, for which he was ultimately disbarred. He served as chief counsel for Senator Joseph McCarthy during the McCarthy hearings and represented Donald Trump in the 1970s and 1980s.

The defense team in the Vivian Gordon murder trial confers at the Bronx County Courthouse on New York, June 20, 1931. From left to right: John Dwight Sullivan, Samuel Greenberg's court-appointed lawyer; Samuel Greenberg and Harry Stein, defendants; and Samuel Leibowitz, representing Stein. Reporters described Stein as "composed and at ease" throughout the trial, but Greenberg was "pale, nervous, and camera-shy."

when they were both assistant district attorneys, "tell this attorney from Brooklyn to behave himself and to remember he is in Bronx County and not in Brooklyn."

Leibowitz then proceeded to challenge the entire jury pool, arguing that the prospective jurors had been "hand-picked" from McLaughlin's neighborhood in the Bronx.

Cohn overruled him.[39]

In addition to eliminating hostile jurors, one of Leibowitz's objectives during the selection process was to psychologically prepare the jury for his arguments. He referred to Vivian Gordon as "a woman of loose morals, a blackmailer and an extortionist of the worst type." Some of the questions he asked jurors weren't designed to evaluate their biases but rather to plant seeds of doubt in their minds. "Do you know any Supreme Court justices or ex-Supreme Court justices?" he asked, an oblique reference to Justice Crater. Did they know any Pinkerton agents? Were they familiar with Noel Scaffa? Had they ever been to Boston (an allusion to Mulrooney's secret trip)? Did they believe that all cops were honest?

Frustrated by Leibowitz's suggestive inquiries, McLaughlin countered with his own question to a prospective juror, "You realize, don't you, that sometimes defense attorneys spread buncombe into a case?"

"You don't believe that every District Attorney is honest, either, do you?" Leibowitz parried.[40]

Leibowitz relished ad hominem attacks and verbal warfare with opposing counsel. McLaughlin, not so much. After three days of heated sparring, the "toy bulldog" bowed out. Pleading illness, he handed off the case to Assistant District Attorney Israel J. P. Adlerman, a bald, portly, phlegmatic prosecutor with less vigor but thicker skin than his irascible boss. If McLaughlin was indeed ill, it can't have been too serious because he was back on another case a couple of days later. Perhaps he was preoccupied by a new campaign against Dutch Schultz's gang in the Bronx, or maybe he underestimated Leibowitz, but it was a decision that he would come to regret.[41]

The trial commenced before a packed courtroom on June 18, 1931. Harry Stein, sitting beside Leibowitz, looked as calm and carefree as if he were just a spectator watching the proceedings with interest. By contrast,

Greenberg, sitting between Stein and his own court-appointed lawyer, John Dwight Sullivan, was pale and nervous.[42]

Once the jury was seated, Adlerman delivered the prosecution's opening statement, a leaden reconstruction of the crime based almost entirely on Schlitten's confession. Most of the details had already been reported by the press, but Adlerman finally addressed the motive, suggesting that Stein murdered Vivian Gordon to help out an unnamed "friend" who needed to put Gordon "out of the way."

"After we have proved these and other facts," he concluded mildly, "we will expect you to return a verdict of guilty, convicting these defendants of the charges in the indictment."[43]

Leibowitz responded with typical panache. "Our claim here is that the whole accusation is a concocted story which has been manufactured out of whole cloth by the cops in this case," he thundered. "It is the most contemptible frameup to railroad two men to the electric chair that has ever been written about or heard of. The whole case rests on the testimony of Noel Scaffa, a sort of liaison between the police and the underworld, a drug peddler named Butterman and a so-called jewel peddler named Broadway Rosenfeldt, who actually is a fence and a relative of Butterman's."[44]

The first day of testimony proceeded with little incident other than occasional bickering between Leibowitz and Adlerman. Emanuel Kamna testified about his discovery of Gordon's body. Several detectives described the crime scene and what they found in Gordon's apartment. The building superintendent, Erich Seibert, said that she had left her apartment around 3:00 p.m. on February 25 and returned two hours later. Elevator operator William Wheaton recounted her departure that evening between 11:00 and 11:30 p.m. The last witness, a shoe store manager, testified that he too had seen Gordon in the afternoon and that she had mentioned an appointment with Radeloff.

"She came to get a pocket-book she'd left for repairs nine days before," he said. "She refused to look at shoes, telling me she had no time because she had an appointment with her lawyer. She was wearing her mink coat and her diamond ring."

"Of all the women that come into your store in a day, do you remember only Vivian Gordon as wearing a mink coat?" Leibowitz asked him in cross-examination.

"Because Vivian Gordon was a striking person and because I spoke to her," he replied.[45]

Leibowitz's cross-examinations were relatively gentle on the first day, but he used every opportunity to inject his counternarratives. He asked one of the detectives if he'd ever seen Noel Scaffa in connection with the case. The witness said that he hadn't but admitted that he knew Scaffa, though not personally. Seibert was asked whether he had ever seen a tall, distinguished-looking man with a high collar visit Gordon's apartment— another oblique reference to Justice Crater, who was known for wearing stiff white collars, three inches high. The superintendent said that he wasn't often in the lobby and that the only visitor he'd seen enter Gordon's apartment was the "fellow named Radeloff."[46]

The second day of testimony featured more detectives, the medical examiner, and employees from the K & S Auto Renting Company. Again, Leibowitz held back from aggressive cross-examination, though he pressed Detective Patrick Walsh about whether Harry Schlitten had been beaten during his interrogation.

"Nobody ever laid a hand on him," Walsh retorted.

"Was there a piece of rubber hose there?" Leibowitz persisted.

"There is no piece of rubber hose in that office or in any other office of the police department," the detective declared.

"If you had given Schlitten a beating, or tortured him with the live ends of cigarettes, would you be man enough to come here and admit it?" Leibowitz pressed.

"Yes, I would," Walsh started to say before Adlerman objected.[47]

On the third day, Harry Schlitten took the stand. Nervous and frightened, the burly witness hung his head and kept his eyes on the floor to avoid looking at the defendants as he recounted the murder plot, including the detail that Adlerman had alluded to in his opening statement. He said that when he met Stein at the Romanian teahouse, he asked him why he needed a car. "If I don't get a certain party out of the way, a friend of mine is going to jail," Stein answered.[48]

Continuing the narrative, Schlitten described how he'd rented the Cadillac with Izzy Lewis, picked up Stein and Greenberg near Gordon's apartment, and continued up to the Bronx to scout out a quiet spot, stopping along the way to drop off Lewis and pick up a rope from Stein's apartment. Then he shuttled Stein back to Gordon's building and returned to "the spot" in the Bronx, where he and Greenberg talked about the diamond ruse. "When this party comes up with Stein, you are only the chauffeur," Greenie instructed him. "If I say, 'Drive to Max's or Abe's place,' you drive down the bottom of the hill."

"I looked at my watch," Schlitten recalled. "It was about five or ten minutes to twelve. I looked up the street and saw Stein crossing the street with a woman and I nudged Green and I said, 'That looks like Stein coming down.' He said, 'Yes, that's him.' I says, 'He has got a woman with him.' Green says, 'That is the party that is supposed to go.'

"They came down to the car. Green got out of the front seat and got in the back. Stein introduced Green to the girl. They got into the car. Green says, 'Drive to Max's please.' I proceeded out Grand Avenue and I overheard some conversation about, 'Do you want a drink?' and then another part of the conversation was, 'Where have you been all my life?' she said. And as I made a right-hand turn on Sedgwick Avenue and passed the last house, the scuffle started. I proceeded up a little further and Stein says, 'She's got me by the balls.' A little further on, I heard this awful gasping sound for breath, like a screech, a cackle. I proceeded up a little further and Stein said, 'She's finished now,' and I turned around and there was Stein and Green down on their knees and Stein pulling the rope on the neck. I turned back and drove.

"I proceeded on along by the reservoir and into Van Cortlandt Park, and Stein told me to stop. Stein got out and grabbed her by the feet. Greenberg picked her up by the arms and carried her out. When we had gone a little further in the car, Stein picked up a slipper of hers and threw it out the window.

"Coming back down Jerome Ave., they asked me if I wanted a drink and I says 'No.' Stein says, 'There's $2.16 in this pocketbook.' He took it out and took out some keys and put them in his pocket and threw the pocketbook.

"Then an argument started. Stein wanted to go back to the apartment and get two diaries. Greenberg said, 'You're crazy if you go back to that apartment.' They argued and argued. Then they had two drinks and as far as I know they didn't go to the apartment.

"Stein told me to go to 49th Street and 8th Avenue to pick up Izzie English. Then Stein showed me the diamond ring. It was a big white stone with small stones around it. He asked me what I thought of it. I said, 'It's all right.'"[49]

After picking up Lewis, Schlitten said, he dropped off Stein and Greenberg, returned the car around 1:15 a.m., and went home. Stein found him at the teahouse the next day and told him that he'd sold the ring for $600, promising to bring some money to his apartment that evening. By the time he arrived and handed Schlitten $212, the news about Gordon's murder and the arrests of Radeloff and Cohen had made the *New York Evening Journal*.

"I had the *Journal* there," Schlitten continued, "and I said to him, 'There's your friend Chowderhead Cohen,' and this Radeloff's picture was on the other end. I says, 'Who is this guy here?' He said, 'Well, that's the party we done it for.' He says, 'He had defended me in a case and I still owe him $1,500.' He left then.[50]

"About four days later, I saw him. He met me in front of 1030 Sixth Avenue and gave me $17. He said, 'We got $50 for the wrist watch.' About three weeks after that, he came into the tea house all aflutter—"

"All a what?" Adlerman interjected.

"All aflutter, excited," Schlitten answered. "He said to me, 'I got to get that coat out of the Times Square checkroom.' I says, 'Well, what are you asking me? Who put it there?' He said, 'Somebody did and I got to get it out. Six people looked at that coat.' I said, 'Don't bother me. I don't want no part of that coat. Leave me alone.'

"The next time I saw him was a few days later. He told me what a smart woman this woman was that owned this house at 294 Riverside Drive. He took the coat up there and she burned it down in the incinerator and she had some company there and this company smelled this awful stink and he told me that she told them that the garbage man was downstairs; what a smart woman she was.

"The day before Stein was arrested, I met him. He had some money for me. 'Some, but not a hell of a lot,' he told me. 'I just got $150 off Radeloff. You take $100 and I'll keep $50. I think I'll be leaving town for a few days.' So I bought some cigarettes."[51]

By the time Schlitten completed his testimony, Harry Stein had lost his poise and turned several shades paler. Greenberg look even more anxious than before. But Samuel Leibowitz had prepared for this moment. He strode up to the witness box and began his cross-examination.[52]

"Would you have any objection, Schlitten, if you could gain something by it, to tell a lie under oath?" he asked.

Adlerman objected immediately, but the unanswered question hung in the air, as Leibowitz had intended. Next, he began to grill Schlitten about his background. Did he know a Chinese man in Berkeley, California, named Mike Woo or Won? Hadn't he been engaged in extorting money from illegal Chinese immigrants? Hadn't he been involved in opium smuggling? Wasn't he known around the garment district as an anti-union "gorilla"? Why did his ex-wife divorce him? How much alimony had he paid her?

Schlitten's answers to Leibowitz's accusations were evasive. "I did business with a lot of Chinamen," he acknowledged, though he denied the extortion and smuggling allegations. He insisted that he wasn't a "gorilla" but conceded that garment factories paid him for protection from unions. He admitted that he dealt poker and owned a pool hall in East Harlem, that he'd previously plotted with Stein and Greenberg to hold up an armored car in Boston, that his ex-wife had divorced him for sleeping around, and that that he'd neglected to financially support his three-year-old child.

After Leibowitz had finished shredding Schlitten's reputation, he asked him to repeat his description of the murder. "Has this story been memorized by you?" he asked, after Schlitten had finished repeating his testimony, almost verbatim.

"No, sir," Schlitten answered. "It is just something I can't forget."

"Is the kind of language that you used on direct examination in describing the occurrence and the sound that came, is that the language you have been in the habit of using every day of your life?"

"Well, when I get around nice people, I talk nice. When I get around people that are not so nice and talk from the side of the mouth, I talk the same way."

"As a matter of fact, that language has been written out for you, this story that you have narrated in this fast, glib fashion?"

"It is a story that is up in my head, I guess."

Then Leibowitz dug into Schlitten's motives for participating in the crime. "Now, what did you tell Stein when he said that he wanted to kill somebody in a car or take somebody for a ride?" he asked. "By the way, you knew that to mean he wanted to kill somebody, didn't you?"

"Yes," Schlitten admitted, cringing a little.

"Were you short of money when it was proposed to you to become an accessory to a murder?"

"No, sir," he answered softly.

"Well, was it friendship for Stein that drove you to take part in a murder?"

"Partly friendship."

"Did you consider it a favor that you were doing?"

"Not exactly . . . he told me I would get a thousand or two thousand dollars out of this thing."

"And you were ready by reason of that to go and take part in a murder?"

"Drive the car."

"Well, to take part in a murder, right?"

"Yes," Schlitten murmured miserably.

"Did your conscience bother you when the proposition was made to you to go out on a murder?"

"It didn't bother me then." It was only later, he said, after Stein's arrest and all the news reports, that his conscience began to gnaw at him.

"Your conscience started to bother you about your part in the crime?" Leibowitz asked innocently, goading his witness on.

"That's right."

"That's why you made the confession?"

"That's right."

"The first time in your life your conscience bothered you?"

"That's right."

"It didn't bother you when you made the plan to go out to murder?"

"I didn't realize the horror of it."

"Did it bother you after you saw the woman, as you say, with a dying gasp coming out of her mouth. Did your conscience bother you?"

"It bothered me a little, but I had company and I forgot that."

By this point, Schlitten was cowering in his seat and mumbling replies into his palm. Leibowitz seized the opportunity to exploit his distress by changing tack. "Would you lie to save your life?" he asked abruptly.

"I would not," Schlitten answered cautiously, starting to discern the trap that the attorney had laid for him.

"Did you try to make a bargain that if you testified for the district attorney, for the prosecution, that you would be allowed to go scot-free? Did you, yes or no?"

"I can't answer it yes or no," Schlitten hedged. After more prodding, he admitted that McLaughlin had promised him immunity, but he insisted that he'd already decided to confess.

"You were ready and willing to tell this story whether you got immunity or not, weren't you?" Leibowitz prodded him.

"I was."

"You were ready to take the consequences of going to the chair, of convicting yourself of murder, weren't you?"

"I was."

Leibowitz turned to the jury and raised his eyebrows, telegraphing astonishment that a professional criminal, a man willing to abet murder for a couple thousand dollars, would sacrifice his life rather than tell a lie.

"In other words, if I understand you correctly," he said slowly, "you would have told the story as you have told it here, even though it meant your going to the electric chair. That is what you want this jury to understand. That's right, isn't it?"

"Yes, sir."

"That is because your conscience bothered you?"

"That's right."

Leibowitz turned to the judge with smug satisfaction. "May we have a five-minute recess?" he asked, giving the jurors time to process what they'd witnessed.[53]

The next day, Adlerman tried to repair the damage by returning the jury's attention to the horror of Vivian Gordon's strangulation. "You were asked yesterday about the 'cackle,'" he said to Schlitten. "Will you demonstrate to the jury what kind of sound it was that you heard in the automobile?"

"Do I have to?" Schlitten asked mournfully.

"Well, if you can, can you repeat it?"

"Can't they use their own judgment about that? Somebody gasping for breath and can't catch it and makes this quizzing noise." Schlitten's face reddened and his eyes bulged as he voicelessly pleaded with the prosecutor. He swallowed once and started to perspire. The courtroom went silent in anticipation. Finally, he gesticulated with his hands and emitted a rasping, gurgling gasp.[54]

Adlerman glanced triumphantly at the jurors, confident that Schlitten's performance would leave a deep impression on them. But Leibowitz countered with another ferocious cross-examination. His objective this time was not to rattle the witness but to present the jury with an alternate narrative.

"Isn't it a fact that you and Izzy Lewis took Vivian Gordon out and murdered her?" he shouted at Schlitten.

"No, sir."

"Isn't it a fact that Izzy Lewis went back to the garage with you because he had been with you all evening?"

"No, sir."

"And aren't you shielding Lewis and hanging it on Stein?"

"No, sir."[55]

After Schlitten was finally released from the witness stand, Leibowitz applied the same tactics to the state's remaining witnesses, Izzy Lewis and David Butterman, who corroborated parts of Schlitten's testimony. During cross-examinations, he cycled between attacking the witness's credibility and promoting counternarratives. "Isn't it a fact that you and Schlitten took Vivian Gordon up to Van Cortlandt Park and murdered her?" he bellowed at Izzy Lewis. Lewis denied the accusation but undermined his own credibility when he proudly described himself as "a man of the underworld" and in the next breadth promised to "tell the truth, and nothing but the truth."

"And you would do it at the risk of your life?" Leibowitz pressed him.

"I ain't afraid of nothing," Lewis answered.

"Never told a lie in your life?"

"No."[56]

With Butterman, Leibowitz focused on the witness's criminal record and his reputation as a fence for stolen goods. Butterman helpfully described himself as a "jobber" and said that he didn't ask questions when people sold him furs and other loot. He also admitted that he knew Noel Scaffa, though he denied asking the private eye to help him sell information to the police.[57]

After Adlerman rested the state's case, the rest of the trial went quickly. Leibowitz did not call Stein or Greenberg to the stand, fearing that their criminal records would bias the jurors against them. Instead, he called their relatives, who presented alibis to the court. Stein's youngest sister, Marguerite Norris, an attractive, stylish young woman who worked as a film extra and occasional cabaret dancer, testified that her brother had taken her to see a movie at the Roxy Theatre at 10:00 p.m. on the night of the murder. When they came out at midnight, she said, they dined and danced at a nightclub in Times Square, then took a subway home.[58]

During her cross-examination, Adlerman raised questions about some of her activities. "Didn't you go out riding with a keeper in Bronx County Jail?" he asked. She initially denied the charge but then admitted that she'd gone to dinner with "an old gentleman there who was very nice." She claimed that he'd insisted on escorting her home in a taxi after the meal.

"Didn't you approach this keeper for the purpose of communicating with material witnesses against your brother, especially David Butterman?" Adlerman pressed her.

"No! No!" she cried as she jumped to her feet and burst into tears. "My brother is innocent—he is innocent, no matter what you say!" she screamed.[59]

Greenberg's older sister, Sophie Wallerstein, was more composed as she testified in Yiddish, through a translator, about her brother's whereabouts on the night of the murder. Their mother had died on February 20. In accordance with Jewish mourning ritual, she sat shiva for seven days, during which she and her family didn't leave home. She said that Sam stayed in her fourth-floor apartment during that time, sleeping in their mother's old bedroom, which had no fire escape. "We have no telephone," she added. "He received no messages during that time and sent none." Her sixteen-year-old son, Sydney, also testified that "Uncle Sam" had stayed with them and recalled that he had gone to bed around midnight on February 25. The Wallersteins were strong witnesses, and Adlerman's cross-examination was less effective than it had been with Marguerite Norris, though he got Sophie Wallerstein to admit that Greenberg hadn't covered his head with a yarmulke while sitting shiva, which suggested that he wasn't particularly observant of Jewish law.[60]

The last witness that Leibowitz attempted to call was Irving Ben Cooper, but when he cried out the investigator's name, he received no answer. He later explained that he'd sent one of his staff members with a subpoena to Seabury's office but that Cooper could not be found there. Rather than delay the trial to track down the witness, Leibowitz decided to rest the case.[61]

He delivered his closing arguments when the court reconvened on Monday, June 29. Given his success during the Schlitten cross-examination, he decided to put aside the more outlandish theories about Scaffa and Crater, focusing instead on Schlitten's credibility and police misconduct. "If I can convince you that Schlitten is a liar, the People's case crumbles," he told the jury. "There is no case, except possible prosecution of stolen goods, but that is all."

He began by reading off ten pages from Schlitten's testimony, noting that the witness had repeated the same story twice. "Does that story of Schlitten, as I have read it to you, sound like the language of a thug, a gorilla? Or does it sound like lawyer talk?" he asked the jury. "That could not have been told as it was unless it was memorized. It is impossible that any human being could tell such a story unless it was coached, drilled and hammered into him . . . I am going to convince you that it is improbable, a fake, a fraud. This whole case is a damnable conspiracy. It is so perfect and tailor-made that its very perfection creates suspicion as to its truthfulness.

"Schlitten is a thief, a crook, a gorilla, a racketeer, a dope peddler, a lying coward," he shouted. "What caused this man to violate the code of the underworld and become a squealer, a rat? Bunk! It was the fear of the cops. Oh, how strong they are—these crooks—when they have a gat* in their hip pocket! How brave they are when they break into the apartment of a woman and rob her! But take them into the back room of a station

---

* A pistol, originally shorthand for gatling gun.

house, and let a six-foot cop smash them once or twice in the face—and see what happens."

At this point, Adlerman objected, but Leibowitz shouted over him, "Then what happened to him on the night of his confession? What happened between 6:30 p.m., when he was brought to police headquarters, and 1:45 the next morning, when he made his statement? Before he gave them the statement, he told officials what he wanted. It was: 'You let me go—you give me my freedom—you save my life—and I'll give Stein to you.'"

Turning to the defendants, he roared, "Stein and Greenberg, they want to strap you in the chair and burn you, to satisfy public clamor. That's what they want to do!" Then he whirled back to the jury. "Are you going to railroad innocent men on the testimony of rats?" he asked rhetorically. "Are you going to send Stein to the chair to vindicate a contemptible police frame-up? All I ask is a square deal and a verdict of not guilty."[62]

After a recess, Adlerman rose to deliver the prosecution's rebuttal. He again recounted the events of the crime, but this time, he explicitly pinned the murder on Radeloff, noting that the defense had not called him to testify. "If I were John A. Radeloff, I would tear down the doors of this courthouse in my eagerness to get here and take the witness and to deny the testimony linking me to the case," he exclaimed. "Why wasn't John A. Radeloff produced by the lawyer who has an office in the same building with him?"

Leibowitz rose to object, but now Adlerman shouted out over him, "If Radeloff did not know Stein why was he not called to testify? Vivian Gordon was about to complain to someone. Was she about to make a complaint to someone about this lawyer? Was she about to complain to the Bar Association or some other authority? Vivian risked and lost her life because she was about to talk, and the gangster code was put into action. Stein took her life, and he took her life for the man who directed and inspired this horrible murder—John A. Radeloff, the lawyer."[63]

In addition to implicating Radeloff, Adlerman spent much of his time attacking the defense lawyer, rather than the defendants. Calling the frame-up allegations "ridiculous and nonsensical," he asked Leibowitz why he hadn't called Noel Scaffa to the stand and accused him of "concocting the whole story and dumping it into the lap of the police commissioner."

"How often have you stood up in a courtroom and proclaimed the innocence of a client when you knew in your heart that he was guilty?" he shouted. "Mr. Leibowitz said he would prove this case a contemptible frame-up by the police," he continued, turning to the jury. "He was groping in the dark for a defense. The alibi he interposed was a trick of defense attorneys." Pivoting back to Leibowitz, he thundered, "You know that the defense of an alibi is a lie. Why didn't you tell that to this jury in your opening?"

When he had exhausted his attacks, Adlerman concluded his statements by urging the jury to consider the symbolic significance of Gordon's murder, alluding not to police corruption but to the crime wave that had swept the city. "There is a greater issue," he said, "that a witness about to give information was killed, and the killing of that witness is a challenge to our American institutions, to law and order. . . . The time has come when hired and paid assassins can no longer ply their nefarious trade in the city of New York. The time has come to stamp out that kind of murder. I say to you that Stein, the mastermind, got Greenberg to help him carry out the mandate of John A. Radeloff."[64]

And yet John Radeloff hadn't set foot in the courtroom. It was true that Leibowitz hadn't called him to testify, but neither had Adlerman. Nor had the district attorney arraigned him with the other defendants, for the case against him was too weak to prosecute. All the evidence of Radeloff's culpability was either circumstantial or based on hearsay, and the incriminating diaries weren't even admissible in court, since there was no one alive to testify that Vivian Gordon had written them. Any successful prosecution of Radeloff would require a confession from Harry Stein, and the only leverage for persuading a hardened criminal like Stein to cooperate was a death sentence. So, though Radeloff wasn't on trial, his fate depended on the same twelve jurors who would determine Stein's guilt.

The all-male jury—women were ineligible to serve as jurors in New York at the time—deliberated for three and a half hours and reached unanimity on the third vote. At 4:15 p.m., the foreman announced the verdict: Not guilty on all counts. Surprised gasps erupted from the gallery, and even Stein looked dazed for a moment before breaking into a grin. Greenberg yelped for joy and tried to rush across the room to thank the jurors before a bailiff steered him back to his seat. "Dank Gott! Dank Gott!" cried his sister, Sophie Wallerstein, as cheering friends and relatives surrounded the defendants.[65]

After Justice Cohn briefly restored order, Adlerman asked to him to "let the jury know what kind of a man this Stein is," adding with disgust, "He's got a police record as long as your arm!"

"The jury's verdict is final," Cohn retorted. When he adjourned the court, Greenberg bolted out to the corridor and began kissing abashed jurors on both cheeks, exclaiming, "Thank you! Thank you!" He exchanged a few more celebratory embraces with his relatives and then dashed outside to a taxicab without even saying goodbye to Stein.[66]

Stein had also begun thanking the jurors—in a more restrained manner—but his gestures of gratitude were cut short by Sheriff Robert Moran, who put a hand on his shoulder and informed him that he was under arrest for the assault and robbery of Lola Baker. They soon departed in a squad car bound for the Manhattan prison colloquially known as the Tombs.[67]

Leibowitz, when he spoke to the press afterward, expressed little concern for the fate of his client. He waved off the new charge as "piffle," preferring to focus on his courtroom triumph. "The verdict shows that what I said at the start is true: the whole case was a contemptible frame-up," he gloated. "I said it would fall flat as a pancake, and it has. A case tailor-made by the police department will never hold water before a jury of twelve sensible men." He concluded with one last dig at Charles McLaughlin. "The Bronx District Attorney ran out on the case," he sneered. "He knew he could never get a conviction of guilt so he refused to try it himself."[68]

McLaughlin didn't respond to the taunt or comment publicly on the verdict at the time, but months later, he described the jury's decision as "one of the rankest miscarriages of justice I have ever known. Verdicts like that—brought in by ignorant juries, juries that have been intimidated or juries that are easily fooled—are responsible for gang conditions in America today. Killers are turned loose—scot free—even with the best of evidence against them. Something—I don't know just what—will have to be done about it."[69]

Neither Commissioner Mulrooney nor Inspector Bruckman spoke to the press about the case after the trial. John Radeloff was also conspicuously silent. The verdict may have frustrated the Bronx district attorney's

The *News* front page of July 8, 1931, reports that the "entire contents of three 'dynamite diaries' of the slain Broadway beauty, Vivian Gordon, became public yesterday. . . . At right, entries in her diary last Feb. 13, in which, referring to Radeloff, she wrote 'if anything happens to me, he is to blame.'" At bottom, a headline for a Seabury probe story inside.

plans to prosecute him for murder, but he still had to contend with the extortion charge brought by his former client, so he may have decided that it would be prudent to lie low. Or perhaps he became reticent because the newspapers were no longer willing to pay for his commentary.

But even as the various men connected with the case went quiet, Vivian Gordon's own voice was at last allowed to be heard. One week after the trial, the *News* published the complete "dynamite diaries," redacting only certain names. The blistering words that tumbled from the tabloid pages defied Gordon's killers' attempt to silence her. Anyone with two cents to spare could read her own account of the last two years of her tempestuous life— from the clover days of 1929, when the champagne flowed and her love affair with Radeloff smoldered, to the bleak winter of 1931, when she stuffed money under her mattress and bitterly tabulated her dwindling assets.

The last few diary entries were like bread crumbs marking the path of her demise. "Saunders, note 1500, due Oct. 5, 1929," she wrote on January 3, 1931, referring to Harry Stein by the alias he'd given her. She evidently began harassing him for repayment because on January 30, she recorded, "Saunders here," confirming that they'd been in contact. The next day, she added, "Greenberg returned from A. C.* Sunday." It's not clear whether she knew Greenie personally, but she knew about him. Stein may have told her that they'd succeeded in establishing the diamond-smuggling operation that they'd scouted in Europe in 1929. The idea that a petty crook like Greenberg would obtain diamonds worth $250,000 was preposterous, but if Stein embellished his friend's reputation, Gordon may have been desperate enough to believe him. "Stoney," she wrote on February 2, meaning that she was broke.

Two days later, she dropped her final, enigmatic bread crumb. "I believe that John A. Radeloff and Sam Cohen pulled that jewelry deal alone," she wrote. Was "jewelry" a reference to the diamonds? Or was she referring to another one of Radeloff's "rotten deals." Either way, the diaries insinuated that her tragic fate was twisted up with his. He may not have gone to prison for her murder, but she had exposed his depravity to the world.[70]

---

* Probably Atlantic City.

In addition to the diary, the *News* article quoted a poignant poem that the detectives had found in Gordon's apartment near the datebooks. She had transcribed the verses by hand from a poem called "The Twilight of Love," by Gilbert Parker, which had been set to music by composer Edward Elgar in 1910. Her version of the poem was abridged, and it sometimes diverged from the original, as if she had reproduced it from a faulty memory.

> ADIEU! The sun goes wearily along.
> The mist creeps in on the sleepy town,
> Hoteens* drift o'er the shadowy mere—
> Adieu, dear heart—for night is near
>
> Sometime shall the veil between
> The things which are and which might have been
> Be lifted back and mine eyes shall see
> And the meaning of all be made clear to me.
> Adieu![71]

---

* It's unclear what Gordon meant by "hoteens," possibly an error in the printed reproduction. The original Parker line reads, "The white sails bend to the shuddering mere."

PART III
CATCH A TIGER

CHAPTER 10
THE TIN BOX BRIGADE

If Vivian Gordon hadn't been murdered, Samuel Seabury's anti-corruption drive might have ended with the magistrates' inquiry. The removal of a few judges, prosecutors, and police officers would have been sufficient for Governor Roosevelt to demonstrate independence from Tammany Hall, leaving him free to devote his attention to the presidential race. Mayor Walker would have continued to play the charming cad and would likely have been reelected to a third term. Seabury would have been commended for his work, and his lengthy reports would have been filed away in the archives of the Appellate Division.

But Gordon's unsolved murder and her daughter's tragic suicide catalyzed the collective fury and frustration that had been simmering below the surface. Amid crippling unemployment, spiraling crime, rampant graft, and chronic institutional incompetence, New Yorkers cried out for a savior, and "Saint" Seabury came marching in. His work ethic and seriousness of purpose delivered results seldom seen from the city's blundering, self-interested officials. His righteous dignity, which might have drawn scorn at the height of the Jazz Age, inspired trust in the depths of the Great Depression.

By April 1931, Seabury was juggling three separate investigations. The original "vice quiz" had been commissioned by the courts, but the Crain inquiry and citywide investigation were empowered by the state, which necessitated a change of headquarters. Seabury promptly moved his growing operation across the street from the County Courthouse to the State Office Building, a nine-story rectangular block of gray granite striated by fluted pilasters and crowned with lion cornices. Today, it houses the Manhattan Marriage Bureau, among other agencies. Brides and grooms loiter in the elegant lobby, nervously checking the numbers on

OPPOSITE: The State Office Building on 80 Centre Street, New York, in an undated photograph. First opened in 1930, it is now called the Louis J. Lefkowitz Building.

their tickets as they await their turn in the chapel. But when construction began in 1928, political officials slated the building for a grander if less romantic purpose, a single edifice large enough to house all the New York State offices in Manhattan.[1]

"The State Office Building is a very crowded building with eight busy elevators discharging passengers, and taking on others," recalled Frances Perkins, FDR's industrial commissioner. Seabury used to break for lunch around 12:30, she said. "Whether an order was given for the purpose of protecting his life or not, I don't know, but as soon as he signaled an elevator all other passengers were discharged on the floor above. The elevator operator came to a pause on Seabury's floor and nobody was allowed in that elevator except Mr. Seabury and his associates. They were brought down with a bang to the ground floor. The elevator operator threw open the door. Seabury was always preceded out of the elevator by a man—whether he was a strong-arm man for his protection I never did know, but he was an impressive looking fellow. Then came Mr. Seabury with a young man on either side of him and a couple bringing up the rear. Any one of those might have been guards or legal aides. It could have been any of these things. I think they were probably a combination of both. Sometimes there would be other people, but there were always at least five who sort of surrounded him.

"Mr. Seabury was always dressed in a dark suit. In the wintertime he wore a black Chesterfield overcoat, with a velvet collar—very elegant and very correct. He wore a black hat, which was not the sombrero type, but smallish and elegant looking. It was very correct, never banged-up, always carefully brushed. He was a very handsome man with white hair and a very ruddy face. . . . As soon as he stepped off the elevator and into the corridor all traffic stopped. Everybody just stopped short wherever they were. People would stop, look and whisper, 'That's Seabury. There's Seabury.' Everybody stopped short, whether they were the baker's boy come to get an order, or whether they were a window cleaner seeking to get a permit to insure his employees, or whether they were a man on crutches looking for the Compensation Bureau to see when he could get his compensation, or whether they'd come about the parkways, or whether they were public officers. They all stopped short. Utter silence would reign while Seabury went out to lunch. Everybody stopped and looked. Traffic stopped and fell away. He walked through it with his head in the air going out to lunch. Nobody said a thing. That was that."[2]

Even as he staffed up and moved to new offices, Seabury still found time to personally attend hearings in the magistrates' investigation. While the Vivian Gordon investigation was ongoing, before Stein's arrest, Seabury called Officer Andrew McLaughlin to the stand. Dressed in a natty, chocolate-colored, double-breasted suit, the handsome vice cop smirked and wisecracked until Seabury finally scolded him: "We don't want your witticisms." Under questioning, McLaughlin breezily confessed to embellishing arrest reports, explaining that he found it necessary to "build up the case on imagination." For example, he said, he only described suspects as "fully clothed" when they were wearing hats and coats. "Any other condition between that and the

Officer Andrew McLaughlin leaves the courthouse after being questioned by Samuel Seabury in New York, March 13, 1931.

nude was called 'partly dressed,'" he admitted. Yet he complained that it had become much harder to win convictions since the magistrates' investigation started. "It used to be that if you saw a woman talking to some men on the street, you could get her convicted on a charge of prostitution," he said, "but now all of the magistrates except Jean Norris throw those kind of cases out."[3]

Then Seabury turned to his finances. After McLaughlin testified that he kept only one savings account, the investigators submitted evidence that he had opened four accounts at three separate banks as well as two brokerage accounts. In the last two years alone, the records showed that he had deposited $35,800 into these accounts, mostly cash. Yet his total earnings from fourteen years at the police department amounted to only $26,950 before taxes, and he'd lost $3,376 in the stock market. Asked to explain the source of his income, he claimed that he'd won money by gambling on horses, prizefights, baseball, elections, and craps, though he refused to provide any details about where he did his betting.[4]

One week later, Commissioner Mulrooney dismissed McLaughlin from the police force, depriving him of his golden goose at the height of the Depression. More than a dozen colleagues suffered the same fate. Six were indicted for perjury, including McLaughlin's partner, Richard Ganley, though not McLaughlin himself.

On April 11, two days after Harry Stein's arrest, Mulrooney dissolved the entire vice squad, demoting almost 400 officers back to patrol beats, and began rebuilding the squad from scratch. He also enacted new rules that restricted vice raids and prohibited the use of stool pigeons. Such radical actions would likely never have happened without the political pressure created by Vivian Gordon's murder. Once again, the Furies unleashed by her killing had exacted retributions far beyond what she'd ever imagined. But her posthumous vengeance was not yet complete.[5]

Magistrate Henry Stanley Renaud had conveniently left the city that winter on a four-month vacation in Del Ray, Florida. When he returned, Seabury immediately put him on the stand. Smartly dressed in a gray suit, green shirt, wide wing collar, and green bow tie, the little magistrate squirmed in the witness chair as investigators grilled him about the harsh sentence he'd meted out to Gordon in 1923. They also questioned his courtroom policies, which had facilitated the shakedown racket, and inquired about his fancy cottage upstate, though they submitted no evidence that he'd taken bribes.[6]

Polly Adler also returned from Florida in the spring. At first, she hid out in a private apartment, but Seabury discovered her address and sent his process servers to stake out the building in rotating shifts. When the madam finally broke down and accepted the court summons, they escorted her downtown to the State Office Building, where she was introduced to Irving Ben Cooper.[7]

"He wasted no time on the amenities and began firing questions at me the moment I came into the room," she wrote in her autobiography. Day after day, Cooper grilled her for hours about her connections in the vice squad and the courts as he stared her down with "sharp blue eyes that seemed to bite into me." She gave him nothing, though, for she couldn't afford to be known as a "squealer." Betraying her clients and associates would have ruined her business and potentially jeopardized her health. "I continued to impersonate a clam so successfully that Irving Ben Cooper was tearing his hair out," she recalled with smug satisfaction.

Finally, Cooper turned Adler over to Seabury, whom she described as "a gray-haired, fine-looking man who treated me with meticulous politeness." He asked her matter-of-factly whether various Tammany officials, including Mayor Walker, had ever held celebrations at her brothels. She answered his queries with a placid "no" or "I don't recall" until he suddenly pulled out a police officer's paycheck with a partial signature on it. "Is this yours?" he asked mildly.

Her face went pale. "It's not my handwriting," she answered feebly.

"Think it over, Miss Adler," Seabury replied. "Refresh your memory, and give me your answer tomorrow."

Her memory needed no refreshing. The check was from Officer Irwin O'Leary, one of her confidantes on the vice squad, who'd given it to her in payment for a stock deal that they'd done together. She'd begun to endorse it but stopped for fear the check might incriminate her, as indeed it had. She admitted nothing to Seabury, however, nor to Cooper, who continued to interrogate her for weeks without success.[8]

But Officer O'Leary wasn't as steadfast when Irving Ben Cooper put him on the stand and demanded, "When did you first meet Polly Adler?" The relentless attorney barraged the officer with sharp questions and incriminating documents until O'Leary broke down and admitted the truth about his stock deals with Polly Adler, though he insisted that he had no idea that she was in the brothel business. No one was fooled by this evasion, however, least of all Commissioner Mulrooney, who promptly dismissed O'Leary from the police force. Polly Adler was furious about O'Leary's capitulation and embarrassed by the press coverage, but she wasn't prosecuted and returned to her business with her reputation for discretion intact. If anything, Seabury's investigation benefited her financially, since she was no longer obliged to pay "protection money" to the vice officers who used to shake her down.[9]

As the pace of the magistrates' investigation slackened, Seabury turned his attention to District Attorney Thomas Crain, the subject of his second investigation. The governor had instructed him to examine Crain's competence, which was trickier than investigating criminal activity. The investigators couldn't build a case by subpoenaing bank accounts or interviewing victims. Moreover, the district attorney's authority was too broad to review everything, so Seabury focused on a specific type of crime, labor racketeering, for which enforcement had been conspicuously lax. He picked a handful of cases that Crain's office had investigated but never prosecuted and proceeded to investigate them himself. In a matter of weeks, his team was able to unearth substantive evidence of criminal racketeering by various union leaders. He determined that Joseph "Socks" Lanza, union rep for the United Sea Food Workers at the Fulton Fish Market, had taken bribes from employers to undercut union negotiations. Similarly, "Tough Jake" Kurzman purported to be a union organizer but had received payoffs from hat manufacturers to suppress millinery unions. Joseph Mezzaco, head of the cloth-shrinking union,* had stashed hundreds of thousands of dollars in a bank account, which the district attorney could have easily subpoenaed the same way Seabury did.[10]

As Seabury examined witnesses, he had to deal with frequent interruptions from the vociferous Samuel Untermyer, who constantly tried to obstruct the hearings and badger witnesses. When Seabury scolded him for hostile cross-examinations, the famously aggressive lawyer complained, "That means we can come here, but we cannot defend ourselves. Why haven't we the right to attack witnesses?

"If your honor plans to prejudge these charges," Untermyer continued, his voice rising to a shout, "I want to know about it right now."

Seabury's face reddened, but his voice was calm and imperious as he admonished the lawyer. "I consider your statement of prejudgment to be

---

* Cloth-shrinking, also known as fulling, is a process for finishing raw wool fabric by using heat and pressure to tighten and smooth the threads.

a gross impertinence," he said coldly. "Whatever your opinion may be, I must ask you not to express it before me again."[11]

The following day, Untermyer began the defense arguments by calling Deputy District Attorney Charles Pilatsky to the stand. Youthful, chubby, and loquacious, Pilatsky described Crain's investigative process in such detail that attorneys on both sides were obliged to ask him to be brief. He boasted that during the previous November, he had examined more than 500 witnesses covering 150 complaints of racketeering, adding that he kept a sign on his office door that read, "Racketeering Complaints Received Here."

"How many indictments came out of your investigation?" asked John Kirkland Clark, Seabury's chief counsel in the Crain investigation.

"Two," the young man replied.

"And how many of those were dismissed without trial?" Clark followed up.

"I understand, both of them," Pilatsky answered.

"I think the whole thing is ridiculous," Untermyer interjected. "There are thieveries, robberies, murders and all sorts of things going on all the time, but the district attorney doesn't have to discover them. If that were the case, you might as well do away with the police department."[12]

Next, Untermyer called Crain himself to the stand. Pale and ill at ease, the district attorney crossed his legs and bit his lip as he defended his decisions not to prosecute the cases that Seabury's investigators had uncovered. He admitted that his office had failed to curb rampant racketeering but blamed Governor Roosevelt for tying his hands.

"Is there a man on the face of the earth who can walk into the district attorney's office and stop racketeering?" Untermyer asked him.

"No," Crain answered. "Not under the present laws."

"What would you suggest might be done?" Seabury inquired.

"I think that the warfare can be waged more effectively if the district attorney is not attacked from the rear," he replied, a sardonic smile on his thin, compressed lips.[13]

Seabury flushed angrily in reaction to the unsubtle dig at his commission, acidly noting that Crain had been elected in November 1929, long before the investigations began. The hearing soon deteriorated as the opposing counsels shouted objections over each other. "The voices of Mr. Untermyer and Mr. Clark blended and jumbled like two radio stations in the same spot on the dials, and their words were indistinguishable," the *New York Times* reported. "Mr. Crain smiled broadly in evident enjoyment, while Mr. Seabury, obviously provoked, struggled to maintain his judicial calm and dignity."[14]

After the courtroom contretemps, Seabury ordered a one-week recess. In the interim, he worked with a Columbia professor named Raymond Moley to analyze Crain's record. Moley was a brilliant, forty-five-year-old, chain-smoking polymath from a small Ohio town. He'd received his PhD in political science, but his roving intellect would not be bound to a single academic field. In addition to government and politics, he wrote about public law, criminal justice, American history, and economics. Nor was he content to be confined to an ivory tower. He had worked on Roosevelt's gubernatorial campaign in 1928 and directed research at a state commission on justice administration after the election. He would later lead President Roosevelt's famous "brain trust" and help write some of his most famous speeches.[15]

Seabury was also impressed by Moley. He initially hired the professor to assist with the magistrates' investigation and later brought him into the Crain inquiry. On April 30, Moley arrived in Seabury's courtroom armed with eleven charts and graphs. One chart, entitled "Homicides 1930," included three bars representing 273 homicides in Manhattan, 144 indictments, and 55 convictions. A 20 percent conviction rate was bad enough, but the third bar was subdivided. Moley explained that the 55 convictions included 47 guilty pleas to lesser charges. Only 8 defendants were convicted as originally charged, he said, and 6 of those were charged for manslaughter. During the deadliest year in Manhattan's history to date, only 2 people were convicted of murder in the first degree. The *Times* summed up the day's hearing with a damning headline, "CRAIN WORST PROSECUTOR IN 25 YEARS, MOLEY SHOWS BY REVIEW OF THE RECORDS."[16]

After Moley's presentation, Seabury moved swiftly to wrap up the hearings and prepare his report to the governor. He took a conservative, legalistic approach to his assignment, drawing a distinction between ineffectiveness and gross incompetence. Though he castigated Crain's inefficiency and negligence, he ultimately concluded that the district attorney's failures were not "so general in scope or so gross in character as to warrant a recommendation that he should be removed," and he recommended that the City Club's charges be dismissed.[17]

Professor Moley criticized this decision when he wrote about the investigation years later. Arguing that his analysis had "proved a case of gross inefficiency," he blamed the outcome on Seabury's "incredible legalism." Yet Seabury had another, more pragmatic reason for not recommending Crain's removal. "There was no question that we could have, if we wanted to," recalled one of his assistants,

A c. 1933 portrait of Professor Raymond Moley, who assisted Seabury with the Magistrates' and Crain investigations.

George Trosk, "but we had advance information that, regardless of what the report said, Tammany's leadership was going to nominate Crain anyway. And that meant he would win in controlled Manhattan. We knew we would be left looking silly—that it would look like a repudiation of our efforts. So we decided to do the practical thing, set out all the damaging evidence that we uncovered but not recommend removal. We knew that there was much more to be gained by continuing the investigation into the whole city's affairs."[18]

Even Crain's exoneration wasn't sufficient to placate Samuel Untermyer, though. "The proceedings were conducted with a degree of bias rarely known by a distinguished judge who appeared to be acting throughout as a prosecutor," he complained to the press. "Judge Crain was entitled to an unstinted, unqualified vindication. . . . I shall wire the governor to ask a hearing for the purpose of arguing the injustice of the criticisms."[19]

Roosevelt quashed this request with a curt rebuke. "The governor considers the statement in this morning's paper by Mr. Untermyer to be a gratuitous and unprofessional attack on the governor's commissioner," he communicated through an intermediary. "The governor resents and has long resented the attitude of counsel for Mr. Crain in this case."

To Seabury, he issued a warm letter of appreciation. "I desire to compliment you and thank you for your painstaking, considerate and tireless efforts in this case," he wrote. "The reading of your report impresses me with the soundness of your reasoning and the complete fairness of your conclusions."[20]

Roosevelt's gratitude was sincere. From his point of view, the outcome was ideal. By assigning the distinguished judge to investigate Crain, he had publicly demonstrated that he wasn't afraid to stand up to the Tammany Tiger. At the same time, Seabury's conclusion had freed him from the necessity of directly confronting the bosses whose support he still sought.

And yet Seabury's third investigation had only just begun, and Roosevelt's greatest test was yet to come.

The first public hearing in the citywide investigation opened on July 21, three weeks after the Vivian Gordon verdict. Though Seabury's offices had moved across the street, the hearings were still held at the County Courthouse, in a huge courtroom with white walls, varnished oak furniture, and four broad windows that allowed sunlight and street noise to profane the solemnity of the proceedings. Attired as usual in a dark business suit, starched collar, and silk tie, Judge Seabury strode into the hearing room, his dark eyes flashing and his face flushed with nervous excitement. He handed his cane and boater hat to an assistant, and sat down at the counsels' table.[21]

His role in these proceedings differed somewhat from his previous investigations. Instead of presiding over the hearings himself, he was to act as chief counsel for a legislative committee made up of four state senators and five members of the Assembly, who sat in a row at the long judge's bench. Samuel Hofstadter, a cherubic up-and-coming state senator with round wire-rim glasses, chaired the committee. He and his fellow Republicans had the majority, but a couple of Tammany stalwarts did their best to impede the proceedings. Assemblyman Louis Cuvillier, bald and hollow-eyed, indulged in long, incoherent rants about the illegality of the citywide investigation, much to the dismay of the court stenographers, who had difficulty transcribing his garbled diatribes. Senator John McNaboe was more comprehensible but completely insufferable. He'd only served a few months in the Senate. Before his election, he'd been an assistant district attorney under Crain. By coincidence, he'd unsuccessfully prosecuted Vivian Gordon in 1930, based on Joseph Radlow's extortion allegations. McNaboe later claimed that he'd "received instructions" from Tammany Hall to obstruct the citywide investigation, which he attempted to do so frequently and obnoxiously that even Cuvillier called him a "disgrace to the Democratic party." Seabury eventually appealed to Hofstadter to remove him from the committee on the grounds that he was "impudent, objectionable, obstreperous, insulting and loud-mouthed." When McNaboe realized that even Cuvillier supported his removal, he finally shut up.[22]

The primary witness at the first hearing was William Doyle, the former horse veterinarian accused of bribing city officials. He was an old-school Tammany loyalist, ruddy and bald, with round glasses like Chairman Hofstadter's. In the early 1900s, he'd used political connections to obtain an appointment as chief veterinarian for the fire department, which still used horses to pull the engines. In 1918, a Tammany mayor appointed him chief of the Bureau of Fire Prevention, but he resigned three years later after a deadly fire killed six people. Indicted for negligently waiving the building's fire code violations he avoided conviction and soon found a more lucrative career as a lobbyist. Exploiting his Tammany connections and knowledge of New York City's regulatory practices, he amassed over a million dollars obtaining elusive permits for businesses and construction projects that violated the city's zoning rules, height restrictions, and fire codes. His clients paid him huge fees, partly in cash, which he used to bribe the relevant officials, a practice known as fee sharing.[23]

Seabury wasn't particularly interested in Doyle himself, but he was eager to find out who had shared those fees. He wasn't the only one. The year before, a federal prosecutor had charged Doyle with tax evasion and tried to pressure him to reveal the recipients of his bribes, but the "millionaire horse doctor" refused to talk. He pleaded the Fifth Amendment in response to every question, and the jury deadlocked.

When Seabury took up the case, he tried to prevent Doyle from employing the same artifice. The Fifth Amendment only protects witnesses from incriminating themselves, so Seabury arranged for the Hofstadter commission to grant Doyle immunity, which would enable him to testify without risk of self-incrimination. But when he took the stand, Doyle invoked the Fifth Amendment anyway, calmly declining to answer any of Seabury's queries as he recited over and over, "I refuse to answer that question because it might tend to incriminate me."[24]

He also received support from McNaboe and Cuvillier, who seemed to have appointed themselves defense counsel. "I think we must appreciate that this witness is not charged with any crime," McNaboe protested. "There is no proof of corruption. Get your proof."

Cuvillier chimed in with a convoluted exposition on the witness's legal rights. At the conclusion of his diatribe, he characterized the investigation as a political charade orchestrated by the Republican state leader.[25]

Seabury never raised his voice nor spoke impolitely in the courtroom. When irritated by troublesome adversaries, he often laced his words with sarcasm, but he delivered them with a smile. After Cuvillier accused him of serving Republicans leaders, however, his faced flushed, and the veins on his neck bulged. "If that were a fair argument," he rejoined, a slight tremor in his voice, "then it would certainly follow with equal logic and equal force that all those who seek to obstruct the activities of this committee . . . were actuated by the leader of Tammany Hall." Cuvillier went quiet, and the courtroom burst into applause.[26]

Seabury resumed his interrogation after the ovation subsided, but when Doyle continued to plead self-incrimination, he finally gave up and appealed to the committee. "In view of the contumacious action taken by this witness," he said to Chairman Hofstadter, "I ask the committee to cite this witness to the Supreme Court of the State of New York." Cuvillier and McNaboe protested vociferously, but the Republican majority granted Seabury's request, citing Doyle for contempt. The sergeant-at-arms then escorted the witness upstairs to the courtroom of Supreme Court Justice William Black, who sentenced him to thirty days in the county jail.[27]

The sentence wasn't immediately carried out, however. That evening, Boss Curry placed a phone call to Justice Henry Sherman of the Appellate Division, who was vacationing in Lake Placid, a resort community 300 miles north of the city. Sherman had been nominated for the Supreme

Court by Curry's predecessor in 1927, so he owed Tammany a favor. After the call, Doyle's attorney secretly took a train to Lake Placid to meet with the judge, who issued an emergency stay the next morning.[28]

Seabury was furious when he learned about the unorthodox intervention. Suspecting foul play, he subpoenaed the phone records of the Park Lane Hotel, where Boss Curry kept a suite that he used for business. When Seabury discovered Curry's phone call to Lake Placid, he leaked the news to the press and publicly accused the Tammany boss of engaging in "trickery and deceit" reminiscent of Boss Tweed's nineteenth-century regime. The full Appellate Division promptly removed the stay and upheld Doyle's sentence. Even Justice Sherman, embarrassed by the disclosure of Curry's call, voted with the majority.* [29]

Doyle spent three weeks in the New York County Jail on West 37th Street before Seabury recalled him to the stand. Rattled by his brief incarceration, the horse doctor changed tack. Instead of pleading the Fifth, he now denied that he'd bribed anyone, despite previously claiming that his testimony would incriminate him.

"Are you now trifling with this committee?" Seabury demanded, exasperated.

"I am making a serious and truthful answer," Doyle insisted.[30]

The courtroom was packed that day. Before the doors opened at 10 a.m., the line to enter had wound through the corridors and spilled down the front steps. Those who arrived early found seats in the gallery or jammed into the aisles. The rest tried to listen to the proceedings from the crowded hallway. When Seabury strode into the room to begin the hearing, many of the spectators clapped and applauded, heedless of the furious percussion from Senator Hofstadter's gavel.[31]

---

* Benjamin Cardozo, chief judge of the New York Court of Appeals (and later a Supreme Court associate justice), subsequently overruled the Appellate Division, arguing that the Hofstadter commission lacked authority to grant Doyle immunity. Seabury praised the ruling as "learned," even though it went against his interests. Following Cardozo's instructions, he then persuaded FDR to call a special legislative session, during which the Republican majority authorized the commission to grant immunity, which prevented Doyle and other witnesses from hiding behind the Fifth Amendment.

They hadn't come to see Doyle's testimony though. The source of the excitement was the second witness that day, John F. Curry. Wearing a businesslike double-breasted suit, his white mustache neatly trimmed, the Tammany boss slipped into the building through a rear entrance and sauntered into the courtroom in the midst of Doyle's testimony. Seabury had just delivered a stinging rebuke to Doyle, eliciting more applause, when another group of spectators spotted Curry and began to cheer. The competing acclamations for Seabury and Curry, accompanied by Hofstadter's rhythmic pounding, resounded through the chamber.

"I will ask you, Chairman, to keep order in this court," McNaboe smirked.

"Senator, you can see that I'm doing everything I humanly can to maintain order," Hofstadter retorted sharply. "If there is any repetition of that again," he warned the spectators as Curry took his seat, "we will have to escort every person participating in it out of the room."[32]

But the cheering resumed when Curry took his turn on the witness stand. Red-faced and sweating in the heat, he freely admitted that he'd called Justice Sherman on Doyle's behalf, adding that he'd solicited two other judges as well. Instead of expressing shame or remorse, he brazenly insisted he had not only a right but a duty to intervene in the case. "I, as the representative of the Democratic organization of the city of New York, was expecting someone to test the constitutionality of the committee's powers," he uttered in a thick New York accent, "and therefore when the request came for my aid, I was glad to be of service."

Seabury, flabbergasted by Curry's audacity, tried to badger him into acknowledging the impropriety of his intervention. "Don't you think it is a great piece of impertinence for you, simply because you are the leader of Tammany Hall, to undertake to find for a lawyer in a litigation pending in the Supreme Court, a judge before whom an application can be made?" he demanded.

But Curry refused to concede, casting himself as a fearless champion protecting his constituents. "This is a *crucification*, if it can be had, of the Democratic party of the City of New York," he declaimed. "I would step on the gas wherever it would be of help to the Democratic party of this city."

"Tell it to him, boss!" someone shouted as Hofstadter pounded away.

The commission's Tammany loyalists also jumped into the fray. "Why do we have to sit here and hear this all over again?" McNaboe complained after Seabury repeatedly tried to elicit remorse from Curry.

"You are not required to sit here if you do not wish to, Senator," Seabury acidly retorted.

"The minority protests to browbeating and insulting witnesses by counsel," Cuvillier chimed in, weaving his body up and down as he spoke. "I warn you now, unless it is stopped, the minority will walk right out of the court now."

"Now, now," Hofstadter wearily chided the Democrats, "this is a joint legislative investigation."

"It is not joint; it is disjointed," Cuvillier grumbled, but neither he nor McNaboe left their seats.[33]

When the objections subsided, Seabury resumed his wrangling with the Tammany boss but made no further headway. At the end of the day, the commission voted along party lines to sustain Doyle's contempt charge, but even this minor victory proved pyrrhic. The next day, Doyle posted $20,000 bail. "Well, we've licked them," he told his cellmates as he departed. A liveried chauffeur delivered him by limousine to his mansion in New Jersey. A few months later, the judges of the Appellate Division dismissed the contempt charges against him.[34]

The newspapers tut-tutted about Curry's intervention in the case, and the New York Bar Association opened an investigation into Justice Sherman's actions, but neither man faced consequences for the incident. Though largely symbolic, Curry's action was celebrated by the Tammany base, and it succeeded in sending a message to other witnesses subpoenaed by the commission.[35]

After the hearing, Seabury, who had consumed nothing but a glass of milk since breakfast, ate dinner and decamped for a few days to his summer home in the Hamptons. The Tiger had parried his first thrust in the citywide inquiry, but his team was busy sifting through bank records and privately interviewing witnesses. They had already found plenty of material for future hearings, and there was more still buried, waiting to be found.[36]

* * *

One of Seabury's most valuable witnesses was a talented police captain named Lewis Valentine. Valentine had once led the department's "shoofly" squad, a special agency tasked with investigating police misconduct. The zeal with which he'd pursued this mandate had not endeared him to his fellow officers, but the real trouble started when he tangled with Tammany leaders. While digging into links between police officers and illegal gambling rings, he discovered that many of the biggest games were hosted at Tammany clubhouses. These operations were protected by barred windows, "icebox doors," and posted sentries, which delayed Valentine's raiders long enough to tip off the gamblers. By the time they gained entry, the officers often found the city's most notorious gamblers playing checkers, dominoes, and double solitaire at two o'clock in the morning.[37]

One of Valentine's lieutenants finally caught the gamblers in the act by ascending to the roof of an adjacent building and dropping suddenly into their den. As he was arresting the perpetrators, Tammany district boss Thomas Farley arrived at the clubhouse and began shouting for him to stop. The arrests continued, but Farley followed the patrol wagon to the station house and arranged bail for the detainees. The charges were later dismissed.[38]

Valentine's exploits caught the attention of Mayor Walker, who pressured the police commissioner, Joseph Warren, to shut down the gambling raids. Warren resisted, but his tenure was brief. In 1928, he was replaced by Commissioner Grover Whalen, who immediately demoted Valentine from deputy inspector to captain and disbanded the shoofly squad. A year later, Tammany nominated Thomas Farley for sheriff of New York County, and he was duly elected. Among other law enforcement tasks, the county sheriff was responsible for suppressing illegal gambling.[39]

But Valentine had kept records from his work, and he told Seabury all about his investigation of gambling rings at Tammany clubhouses. The judge also subpoenaed Farley's bank records, which revealed that the sheriff had deposited $360,000 in seven years—equivalent to $7 million today. Of those deposits, $53,000 had come from his official salary. The rest was cash.[40]

In October, Seabury called Farley to the stand to explain the source of his substantial wealth. "Will you tell the committee where you could have gotten that sum of money?" he asked.

Farley, a strapping man of 250 pounds with prodigious black eyebrows that dominated his face, spoke with an incongruously high voice. "It represented moneys I had saved," he answered.

"Where did you keep these moneys that you had saved?" Seabury continued.

"In a safe-deposit box at home in the house."

This answer amused Seabury. During the magistrates inquiry, several witnesses had claimed to have stockpiled their money in tin cashboxes, and it had become a running joke in the courtroom. "In a little box in a safe?" Seabury asked with a smile.

"A big safe," Farley answered.

"But a little box in a big safe?"

"In a big box in a big safe."

"And, Sheriff, was this big box that was safely kept in the big safe a tin box or a wooden box?"

"A tin box," Farley replied earnestly, provoking titters from the spectators.

Seabury, smiling again, returned to the mysterious bank deposits. "Now, in 1930, where did the extra cash come from, Sheriff?" he asked.

"Well, that is . . ." Farley hesitated. "My salary check is in there."

"No, Sheriff," Seabury countered, "your salary checks are exclusive of the cash deposits."

"Well, that came from the good box I had," Farley replied. Laughter now rippled through the courtroom.

"Kind of a magic box?"

"It was a wonderful box."

"A wonderful box," Seabury said, pausing as the laughter continued. "What did you have to do—rub the lock with a little gold, and open it in order to find more money?"

"I wish I could." Farley answered.[41]

Sheriff Farley's choice of financial repository wasn't unique. John Theofel, the Tammany boss in Queens, had enriched himself by selling Supreme Court appointments. He too told Seabury that he kept his money in a box, much to the amusement of the court.

"What kind of box?" Seabury asked.

"A metal box," Theofel answered, eliciting more laughter.

"Was it a gold box?" Seabury pressed.

"No."

"Was it a silver box?"

"No, sir."

"Was it a tin box?"

"I don't know whether it is tin or what other metal it is. I can bring it."

The irrepressible Senator McNaboe chose this opportune moment to intercede. "I don't think the State of New York is warranted in spending $500,000 to find out whether anyone has any money in a tin box or not," he protested.

"Or a diamond box or a gold box," added Assemblyman Cuvillier, helpfully.

"It could be done more economically if the Senator did not interrupt," Seabury rejoined.

But McNaboe would not be silenced. "There is no law in this country that says a man must keep it in a bank," he retorted earnestly. "He can keep it in a sock, if he wants to."

"With that vindication of tin boxes, may I come back and ask the witness if he kept it in a tin box?" Seabury asked the chairman. Then he returned to grilling Theofel about his misbegotten wealth.[42]

These exchanges provided plenty of fodder for the papers, which mocked the "Tin Box Brigade" parading through Seabury's courtroom. Yet the charges against the witnesses were serious. In addition to the gambling clubs and the sale of judicial appointments, Seabury's investigators uncovered evidence of bribery in the award of pier leases in Manhattan and a bus franchise in Staten Island. They revealed that the city clerk responsible for administering marriage licenses banked $64,000 a year with the help of "voluntary" contributions from happy couples. They chronicled the activities of the district boss in the Bronx, who manipulated city permits to benefit his businesses and crush his competitors. Most egregious of all, they demonstrated that Tammany leaders had diverted millions of dollars of unemployment relief to undeserving loyalists.[43]

Seabury's revelations were politically damaging to Tammany, but few of the perpetrators suffered direct consequences. The massive bank accounts he uncovered were damning, but the witnesses had been granted immunity, and most of the evidence was too circumstantial to prosecute in any case. The marriage clerk was forced to return his gratuities to the city, and Sheriff Farley was reluctantly dismissed by Governor Roosevelt, but most of the officials who testified in Seabury's hearings kept their jobs, and some were even promoted. As long as the Tammany regime held power, the abuses were destined to continue. To ensure that his efforts wouldn't wash back into the sea once the outrage subsided, as so many other attempts to clean up the city had done, Seabury needed a knockout blow, a scandal from which the Tiger could not recover.

CHAPTER 11
LITTLE BOY BLUE

JAMES ELLIS, A THIRTY-ONE-YEAR-OLD ACCOUNTANT FROM BROOKLYN, spent the summer of 1931 combing through bank records. His boss, Samuel Seabury, had tasked him with examining Jimmy Walker's finances in hopes of discovering how the mayor supported his extravagant lifestyle. Chase National Bank, where Walker held an account, dutifully complied with Seabury's subpoenas and assigned a teller to assist his staff with its research. Ellis found nothing improper or suspicious among the canceled checks and deposit slips during his first review, but he decided to examine the records a second time in case he'd missed something. During the next pass, the teller who was assisting him asked for two days' leave to care for his ailing wife. The bank initially refused the request, but Ellis contacted the teller's boss, assuring him that his research could wait for a couple of days.

When the teller returned to work, he expressed his appreciation for Ellis's kindness by offering him a tip. "This will probably cost me my job," he said, "but you fellows left out one thing on your subpoena."

"What's that?" Ellis asked.

"Letters of credit," the teller replied.

Hearing this, Ellis put on his hat and raced back to the State Office Building. "I may be onto something," he told two of his colleagues, Louis Molloy and Phil Haberman. "Quick, make out a subpoena for letters of credit."

When it was done, all three returned to the bank and delivered the new subpoena to a bank executive who had assisted them with previous information requests. This time, however, the executive gave them a runaround, stalling until closing time without providing the documentation.

Dismayed, Ellis, Molloy, and Haberman hurried back to headquarters and charged into Seabury's office. As they described the bank executive's stonewalling tactics, the judge became uncharacteristically agitated. Then he settled himself and thought silently for a while.

"I will make a suggestion," he said at last. "If you think well of it, why don't you go over to the Chase right now, present my compliments to Mr. Winthrop Aldrich, and say that if there is such a needed document in his bank and it is not in my possession by tonight, his bank will not be open tomorrow."

This matter-of-fact threat astonished the three assistants, for the Hofstadter commission's authority didn't extend to shutting down banks. But Seabury explained that he would subpoena every teller and officer at the bank, if needed, leaving no one available to conduct business.

Ellis, Molloy, and Haberman returned to the bank, but when they asked to see Winthrop Aldrich, the bank president, a secretary told them that he wasn't available. They asked for the first vice president, but he wasn't available either. They asked to see any vice president, but the secretary explained that, unfortunately, they were all with Mr. Aldrich. "It was obvious that the impregnable Chase Bank was scared to death," one of the investigators recalled.

Finally, they delivered Seabury's bold threat to close down the bank. The stunned secretary hurried away and returned sometime later with a vice president who handed them a document—a record of a $10,000 letter of credit issued by Chase Bank on behalf of James J. Walker on August 9, 1927. The document listed six checks drawn against the credit at various locations in Rome, Venice, and Paris. The dates coincided with a European tour that Walker had taken that autumn.

Letters of credit were commonly used to facilitate foreign transactions, so the existence of the letter wasn't in itself remarkable. But who had paid the bill? The document was stamped "CASH," which made the payer impossible to trace. Or at least it would have been if Mayor Walker had stayed within his budget. The $10,000 cash payment covered his first five checks, but he also drew a sixth check for $3,000 in Paris on October 4. The bank apparently had trouble obtaining payment for the overdraft because the transaction wasn't closed until January. Next to the final check, a clerk had scrawled, "Paid J. A. Smith check on First Trust & Deposit Company, Syracuse, for $3,047.50. Int. 5%."

The three investigators raced back to Seabury's office. As he read the document, the phlegmatic judge couldn't mask his excitement. Even without knowing the details, he had no doubt what the letter of credit signified. "This is a fatal blow to Tammany Hall," he gloated. "It is the first time in the history of New York that a mayor is caught taking money with his actual receipts for the bribe."[1]

It took Seabury's team months to unravel all the secrets portended by the mysterious letter of credit. Their first step was to identify the person who'd paid Walker's overdraft, easily accomplished with a subpoena to the Syracuse bank that had issued the check. The man's name was J. Allen Smith. He lived in Syracuse but had an office in Manhattan, where he served as a sales executive for an Ohio-based manufacturer of buses. For the past few years, however, he'd spent much of his time promoting a transit company in New York City called the Equitable Coach Company, incorporated in 1925.[2]

The transit venture was the brainchild of a Tammany state senator from Brooklyn named John Hastings. Thick-set and dough-faced with slicked-back hair, Hastings wore expensive English suits and custom-tailored shirts, drove big cars, and kept his cigars in a box labeled, "THESE CIGARS ARE MADE ESPECIALLY FOR SENATOR JOHN A. HASTINGS." He had a talent for exploiting other people's money and a history of attaching himself to highly speculative ventures, including Mexican gold mines, experimental jet engines, synthetic marble tiles, and a chemical process for allegedly converting copper into gold.[3]

The Equitable Coach Company was the most elaborate of his pet projects. He persuaded several businessmen from Ohio to invest $40,000 each in a financial institution called the Equitable Trust Company, which was used to fund the transit venture. The partners hoped to obtain an exclusive franchise to provide bus service in four of the five boroughs, but their ambitions went beyond buses. Internal documents laid out an audacious scheme to take over all of New York City's surface transportation facilities, and possibly its subways as well, with the expectation of multimillion-dollar profits.

To accomplish their plan, they needed political connections. This was Hastings's contribution to the venture. He was close to Jimmy Walker, whom he'd befriended while serving with him in the state Senate. After Walker became mayor, Hastings asked for his help to win the bus franchise. The assistance was sorely needed, for the Equitable Coach Company was among the weakest candidates to apply for the franchise in 1927. Its backers had no transit service experience and woefully insufficient capital. But Walker agreed to help, and he succeeded in muscling past the objections of the other members of the Board of Estimate, who eventually consented to award the franchise to Equitable.

His intervention wasn't motivated entirely by friendship, though. After Seabury's investigators connected J. Allen Smith to the overdraft check, they subpoenaed the Equitable Trust Company's records and confirmed that Walker's original letter of credit had been paid by the trust as well. The timing was telling. Chase Bank issued the letter the day before Walker signed the bus franchise authorization.[4]

The letter of credit was obviously a kickback, but Seabury hoped to build a stronger case before he went public with the evidence, and he doubted that the mayor's indiscretions were limited to a single bribe. His investigators continued hunting for accounts in Walker's name at banks and brokerage offices but kept coming up dry until, once again, an off-the-record tip pointed them in the right direction. The source this time wasn't a lowly teller but John Prentiss, senior partner at Hornblower & Weeks, a large brokerage firm. After a representative from the firm reported that Walker had no account there, Prentiss paid a confidential visit to Judge Seabury and told him about an anonymous account that hadn't been mentioned in the report. It had been opened in March 1927 with $102,000 in cash and supplemented by large deposits for several months until the total reached $263,000. Then, on August 9, the same day that Walker received the letter of credit from Equitable, the account holder suddenly withdrew the entire amount in cash and closed the account. Prentiss was the only person at Hornblower & Weeks who knew the identity of the account owner, a forty-six-year-old accountant named Russell Sherwood.

At the time he made the deposits, Sherwood was working as a bookkeeper at Walker's old law firm, where he earned $3,000 a year. Handsome and mild-mannered, with round, shell-rimmed glasses, Sherwood came from an old upstate family. In addition to his financial acumen, his employers valued his discretion, and he was often called upon to handle sensitive personal matters. Both of these attributes were particularly valuable to the mayor. Walker was a great spender, but he had no head for personal finance. Even writing checks was too much of a chore for him. So he employed Sherwood, unofficially, as his money manager. Not a money manager in the usual sense of a financial expert who handles investment portfolios, though he did that too. Sherwood literally managed all of Walker's money. He personally picked up his boss's paychecks and deposited them with various banks and brokerages. He drew up checks for Walker's expenses and took them to the mayor to sign. He also disbursed money to Walker's wife, his sister, and, more discretely, his mistress, Betty Compton, who received a total of $75,000 in cash, securities, and a letter of credit.

The magnitude of the capital that passed through Sherwood's hands made the original $10,000 letter of credit look paltry. Seabury's investigators uncovered deposits of nearly $1 million—equivalent to $20 million today—between January 1, 1926, when Walker took office, and August 5, 1931. Three-quarters of those deposits were cash. Most were at brokerage accounts, which, unlike bank accounts, permitted anonymity. The money had come from numerous parties in a variety of ways, but the contributors shared one thing in common. Like the backers of the Equitable Coach Company, they all wanted something from the city of New York.[5]

William Scanlan, salesperson for the Butler Manufacturing Company, paid Sherwood $6,000 after receiving a $10,000 commission for selling ten streetsweepers to the city. The deal was consummated over objections from the city's chief engineer, who protested that Butler's "so called dustless sweeper is not dustless, and it does not sweep clean."[6]

Investment bankers Samuel Ungerleider and J. A. Sisto held large stakes in the Checker Cab Corporation, which was lobbying for regulation to shut down independent taxi drivers. Ungerleider paid Sherwood $52,000 for stock that was worth $30,000. Sisto brought Walker into a stock deal that netted the mayor $26,000 without having to put up a cent.[7]

Paul Block, an advertising tycoon and newspaper owner, had invested heavily in a new kind of synthetic marble tile, another one of Senator Hastings's schemes. Block and Hastings hoped to sell the newfangled tiles to city contractors for subway station walls. In addition to the financial opportunity, Block was starstruck by the famous mayor and hoped to buy his favor and friendship. He opened a joint brokerage account with Walker, to which he contributed half a million dollars over two years. Walker contributed nothing, but Sherwood withdrew $246,693 on his behalf.[8]

Seabury and his assistants spent months following the money trail, yet the provenance for much of it remained mysterious. They would have benefited greatly from Sherwood's testimony on the subject, but he'd skipped town. Seabury, hoping to keep his discoveries from the press, had originally invited the accountant to come in voluntarily for a private interview in August. When the offer was declined, Seabury issued a subpoena, but Sherwood left the city before the process servers found him. He was located a week later at a hotel in Atlantic City. Seabury had no authority outside the state, so he persuaded the United States Attorney for the Southern District of New York to open an investigation for tax evasion. But when the news broke, Sherwood vanished again.

He resurfaced a couple months later in Mexico City. Reporters tracked him down at the Ritz Hotel, where he was relaxing with a new bride, whom he'd secretly married while on the lam. "I do not know whether my honeymoon will last one month or six months," he told the journalists. "If there's anything I don't like it's publicity."

Russell T. Sherwood (second from left), would not return to the United States until June 1, 1933. He is seen here with his attorney, Michael Dee (left, with coat over arm), at a Hoboken, New Jersey, beer garden the day of his reappearance, where he told reporters that he had been hiding because he did not want to interfere with "personal matters" involving the former mayor.

Mexico's extradition treaty didn't extend to tax evasion, so even the feds couldn't reach him there, but Seabury dispatched two of his process servers to Mexico City anyway. They staked out the hotel lobby from the comfort of easy chairs until Sherwood arrived, then introduced themselves and handed him a subpoena. Though they couldn't compel him to return, the delivery of the subpoena empowered a New York judge to hold Sherwood in contempt. Yet even a $50,000 fine wasn't sufficient incentive to induce the fugitive witness to return to Manhattan.[9]

While Seabury struggled to retrieve Russell Sherwood from Mexico, echoes of the Vivian Gordon case resonated from two trials in the Criminal Courts Building, just up the street from Seabury's office. In one courtroom, Lola Baker testified that Harry Stein, whom she knew as Charlie Brooks, had chloroformed her at her apartment after they returned from a date in April of 1930. "When I regained consciousness, I was on the floor, a comforter was on my head and something was wound around my neck, choking me," she recounted. "He was stooping over me. I tried to bite him and he hit me on the jaw with his fist." She survived the attack but said that Stein broke two of her ribs and stole $2,100 worth of jewelry.[10]

Once again, Stein's family members offered an alibi, but his new lawyer lacked Sam Leibowitz's genius, and the Baker case wasn't so heavily influenced by sensational press coverage. This time, the jury convicted him, and the judge sentenced him to 25 years in prison.[11]

Meanwhile, in a second courtroom, John Radeloff faced extortion charges from a tailor named Jacob Garber. Echoing the shakedown schemes in the Woman's Court, Garber accused Radeloff of conspiring with the owners of the tailor shop where he worked to frame him for stealing clothes worth $110. He testified that Radeloff and his employers forced him into a car and threatened to charge him with grand larceny unless he paid them $1,600.[12]

Radeloff admitted receiving $1,600 from Garber but claimed that it was merely a legal fee. If so, the fee was exorbitant, especially since Radeloff didn't even represent Garber in court, leaving the unfortunate tailor to plead guilty. Nonetheless, the smooth-talking lawyer managed to convince the jurors, who acquitted him hours after his old associate, Harry Stein, was convicted.[13]

In contrast to the breathless coverage of Vivian Gordon's murder trial in the spring, news of the two verdicts was consigned to brief articles in the back pages of the papers at the end of October 1931. New Yorkers had moved on from the Vivian Gordon, and a new scandal had seized their attention. The flight of Mayor Walker's mysterious "personal business agent" from Manhattan to Mexico City with Seabury's process servers at his heels signaled a thrilling twist in the Seabury saga.

The Tammany members of the Hofstadter committee, outraged by the prospect of Walker being dragged into the citywide inquiry, went ballistic. "Why is it that the mayor of the city of New York is not called instead of pussyfooting, wire-tapping, and peeking through key holes to get his agent?" Senator McNaboe demanded. "I protest vigorously against this kind of tactics."

"I say it is an insult to the citizens of the city of New York," Cuvillier added, "and an insult to the city of New York and its fair name."[14]

In response to these objections, Seabury introduced evidence that Sherwood and Walker shared a safe-deposit box at Chase Bank. The revelation first elicited gasps from the spectators, then laughter when Seabury noted that the rental agreement included two keys to a tin box. "WALKER'S BANK BOX SHARED BY SHERWOOD," the *News* proclaimed on its front page the next day, followed by a two-page report on the "surprise testimony," including photos of Walker, Sherwood, and a copy of rental agreement signed by both men.[15]

But no one outside Seabury's office had any clue about the immense graft that he and his staff had uncovered. After dropping the bank box bombshell on October 29, 1931, the investigators managed to keep the findings secret for five more months while they methodically built a case against the mayor. "By the time we were ready to present the evidence, we knew all about his finances and financial dealings," recalled Seabury's assistant, George Trosk. "Perhaps more than Walker knew about himself."[16]

Finally, in April 1932, one year into the citywide investigation, Seabury began summoning Walker's benefactors to the stand. One by one, he grilled the witnesses about the money and securities that they'd given the mayor.

William Scanlan, the streetsweeper salesman, professed ignorance of his $6,000 payment to Sherwood, even though Seabury had the canceled check. Unfortunately, he testified, he'd recently burned all his financial records in a bonfire in his backyard. J. A. Sisto, the Checker Cab investor, admitted sharing stock market profits with Walker and acknowledged speaking to him about taxi regulation but insisted that he invited the mayor into the stock deal because he "felt a great deal of admiration for him." Sisto's coinvestor, Samuel Ungerleider, claimed that he'd paid Sherwood an exorbitant price for stock as a favor to a mutual friend who'd asked him to give the accountant a hand. Yet the friend subsequently testified that he'd had nothing to do with it.[17]

Paul Block, the synthetic tile investor, claimed that the $246,000 he'd lavished on Walker was simply a gift for a dear friend. He described a conversation with his ten-year-old son, who asked him how much the mayor was paid. "Can he live on what he gets?" the boy wondered. "Well, I suppose he can," Block recalled answering, "but it probably is a difficult problem." Turning to Seabury, Block said, "And, Judge, I want you to believe me that it entered my mind then that I was going to try and make a little money for him."[18]

Senator Hastings's name came up repeatedly during the hearings. He had a hand in several of the ventures connected to Walker, especially the Equitable Coach Company. During the testimony of one of the bus company promoters, Seabury presented two telegrams in which the partners had encoded Walker's name by referring to him as Hastings's "boy friend." Hastings became so agitated by the allegations that he barged into the anteroom where Seabury was relaxing between hearings and seized the fifty-nine-year-old judge by the label of his coat. "You coward!" he screamed, shaking his fist in front of Seabury's pince-nez. "You political blackmailer you! You're afraid to call me to the stand!" One of Seabury's assistants rushed over and restrained Hastings until a police officer dragged the senator, still shouting, out of the room.[19]

Hastings finally received his invitation to take the stand the following week. At the hearing, he behaved so obnoxiously that Seabury commanded him to "stop bellowing and answer the question." In his calmer moments,

Hastings admitted that he'd helped arrange the $10,000 letter of credit at Chase Bank but claimed that the money had come from his colleague, former New York State Senate Minority Leader Bernard Downing, who had accompanied Walker to Europe. According to Hastings, Downing had collected a shared fund to cover the group's travel expenses, which he'd planned to convert to American Express checks before the trip. Hastings persuaded him to route the money instead through the Equitable Trust Company as a favor to his business partner, J. Allan Smith, one of the trustees. So Downing gave the $10,000 in cash to Hastings, who delivered it to Smith, who deposited it briefly in the Equitable trust before withdrawing it to purchase the letter of credit for Walker.[20]

At least that was Hastings's story. But the convoluted tale raised several questions that he was unable to answer. Where did Downing get the cash? Why did Smith want to pass the money through Equitable? And why was the letter of credit given to Walker? Neither Smith nor Downing were available to disentangle these mysteries. Smith had gone abroad and could not be found, and Downing had conveniently passed away in 1931.

Seabury rarely criticized his witnesses' explanations directly. He just raised his eyebrows and kept asking questions, encouraging them to dig themselves deeper into the farce. After Hastings testified about receiving $10,000 from Downing, Seabury asked him whether he'd given his colleague a receipt.

"I don't know. I may have," Hastings replied.

"Well, did you, Senator?" Seabury pressed.

"I have a hazy recollection that I did."

Seabury grilled Hastings about the supposed receipt for several minutes. What did it say? Who wrote it out? Did anyone else see the receipt? What kind of stationery was it written on? Was it handwritten or typed? Had he tried to locate it? Hastings became increasingly flustered by this barrage of questions and at one point accused Seabury's investigators of illegally seizing the receipt from his personal papers.

"How do you think a receipt that you wrote out and gave to Senator Downing could have gotten into your papers?" the judge asked incredulously, prompting laughter in the court, which only made Hastings more agitated.[21]

By the end of the exchange, Seabury, without ever contradicting his witness or accusing him of lying, had made clear to all that there was no receipt, and indeed, that Hastings had fabricated the entire transaction.

Day by day, hearing by hearing, Seabury spooled out the story of Mayor Walker's corruption, using the absurdity of the witnesses' answers to bolster his case. Newspapers printed the highlights on their front pages and savaged the witnesses in their editorials. The *Times* and the *Herald Tribune* published complete transcripts of noteworthy testimonies.

With each hearing, the public anticipation intensified. Few were shocked by the greed or mendacity of little-known politicians and businessmen, but Jimmy Walker was a beloved figure. Many New Yorkers didn't believe, or didn't want to believe, the accusations emanating from Seabury's courtroom. Fans and critics alike were eager for the mayor to come to the courthouse and pit his agile wit against the judge's formidable intellect.

No one looked forward to the confrontation more than Seabury himself. He'd spent nearly two years ripping away the plaster façade of New York City's bureaucracy to expose the rot that lay behind it. Starting with magistrates and vice cops, he'd worked his way up the municipal hierarchy, and now, at last, he would call the mayor himself to answer for his transgressions. Seabury and his staff had prepared for this moment, staging mock hearings in which one of his assistants played the wisecracking mayor and others the truculent members of the committee. "Don't look him straight in the eye when he's on the stand," one of Seabury's associates advised him. "He has an uncanny ability to stare you down. Once he's caught you, you're liable to be stunned and confused."[22]

Yet even the mayor was only a means to an end, for mayors come and go. By taking down Walker in spectacular fashion, Seabury hoped to cripple the terrible Tiger, which he'd been battling all his life, and finally bring good government to the citizens of New York. He saw these hearings as an opportunity to redeem his hometown and to secure his place, at last, in the pantheon of the great Samuel Seaburys.

Though he would never admit it in public, the judge also harbored other ambitions. The Walker hearings had garnered national and international press coverage. Nearly every day, Seabury's secretary showed him clippings from newspapers across the country praising his work and mentioning him as a possible presidential nominee. The Democratic National Convention was only a month away. He hadn't done any campaigning and had no pledged delegates, but if the convention deadlocked, anything was possible. While a presidential nomination was highly unlikely, a vice-presidential opportunity seemed conceivable—provided, of course, that the presidential nominee wasn't also from New York.[23]

Unfortunately for Seabury, the governor of New York happened to be the frontrunner in the primary race, and Roosevelt certainly wouldn't select a running mate from the same state. Seabury's only hope for a spot on the ticket was to stop FDR from winning the nomination. If Roosevelt stumbled, a "dark horse" candidate might have a chance. Former Secretary of War Newton Baker of Ohio was regarded as the most likely compromise candidate if the convention deadlocked. He and Seabury were politically aligned, and a presidential ticket that featured two large swing states, Ohio and New York, would be formidable in the general election, so Seabury decided to campaign for Baker—and against Roosevelt.[24]

To this end, he delivered an attention-grabbing speech at a dinner in Cincinnati at the end of February 1932. While discussing the governor's recent dismissal of Sheriff Farley, he complained that Roosevelt had refused to act on his findings until forced to do so. "Nothing having been done about it, I, myself, filed charges before the governor and after two months' delay we got some action," he said. Later in the speech, he spoke of well-intentioned politicians who were paralyzed by fear. "They know the conditions are evil, but they fear to antagonize the power of Tammany Hall," he argued. "They soften their opposition so that while the public will not regard them as pro-Tammany, Tammany Hall will not regard them as opposed to it." He didn't name Roosevelt this time, but everyone knew whom he meant.[25]

After the dinner, Seabury delivered an abridged version of the speech on a national radio network, which attracted press coverage across the country. "Seabury in Attack on Tammany Strikes Blow at Roosevelt," the *New York Times* blazoned on its front page. "Seabury Seen as Candidate," the *Los Angeles Times* announced. "Seabury Slaps Roosevelt," the *News* trumpeted, describing the speech as "an attempt by Seabury to link up directly with the

Mayor James J. Walker, center right with hand in air, waves his fedora at the cheering crowd gathered outside the County Courthouse in Lower Manhattan, New York, May 26, 1932, before his appearance in front of the Hofstadter committee.

candidacy of Newton D. Baker, perhaps as the latter's running mate on the Vice Presidential ticket."[26]

Mayor Jimmy Walker also looked forward to taking the stand, but for a different reason. Following his advisers' counsel, he'd maintained a studied silence during the investigation, refusing to comment on the hearings, but he found it difficult to restrain himself and itched to rebut Seabury's allegations. So when the summons finally came for him to appear before the Hofstadter committee on May 25, he felt a sense of relief. After he shared the news with reporters, one of them remarked, "I wouldn't want to meet the judge."

"That's where you differ from me," Walker said cheerfully. "I'll be very pleased to meet him."[27]

The night before the hearing, three Democrats from the committee came to discuss strategy with him, but he waved them off. "There are three things a man must do alone," he declared, "be born, die, and testify."[28]

But Walker wasn't exactly alone. When his limousine pulled up to the courthouse the next morning, he found thousands of cheering supporters crammed into the square. A jubilant roar went up as he stepped out of the car wearing a one-button, double-breasted blue suit, blue shirt, and blue tie, with a blue handkerchief sprouting from his breast pocket. "Little boy blue is about to blow his horn—or his top," he'd joked with his valet while dressing.

Walker waved his fedora at the crowd and followed his police body-guards as they cleared a path through the masses. Shouts erupted as he passed, "Good luck, Jimmy!" "Atta boy, Jimmy!" "Go get 'em, Jimmy!" One spectator begged for his help to gain admittance to the courtroom. "I'd be most happy to give you my seat," Walker quipped. When he reached the top of the steps, he threw his left fist like a boxer, ducked, and grinned, and the crowd went wild.[29]

The cheers followed him through the rotunda as he made his way to the courtroom. It had been designed to hold 300 occupants, but more than twice that number had squeezed into the chamber. The fortunate ones found seats on benches, railings, camp chairs, or the floor. The rest stood in the aisles. When Walker came through the door, a cheer erupted from the back of the room and surged forward, drowning out all sounds except the pounding of Hofstadter's gavel. When the acclamations finally subsided, the chairman admonished the spectators and threatened to clear the room, a threat that he repeatedly invoked during the hearings but never carried out. "Judge Seabury," he said at last, "the committee is ready, if you are."

Seabury rose from his seat and turned to Walker. "Mr. Mayor, would you be good enough to take the stand," he said courteously. Walker stepped briskly to the simple walnut armchair chair near the judges' bench, where the committee sat. He swore an oath to tell the truth, and the long-awaited showdown commenced.[30]

Walker was much cannier than Seabury's previous witnesses and more difficult to pin down. He met the judge's questions with a fusillade of self-deprecating wisecracks, indignant tirades, and acid jibes that knocked Seabury off-balance and derailed his methodical line of questioning.

"Can't you say yes or no?" Seabury asked in frustration at one point.

"Is this an inquiry or is this a persecution of me?" Walker countered.

"There is no sign of the latter," Seabury declared.

"There is no sign of the former," Walker shot back.

At another point, Seabury chided the mayor for answering his question by "making a speech."

"Well, they're not so bad," Walker quipped. "Did you ever listen to any of them?"[31]

He played to the crowd rather than the committee members, raising an eyebrow or waggling a finger to punctuate his one-liners. The financial technicalities of the inquiry were difficult for most spectators to follow, but they gleefully responded to the mayor's punch lines with laughter and applause. When he tossed barbs at Seabury's expense, Tammany supporters in the gallery shouted, "How do you like that, Sam?" and "Let him have it, Jimmy!" until Hofstadter gaveled them into silence.[32]

"You have an appreciative audience, Mr. Mayor," Seabury drily observed after one such outburst.

The remark prompted an indignant retort from Senator McNaboe. "You have had your appreciative audience for six months!" he shrieked. "You have had Communists and Reds in here!"

Walker didn't welcome McNaboe's hysterics, though. "Please don't help," he chided the unruly senator. "I don't have to come here for an appreciative audience."[33]

He also employed a more surreptitious tactic to get under Seabury's skin. In between questions, he occasionally whispered, "You and Frank Roosevelt are not going to hoist yourself to the Presidency over my dead body," so quietly that even Seabury wasn't sure what he said.

"The Mayor keeps muttering something," Seabury mentioned to Louis Molloy during a recess. "I don't seem to be able to hear him. Do you?" Molloy had heard Walker make the remark several times but decided that telling his boss would only serve Walker's purpose. "I'm not sure, Judge," he answered evasively.[34]

Seabury spent most of the first day interrogating Walker about the Equitable Coach Company. The bus deal had proven disastrous. Four years after the mayor signed the franchise papers, the company still hadn't secured financing and was finally forced to surrender the franchise in

Samuel Seabury, left, interrogates Mayor Walker at the New York County Courthouse, May 26, 1932.

1931. During this period, Walker had repeatedly advocated for Equitable, not only in 1927 but also when the contract came up for renewal two years later, despite the company's obvious financial difficulties. In response to Seabury's questions, he acknowledged voting for Equitable's application both times, but he claimed that his friend Senator Hastings had never tried to influence him, and he flatly denied pressuring the other members of the Board of Estimate to approve the deal.

When Seabury asked him about the mysterious letter of credit, Walker offered the same dubious explanation that Hastings had provided, but his answers to the follow-up questions were slicker. He claimed that he'd contributed $3,000 in cash to Senator Downing's joint travel fund, delivered by his secretary in an unsealed envelope. No, he hadn't asked Downing for a receipt. "We weren't that kind of friends," he quipped, and laughter floated from the galleries. He had no explanation, though, for why the money had been routed through the Equitable Trust Company.[35]

The weather was unusually hot for May, reaching a high of 84 degrees in the afternoon, and the temperature was far hotter inside the packed courtroom. Seabury and Walker, in stifling wool suits, mopped their faces until their handkerchiefs soaked through. Several spectators fainted. Yet the proceedings continued all afternoon until Hofstadter finally adjourned at 5:10 p.m. "I think it has been rather a hard day for everyone," he said wearily.[36]

Walker looked triumphant when he emerged from the courthouse, but the hours of heat and strain had worn him down too. The next day, he made fewer wisecracks and shorter speeches. His voice rasped, and his temper frayed. "I am here on an inquiry, but it looks as if somebody wants my life," he railed at one point. A few minutes later, he angrily accosted one of Seabury's assistants for allegedly sneering at him.[37]

Under questioning, he cast aside his money manager, Russell Sherwood, insisting that he didn't know him well, had never touched their joint safe-deposit box, and knew nothing of the secret account at Hornblower & Weeks. He admitted that Sherwood had deposited his paychecks, drawn up checks for him, and paid his and his wife's expenses, but he claimed that the accountant had performed these services only as an employee of his former law firm. "He was never a representative of mine," he declared. "He was never an employee of mine."

Seabury had chivalrously refrained from naming Walker's mistress to avoid embarrassing the couple, but he questioned the mayor about $75,000 that Sherwood had transferred to an "unnamed person." Walker confessed to authorizing one payment of $7,500 to her, adding "there was a circumstance attached to it," but he professed ignorance about the rest.

Despite his disavowals, Walker couldn't deny or find excuses for all the financial records Seabury had accumulated, and he was forced to admit that he'd received enormous gifts from various businessmen. "I have had countless kindnesses from people," he shrugged. The $250,000 brokerage account that Paul Block, the tile investor, had shared with him was particularly egregious. Walker confessed that he'd drawn freely from the account and had transferred the money to a safe. "Not a vault, not a tin box—a safe in my house," he added.[38]

"His conduct as a witness was unbelievably inadequate," recalled Raymond Moley, the Columbia political scientist who'd worked with Seabury on the earlier investigations. "He was undocumented and unrehearsed. He could not defend his administration, because he apparently knew little of the vast government over which he had presided for six and a half years. He was quite innocent of any knowledge of his own personal finances, his own bank account or the safe-deposit box of which he had been a joint owner for years. Faced by the flood of evidence accumulated by his enemy, he stood helpless. A sea of deadly facts rolled over him—neglected duty, misplaced trust and colossal indiscretions. Walker had no defense but evasion, amnesia, cheap theatrics and shallow, unbelievable rationalizations."[39]

At the conclusion of his testimony, the exhausted mayor struck a note of humility and contrition. "Let us have done with it all," he said to the committee members. "I've had my day in court. It hasn't all been pleasant. If I have irritated the committee and if I have appeared to have been annoyed myself, I ask you to accept my apology for any discourtesy that I might have been guilty of. You will appreciate, I think, that I am a bit human and I am subject to human emotions, especially when I am forewarned for twelve months that I am going to be put on the spot."[40]

Seabury and his staff were weary too. They felt proud of their accomplishments but were dismayed by the popular support that the mayor still enjoyed despite the damning evidence they'd produced. Back at the State Office Building, Seabury looked around at their downcast faces. "This is the most discouraged group of lawyers I have ever seen," he said. "All of you are to go to your homes immediately, pack a bag, and meet in front of my house on 63rd Street two hours from now."

They spent the weekend at Seabury's house in East Hampton, roaming the sand dunes and drinking cocktails in the library. The judge had forbidden them to discuss the investigation while they unwound, but at the end of the weekend, one of his assistants violated the rule. "I think that Walker talked himself out," he mused. "I don't think that he really made a good showing, and I think that the facts we brought out are going to sink into the public's mind after the wisecracks are forgotten."

Seabury's eyes sparkled. "Well, I daresay your spirits are revived now," he said. "Let's get down to cases again."[41]

On the evening of June 8, at around 10:00 p.m., two of Seabury's assistants arrived at the Executive Mansion in Albany bearing heavy parcels.

The butler informed them that the governor had retired to his chambers, but he accepted their delivery: eight volumes of transcripts and analysis from the Walker hearings and a long letter from Judge Seabury. "The Mayor's conduct has been characterized by such malfeasance and nonfeasance in disregard of the duties of his office, and he has conducted himself, to the prejudice of the City of New York and its inhabitants, in a manner so far unbecoming the high office which he holds, as to render him unfit to continue in the office of Mayor," Seabury wrote. "In my judgment, the evidence presents matters of the gravest moment to the people of the City of New York. I therefore present it to Your Excellency, who alone, under the Constitution and the laws, is empowered to act."[42]

Roosevelt wasn't pleased to receive Seabury's gift. The political crisis that had engulfed New York City for the past two years had been harrowing, but he'd managed to navigate the perilous strait between Tammany's fangs and Seabury's vortex. With only three weeks to go before the Democratic National Convention in Chicago, he'd established himself as the frontrunner, with 494 pledged delegates out of a total 1154, and his campaign manager promised 200 more before the convention opened. But now, just as the golden fleece of the nomination seemed within reach, the current was dragging him back toward the maelstrom.[43]

A few days earlier, three national Democratic leaders had come to see him. They'd exhorted him to dismiss Mayor Walker immediately, warning that if he lacked the courage to confront Tammany, he would surely lose the nomination. Roosevelt remained calm during the visitors' harangue and courteously bid them good night once they'd said their piece. One of his aides, Marion Dickerman, had been present during the conversation. "They're right, Franklin!" she blurted out after the visitors left. "You know they are! The convention will never nominate a Tammany-controlled candidate, and that's what your enemies will call you. You must remove the mayor."

Roosevelt glared up at her from his wheelchair, angrier than she'd ever seen him. "Never," he snapped, "never will I let it be said that I climbed to a position of power on the back of someone else!" When he saw how his outburst had frightened her, he composed himself and opened up about his dilemma. He admitted that he had less to fear from Tammany than from the nation's scorn if he allowed Walker to remain, but to convict a man for the sake of his own gain would be unjust and contrary to his own principles. "This is a vital matter," he declared. "It's more important than any immediate political advantage. You must let me be myself."[44]

Yet the political calculus wasn't as clear-cut as the visitors let on, for there were also risks to alienating Tammany Hall, even if Roosevelt didn't need their delegates. He was the frontrunner because of his perceived electability. "The delegates in that convention want victory more than they want any one candidate," opined political journalist Mark Sullivan, "and capacity to carry New York is almost a guarantee of victory." But to win New York, FDR would need Tammany's support in the general election, and that support had come into question. "Roosevelt may still be nominated," Sullivan continued, "but he is a little less certain to be nominated than he was before Mr. Seabury laid the Mayor Walker scandal on his doorstep—at the most embarrassing possible time."

"Parenthetically," Sullivan added, "has it ever occurred to any Democratic leader to inject Seabury into that convention as a dark horse? Suppose somebody should make the right kind of speech about that able, patient and dogged exposer of Tammany, and make it at just the right time."[45]

Roosevelt was well aware of Seabury's undeclared presidential ambitions. He had hired Seabury's colleague, Professor Moley, to assemble a "brain trust" of academics to advise his presidential campaign. Moley revealed that the judge had asked him to write an introduction to an upcoming biography. Presidential aspirants often commissioned hagiographies to bolster their campaigns; Roosevelt had one himself. The purpose of Seabury's biography was soon confirmed by Louis Howe, one of FDR's trusted advisers. "Walter Chambers, the man who wrote the book on Seabury, on a leave of absence from the *World-Telegram*, has been in Washington and talked to some newspaper people," Howe wrote to Roosevelt. "He approached some people on Capitol Hill, especially Wheeler of Montana, to get his viewpoint on Seabury as a presidential candidate."[46]

Seabury's long-shot candidacy wasn't Roosevelt's chief concern, though. His old ally, former New York governor Al Smith, the "Happy Warrior," was a far greater threat. After losing the 1928 presidential election to Herbert Hoover, Smith had vowed never to run for office again, but during the next four years, he changed his mind. No one was quite sure why Smith had decided to run again, but one factor was resentment against the frontrunner. Having recruited FDR for governor in 1928, he'd expected more deference from his successor and was dismayed when Roosevelt replaced his cabinet officials, including Robert Moses, and neglected to consult with him on political matters.[47]

Smith's candidacy split the New York delegates. Roosevelt was popular upstate, but Smith dominated New York City and the suburbs, where Tammany held sway. He also prevailed in several other Northeast states. Had Roosevelt won those delegates, he could have reached the two-thirds majority required to win the nomination on the first ballot. At that time, most state primaries were nonbinding, so convention delegates could change their votes, a common occurrence when no one reached the two-thirds threshold. After the first ballot, the convention would become a free-for-all in which supporters of the leading contenders would compete to recruit delegates pledged to other candidates.

Roosevelt was still optimistic about his chances even if he didn't win on the first ballot, but the Walker scandal had complicated his plans. Given Seabury's evident political aspirations, Roosevelt suspected that the judge had deliberately timed the hearings in an attempt to sabotage his nomination. "This fellow Seabury is merely trying to perpetrate another political play to embarrass me," he complained to one his advisers. Professor Moley, who knew the judge fairly well, reached the same conclusion. "A month or less before the Democratic convention, Judge Seabury, as a deliberate means of embarrassing Roosevelt, threw his report on Walker onto the governor's desk," he later recounted.[48]

As usual, Roosevelt bided his time. After receiving the Walker report from Seabury, he made a public show of reviewing the documents. "I intend to devote all my spare moments to the reading and studying of the charges," he promised reporters. On June 21, he formally sent Walker the allegations and asked for a response, as he had previously done with the City Club charges. Walker acknowledged receipt and promised a reply after the convention, to which he was a delegate. And with that, all eyes turned to Chicago.[49]

At the end of June, four of Seabury's assistants, including Louis Molloy and Phil Haberman, piled into an Essex sedan and set off for Chicago. They took the northern route through Ontario so that they could stock up on Canadian Club whiskey. Seabury's biographer Walter Chambers, who'd taken on the role of campaign manager, advised them to bring booze to entice delegates. They were ostensibly supporting Newton Baker of Ohio, but their real purpose was to promote their boss.

"We had a terrific esprit de corps, even though we didn't know precisely what role to play," one of them later recalled. "We buttonholed delegates and told them we were New Yorkers for Baker of Ohio, that neither Smith nor Roosevelt would do, and that the only New Yorker respected in all parts of the country was Seabury. If they wavered, we invited them to our rooms for shots of Canadian. And, if they were considered important enough, we gave them free copies of the campaign biography."[50]

They roomed at the iconic Drake Hotel downtown, which coincidentally hosted a large Tammany contingent as well. More than a thousand district leaders, captains, families, and friends arrived on four reserved trains, each nicknamed the "Tammany Special." After disembarking in Chicago, they paraded boisterously through the streets in their straw hats to the beat of brass bands. Former sheriff Thomas Farley marched at the head of one group. Asked which candidate he supported, he replied, "Whoever Curry picks for us. We would go up and down through hell behind him."*[51]

---

* According to *The Last Testament of Lucky Luciano* (1975) by Martin A. Gosch, Richard Hammer, and Lucky Luciano, the Tammany crowd also included three mobsters: Luciano, Frank Costello, and Meyer Lansky. The disputed biography describes a supposed deal between Luciano and a Roosevelt representative to deliver Tammany votes in exchange for shutting down the Seabury investigations. "Every goddamn fuckin' move we made was getting' into the newspapers, and that bastard Seabury was really diggin' deep," Lucky allegedly told biographer Martin Gosch. "The only guy who could control Seabury was Roosevelt, and we figured that's where we had our ace. We had most of the city's delegates to the convention in our pocket, so we could stop the Governor from winnin' the state of New York; maybe that'd cost him the nomination—if a guy couldn't carry his own state, he looked like a bum."

Even if the Luciano quotes are authentic, which is doubtful, the swaggering assertions are certainly fanciful. Beyond the implausibility of Roosevelt cutting a deal with mobsters who claim to speak for Tammany Hall, Lucky's alleged recollections are historically inaccurate. Most Tammany delegates did not vote for Roosevelt; he didn't carry New York at the convention, Seabury wasn't focused on ties between Tammany and the Mafia, and the investigations were almost over by then anyway. But it's a great story.

Seabury's assistants gaped from the doorway as the Tammany horde stormed the hotel. "Wow. What we couldn't do with some subpoenas now!" Haberman joked. Ironically, the puny Seabury squad and the Tammany juggernaut were allies of sorts at the convention, both determined to stop Roosevelt. Judge Seabury, who arrived separately from his assistants, made his views on the subject clear to Professor Moley. "He was most uncomplimentary in his remarks to me about Roosevelt," Moley recalled. Seabury had brought along with him his nephew, who piped in, "Do you think Uncle Sam has any chance for the nomination?"

"Of course, the lightning might strike anybody," Moley replied, skeptically, "but you have to have a reasonable cause to support it."[51]

The convention was held in the new Chicago Stadium, the largest indoor arena in the world at that time, equipped with novel facilities like air-conditioning and a colossal pipe organ built into the ceiling. The air-conditioning was no match for the heat of 20,000 bodies in the middle of summer, though, and even the great organ struggled to be heard over the cheers and chants that constantly erupted from various delegations.[52]

On the first day of the convention, Jimmy Walker received a huge ovation when he entered the hall with Boss Curry at his side. Al Smith received a big one as well when he took his place in the Tammany section. Samuel Untermyer was there too, sporting his signature orchid in his lapel.[53]

One of the only eminent New York Democrats missing from the convention was the governor himself. According to tradition, presidential candidates were expected to feign disinterest in the dirty business of politics and to only reluctantly accept the nomination at the behest of their supporters. As a delegate, Al Smith attended the early proceedings but stayed in his hotel room during the nominations. Roosevelt remained in Albany for appearances' sake, but like the other candidates, he received frequent updates and issued orders to his staff via telephone.[54]

The nomination speeches began at 3:00 p.m. on June 30 and continued until 3:00 a.m. the next morning, interrupted only by a dinner break in the evening. After each candidate was nominated, his supporters would cheer as wildly as they could for as long as possible, competing to prove which candidate generated the most excitement. After Roosevelt's nomination, his twenty-four-year-old son, James, seized the New York delegation's standard from beside Boss Curry and charged down the aisle with it; Curry

Delegates supporting Franklin D. Roosevelt cheer for him during the Democratic National Convention in Chicago, June 30, 1932.

smiled but did not move. The cheering lasted forty-three minutes, but that was only the third-best showing. Top honors went to Al Smith's supporters, who shouted and whooped for over an hour.[55]

But in the end, it was the delegate count that mattered. The roll call began at 4:28 a.m. While some states demanded unanimity from their delegates, New York's delegation was too sharply divided, so each delegate voted separately. Jimmy Walker was fast asleep at a friend's apartment when one of his colleagues shook him awake and told him that it was time to vote. He hurriedly threw on clothes over his pajamas and took a taxi to the arena in his slippers. Though he'd missed his turn, he was still permitted to vote. "I desire that my vote be cast for Alfred E. Smith," he declared in a defiant tone, and the Tammany crowd went wild. "Good old Jimsie!" Smith gushed. "Blood is thicker than water!"[56]

Smith outperformed Roosevelt in the New York delegation, 66 to 28, but Roosevelt was the frontrunner overall, with 666 votes to Smith's 201. House Speaker John Garner of Texas came in third with 90 votes, and the remainder went to various "favorite sons"—candidates with strong regional support but small chance of winning the nomination. Despite Roosevelt's strong opening, he was still 104 votes shy of a two-thirds majority. To reach the threshold of 770, he would need to peel off delegates from his rivals while holding his own coalition together. He made slight progress in the second and third ballots, increasing his total to 683, but remained well short of the goal.[57]

When the convention finally adjourned at 9:15 a.m., Roosevelt's opponents were optimistic. His support was broad but shallow. His delegates in Iowa, Minnesota, and Mississippi were especially restive. If even one state broke for another candidate, it could trigger a stampede away from FDR, and then the convention would be wide open.

But Roosevelt's sharp-witted campaign director, Jim Farley (no relation to the former sheriff), had a plan. During the recess, he negotiated with party leaders in Texas and California. To win over the Texans, he offered Speaker Garner of Texas the vice presidency. The chairman of the California delegation, former treasury secretary William McAdoo, didn't ask for an appointment, but he requested veto power over key cabinet officials to ensure that they were sufficiently progressive. Roosevelt personally approved both offers by telephone.[58]

The fourth roll call began at 9:22 that evening, starting alphabetically with Alabama. When California's turn came, McAdoo stepped up to the microphone. "We believe that California should take a stand to end this contest," he declared. "Our belief in democracy is so strong that we feel, when a candidate comes to a convention as the choice of the popular will and has behind him almost 700 votes . . ."

As he said these words, the shouts of nearly 20,000 people filled the arena. Roosevelt supporters cheered wildly and began parading through the aisles, while his opponents booed and cursed. It took fifteen minutes for the chairman to regain control of the convention. When the shouting subsided, McAdoo resumed his speech, announcing that the California and Texas delegations had agreed to change their votes from Garner to Roosevelt.[59]

When the roll call resumed, most of the delegates who had voted for other candidates switched to Roosevelt in order to present a united front. Only the Smith supporters resisted. "Now, John!" Walker urged Curry. "Now is the time to join in." But the boss refused to embrace Roosevelt, so Walker and the other Tammany delegates followed his lead. Not a single

Smith delegate broke rank on the fourth ballot, and Smith himself refused to concede. Their intransigence caused some to worry that Tammany wouldn't support Roosevelt in the general election. To allay these fears, Boss Curry promised to back the nominee. "The convention has decided," he said brusquely to reporters. "We are good Democrats." But he didn't utter Roosevelt's name.[60]

Judge Seabury had remained quiet during the uproar. "That's it. It's all over," he said to his nephew after McAdoo spoke. That evening, he invited his despondent assistants to dinner. "There was never any danger of my being nominated," he told them good-naturedly. In any case, they still had work to do in New York. The citywide investigation was ongoing, and the charges against the mayor remained unresolved.[61]

The day after his nomination, Roosevelt flew to Chicago with his family. In a historic breach of tradition, he delivered his acceptance speech at the convention rather than waiting for party leaders to formally notify him in person. The speech had been largely formulated by Professor Moley, but Roosevelt, gripping the lectern in a blue suit with a red rose in the lapel, made it his own. Enunciating clearly and confidently in his upper-class mid-Atlantic accent, he promised bold action to combat the Depression, including public works, tax relief, tariff reduction, home mortgage guarantees, and farm relief, as well as a repeal of Prohibition. "I pledge you, I pledge myself, to a new deal for the American people," he proclaimed. "This is more than a political campaign; it is a call to arms. Give me your help, not to win votes alone, but to win in this crusade to restore America to its own people."[62]

After the speech, Roosevelt returned to Albany to prepare for the general election campaign. President Herbert Hoover was deeply unpopular, and the Democrats' prospects were favorable, but Roosevelt worried that the Walker scandal could cost him his home state. During the previous half century, only one president, Woodrow Wilson, had been elected without New York's massive delegate bloc, and there was no telling how Tammany would react to the mayor's dismissal.[63]

Over the next few weeks, he received a flood of entreaties and unsolicited advice about the Walker problem. Some warned that if he removed the mayor, he would certainly lose New York and likely Massachusetts, New Jersey, Illinois, and Connecticut. Others insisted that if he didn't remove Walker, he'd lose independents and progressive Republicans, which could jeopardize the western states. Roosevelt's campaign manager, Jim Farley, who counted Walker as a personal friend, also urged FDR to spare the mayor.[64]

In response to these conflicting appeals, Roosevelt vacillated. "On one occasion while talking over the subject," Raymond Moley recalled, "Roosevelt said, half to me and half to himself, 'How would it be if I let the little mayor off with a hell of a reprimand?' Then suddenly, as if answering himself, Roosevelt said sharply, 'No. That would be weak.'"[65]

Mayor Walker delivered his official response to Seabury's allegations at the end of July. The 27,000-word reply was even longer and more strident than his previous response to the City Club charges. Alleging that the accusations against him were founded on nothing but "malice and slander and rancorous ill-will," he cast himself as the victim of a Republican conspiracy to "blacken the reputation of the city administration," and he accused Seabury of putting him on the stand before the Democratic convention "to make me a political football."[66]

Yet Seabury's charges were far more serious and detailed than the City Club's, and Walker's rebuttals utterly failed to refute them. He spuriously claimed that most of the charges should be dismissed outright, since they related to events that occurred during his first term. Mainly, he reiterated the excuses that he'd presented at the hearings. There was not much else that he could say. "The charges against Walker were couched in such clever, overlapping technical language that they were unanswerable," one of his attorneys recalled. "If one of the charges was denied, Walker was trapped into a confession on one of the others."[67]

A week later, Governor Roosevelt summoned Mayor Walker and Judge Seabury to appear before him at a special hearing in the Capitol, beginning August 11. Reporters noted that the first hearing would overshadow Herbert Hoover's acceptance speech, which was scheduled for the same day.

"By George! That is the day, isn't it?" Roosevelt innocently replied. "I want you all to know that there is absolutely no connection with the Walker case and my campaign for the presidency."[68]

The day before the hearing, thousands congregated at Grand Central Station to see the mayor off. Fifty police officers and a contingent of Tammany leaders escorted him through the cheering crowd to the platform. Another huge assembly welcomed him when he arrived in Albany that evening. Fireworks exploded in the air, and a thirty-piece brass band belted out "For He's a Jolly Good Fellow," courtesy of the city's Democratic boss. Walker raised his clenched fist over his head, and the crowd roared.

Seabury departed the same day by automobile, without fanfare, accompanied only by his wife and two assistants. Several other assistants, traveling in a second car loaded with documents, were stopped by a police officer, who poked suspiciously at their cargo before waving them on. There was no welcoming committee in Albany. The Seaburys quietly checked into their hotel and went to bed.[69]

Both parties assembled in the Executive Chamber of the capitol the following afternoon. Seabury and his assistants sat at a long table to the right of the governor's great mahogany desk. Walker sat with two attorneys at a table on the left. A waist-high brass rail, borrowed from the Assembly Chamber, separated sixty reporters and roughly the same number of spectators at the back of the room. Portraits of governors past gazed down upon the proceedings as sunlight filtered through stained-glass windows.

At 1:40 p.m., the door to the governor's private office opened, and the room hushed. Roosevelt stood in the doorway, looking about the chamber with his chin in the air. Then, with his secretary gripping one arm, he began to stagger across the red carpet. Only the thump of his feet and the creak of his braces broke the silence as he labored over to the desk and dropped wearily into the high-backed leather chair.[70]

The governor's hearings focused on the same topics that Seabury had addressed during Walker's previous appearance at the County Courthouse, but the setting was completely different. Gone were the mayor's crowd-pleasing witticisms, the rowdy spectators, and the disruptive committee members. Walker's lead attorney, John Curtin, was a truculent Tammany loyalist, but Roosevelt rebuffed his attempts to call witnesses who hadn't previously testified. The governor made clear that he would be the judge and jury, and he brooked no attempt to obstruct or derail the proceedings, repeatedly reminding Walker and Curtin to stick to the

Police Commissioner Edward P. Mulrooney, Mayor James J. Walker, and the mayor's counsel, John. J. Curtin, leave the capitol in Albany, during lunch recess on the fifth day's hearing of the removal charges against Mayor Walker, August 17, 1932.

evidence. When Walker compared the hearings to Soviet tribunals and medieval trials, Roosevelt patiently assured him that he would be given a "square deal." When Curtin presumed to lecture him about the law, Roosevelt retorted, "Mr. Curtin, I happen to be a lawyer, and remarks of that kind are wholly unnecessary to the governor of this state."

Seabury's role at the hearings was passive. "In view of my letter of June 8, 1932, the analysis of the evidence that accompanied it, and the evidence itself," he told Roosevelt on the first day, "I feel that as to specific matters or details, unless Your Excellency desires anything, I should not add anything further to it." He occasionally corrected and clarified misrepresentations of the evidence by reading from court records, but otherwise, he sat back and allowed the governor to conduct the inquiry.[71]

For the next two weeks, Roosevelt methodically led Walker through Seabury's accusations, interjecting incisive questions when the mayor gave evasive answers. After Walker declared that he hadn't even looked at the

) in bonds that he'd received from investment banker J. A. Sisto,
elt asked, "How many shares did you think you were getting?"

"I beg your pardon?" Walker replied.

"How many shares?"

"I don't know that . . . ," Walker stammered, "if I did know . . .
but I . . . my understanding was . . . in view . . . there were no questions
about it . . . in fact, if I never heard of it again it would been all right with
me. . . . I wouldn't have probably complained about it. I mean, there was
no definite agreement about it."[72]

Roosevelt also grilled the various businessmen who had been so generous to the mayor. As Samuel Ungerleider tried to explain the complex
arrangement whereby Russell Sherwood, as Walker's agent, was permitted to earn profits from a stock market investment without risking any
capital or even paying taxes, Roosevelt shook his head in disbelief. "Most
extraordinary business proposition I ever heard of!" he scoffed. "How was
it you conferred this valuable privilege on Mr. Sherwood when thousands
of other people in every State in the Union didn't get it?"[73]

Later, when questioning the mayor about Sherwood's disappearing
act, Roosevelt expressed incredulity that Walker hadn't tried to contact
him "Isn't it a curious thing for you," he asked, "when a man with whom
you had a safe-deposit box, and who looked after your personal affairs,
disappears, and the whole town is looking for him, and he turns up, not
to communicate with him?"

Walker responded with a series of evasions, denying that he knew
Sherwood well, that the "whole town" was looking for him, or that he had
a way to reach him—even though Sherwood's hotel had been reported by
every newspaper in the city.

As the mayor continued to hedge, Roosevelt crossly exclaimed, "So
you just let it ride?"

"Well, now, your Excellency may characterize it as you will," Walker
answered, taken aback. "I would so much rather he were here today."

"*I* wish he were here," the governor rejoined.[74]

Roosevelt also pressed the mayor about letters of credit that Sherwood
had authorized for the "unnamed person." Like Seabury, he avoided publicly identifying Walker's mistress. "Did you know anything about those
letters of credit?" he asked.

"I did not!" Walker angrily replied, throwing his hand in the air as he launched into a convoluted diatribe. "I assume also, as counsel might in any effort for fairness, that the same person might have had charge accounts, the same person might have bought clothes, might have bought real estate, and that assumption wouldn't anymore follow except for publicity purposes!"

"Strike out that answer," Roosevelt commanded the stenographer. "It is not responsive to the question. Strike out everything he said after 'I did not.'" Then he scolded the mayor, "You have got to stick to this issue."[75]

Later, as Walker was leaving the chamber, a reporter asked him, "Why don't you tell us her name?"

The mayor laughed. "Who are you? How long have you been around?" he mocked. "They profess they are trying to protect her when actually they are focusing attention on her. I don't care if they make it public."

"Was it Betty Compton?" the reporter pressed.

"Who else could it be?" Walker replied with a grin as he stepped into the elevator.[76]

His glee was fleeting, though. The hearings weren't going well, and he knew it. Any hope that he harbored of leniency from the governor was dashed when Tammany district leader John Ahearn came to his hotel one evening to warn him that Roosevelt had already decided to remove him.

"I don't know why he'd make up his mind to do that," Walker responded. "Who told you he would?"

Ahearn said that he couldn't reveal his source but vouched for his dependability. He advised Walker to resign and run for governor himself to seek vindication from the voters.[77]

When the hearings adjourned for the weekend on August 26, Seabury returned to New York City by train. A crowd of spectators and a ten-piece brass band were waiting on the platform when he disembarked at Grand Central Station. Realizing that the welcoming party was meant for the mayor, who'd traveled on the same train, he made light of the mix-up. "Unaccustomed as I am—and so forth," he joked.

Walker was in a darker mood when he stepped onto the platform after Seabury. "My God, I thought I asked them not to come again," he groaned when he heard the band playing "Happy Days Are Here Again," which happened to be Roosevelt's campaign theme song. An odd procession paraded down the platform: a grinning Seabury with his assistants, followed by the exuberant brass band, and then Walker, drawn and weary, with his entourage.[78]

Feeling ill, Walker returned to his apartment and retired for the night. The next day, he received more unhappy news from another quarter: his younger brother, George, had died of tuberculosis. The hearings were delayed for a week, and the mayor kept to his bed until the funeral on September 1.[79]

Six thousand people, mostly Tammany supporters, came to the service at St. Patrick's Cathedral. Fewer than half fit inside; the rest spilled out onto Fifth Avenue. Mayor Walker, looking haggard and frail, ascended the steps on the arm of his brother's widow. During the service, he gritted his teeth and pulled himself erect as if trying to resist a breakdown. "Jim looks terrible," Jim Farley remarked. "In fact, he looks worse than George."[80]

After the service, Walker spoke with a friend, Dan McKetrick, about his prospects. "I think Roosevelt is going to remove me," he said gloomily. "I've got a conference at the Plaza with John McCooey, Curtin, Curry, and the rest. What am I to say to them?"

"Will you wait, until I talk to Jim Farley before you commit yourself to anything?" McKetrick asked.

"I don't know," Walker replied.

At the cemetery, he had another conversation on the topic with his sister, Nan. "Sis, take a short stroll with me," he said. "I've got something to tell you." He led her over to the gravesite of former Tammany boss Charles Murphy and reflected silently for a few moments before the tombstone. "Mr. Murphy once told me that most of the troubles of the world could be avoided if men opened their minds instead of their mouths," he said to Nan. "I'm going to resign."

"When, Jim?" she asked, shocked.

"Now," he said, "Or as soon as I leave the meeting at the Plaza."

Eighteen Tammany leaders met him the Plaza Hotel that afternoon, including Boss Curry and Al Smith. "We sat at a round table, Smith at my left," Walker later recalled in an interview. "One by one the boys rose to say to me, 'Jim—stick! Let that man toss you out. We'll nominate you again, and the people will send you back to City Hall.'" Seventeen of the participants encouraged him to fight the charges. Only Smith remained silent. "What does my friend Al say?" Walker finally asked.

"Smith rose and looked directly across the table, without even facing me," he continued. "Speaking out of the corner of his mouth, he snarled, 'You're through. The public don't want you. If you're nominated, you'll be licked. You're through.'"

Walker didn't reveal his decision to the Tammany leaders. When he returned home, he received a message to call Dan McKetrick, the friend he'd spoken to at the funeral. McKetrick had reached Jim Farley, who urged him to tell the mayor to wait. But Walker silenced his telephone and called no one.[81]

That evening, several of Roosevelt's advisers, including Jim Farley, came to see the governor at the Executive Mansion. At the stormy meeting, the visitors emphatically urged him to spare the mayor. Toward the end of the conference, Basil O'Connor, a member of the brain trust, lit a cigarette and hurled the spent match in Roosevelt's direction. "So you'd rather be right than President!" he snapped.

"Well, there may be something in what you say," Roosevelt calmly replied.

At that moment, the telephone rang. There was news. Jimmy Walker had sent a message to the city clerk: "I hereby resign as Mayor of the City of New York, the same to take effect immediately."[82]

Samuel Seabury was at his home on East 63rd Street when he heard the news. Though it was past midnight, he was still hard at work preparing material for the hearings that were scheduled to resume after the weekend. "We were about to go into Walker's finances," George Trosk recalled, "and the details would have completely destroyed him."[83]

But the mayor's resignation put an end to the inquiry. Only a few journalists and visitors were present the next day when Governor Roosevelt lowered himself into his high-backed chair in the Executive Chamber and addressed the room. "The Honorable James J. Walker has resigned his office as Mayor of the City of New York," he declared. "His action in doing so has terminated the proceedings before me, as governor of this state, and I, therefore, declare the hearing closed."[84]

Hours later, Samuel and Maud Seabury boarded a French liner bound for England to resume the vacation that had been cut short two years earlier. The judge refused to answer specific questions from journalists as he boarded the ship, but he released a statement denouncing Walker and, unexpectedly, praising Roosevelt. "The whole odious picture revealed by the investigation of the affairs of Mayor Walker shows him to have been recreant in every obligation of his high office. He betrayed the people of this city, whom he was pledged to serve," he declared. "I know the pressure to which Governor Roosevelt must have been subjected . . . His firmness in standing up against the pressure, and the fair and thorough manner in which he conducted the hearing, have won for him the admiration of fair-minded people throughout the nation."[85]

With that, he boarded the ship and set off for England in search of rare books for his long-neglected library.[86]

EPILOGUE: A NEW YEAR

FOUR HUNDRED POLICE OFFICERS COULD BARELY CONTAIN THE HUNDREDS of thousands of raucous visitors who jammed Times Square on December 31, 1933, sixteen months after Mayor Walker's resignation. The revelers tooted tin horns, tossed confetti, and swigged from hip flasks as they swarmed into the square while trying to avoid the snowmelt that dribbled from store awnings and puddled in the gutters. Honking automobiles, reduced to a crawl by the mass of pedestrians, added to the din. Wandering buskers serenaded the crowd with songs and saxophones, as ragged peddlers hawked noisemakers and trinkets, shouting, "A nickel, a nickel, they are yours, folks, for a nickel!"[1]

New Yorkers had much to celebrate that New Year's Eve. They'd just elected a new mayor, Fiorello La Guardia, who promised to end corruption and provide jobs for the unemployed. Wall Street had begun to rebound, and the economy, bolstered by President Roosevelt's New Deal policies, was showing faint signs of recovery. Finally, to the delight of those who descended on Times Square that night, Prohibition had been repealed a few weeks earlier, and champagne toasts were legal for the first time in fourteen years. "It was the wettest, happiest, biggest, and loudest greeting to a New Year since 1920," enthused the *Herald-Tribune*.[2]

The crowd continued to swell as dusk slipped into darkness. Photojournalists and newsreel operators set off flares from the rooftops and shouted for people to look up at the cameras. The police called in reinforcements, but it wasn't enough. Three minutes before midnight, the mob surged over the barriers, carrying the helpless officers along with them. They massed in the middle of the square and craned their necks to watch a four hundred-pound iron sphere, glowing white like the moon, slowly descend above the roof of the Times Building. When it disappeared from view, giant neon signs flashed "1934" on all four sides of the building, and a cacophony of shouts and horns and bells echoed through the square.[3]

* * *

A few blocks away, Edward Mulrooney rang in the New Year with hundreds of New York elites in the elegant ballroom of the Warwick Hotel. Though a teetotaler, he, too, welcomed the end of Prohibition, which he blamed for the rise of organized crime. Arresting gangsters was no longer his responsibility though. After thiry-four years with the force, he'd resigned to become chairman of the new State Alcoholic Beverage Control Board. Administering liquor licenses was far less taxing than managing the police department, yet it required all his diligence to keep the new liquor inspectors honest.[4]

John Curry also attended the gala at the Warwick Hotel, though he didn't welcome the New Year with as much gusto as the other guests. The Seabury investigations had dealt a severe blow to Tammany Hall, and his efforts to repair the damage weren't going well. After Jimmy Walker's resignation, the city had held a special election for a mayor to serve out the remainder of his term. Curry had nominated a Tammany lawyer named John O'Brien—a poor choice. Though O'Brien managed to win the special election, he proved a weak and unpopular mayor, so obviously beholden to the Hall that he alienated all but the most loyal Tammany supporters. After Mulrooney resigned, O'Brien insinuated that he wouldn't consider a replacement for police commissioner until he'd received instructions from Curry. "I have had no word on that yet," he told reporters. "I don't know if I will have word tomorrow or not, but I will give the matter immediate attention."[5]

O'Brien served less than a year before La Guardia trounced him in a three-way mayoral race on November 7, 1933. As the New Year dawned, Curry's prospects were bleak. Deprived of his power to steer city jobs to loyalists, widely blamed for Seabury's onslaught and La Guardia's election, his popularity among the Tammany rank-and-file had plummeted. Four months later, he was out. "John Francis Curry was not the worst leader Tammany Hall ever had," opined *TIME* magazine, "But he was afflicted with such stubbornly bad judgment that last week he had the distinction of being the first Tammany boss to be booted out of his job by his disgruntled followers."[6]

Twenty blocks northeast of the chaos in Times Square, Samuel and Maud Seabury quietly rang in the New Year at their home on East 63rd Street.

Several city officials and political leaders joined them in their elegant library, including Mayor-Elect La Guardia and his wife, Marie. Five minutes after midnight, La Guardia placed his hand on a Bible. Under the august gaze of generations of Seaburys, the diminutive Italian American politician solemnly swore to support the constitutions of the United States and New York State and to faithfully discharge the duties of the office of mayor of the city of New York.

"Now we have a *mayor*," Seabury gloated after the oath was sworn, implying that La Guardia's predecessor had only been a placeholder.[7]

His pride in the outcome of the election was well-earned, for it wouldn't have happened without him. Well aware of the fleeting success of previous anti-Tammany reformers, Seabury hoped to establish a new city charter that would permanently enshrine good government principles and prevent the tidal wave that he'd unleashed from washing back into the Tammany sea. To fulfill his plan, it was essential to elect an honest and effective mayor who shared his vision. To this end, he had organized a Fusion ticket to unite anti-Tammany politicians from both parties. His allies in the effort exhorted him to run for mayor himself, but Seabury declined on principle. "When I undertook to conduct the investigation into the affairs of the city, I determined that it would be as thorough, as fair and as nonpartisan as I could make it," he declared. "Never had I any desire to capitalize the results of the investigation by election to office. To make that clear I announced that I would not accept any nomination for office in the municipality. I feel bound to adhere to that decision."[8]

Even though he chose not run for mayor himself, Seabury retained tremendous influence over the Fusion campaign. He adamantly rejected the organizers' second choice, Robert Moses, because of the power broker's ties to former governor Al Smith. At a meeting with other Fusion leaders, Seabury slammed his fist on the table and declared that he would have no further dealings with the group if they sold out to Tammany, even to a "New Tammany" reformer like Smith. When Moses got word of Seabury's opposition, he withdrew his candidacy, knowing that he could not win without the judge's support.[9]

Seabury believed that the only leading candidate who could be counted on to battle the bosses to the death was La Guardia, a Republican, who shared his progressive ideas and his loathing of the Hall. The two men had been introduced in spring 1933. La Guardia's flamboyant personality and explosive temperament contrasted with Seabury's cool formality, but their political views aligned, and they quickly developed a personal bond founded on mutual respect. Seabury called La Guardia "Major," a reference to his army rank during World War I. La Guardia called him "Judge," though he jokingly referred to him as "the Bishop" in private. "Fiorello considered Seabury dignified and learned," Marie La Guardia recalled. "When I first met the Judge he seemed cold and stiff, yet he was very kindly and courtly. But he relaxed around Fiorello. . . . Fiorello would josh the Judge a little, and the Judge had quite a sense of humor, in his gentlemanly way."[10]

On August 3, three months before the election, Seabury met again with the other Fusion organizers to choose a nominee. The majority supported John O'Ryan, a Democratic lawyer and former army general, but Seabury rejected him for having too many Tammany ties. He advocated so forcefully for La Guardia that one of O'Ryan's backers finally shouted, "Sit down, Sam, sit down!" shocking the other participants, who had never heard the judge referred to by his first name in public. But Seabury refused to budge, and such was his influence that the others realized that they had to concede if they hoped to win the election. "Congratulations, Major," Seabury's assistant Louis Molloy told La Guardia after the meeting. "You've just been nominated."[11]

Seabury's perseverance was soon validated. Upon taking office, the new mayor began purging corrupt civil servants and replacing them with capable officials, starting with the police department. "I want every district cleaned up," he warned two hundred ranking officers, hours after taking the oath on January 1. "All who have been put in high places by 'pull' are to be taken out. . . . Any type of gift, no matter how small and no matter what the rank of the officer, must not be accepted." His orders were faithfully executed by Lewis Valentine, whom he promoted first to chief inspector and then to police commissioner the same year. Valentine cleaned up the police force, dismissing more than 300 officers and fining more than 8,000 over the course of his eleven-year tenure. He established strict discipline and promoted competent officers to the top of the force, including Henry Bruckman, whom he appointed assistant chief inspector in charge of the entire detective bureau.[12]

Mayor Fiorello La Guardia and President Franklin D. Roosevelt together in Hyde Park, New York, August 1938.

Mayor La Guardia's greatest challenge was to shepherd New York through the Great Depression. Though he and FDR represented different political parties, they collaborated on huge public works projects to reduce unemployment and bring modern infrastructure to the city. With the able assistance of Robert Moses, La Guardia oversaw construction of the Triborough Bridge, FDR Drive, the West Side Highway, La Guardia Airport, and three major tunnels, as well as numerous parks, playgrounds, swimming pools, and public housing.

The new mayor's dynamism and integrity impressed New Yorkers, long accustomed to corruption and incompetence. Voters reelected him twice, in 1937 and 1941, before he finally retired in 1945 after twelve years in office, a record that has been tied but never broken. Historians credit La Guardia for reforming the bureaucracy, reducing crime, consolidating the subway system, building modern infrastructure, and holding the city together during the Depression. In a 1993 survey of urban history scholars, more than half ranked La Guardia as the greatest mayor in US history.[13]

Yet his most important achievement, from Seabury's perspective, was the emasculation of Tammany Hall. After purging dishonest and ineffective Tammany stooges from city government, La Guardia instituted civil service exams to help ensure that their replacements would have relevant expertise. He also promoted Seabury's proposed revisions to the city charter, which won voters' approval in 1936. The new charter abolished the board of aldermen and replaced it with a new city council elected by proportional representation, an idea that Seabury had long championed. For most of New York's history, each district elected an alderman, who was usually linked to the local Tammany clubhouse. Under the new system, every borough elected a slate of city council members, which diminished the influence of local powerbrokers in the election.[14]*

While these actions depleted the ranks of Tammany loyalists in city government, the biggest blow to the machine was La Guardia's political longevity. Since taking control of City Hall in 1839, Tammany had never had to endure more than four years under an unfriendly mayor. Twelve years in the political wilderness during La Guardia's tenure undermined the source of the bosses' leverage—the power of patronage. Unable to attract recruits and enforce party discipline by rewarding loyalists with lucrative jobs, the organization began to wither.

In 1943, Tammany sold its grand clubhouse on Union Square to the International Ladies Garment Workers Union. Jimmy Walker, sixty-two years old and dapper as ever, spoke at the dedication. After resigning in 1932, he'd fled to Europe with Betty Compton to escape his creditors and a federal tax investigation. His wife divorced him after he went aboard, and he promptly married Compton at a simple civil ceremony in Cannes. Three years later, the couple returned to New York City after a federal grand jury absolved Walker of tax evasion.[15]

He remained enormously popular and was often sought out to deliver speeches and toasts, but he rebuffed his supporters' entreaties to run for office again. In 1938, President Roosevelt invited Walker to the White House for a well-publicized social visit, an implicit act of amnesty that improved FDR's standing among the former mayor's supporters. Two years later, as the presidential election approached, Roosevelt privately urged Mayor La Guardia to find Walker a job. To Samuel Seabury's dismay, La

---

* Proportional representation was repealed in 1947, but the City Council remained.

Guardia complied with the president's request by appointing Walker to mediate labor disputes between the Ladies Garment Workers Union and various manufacturers, an administrative position with an annual salary of $20,000 plus expenses (almost $435,000 today).[16]

It was in this official capacity that Walker spoke at the dedication of the union's new headquarters, but he spent more time eulogizing Tammany Hall than saluting the building's new owner. In his speech, he acknowledged Tammany's abuses but defended the organization's progressive legacy, including workmen's compensation, widows' pensions, and child welfare.

When La Guardia took his turn at the podium, he added, "I can't help but think how fitting and proper it is that Jimmy and I should meet here. This building was erected in the flourishing days of Walker's administration. And it was put on the bum by the La Guardia administration!"[17]

After selling the clubhouse, Tammany moved uptown to the fifth floor of a building on Madison Avenue. All the banners, flags, busts, and portraits of bygone leaders went into storage. The only adornment that made the migration to the new nondescript headquarters was an oil painting of Charles Murphy.[18]

Even when a Tammany-backed mayor, William O'Dwyer, succeeded La Guardia in 1946, the organization continued to atrophy. "Tammany will never recover from the prodigious blows inflicted by Seabury," Professor Sam Moley predicted in 1949. "One after another of its overlords have fallen, either directly from the Seabury attack or from the weakness and incompetence that followed its defeats at the polls.[19]

But Samuel Seabury didn't live long enough to witness Tammany's final dissolution in 1967. After his wife died in 1950, he slipped into senility. A psychiatrist who interviewed him in 1955 to assess his competence found his responses to be incoherent. When he asked Seabury questions about La Guardia and other aspects of his public life, the octogenarian judge only mumbled over and over, "We'll get them, we'll get them."

He died three years later at eighty-five. Two hundred and fifty people attended his funeral at Trinity Church on Wall Street, including relatives, former assistants, and numerous officials and dignitaries. "New York City owes a lasting debt to Judge Seabury, a giant of righteousness," opined the *Herald-Tribune*. "It was Seabury who toppled Jimmy Walker from office, forcing that amiable but faithless Mayor to quit under fire of Governor

Roosevelt's hearing in August, 1932. It was Seabury who exposed the corruption of Tammany politicians . . . It was Seabury who personally picked Fiorello La Guardia to run for Mayor. . . . And we rather imagine that Samuel Seabury, who once routed a wise-cracking Mayor and corruption, would like to be remembered as the driving individual force that brought La Guardia and reform to City Hall."

A friend of Seabury's who attended the funeral eulogized the judge more succinctly: "Seabury really cared for New York," he reflected.

Harry Stein rang in 1934 in a cold prison cell, where he was serving out his larceny sentence at Clinton Prison in Dannemora, New York, known as "Little Siberia" because of its isolation and frigid winters. He was later transferred to the more hospitable Great Meadows Prison to the south, but he didn't stay long. When Edward Mulrooney became state commissioner of correction in 1936—after relinquishing his position on the alcohol control board to his old colleague, Henry Bruckman—the former police commissioner promptly transferred Stein back to Dannemora.[20]

Harry Stein was finally paroled in 1948, but his long incarceration failed to reform him. Two years later, he and three associates from Dannemora, armed with pistols and driving a dilapidated rental truck, held up a *Reader's Digest* van enroute to the bank to deposit subscription receipts. One of Stein's accomplices shot the man in the passenger's seat between the eyes, killing him instantly. As they drove off with the loot—about $5,000 in cash—Stein muttered, "We should have gave it to the other one too."[21]

Detectives cracked the case a few weeks later and arrested Stein at the apartment of his brother, Louis, on the Lower East Side. Confessions that the cops obtained from the suspects were allegedly coerced, but the jury convicted them anyway, and the judge sentenced Stein and two co-defendants to death.

As Stein waited on death row, rumors circulated that he knew what had happened to the missing Justice Crater. According to unnamed underworld sources cited by the *Daily News* and other papers, Crater had been accidentally killed during an argument in Vivian Gordon's apartment as she attempted to blackmail him. Stein and Chowderhead Cohen had then disposed of the body by encasing it in cement and dumping it in the East

River. But Stein denied the rumors and even offered to take a lie detector test. "Any effort to connect me with the disappearance of Judge Crater is absurd," he stated. "If I knew anything about him, or could save the life of myself or codefendants, and knew any secret, I'd let it out."[22]

On July 9, 1955, Harry Stein, age fifty-six, shuffled into the brightly lit, hospital-green execution chamber at Sing Sing and dropped awkwardly into the chair. As the prison guards strapped him in and attached electrodes to his shaven legs, he stared grimly at the spectators with a look of hatred until the guards covered his eyes with a black mask. A loud *wharrumpp* filled the room, and his body jerked taut against the bonds. When it was done, a doctor put a stethoscope to his chest and declared, "I pronounce this man dead."[23]

Stein's death was the most sensational of Vivian Gordon's circle. Her other accomplices and assailants drifted in and out of prison as they faded into obscurity. Sam Greenberg received a two-year sentence for conspiracy to obtain false passports for the Oslo expedition. Harry Schlitten was convicted in Hollywood for selling narcotics to movie stars. Chowderhead Cohen was arrested for strikebreaking and later pleaded guilty to fraudulently obtaining federal unemployment relief. Of the group, only John Radeloff escaped jail time, though his wife finally divorced him in 1932 after catching him in bed with another woman. He continued to practice law for several years and eventually moved out to Colorado Springs, where he became an editor at Shepard's Citations, publisher of a venerable legal citation index.[24]

As for Vivian Gordon, her name gradually receded from New Yorkers' collective memory. In the thirties and forties, journalists often referred to her and drew comparisons to her case, trusting that their readers would be familiar with the story. As the events of 1931 dwindled into the distance, the Vivian Gordon references became rarer, and when her name came up, longer explanations were required. Every couple of decades, the *News* published a retrospective article about the case to enlighten a new generation of readers, but later versions downplayed the Seabury connection, reducing the story to a titillating but inconsequential murder mystery.

In 1987, Vincent Bugliosi—who prosecuted Charles Manson and wrote the bestselling book about the case, *Helter Skelter* (1974)—collaborated with author William Stadiem on a novel titled *Lullaby and Good Night: A Novel Inspired by the True Story of Vivian Gordon*. Their treacly reimagining of Gordon's story delivers the happy-ever-after that she imagined when she wrote the letter to Isidore Kresel on February 7, 1931. The novel's heroine lives to testify against her ex-husband and the cop who framed her, ultimately achieving the public vindication and joyful reunion with her daughter that Gordon craved so desperately.[25]

The real story was far bleaker, offering neither redemption nor reunion, only death. Yet Vivian Gordon did exact vengeance in the end, not on one or two men but on the entire institution that had destroyed her life and so many others. Without the popular outrage unleashed by her murder, Governor Roosevelt might never have authorized Seabury's city-wide investigation. Jimmy Walker might never have resigned in disgrace. Fiorello La Guardia might never have been elected mayor. Tammany Hall might not have fallen so far and so fast. Vivian Gordon's body lies buried in Westchester, but her spirit is woven into the history of her adopted city, one small forgotten thread in the glorious tapestry of New York City.

ACKNOWLEDGMENTS

WRITING A BOOK IS OFTEN DESCRIBED AS A SOLITARY PROCESS, BUT I couldn't have managed it without the help of so many others. I'm especially grateful to my wife, Tanya, for taking up the slack at home and indulging me in occasional writing retreats; for patiently suffering my distraction and the postponed projects and vacations; for listening to every word I wrote and offering me honest and wise advice; and for loving and supporting me through this challenging time. I also wish to thank my parents, Mark and Debra, for their boundless love and encouragement, and my daughter, Hanna, for all the hugs and kisses a daddy could desire. I'm indebted to my readers for their generous time and assistance: Colin Asher, Nora Caroll, Alan Feuer, Lucile Scott, Bernie Kluger, Darren Chervitz, David Rodnitzky, and my brother, David. I'd like to offer special thanks to Mark Taylor for his pro-bono legal counsel and Debby Applegate for so generously sharing her research and her time with a fellow author. Thank you to my editor at Union Square & Co., Barbara Berger, who believed in this book and partnered with me to bring it to fruition, and to my agents, Jane Dystel and Miriam Goderich, who have loyally stood by me every step of the way. I'd also like to thank the Union Square & Co. team for their fantastic work, including production editor Michael Cea, interior designer Kevin Ullrich, photo editor Linda Liang, and cover art director Jo Obarowski—as well as cover designer Studio Gearbox and copyeditor Patricia Fogarty. Finally, I'd like to thank all my friends and family—too numerous to name—whose enthusiasm inspired me to complete this book.

NOTES

Abbreviations Used

Baltimore Sun	BS	*New York Tribune*	NYTr
Brooklyn Daily Eagle	BDE	*New York Herald Tribune*	NYHT
Brooklyn Daily Times	BDT	*Standard Union*	SU
Chicago Tribune	CT	*Washington Post*	WP
Daily News	DN	*National Archives and*	
Los Angeles Times	LAT	*Records Administration*	NARA
New York Times	NYT		

Chapter 1: A Moth That Loves the Flame

1 "The Red Ball Goes Up," *NYTr*, Jan. 12, 1908; "Mild Breezes Lure Throngs to the Beaches; Mercury, 8 above Normal, Ruins Skating," *NYT*, Jan. 19, 1931; "The Weather," *NYT*, Feb. 26, 1931; Grace Robinson, "Girl Vice Quiz Witness Found Murdered in the Park," *DN*, Feb. 27, 1931.

2 Andrew L. Yarrow, "The Bucolic Pleasures of Van Cortlandt Park," *NYT*, July 31, 1987, sec. Arts; Robert S. Grumet, *Manhattan to Minisink: American Indian Place Names of Greater New York and Vicinity* (Norman: Univ. of Oklahoma Press, 2013), 219; William Bright, *Native American Placenames of the United States* (Norman: Univ. of Oklahoma Press, 2004), 270, 298.

3 "Emanuel Kamna," in *1925 New York State Census*, 1925; "Emanuel Kamna," in US Army, Register of Enlistments, 1798–1914, 1914; "Emanuel Kamna," in New York, Mexican Punitive Campaign Muster Rolls for National Guard, 1916–1917, 1917; "Emanuel Kamna," in Abstracts of World War I Military Service, 1917–1919, 1919; "Emanuel Kamna," in New York National Guard Service Cards, 1917–1954, 1911; "Emanuel Kamna," *City Record*, July 31, 1975.

4 Fred D. Pasley, *Not Guilty! The Story of Samuel S. Leibowitz* (New York: G. P. Putnam's Sons, 1933), 201; "Woman Vice Case Witness Found Strangled in Park; Her Lawyer Is Arrested," *NYT*, Feb. 27, 1931.

5 Russell Owen, "Police Shifts Made to Strike at Crime," *NYT*, July 14, 1935; "H. E. Bruckman, Foe of Gangsters, Dies," *NYT*, Feb. 3, 1947; "New State Liquor Czar a Bird Fancier and Nature Lover, But Record Shows Him Bad Medicine for Lawbreakers," *BDE*, Mar. 12, 1936; "Henry E. Bruckman Is Dead; Ex-Detective Chief, S.L.A. Head," *NYHT*, Feb. 3, 1947; Martin M. Frank, *Diary of a D.A.* (New York: Henry Holt, 1960), 13.

6 Owen, "Police Shifts Made to Strike at Crime."

7 Leo Katcher, *The Big Bankroll: The Life and Times of Arnold Rothstein* (Potomac, MD: Pickle Partners, 2016), 9, 26, 34, 104–13, 134–37, 140, 213; Robert G. Folsom, *The Money Trail: How Elmer Irey and His T-Men Brought Down America's Criminal Elite* (Lincoln: Univ. of Nebraska Press, 2011), 102–3.

8 Katcher, *The Big Bankroll*, 216–23.

9 Ibid., 218–19, 255; J. Anne Funderburg, *Bootleggers and Beer Barons of the Prohibition Era* (Jefferson, NC: McFarland, 2014), 109–10; Folsom, *The Money Trail*, 103.

10 J. Richard "Dixie" Davis, "Things I Couldn't Tell Till Now," part 2, *Collier's Weekly*, July 29, 1939, 38; Katcher, *The Big Bankroll*, 219–20, 295–99; Folsom, *The Money Trail*, 104–5; Funderburg, *Bootleggers and Beer Barons*, 110–11; Joel Sayre, "Jack Diamond Is Acquitted in Torture Case," *NYHT*, July 15, 1931.

11 Jeffrey Sussman, *Big Apple Gangsters: The Rise and Decline of the Mob in New York* (Lanham, MD: Rowman & Littlefield, 2020), 33; "Homicide Rate Up; Prohibition Blamed," *NYT*, Mar. 20, 1930.

12 "Gamblers Hunted as Rothstein Lies at Point of Death," *BDE*, Nov. 5, 1928; "Jack Diamond Shot 5 Times by Gunmen in a 64th St. Hotel," *NYT*, Oct. 13, 1930; "Hunt Capone Gangster in Diamond's Shooting," *DN*, Oct. 14, 1930; Emanuel Henry Lavine, *"Gimme": Or, How Politicians Get Rich* (New York: Vanguard Press, 1931), 99–102.

13 Thomas A. Reppetto, *American Detective: Behind the Scenes of Famous Criminal Investigations* (Lincoln: Univ. of Nebraska Press, 2018), xiv.

14 Funderburg, *Bootleggers and Beer Barons*, 111–12; J. Richard "Dixie" Davis, "Things I Couldn't Tell Till Now," part 3, *Collier's Weekly*, Aug. 5, 1939, 44.

15 Funderburg, *Bootleggers and Beer Barons*, 108–18; J. Richard "Dixie" Davis, "Things I Couldn't Tell Till Now," part 4, *Collier's Weekly*, Aug. 12, 1939, 29.

16 Pasley, *Not Guilty!*, 201–2; "Girl Vice Witness Murdered on the Eve of Her Testimony," *BDT*, Feb. 26, 1931; Robinson, "Girl Vice Quiz Witness Found Murdered in the Park"; "Woman Vice Case Witness Found Strangled in Park; Her Lawyer Is Arrested."

17 Pasley, *Not Guilty!*, 201; "Girl Vice Witness Slain, 100 Police Seek Strangler," *NYHT*, Feb. 27, 1931; "Girl Vice Witness Murdered on the Eve of Her Testimony"; "Victim Is Left Strangled in Park Thicket," *SU*, Feb. 26, 1931.
18 "Vivian Gordon Diary Accuses Her Attorney," *NYHT*, Mar. 3, 1931; "Gordon Quiz Runs in Circles," *DN*, Mar. 11, 1931; Grace Robinson, "Blackmail, Rum, Drugs Mark Vice Murder Trial," *DN*, Feb. 28, 1931; "Woman Vice Case Witness Found Strangled in Park; Her Lawyer is Arrested."
19 "Vivian Gordon Excited in Hotel—Night in Jail," *Variety*, Mar. 30, 1927; "Vivian Gordon Dismissed," *Variety*, Apr. 13, 1927.
20 "Girl Held in Theft," *DN*, May 28, 1929; Louis Davidson, "Gangster's Girl Links Diamond's Pals in Shooting," *DN*, Oct. 29, 1930.
21 Grace Robinson, "Vivian Gordon's Diary Used to Hold Radeloff, Cohen," *DN*, Mar. 3, 1931; "Miss Gordon's Diary Says Three Sought to Kill Her," *NYT*, Mar. 3, 1931; "The Man Who Prints the Magazines," *McClure's Magazine*, Sept. 1913, 111–12.
22 Robinson, "Blackmail, Rum, Drugs Mark Vice Murder Trial"; "Girl Vice Witness Murdered on the Eve of Her Testimony"; "Ad," *DN*, Sept. 25, 1930.
23 "Attorney for Slain Woman in Vice Quiz Held After Grilling," *BDE*, Feb. 27, 1931.
24 "Woman Vice Case Witness Found Strangled in Park; Her Lawyer Is Arrested"; Robinson, "Girl Vice Quiz Witness Found Murdered in the Park"; "Police Check Gordon Diary Clues," *SU*, Feb. 27, 1931.
25 Robinson, "Girl Vice Quiz Witness Found Murdered in the Park"; "Brother of Vivian Gordon Defends Slain Butterfly as Woman of High Taste," *The SU*, Mar. 14, 1931; "Police Check Gordon Diary Clues"; "Maid Tells New Story After Quiz," *Yonkers Statesman*, Mar. 6, 1931; "Gordon Defense Hints at 'Higher-Up,'" *DN*, June 21, 1931; "Behind the Scenes in the Vivian Gordon Case," *True Detective*, Nov. 1931.
26 Jay Maeder, "Vivian Gordon Moth to the Flame," *DN*, Feb. 28, 1999.
27 "Vivian's Complete Diary Lights Up Murder Stage," *DN*, July 8, 1931.
28 "Vivian's Diary Recounts Last Tragic 14 Months," July 9, 1931.
29 Grace Robinson, "Strangler-Thief Accused as Vivian Gordon Slayer," *DN*, Apr. 10, 1931.
30 Robinson, "Girl Vice Quiz Witness Found Murdered in the Park"; "Girl Vice Witness Slain, 100 Police Seek Strangler"; Robinson, "Strangler-Thief Accused as Vivian Gordon Slayer."
31 "Note Reveals Fight Vivian Gordon Made to Clear Her Name," *Philadelphia Inquirer*, Mar. 1, 1931; Robinson, "Vivian Gordon's Diary Used to Hold Radeloff, Cohen"; "Attorney for Slain Woman in Vice Quiz Held After Grilling"; "Quiz Millionaire Friends for Vivian Murder Clew," *DN*, Apr. 3, 1931; "3 Millionaires Admit Meetings with Vivian," *DN*, Mar. 31, 1931; "10 Drivers Rounded Up in Gordon Murder Quiz," *DN*, Apr. 2, 1931.
32 Robinson, "Vivian Gordon's Diary Used to Hold Radeloff, Cohen."
33 "3 Millionaires Admit Meetings with Vivian"; "Woman Vice Case Witness Found Strangled in Park; Her Lawyer Is Arrested"; "Gordon Death Threats Kept Secret by Police," *DN*, Mar. 29, 1931; Grace Robinson, "Gangland Dooms 2 Gordon Squealers," *DN*, June 1, 1931.
34 "Woman Vice Case Witness Found Strangled in Park; Her Lawyer Is Arrested."

Chapter 2: Nothing to Be Concerned About

1 Jean Edward Smith, *FDR* (New York: Random House, 2007), 24.
2 Ibid., 15–19, 55.
3 H. W. Brands, *Traitor to His Class: The Privileged Life and Radical Presidency of Franklin Delano Roosevelt* (New York: Anchor Books, 2009), 50; Smith, *FDR*, 83–93; Rita Halle Kleeman, *Gracious Lady: The Life of Sara Delano Roosevelt* (New York: D. Appleton-Century, 1935), 253; "Franklin D. Roosevelt, 1882–1945: Five Harvard Men Pay Tribute to His Memory," *Harvard Alumni Bulletin*, Apr. 28, 1945, 452.
4 Elliott Roosevelt, James Brough, and Eleanor Roosevelt, *An Untold Story: The Roosevelts of Hyde Park* (New York: G. P. Putnam's Sons, 1973), 127; Derek Strahan, "New York State Executive Mansion, Albany, New York," *Lost New England*, Jan. 29, 2021, https://bit.ly/43jOxj7; "Creepy Noises in the Governor's Mansion Are Spooking Cuomo," *New York Post*, May 4, 2017, https://bit.ly/3C8yDw2.
5 Roosevelt, Brough, and Roosevelt, *An Untold Story*, 258; Samuel I. Rosenman, *Working with Roosevelt* (New York: Harper, 1952), 164.
6 "Woman Vice Case Witness Found Strangled in Park," *NYT*, Feb. 27, 1931; Earle Looker, *This Man Roosevelt* (New York: Brewer, Warren & Putnam, 1932), 185.
7 *Tammany Hall* (New York: Landmarks Preservation Commission, Oct. 2013); "Egan Is First on Job at New Tammany Hall," *NYHT*, Jan. 3, 1929; "John F. Curry Is New Chief of Tammany," *BS*, Apr. 24, 1929; Charles S. Salomon, "Tammany Hails Curry as Great Chief in Victory," *NYHT*, Nov. 6, 1929; James A. Hagerty, "Tammany Hall," *NYT*, Oct. 5, 1930, sec. Special Features.
8 Oliver E. Allen, *The Tiger: The Rise and Fall of Tammany Hall* (Reading, MA: Addison-Wesley, 1993), 2–7, 24; Terry Golway, *Machine Made: Tammany Hall and the Creation of Modern American Politics* (New York: W. W. Norton, 2014), 5–6.
9 Allen, *The Tiger*, 13–17.

10 Ibid., 30–35; Gustavus Myers, *The History of Tammany Hall* (Gustavus Myers, 1901), 87–90.

11 Allen, *The Tiger*, 33–36.

12 Ibid., 61–62, 102, 112–13, 142; Kenneth D. Ackerman, *Boss Tweed: The Rise and Fall of the Corrupt Pol Who Conceived the Soul of Modern New York* (New York: Carroll & Graf, 2006), 2, 87; Golway, *Machine Made*, 91–92; Ray Stannard Baker, "The Trust's New Tool—The Labor Boss," *McClure's Magazine*, Nov. 1903, 35–36.

13 William L. Riordon, *Plunkitt of Tammany Hall: A Series of Very Plain Talks . . .* (New York: McClure, Phillips, 1905), 3–5.

14 Ibid., 34; Lincoln Steffens, *The Autobiography of Lincoln Steffens* (New York: Harcourt, Brace, 1931), 280–81.

15 "Shepard Boom Flare-Up," *NYTr*, Dec. 24, 1910.

16 W. A. Warn, "Senator F. D. Roosevelt, Chief Insurgent at Albany," *NYT*, Jan. 22, 1911, Mag. section part 5; Robert Cruise McManus, "The Rise of a Roosevelt," *The Outlook*, Nov. 5, 1930, 374.

17 Smith, *FDR*, 112–13.

18 "Senator Roosevelt Assails the Bosses," *NYT*, Dec. 24, 1911.

19 Smith, *FDR*, 180–81; Charles LaCerra, *Franklin Delano Roosevelt and Tammany Hall of New York* (Lanham, MD: Univ. Press of America, 1997), 50–51.

20 "Wigwam Rings with Patriotic Oratory," *New York Sun*, July 5, 1917; "Tammany's Fourth Given Over to War," *NYT*, July 5, 1917.

21 Robert A. Slayton, *Empire Statesman: The Rise and Redemption of Al Smith* (New York: Free Press, 2001), 10–16, 39–40, 59–62; Terry Golway, *Frank & Al: FDR, Al Smith, and the Unlikely Alliance That Created the Modern Democratic Party*, Kindle. (New York: St. Martin's Press, 2018), 27–29, 33–34, 47–48, 78–80.

22 Golway, *Frank & Al*, 139–140, 147–148; Jean Edward Smith, *FDR*, 295.

23 Golway, *Frank & Al*, 149–150, 154–155; James Roosevelt and Sidney Shalett, *Affectionately F.D.R.: A Son's Story of a Lonely Man* (New York: Harcourt, Brace, 1959), 205.

24 Frances Perkins, Notable New Yorkers, Columbia Univ. Oral History Research Office, part 2, session 1, p325, accessed Nov. 11, 2019, http://www.columbia.edu/cu/lweb/digital/collections/nny/perkinsf/.

25 Frank Freidel, *Franklin D. Roosevelt: The Ordeal* (Boston: Little, Brown, 1954), 254–55; Geoffrey C. Ward, *A First-Class Temperament: The Emergence of Franklin Roosevelt* (New York: Harper & Row, 1989), 794.

26 Ward, *A First-Class Temperament*, 794; Golway, *Frank & Al*, 211–212; St. Clair McKelway, "Smith to Quit Public Life at Close of Term," *NYHT*, Nov. 8, 1928.

27 "Murphy Eulogized by Governor Smith," *NYT*, 1924.

28 Henry F. Pringle, "What's Happened to Tammany?" *The Outlook*, May 15, 1929, 83; Milton MacKaye, *The Tin Box Parade: A Handbook for Larceny* (New York: R. M. McBride, 1934), 28–30.

29 Francis Scott Fitzgerald, *The Crack-Up* (New York: J. Laughlin, 1945), 87.

30 Debby Applegate, *Madam: The Biography of Polly Adler, Icon of the Jazz Age* (Garden City, NY: Doubleday, 2021), 109; Burton W. Peretti, *Nightclub City: Politics and Amusement in Manhattan* (Philadelphia: Univ. of Pennsylvania Press, 2013), 10–11; "Whalen Says City Has 32,000 Speakeasies and Lays Crime Increase to Prohibition," *NYT*, Apr. 5, 1929.

31 Peretti, *Nightclub City*, 2–3, 20–21, 94–95; Polly Adler, *A House Is Not a Home* (New York: Rinehart, 1950), 71–72; Leo Katcher, *The Big Bankroll: The Life and Times of Arnold Rothstein* (Potomac, MD: Pickle Partners, 2016), 224.

32 George Walsh, *Gentleman Jimmy Walker, Mayor of the Jazz Age* (New York: Praeger, 1974), x; Frances Perkins, Notable New Yorkers, part 3, session 1, p451; Herbert Mitgang, *Once Upon a Time in New York: Jimmy Walker, Franklin Roosevelt, and the Last Great Battle of the Jazz Age* (New York: Free Press, 2000), 74–79.

33 Alva Johnston, "The Jimmy Walker Era," *Vanity Fair*, Dec. 1932, 41; Donald L. Miller, *Supreme City: How Jazz Age Manhattan Gave Birth to Modern America* (New York: Simon & Schuster, 2014), 3–9.

34 "Tammany Hushed as Walker Makes a Solemn Pledge," *NYT*, Oct. 21, 1925; "Walker Reaffirms Tammany Fealty," *NYT*, Oct. 4, 1929; Mitgang, *Once Upon a Time in New York*, 58, 164.

35 Mitgang, *Once Upon a Time in New York*, 53–61.

36 Mason B. Williams, *City of Ambition: FDR, La Guardia, and the Making of Modern New York* (New York: W. W. Norton, 2013), 1401–27.

37 Mitgang, *Once Upon a Time in New York*, 53; "Walker Ridicules Charges of Graft," *NYT*, Oct. 23, 1929; Williams, *City of Ambition*, 1420.

38 Fitzgerald, *The Crack-Up*, 21; Adler, *A House Is Not a Home*, 164–66.

39 "$5,000 Loot Taken at Vitale Dinner," *NYT*, Dec. 9, 1929; "Vitale Party $3,300 Shy by Holdup Raid," *DN*, Dec. 9, 1929; "Call Vitale Hold-up Fake to Recover the 'Contract' for Yale-Marlow Murders," *NYT*, Dec. 27, 1929; "Terranova Free In $10,000 Bail On Plot Charge," *NYHT*, Jan. 17, 1930.

40 "Judge Vause Got $250,000 in Fees in City Pier Lease, Tuttle Tells Prosecutor," *NYT*, May 11, 1930; "Federal Jury Indicts Doyle as Perjurer," *NYHT*, June 14, 1930; "Ewald Indicted with Five for Fraud in Mine Project; to Be Asked to Quit Bench," *NYT*, July 8, 1930; C. G. Poore, "Scandals Arising Over Judgeships," *NYT*, Aug. 24, 1930, sec. Special Features; William B. Northrop, *The Insolence of Office:*

The Story of the Seabury Investigations (London: G. P. Putnam's Sons, 1932), 6–7; Herbert Mitgang, *The Man Who Rode the Tiger: The Life and Times of Judge Samuel Seabury* (New York: Oxford Univ. Press, 1996), 222–23.

41 MacKaye, *Tin Box Parade*, 30–32; Stephen J. Riegel, *Finding Judge Crater: A Life and Phenomenal Disappearance in Jazz Age New York* (Syracuse, NY: Syracuse Univ. Press, 2022); "Crain Lifelong Tammany Man; Jurist 23 Years," *NYHT*, Mar. 8, 1931; "Thomas C. T. Crain, Ex-Justice, Dies, 82," *NYT*, May 30, 1942, 82; "Thomas C. T. Crain Is Dead; Former Judge and Prosecutor," *NYHT*, May 30, 1942.

42 "Magistrates Facing Inquiry in 2 Counties," *NYT*, Jan. 22, 1930.

43 "Republicans at Odds on Plan for Inquiry into Graft in City," *NYT*, Jan. 15, 1930.

44 Kenneth S. Davis, *FDR: The New York Years, 1928–1933* (New York: Random House, 1985), 163, 167–81; "Gov. Roosevelt Bars Politics Until Fall," *NYT*, Apr. 23, 1930; "Roosevelt Remains Silent on New Rothstein Facts," *NYHT*, Sept. 29, 1929; "Roosevelt Pleads for Home Rule as Nation's Salvation," *NYHT*, Mar. 2, 1930; "Charges Roosevelt Side-Steps Inquiry," *NYT*, June 19, 1930.

45 FDR to Herbert H. Lehman, July 29, 1930, in Franklin D. Roosevelt, *FDR: His Personal Letters*, ed. Elliot Roosevelt, vol. 3 (New York: Duell, Sloan and Pearce, 1950), 136; Public Papers of Franklin D. Roosevelt, Forty-Eighth Governor of the State of New York 1930 (Albany, NY: J. B. Lyon Co., 1931), 368. Davis, *FDR: The New York Years, 1928–1933*, 170–71; "Republicans Assail Walker's Inquiry," *NYT*, July 20, 1930.

46 "Mrs. Ewald Admits She Lent Tommaney $10,000 for Healy," *NYT*, Aug. 9, 1930; "Mayor Denies $10,000 Got Ewald His Job, or That Healy Was Consulted About It; Olvany Backs Walker at Crain Inquiry," *NYT*, Aug. 13, 1930; Riegel, *Finding Judge Crater*, 101–5; MacKaye, *Tin Box Parade*, 33–34.

47 "Governor Calls for All the Records in Ewald Case When Dr. Wise Protest," *NYT*, Aug. 16, 1930; "Governor Orders Crain to Send Him at Once All Evidence Relating to the Judgeship-Buying Charge," *NYHT*, Aug. 16, 1930.

48 Davis, *FDR: The New York Years, 1928–1933*, 172; W. A. Warn, "City Inquiry Bill Vetoed," *NYT*, Mar. 30, 1930; A. Staff Correspondent, "Roosevelt Asks Dowling To Check on Magistrates; Inquiry on Mayor Sought," *NYHT* (1926–1962), Aug. 22, 1930.

49 Gene Fowler, *Beau James: The Life & Times of Jimmy Walker* (New York: Viking, 1949), 272–273.

50 "Walker Avowal He Wasn't in Raid Interests Suffolk," *Times Union*, Aug. 27, 1930.

51 "Walker's Touch of Comedy Ends Montauk Raid Incident," *The BDE*, Aug. 27, 1930.

52 Davis, *FDR: The New York Years, 1928–1933*, 172–73.

53 Ibid.; Samuel Seabury, *In the Matter of the Investigation of the Magistrates' Courts . . . Final Report* (NYC: New York State Supreme Court Appellate Division, Mar. 28, 1932), 226; "Appellate Division Expected to Refuse City Bench Inquiry," *NYHT*, Aug. 25, 1930; "Appellate Justices Act Today on Inquiry into Magistrates," *NYT*, Aug. 25, 1930; "Cash Says He Paid Healy $2,000 for Marshal's Job; Inquiry on Bench Decided," *NYT*, Aug. 26, 1930.

54 "Mayor Welcomes City Hall Inquiry," *NYT*, Aug. 24, 1930; "Tuttle Obtains Pay Record of City Officials," *NYHT*, Sept. 10, 1930.

55 Perkins, Notable New Yorkers, Columbia Univ. Oral History Research Office.

Chapter 3: Old Heads for Counsel, Young Heads for War

1 Mitgang, *Man Who Rode the Tiger*, 7, 15–16, 19–20.

2 MacKaye, *Tin Box Parade*, 298; Richard O. Boyer, "Inquisitor," *New Yorker*, June 23, 1931, 20.

3 Mitgang, *Man Who Rode the Tiger*, 23–24, 31–33, 36–41.

4 Ibid., 42–45, 60–64.

5 Ibid., 80–88.

6 Ibid., 112.

7 Ibid., 113–14.

8 Ibid., 115–16; "Seabury Men Defy Murphy at Saratoga," *NYTr*, Aug. 11, 1916; "Seabury Still Worries Murphy," *NYTr*, Aug. 10, 1916.

9 Mitgang, *Man Who Rode the Tiger*, 116–18; "Seabury Leaves Bench to Fight," *NYTr*, Aug. 29, 1916; "Progressive Vote Factor in Primaries," *NYT*, Sept. 17, 1916.

10 Mitgang, *Man Who Rode the Tiger*, 118–23, 154.

11 Ibid., 155–59; Boyer, "Inquisitor," 23; "Seabury Sails Sept. 3rd to Begin Probe," *Brooklyn Citizen*, Aug. 26, 1930.

12 Stephen J. Riegel, *Finding Judge Crater: A Life and Phenomenal Disappearance in Jazz Age New York* (Syracuse, NY: Syracuse Univ. Press, 2022), 10–17.

13 Mitgang, *Man Who Rode the Tiger*, 160; "Seabury Back; Walker, Olvany Face Jury Quiz," *BDE*, Sept. 5, 1930.

14 "History and Architecture of New York County Supreme Courthouse," *Historical Society of the New York Courts*, https://bit.ly/3N8vv9Z, accessed Aug. 13, 2022/; "George Denied His Due," *New York Post*, Feb. 16, 2009.

15 "Five More Leaders Defy Grand Jurors; 23 Others Called," *NYT*, Sept. 26, 1930; Northrop, *Insolence of Office*, 41; Mitgang, *Once Upon a Time in New York*, 104–5.

16 Mitgang, *Man Who Rode the Tiger*, 172–73; Northrop, *Insolence of Office*, 14; MacKaye, *Tin Box Parade*, 144–45; "Bar Admits Curry Ignored Its Choices," *NYT*, Sept. 27, 1930.

17 Mitgang, *Man Who Rode the Tiger*, 179; Michael A. Perino, *The Hellhound of Wall Street: How Ferdinand Pecora's Investigation of the Great Crash Forever Changed American Finance* (New York: Penguin, 2010), 54–55; "Irving Ben Cooper Keeps Up the Battle Against Tammany, Corruption, Rackets," *Jewish Daily Bulletin*, Oct. 15, 1933.

18 Mitgang, *Man Who Rode the Tiger*, 173; "Demands Bank Data of 24 Magistrates," *NYT*, Oct. 7, 1930.

19 Mitgang, *Man Who Rode the Tiger*, 189–90; "Brodsky on Stand Fights to Keep Post," *NYT*, Dec. 17, 1930.

20 Chile Acuna, *Women for Sale* (New York: William Godwin, 1931), 128–31.

21 Herbert Mitgang, "The Downfall of Jimmy Walker," *The Atlantic* 210, no. 4 (Oct. 1962): 100–101.

22 Acuna, *Women for Sale*, 26–31; Northrop, *Insolence of Office*, 67–68.

23 Acuna, *Women for Sale*, 37–39.

24 Seabury, *Investigation of the Magistrates' Courts*, 83–86; Acuna, *Women for Sale*, 56, 137–42; Northrop, *The Insolence of Office: The Story of the Seabury Investigations*, 23; "Old Jefferson Market Soon to Be Demolished," *NYT*, 1929; "Women's House of Detention Protects the First Offenders," *NYT*, 1931; Mae West, "How I Was Jailed for Sex," *London Observer*, Nov. 30, 1980.

25 "Innocent Girls Arrested," *NYT*, Nov. 27, 1930; "At It Again," *Daily Worker*, Dec. 1, 1930.

26 Acuna, *Women for Sale*, 40–42, 48–51, 57, 101–2.

27 Ibid., 131–32, 136–37; Seabury, *Investigation of the Magistrates' Courts*, 85–86; Mitgang, *Man Who Rode the Tiger*, 204.

28 Robert Leibowitz, *The Defender: The Life and Career of Samuel S. Leibowitz, 1893–1933* (Englewood Cliffs, NJ: Prentice-Hall, 1981), 112–113; Wilbur Forrest, "Paid Vice Informer Lists 28 Police and Inspector," *NYHT*, Nov. 27, 1930; "13 Policemen Identified as 'Framers' in Vice Cases," *NYT*, Dec. 4, 1930.

29 "Acuna's Smirk Stirs Vice Trial," *DN*, Apr. 9, 1931.

30 Leibowitz, *The Defender*, 110–113; John O'Donnell, "Girls Accuses Acuna as G. O. P. Starts City Quiz," *DN*, Jan. 4, 1931.

31 Acuna, *Women for Sale*, 160–73.

32 "Got $20,000 to Free 900 in Vice Cases, Prosecutor Confesses, Exposing Ring," *NYT*, Nov. 25, 1930; "Hunt Vice Ring Higher-Ups; Jean Norris Faces Ouster," *DN*, Feb. 14, 1931; Northrop, *Insolence of Office*, 41–53; Walter Chambers, *Samuel Seabury: A Challenge* (New York: Century Co., 1932), 243–44.

33 "Mysterious $65,000 Traced to 2 Police at 'Fixer' Hearing," *NYT*, Jan. 25, 1931.

34 "Vice Spy Says Police Forced Him to Flee," *NYT*, Feb. 4, 1931.

35 Ibid.

36 "Roosevelt Pardons Six Women 'Framed' by Police Vice Ring," *NYT*, Dec. 23, 1930; "Walker, 'Shocked,' Asks Drive on Vice," *NYT*, Mar. 5, 1931.

37 Mitgang, *Man Who Rode the Tiger*, 196–97; "Seabury Accuses Walker of Obstructing His Inquiry When Disclosures Loomed," *NYT*, Jan. 1, 1931.

38 Mitgang, *Man Who Rode the Tiger*, 198–99.

39 "Seabury to Press Inquiry," *NYT*, Feb. 11, 1931; Mitgang, *Man Who Rode the Tiger*, 176.

40 Mitgang, *Man Who Rode the Tiger*, 146, 178; "Jean Norris Faces New Inquiry Today," *NYT*, Jan. 26, 1931.

41 "Dancer's $310 Shakedown Puts Lawyer on Vice Grill," *DN*, Jan. 9, 1931, 310; "Ballet Teacher Says She Was 'Framed' in Raid," *BDE*, Feb. 2, 1931; "Girl Vice Witness Murdered on the Eve of Her Testimony," *BDT*, Feb. 26, 1931 ; "Judge Norris on Stand Today in Vice Probe," *SU*, Feb. 26, 1931.

42 "Victim Is Left Strangled in Park Thicket"; "Girl Vice Witness Murdered," *SU*, Feb. 26, 1931; "Gordon Slaying Closely Linked to Vice Inquiry," *NYHT*, Feb. 27, 1931.

43 "Victim Is Left Strangled in Park Thicket"; Ibid.

44 "Woman Vice Case Witness Found Strangled in Park; Her Lawyer Is Arrested"; "Cooper Affidavit Details Charges of Slain Woman," *NYHT*, Feb. 28, 1931.

45 "Woman Vice Case Witness Found Strangled in Park; Her Lawyer Is Arrested"; "Cooper Affidavit Details Charges of Slain Woman."

46 "Woman Vice Case Witness Found Strangled in Park; Her Lawyer Is Arrested."

47 "Girl Vice Witness Is Murdered"; "Police Check Gordon Diary Clues"; "Cooper Affidavit Details Charges of Slain Woman."

48 "Cooper Affidavit Details Charges of Slain Woman."

49 "Mate and Police Framed Girl, She Told Probers," *BDT*, Feb. 27, 1931.

Chapter 4: Don't Worry, Little Girl

1 Frederick L. (Frederick Lewis) Collins, *Homicide Squad: Adventures of a Headquarters Old Timer* (New York: G. P. Putnam's Sons, 1944), 162–63; Grace Robinson, "Girl Vice Quiz Witness Found Murdered in the Park," *DN*, Feb. 27, 1931; John Arthur Chapman, *Tell It to Sweeney: The Informal*

History of the New York DN (Garden City, NY: Doubleday, 1961), 104; S. J. Woolf, "Mulrooney Talks of Youth and Crime," *NYT*, Mar. 15, 1931, magazine sect.

2 "Mulrooney Joined the Force in 1896," *NYT*, May 21, 1930; "Mulrooney Heads Police; 34 Years on the Force; Whalen Farewell Today," *NYT*, May 21, 1930; "Mulrooney Sworn; Policy Is Restraint," *NYT*, May 22, 1930.

3 Woolf, "Mulrooney Talks of Youth and Crime"; Will Irwin, "Receiver for Prohibition," *NYHT*, Apr. 23, 1933; "Good Chances on the Police Force," *New-York Tribune*, July 31, 1895; Kenneth Campbell and James Thurber, "Mulrooney," *New Yorker*, June 21, 1930.

4 Gerald W. Johnson, "The Policeman's Bed of Roses," *Harper's Magazine*, May 1931, 735; "Girl Vice Witness Slain, 100 Police Seek Strangler."

5 "Vivian Gordon's Murder Brings Boro Lawyer into Murder Inquiry," *BDT*, Feb. 27, 1931; Robinson, "Girl Vice Quiz Witness Found Murdered in the Park."

6 "Two Held in $100,000 Bail in Gordon Murder Case," *NYT*, Feb. 28, 1931.

7 "Woman Vice Case Witness Found Strangled in Park; Her Lawyer Is Arrested"; "Mate and Police Framed Girl, She Told Probers," *BDT*, Feb. 27, 1931.

8 "Woman Vice Case Witness Found Strangled in Park; Her Lawyer Is Arrested."

9 Grace Robinson, "Vice Girl, Killed in Park, Feared Lawyer, Says Diary," *DN*, Feb. 27, 1931.

10 Stanley Walker, *City Editor* (Baltimore, MD: Johns Hopkins Univ. Press, 1999), 256; Ishbel Ross, *Ladies of the Press: The Story of Women in Journalism by an Insider* (New York: Harper & Brothers, 1936), 271–79.

11 Ross, *Ladies of the Press*, 279–80; "Grace Robinson Papers, 1892–1991," Archives West, https://bit.ly /3o16Nnv, accessed June 2, 2022.

12 Chapman, *Tell It to Sweeney*, 13, 26, 61, 76, 87; "How NY DN Found Success as First U.S. Tabloid in 1919," *DN*, June 23, 2019; DN Building (Landmarks Preservation Commission, July 28, 1981).

13 Ross, *Ladies of the Press*, 271–80; Leo E. McGivena, *The News: The First Fifty Years of New York's Picture Newspaper* (New York: News Syndicate Co., 1969), 281; Chapman, *Tell It to Sweeney*, 219; Grace Robinson, "Flames Raze Breakers Hotel," *DN*, Mar. 19, 1925.

14 Robinson, "Vice Girl, Killed in Park, Feared Lawyer, Says Diary."

15 Seabury, *Investigation of the Magistrates' Courts*, 83–86, 131; "Renaud Backs Convictions on Word of Cops," *Brooklyn SU*, Mar. 9, 1931; Wilbur Forrest, "Renaud Took Word of Police on Vice Cases," *NYHT*, Mar. 10, 1931.

16 Robinson, "Vice Girl, Killed in Park, Feared Lawyer, Says Diary"; "Gordon Sentence Defended by Renaud," *NYT*, Mar. 10, 1931; "Grace Robinson Papers," box 36, folder 3.

17 Robinson, "Vice Girl, Killed in Park, Feared Lawyer, Says Diary."

18 Ibid.

19 "Vice Squad 'Lone Wolf' Had $36,280 on Deposit," *BDT*, Mar. 14, 1931; Grace Robinson, "Vice Cop Banked $35,800," *DN*, Mar. 14, 1931; "Dancers' Writhes and Wriggles Get Magistrate's O.K.," *DN*, Mar. 22, 1922.

20 Robinson, "Vice Girl, Killed in Park, Feared Lawyer, Says Diary."

21 Ibid.

22 "Gordon Murder Witnesses Tell of Girl's Scream," *NYHT*, Mar. 10, 1931; Rosemary McClure, "Cruise News: Being Charming Is Job One; Lines Are Using Gentlemen Hosts to Sweep Single Women off Their Feet and onto the Dance Floor," *LAT*, Apr. 23, 2017.

23 "Attorney for Slain Woman in Vice Quiz Held After Grilling."

24 Ibid.

25 Ibid.

26 "Night of Terror," *WP*, Nov. 10, 2017; "Occoquan Workhouse," US National Park Service, https:// www.nps.gov/places/occoquan-workhouse.htm, accessed June 6, 2022.

27 "Lorton 'Graft College' Flayed in Congress," *WP*, Feb. 16, 1934; "High Official of D.C. Jails Admits 'Fees,'" *WP*, Mar. 4, 1934.

28 "Two Held in $100,000 Bail in Gordon Murder Case"; Grace Robinson, "Fear Drove Vivian to Hire Gangster Guard," *DN*, Mar. 1, 1931; "Sophomore Class," *The Tiger*, Dec. 17, 1908; US, World War I Draft Registration Cards, 1917–1918, digital images, Ancestry.com, John E. C. Bischoff, accessed Oct. 7, 2020.

29 Robinson, "Fear Drove Vivian to Hire Gangster Guard."

30 "Two Held in $100,000 Bail in Gordon Murder Case;" Philadelphia County, PA, divorce file 2261 (July 2, 1924), Benita Bischoff and John E. C. Bischoff, Office of Judicial Records, Philadelphia.

31 Grace Robinson, "Quiz Chauffer in Murder," *DN*, Mar. 10, 1931.

32 "Slain Girl's Diary Bares Her Fear of Her Own Lawyer," *Wilmington Morning News*, Feb. 28, 1931.

33 "Policeman and Ex-Husband Deny Framing Miss Gordon," *NYT*, Mar. 2, 1931; Grace Robinson, "Vice Cop Accused by Slain Vivian Whitewashed," *DN*, Mar. 2, 1931.

34 Robinson, "Vice Cop Accused by Slain Vivian Whitewashed"; "Vice Raider Denies Knowing Slain Girl Who Accused Him," *NYHT*, Mar. 2, 1931; "Policeman and Ex-Husband Deny Framing Miss Gordon."

35 Robinson, "Vice Cop Accused by Slain Vivian Whitewashed."

36 Ibid.

37 Ibid.
38 Ibid.
39 Ibid.; "Policeman and Ex-Husband Deny Framing Miss Gordon"; "Miss Gordon's Diary Says Three Sought to Kill Her," *NYT*, Mar. 3, 1931.
40 "Miss Gordon's Diary Says Three Sought to Kill Her"; Robinson, "Vice Cop Accused by Slain Vivian Whitewashed."
41 Robinson, "Vice Cop Accused by Slain Vivian Whitewashed."

Chapter 5: A Woman of Many Acquaintances
1 Grace Robinson, "Fear Drove Vivian to Hire Gangster Guard," *DN*, Mar. 1, 1931; "Woman Doctor Offers Clues in Gordon Murder," *BDE*, Mar. 1, 1931; "Seabury Hunts Slayer of Vice Witness as He and His Aides Receive Threats," *NYT*, Mar. 1, 1931.
2 "Seabury Hunts Slayer of Vice Witness as He and His Aides Receive Threats"; "Slain Girl's Friend, Here for Secret Quiz, Guarded by Seabury," *BDT*, Mar. 2, 1931.
3 "Recipient of Note Quizzed in Slaying of Vivian Gordon," *Philadelphia Inquirer*, Mar. 2, 1931; "Bischoff Quiz in N.Y. Murder Set for Today," *Camden Evening Courier*, Mar. 2, 1931.
4 Ann Tomkins Gibson, "Now My Idea Is This!," *Evening Public Ledger*, Nov. 29, 1920; "Singing Eagle Lodge Girls Visit Shoals," *Portsmouth Herald*, Aug. 20, 1930; Frank A. Pattie, "William McDougall: 1871–1938," *American Journal of Psychology* 52 (2) (1939): 304–5; "Urges Old-Time Parties," *Philadelphia Inquirer*, Nov. 11, 1920; "Slain Girl's Friend, Here for Secret Quiz, Guarded by Seabury."
5 "Woman Vice Case Witness Found Strangled in Park; Her Lawyer Is Arrested"; "John W. Franklin," in Michigan City, IN, US, Directories, 1890–1894, accessed June 17, 2022; "Patents Issued to Hoosier Inventors," *Indianapolis Journal*, Oct. 1, 1890.
6 "Benita Franklin," in 1900 US Federal Census [Chicago Ward 4, Cook, Illinois] (Washington, DC: NARA, 1900), 1 (roll 248); "Comes from Distant Land and Accuses Her Husband," *CT*, Oct. 28, 1904; "Sister Ignorant of Vivian Gordon's Manner of Living," *BDE*, Mar. 10, 1931; "Sister Talks of Miss Gordon," *Windsor Star*, Mar. 10, 1931.
7 "Woman Vice Case Witness Found Strangled in Park; Her Lawyer Is Arrested"; "Benita Franklin," in 1910 US Federal Census [Precinct 7, Denver, Colorado] (Washington, DC: NARA, 1910), 16B (roll T624_116); "Housemaid Tells of Midnight Ride," *Montreal Gazette*, Mar. 3, 1931; "Sister Ignorant of Vivian Gordon's Manner of Living."
8 "American Variety Stage: Vaudeville and Popular Entertainment 1870–1920," *American Memory*, https://bit.ly/43jJJKP, accessed Nov. 13, 2020; "The Phrase That Put Peoria on the Map," PeoriaMagazines.Com, https://bit.ly/3MOWkPd, accessed Aug. 14, 2022; Rebecca Read Shanor, "Hippodrome," *The Encyclopedia of New York City: 2nd Ed.*, ed. by Kenneth T. Jackson (New Haven, CT: Yale Univ. Press, 2010).
9 Paul M. Levitt and Ed Lowry, *My Life in Vaudeville: The Autobiography of Ed Lowry* (Carbondale: Southern Illinois Univ. Press, 2011), 1–35, http://muse.jhu.edu/book/693.
10 Robinson, "Fear Drove Vivian to Hire Gangster Guard"; "Two Held in $100,000 Bail in Gordon Murder Case," *NYT*, Feb. 28, 1931; *U.S., World War I Draft Registration Cards, 1917–1918*, digital images, Ancestry.com, John E. C. Bischoff, accessed Oct. 7, 2020.
11 "Slain Girl's Friend, Here for Secret Quiz, Guarded by Seabury"; "Last Vivian Gordon Admirer Prepares to Tell His Story," *SU*, Mar. 2, 1931.
12 Grace Robinson, Louis Davidson, and Doris Fleeson, "Shame Drives Vivian's Daughter, 16, to Suicide," *DN*, Mar. 4, 1931.
13 Sonia Benson and et al., "Broadway," *U-X-L Encyclopedia of U.S. History*, vol. 1 (Farmington Hills, MI: U-X-L, 2009).
14 Jeff Lunden, "'Shuffle Along' Changed Musical Theater 100 Years Ago," NPR, May 23, 2021; Allen L. Woll, *Black Musical Theatre: From Coontown to Dreamgirls* (Baton Rouge: Louisiana State Univ. Press, 1989), 58–63, 160–63; David Savran, "The Search for America's Soul: Theatre in the Jazz Age," *Theatre Journal* 58 (3) (2006): 459–76.
15 Tom Miller, "The 1894 Hotel Gerard–123 West 44th Street," *Daytonian in Manhattan*, Oct. 18, 2010, https://bit.ly/3NlgstP; "Louis Cohen Robbed," *The Billboard*, Feb. 19, 1921; "Fight Duel in Hotel," *NYT*, Oct. 30, 1923.
16 "Benita Takes Her Diary to Grave Today," *Camden Morning Post*, Mar. 6, 1931.
17 Grace Robinson, "Blackmail, Rum, Drugs Mark Vice Murder Trial," *DN*, Feb. 28, 1931; Anne E. Bowler, Chrysanthi S. Leon, and Terry G. Lilley, "'What Shall We Do with the Young Prostitute? Reform Her or Neglect Her?': Domestication as Reform at the New York State Reformatory for Women at Bedford, 1901–1913," *Journal of Social History* 47 (2) (Dec. 11, 2013): 461–66.
18 "Grace Robinson Papers," Univ. of Wyoming, American Heritage Center, box 36, folder 3; "Dragged by Hair, Bedford Girl Says," *NYT*, Dec. 13, 1919; "Expert Condemns Stringing Up Girls," *NYT*, Dec. 14, 1919; "Initiated Water Cure," *BS*, Dec. 21, 1919.
19 Peter Levins, "The Vivian Gordon Murder Still Unsolved One Year After the Crime," *DN*, Feb. 21, 1932; "Data Disappears in Examination of Vivian Gordon," *Times Union*, Mar. 11, 1931.

20 "Bischoff Quiz in N.Y. Murder Set for Today;" "Slain Girl's Friend, Here for Secret Quiz, Guarded by Seabury."
21 Grace Robinson, "Vice Cop Accused by Slain Vivian Whitewashed," *DN*, Mar. 2, 1931
22 "Benita Takes Her Diary to Grave Today"; Martin Sommers, "Radeloff Ties Police Lieutenant to Vivian," *DN*, Mar. 27, 1931.
23 "Benita Takes Her Diary to Grave Today."
24 Ibid.
25 Ibid.; Robinson, Davidson, and Fleeson, "Shame Drives Vivian's Daughter, 16, to Suicide."
26 "Policeman and Ex-Husband Deny Framing Miss Gordon," *NYT*, Mar. 2, 1931; "Woman Doctor Offers Clues in Gordon Murder."
27 Robinson, "Vivian Gordon's Diary Used to Hold Radeloff, Cohen"; "Miss Gordon's Diary Says Three Sought to Kill Her," *NYT*, Mar. 3, 1931.
28 Robinson, "Blackmail, Rum, Drugs Mark Vice Murder Trial."
29 Ibid.; Irene Kuhn, "Tuttle's Ex-Aid Linked to Bribe by Gordon Clew," *DN*, Mar. 13, 1931.
30 Edith Twedell, "Frauds Change but Never Die," *NYT Magazine*, Sept. 20, 1930; "Three Glib Brokers Held as 'Reloaders,'" *NYT*, Mar. 4, 1923.
31 "Score of Trails Criss-Cross in Gordon Murder," *NYHT*, Mar. 5, 1931; Robinson, "Fear Drove Vivian to Hire Gangster Guard"; "Smooth Stock Salesman Gets 3 Years in Theft," *DN*, May 8, 1929; "'Undercover' Man Guilty of Theft," *Times Union*, May 8, 1929.
32 John O'Donnell, "Walker's Foes List Charges," *DN*, Mar. 12, 1931; Robinson, Davidson, and Fleeson, "Shame Drives Vivian's Daughter, 16, to Suicide"; Robinson, "Blackmail, Rum, Drugs Mark Vice Murder Trial"; "Testimony Is Missing," *NYT*, Mar. 11, 1931; Robinson, "Fear Drove Vivian to Hire Gangster Guard."
33 "Mrs. Radeloff Loyal to Mate Loved by Slain Vivian Gordon," *BDT*, Mar. 4, 1931.
34 Ibid.
35 "Ad: Apartment Hotels of Distinction," *NYHT*, Mar. 20, 1927; "Park Central Hotel Ready for Tenants," *NYT*, June 12, 1927; "$15,000,000 Park Central Hotel Now Nearing Completion," *NYHT*, Mar. 27, 1927; "Park Central Hotel, New York City," *Architecture and Building*, Oct. 1927; "Park Central Hotel New York Unveils Extensive Multi-Million Dollar Renovation and Inspired Redesign," PR Newswire, Sept. 12, 2013; James Barron, "An 86-Year-Old's Head-to-Toe Makeover Is Complete," *NYT*, sec. City Room, Sept. 11, 2013; Leo Katcher, *The Big Bankroll: The Life and Times of Arnold Rothstein* (Potomac, MD: Pickle Partners, 2016), 8.
36 Robinson, "Vivian Gordon's Diary Used to Hold Radeloff, Cohen"; "Vivian Gordon Diary Accuses Her Attorney"; "Grace Robinson Papers," Univ. of Wyoming, American Heritage Center, box 36, folder 4.
37 Timothy J. Gilfoyle, *City of Eros: New York City, Prostitution, and the Commercialization of Sex, 1790–1920*, 1st ed. (New York: W. W. Norton, 1992), 146, 170–75, 207, 309; Debby Applegate, *Madam: The Biography of Polly Adler, Icon of the Jazz Age* (Garden City, NY: Doubleday, 2021), 108.
38 Applegate, *Madam*, 166–69; Earl G. Talbott, "Polly Adler Funeral Plans?" *NYHT (1926–1962)*, June 11, 1962; Karen Abbott, "The House That Polly Adler Built," *Smithsonian Magazine*, Apr. 2012, https://www.smithsonianmag.com/history/the-house-that-polly-adler-built-65080310/.
39 Polly Adler, *A House Is Not a Home* (New York: Rinehart, 1950), 56, 117.
40 Applegate, *Madam*, 189, 209, 257–58, 300–1; Gail Sheehy, "Caste and Class in the Hustling Trade," *New York Magazine*, Apr. 24, 1972, 40.
41 Applegate, *Madam*, 6–9, 112, 193; Talbott, "Polly Adler Funeral Plans?"
42 "Grace Robinson Papers," box 36, folder 3.
43 Ibid.; Robinson, "Blackmail, Rum, Drugs Mark Vice Murder Trial."
44 Applegate, *Madam*, 128–29; Adler, *A House Is Not a Home*, 169.
45 Adler, *A House Is Not a Home*, 173–74; Applegate, *Madam*, 322.
46 "Vannie Higgins, Driving Zigzag, Bumps Into Law," *NYHT*, Mar. 2, 1931; Robinson, "Vice Cop Accused by Slain Vivian Whitewashed."
47 Martin Wurster, "The Rise and Fall of the Racketeer Barons," *Philadelphia Inquirer*, Oct. 30, 1938; Lavine, *Gimme*, 99–102.
48 Robinson, "Vice Cop Accused by Slain Vivian Whitewashed."
49 Ibid.; Louis Davidson, "Gangster's Girl Links Diamond's Pals in Shooting," *DN*, Oct. 29, 1930; *Hotel Monticello: 35–37 West 64th Street, New York City*, 1904; "Hunt Capone Gangster in Diamond's Shooting," *DN*, Oct. 14, 1930.
50 Davidson, "Gangster's Girl Links Diamond's Pals in Shooting."
51 Robinson, Davidson, and Fleeson, "Shame Drives Vivian's Daughter, 16, to Suicide."
52 Robinson, "Blackmail, Rum, Drugs Mark Vice Murder Trial"; Robinson, Davidson, and Fleeson, "Shame Drives Vivian's Daughter, 16, to Suicide"; Adler, *A House Is Not a Home*, 70.
53 Robinson, Davidson, and Fleeson, "Shame Drives Vivian's Daughter, 16, to Suicide."
54 Ibid.
55 Ibid.; "Miss Gordon's Diary Says Three Sought to Kill Her," *NYT*, Mar. 3, 1931; Applegate, *Madam*, 215–18.

61 Fowler, *Beau James*, 316–17; John C. O. Brien, "N.Y. Vote Shows Tiger's Dislike for Roosevelt," *NYHT*, July 2, 1932; Theodore C. Wallen, "Roosevelt Nominated on 4th Ballot by Democrats; Rolls Up 945 Votes in Stampede After Garner Quits," *NYHT*, July 2, 1932.

62 Mitgang, *Man Who Rode the Tiger*, 280–81.

63 Davis, *FDR: The New York Years, 1928–1933*, 306–7, 328–35; "Franklin D. Roosevelt: Address Accepting the Presidential Nomination at the Democratic National Convention in Chicago," American Presidency Project, accessed Mar. 27, 2023, https://bit.ly/3qfyvIv.

64 Tugwell, *The Brains Trust*, 347, 360, 367.

65 Davis, *FDR: The New York Years, 1928–1933*, 353; Mitgang, *Man Who Rode the Tiger*, 292; James A. Farley, "Patronage and the New Deal," *American Magazine*, Sept. 1938, 60–61.

66 Raymond Moley, *27 Masters of Politics in a Personal Perspective*, 209.

67 "Governor to Act Quickly," *NYT*, July 29, 1932; A. Staff Correspondent, "Text of Walker's Answer to Accusations Filed by Seabury with Governor Roosevelt," *NYHT*, July 29, 1932.

68 Mitgang, *Man Who Rode the Tiger*, 290.

69 "Roosevelt Calls Walker for Hearing Thursday," *NYHT*, Aug. 7, 1932.

70 Mitgang, *Man Who Rode the Tiger*, 284; "Mayor Entrains as 5,000 Cheer, and Jeer Him," *NYHT*, Aug. 11, 1932; Hickman Powell, "Walker Ready to Fight Ouster Charges Today," *NYHT*, Aug. 11, 1932; "Walker Hailed in Albany with Band and Fireworks; Has 'No Fear of Removal,'" *NYT*, Aug. 11, 1932.

71 Mitgang, *Man Who Rode the Tiger*, 282–85; Powell, "Walker Ready to Fight Ouster Charges Today"; "Up on the Big Red Carpet," *Press and Sun-Bulletin*, Feb. 12, 1932.

72 Mitgang, *Man Who Rode the Tiger*, 286–90; "Transcript of Hearing Before Governor Roosevelt in Walker Removal Case," *NYT*, Aug. 12, 1932.

73 Walsh, *Gentleman Jimmy Walker, Mayor of the Jazz Age*, 320; "Text of Testimony Before Roosevelt as Walker Hearing on Ouster Charges Opens," *NYHT*, Aug. 12, 1932.

74 "Block Says $246,00 Beneficence to Walker Gains Him No Favors," *DN*, Aug. 24, 1932; "Defense Testimony at Yesterday's Hearing in the Walker Removal Proceedings," *NYT*, Aug. 24, 1932.

75 "Transcript of the Fourth Hearing Before Governor in the Walker Removal Case," *NYT*, Aug. 17, 1932.

76 Hickman Powell, "Roosevelt Tells Walker His Private Affairs Fall Within Scope of Inquiry," *NYHT*, Aug. 16, 1932.

77 "Betty Compton Named!," *DN*, Aug. 17, 1932.

78 Fowler, *Beau James*, 324.

79 "Sherwood Was Bank of All Trades, Say Walker's Witnesses," *DN*, Aug. 27, 1932; "Mayor Returns on Same Train with Seabury," *NYT*, Aug. 27, 1932; "Seabury Leads Walker Parade on His Return," *NYHT*, Aug. 27, 1932.

80 Fowler, *Beau James*, 324.

81 "George Walker Funeral Is Held at St. Patrick's," *NYHT*, Sept. 2, 1932; "Mayor Ready to Bolt Quiz, Resign Today," *DN*, Sept. 2, 1932; Fowler, *Beau James*, 325.

82 Fowler, *Beau James*, 325–26.

83 Raymond Moley, *27 Masters of Politics in a Personal Perspective*, 210–11; Mitgang, *Man Who Rode the Tiger*, 295–97.

84 Mitgang, *Man Who Rode the Tiger*, 297; "Seabury Holds Walker's Act 'Confession of Guilt,'" *NYT*, Sept. 2, 1932.

85 "Roosevelt Maintains Silence on Walker's Attack," *NYT*, Sept. 3, 1932.

86 "Seabury, Sailing, Praises Governor," *NYT*, Sept. 3, 1932; Mitgang, *Man Who Rode the Tiger*, 298–99.

Epilogue

1 "First New Year's Revel Since Repeal Is Orderly; the Gayest in 14 Years," *NYT*, Jan. 1, 1934; "City Hails '34 In Legal Sips," *NYHT*, Jan. 1, 1934.

2 "City Hails '34 In Legal Sips."

3 "First New Year's Revel Since Repeal Is Orderly; the Gayest in 14 Years"; "City Hails '34 In Legal Sips"; "NYE History & Times Square Ball," *Times Square: The Official Website*, May 10, 2017, https://bit.ly/3qqsAR6.

4 "City Hails '34 In Legal Sips"; "First New Year's Revel Since Repeal Is Orderly; the Gayest in 14 Years"; "Mulrooney to Resign Today," *NYHT*, Apr. 11, 1933; "Mulrooney Ousts 5 Aides for Graft," *NYT*, Jan. 1, 1934.

5 "City Hails '34 In Legal Sips"; "O'Brien Will Name Man from Force to Head the Police," *NYT*, Apr. 12, 1933; Golway, *Machine Made*, 283–84, 292–95; Williams, *City of Ambition*, 1830–36, 1979–2007.

6 "POLITICAL NOTE: Curry Out," *TIME Magazine*, Apr. 30, 1934, 16.

7 Dick Lee, "LaGuardia Sworn In as City Greets 1934," *DN*, Jan. 1, 1934; "LaGuardia Takes Office to Give City a New Deal," *NYT*, Jan. 1, 1934; Mitgang, *Man Who Rode the Tiger*, 326–27.

8 Mitgang, *Man Who Rode the Tiger*, 314–15.

9 Ibid., 317–18. | Ibid., 316–18, 341–42.

10 Ibid., 320; "Fusion Picks Gen. O'Ryan For Mayor; 'Sell-Out' to Tammany, Says Seabury," *NYHT*, July 28, 1933.

11 "Rid City of Gangs, Is Order to Police," *NYT*, Jan. 2, 1934; A. G. Sulzberger, "La Guardia's Tough and Incorruptible Police Commissioner," *NYT* City Room, Nov. 11, 2009, https://bit.ly/43IdLrc; "Bruckman Slated as Detective Head," *NYT*, July 3, 1935.

12 "Rid City of Gangs, Is Order to Police"; Sulzberger, "La Guardia's Tough and Incorruptible Police Commissioner"; "Bruckman Slated as Detective Head."

13 Melvin G. Holli, *The American Mayor: The Best & the Worst Big-City Leaders* (University Park, PA: Penn State Press, 1999), 3–4; Erin Durkin, "Greatest Mayor Ever?," *New York DN*, Dec. 13, 2010; Edward L. Glaeser, "Fiorello!," *NYT*, July 18, 2013.

14 Mitgang, *Man Who Rode the Tiger*, 152, 346–47; Williams, *City of Ambition*, 2115–27, 3334–45; Theodore Landsman, "Proportional Representation in New York City, 1936–1947," *FairVote*, accessed May 1, 2023, https://bit.ly/3WMssHE.

15 Fowler, *Beau James*, 333–51.

16 Ibid., 352–58; Mitgang, *Man Who Rode the Tiger*, 354–55; "Mayor Gives Walker Labor Post; White House Influence Is Seen," *NYT*, Sept. 6, 1940.

17 Robert S. Bird, "Tammany Hall Comedy," *NYHT*, Dec. 19, 1943.

18 Golway, *Machine Made*, 297–301.

19 Raymond Moley, *27 Masters of Politics: In a Personal Perspective, A Newsweek Book* (New York: Funk & Wagnalls Company, 1949), 216.

20 "Mulrooney Puts 3 Convicts Out Of Soft Berths," *NYHT*, May 27, 1936; "Bruckman Is Named State Liquor Czar," *DN*, Mar. 4, 1936.

21 "Three Confess Digest Killing, 4th Is Hunted," *DN*, June 9, 1950; "Dorfman Details Killing," *White Plains Reporter Dispatch*, Nov. 18, 1950.

22 "Stein Held Key to 3 Great Mysteries," *DN*, July 10, 1955; "Killer Takes Crater Solution to Grave," *Bergen Evening Record*, Aug. 5, 1955.

23 "Digest Killers' Rites; Few Come to Mourn," *DN*, July 11, 1955; "Witness Recalls Triple Execution at Sing Sing," *Journal News*, June 5, 1989.

24 "3 Get Two Years in Passport Ruse," *Times Union*, Oct. 26, 1933; "Gordon Case Witness Held in Movie Dope Ring Raid," *DN*, July 7, 1934; "Two in Dope Ring Guilty," *The BDE*, Sept. 14, 1934; "Chowderhead and Wife Admit Fraud," *DN*, Aug. 28, 1937; "Mrs. Radeloff Cites Raid in Divorce Suit," *DN*, Nov. 17, 1932; "John A Radeloff," in 1940 US Federal Census [New York, Kings, NY] (NARA, 1940), 61B (roll m-t0627-02599); "Colorado Springs" (US, City Directories, 1822–1995–Ancestry.com), accessed Apr. 29, 2023.

25 Vincent Bugliosi, *Lullaby and Good Night: A Novel Inspired by the True Story of Vivian Gordon* (New York: Dutton Books, 1987).

PICTURE CREDITS

INDEX